SEA CHANGE

SEA CHANGE:
the unfinished agenda of the 1960s
by Dorothy May Emerson

SEA CHANGE: *the unfinished agenda of the 1960s*

ISBN: 978-1-946088-07-9

Library of Congress Control Number: 2018936955
1. Memoir   2. Title

Matrika Press
164 Lancey Street
Pittsfield, Maine
(760) 889-5428
Editor@MatrikaPress.com

Matrika Press

www.MatrikaPress.com

Logo design: Howard Emerson
Cover photos: Donna Clifford
Tie-dye: Cali Kind T-shirts, Cotati, CA
Cover design & interior layout: "Twinkle" Marie Manning
Website: Gretchen Ohmann, Ladyweave
SeaChange1960s.net

DEDICATION

To Zade and his generation
May you keep the vision alive
And find new ways to make more of it real

SEA CHANGE: *the unfinished agenda of the 1960s*

Dorothy May Emerson

TABLE OF CONTENTS

SEA CHANGE: *the unfinished agenda of the 1960s*

Dorothy May Emerson

PROLOGUE: *the unfinished agenda of the 1960s*

"Story—the abundance of it and the lack of it—shapes us. Story—the abundance of it and the lack of it—gives us place, lineage, history, a sense of self. ... What we preserve in larger human story determines what we believe is possible in the world."
        –Christina Baldwin[1]

We who lived in the 1960s[2] need to tell our stories to claim place, lineage, and our sense of self. If we do not tell our stories, if we do not link who we are now with who we were in the process of becoming back then, if we do not articulate this era as an important source of inspiration for the lives that followed, then the world loses the experiences, imagination, and vision that shaped our lives. Through our stories, we can identify and amplify our collective understanding of the mechanisms of culture change.

I can share my story in some detail thanks to letters and papers my mother saved for me, plus my journals and miscellaneous writings from the Sixties. By bringing together my young adult voice with reflections from the perspective of who I am now, I hope to bring to light some of the key changes of the era and how these changes changed me.

"History is what scholars and conquerors say happened; story is what it was like to live on the ground,"[3] writes Christina

---

1   Christina Baldwin, *Storycatcher: Making Sense of Our Lives through the Power and Practice of Story*, 3.
2   When I speak of the decade from 1960 to 1969, I use the terms "1960s." When I want to include the early 1970s, I use the term "Sixties era" or simply "the Sixties."
3   Baldwin, 4.

9

Baldwin. Who were the "conquerors" of this era? By the mid-1970s, the new right, the moral majority, and neoconservatives began to dominate public sentiment. In putting forth their new agenda, they denigrated the previous decade's radicalism as exemplifying all that was wrong in America. Some blamed overindulged white middle class youth, who rebelled against their parents' values of hard work, achievement, and material success. Others focused on the outward manifestations of drugs, sex, rock and roll, and campy clothes and hair styles, belittling the real accomplishments of the decade. These conquerors failed to see the Sixties as significant and called for a return to the values of the 1950s.

More recently, David Sirota and others have described conscious efforts to discredit the experimental ideas and passion for social justice of the Sixties era. He writes: The 1980s-created narrative of the Bad Sixties can still be found in everything from national Tea Party protests to never-ending culture-war battles on local school boards. The message is always the same: If only America can ... get past its Sixties immaturity and liberalism, everything will be A-okay."[4]

I have a different message. I want future generations to know there was a time when people believed peace, love, equality, and freedom were possible, when trusting ourselves and others was natural and easy, when it was exciting to explore the boundaries of our minds and bodies, when little was forbidden except saying that anything was impossible. I want my grandson, his generation, and those that follow to know there were people who believed life could be different, that we could live and love in new ways and move beyond the barriers and social conventions that strangled our cultural imagination and limited the creation of a better future for everyone everywhere. I hope my story will help counter the media and political commentaries that discredited the Sixties and sought to bury our hopes and dreams.

I believe it is essential to remember what happened then and why, because the sea change of the 1960s is unfinished. We

---

4   David Sirota, *Back to Our Future: How the 1980s Explain the World We Live in Now*, 2011.

need to revive and share our buried hopes and dreams before our generation is dead. To do so, though, may require us to deal with painful memories, situations where we now know we could have done better. Back then, as we struggled to live liberated lives, we carried with us cultural attitudes from the past. We couldn't change everything at once, and sometimes we hurt ourselves and each other. For me, writing this memoir has been a chance to heal the past and mend relationships. Most of all, writing this has helped me honor what I learned from my experiences, including my mistakes.

Today more than ever we need the dreams of the Sixties and its daring vision that equality, freedom, love, and peace are possible. Remembering what happened then in a more than superficial way is essential, if we are to complete that unfinished agenda. Harvesting our dreams and visions and remembering them into being might help us complete the sea change begun in the era we call the Sixties.

I. SOMETHING RICH AND STRANGE:
an introduction

"Full fathom five thy father lies
Of his bones are coral made
Those are pearls that were his eyes
Nothing of him that doth fade
But doth suffer a sea-change
Into something rich and strange."
-Shakespeare, The Tempest

The 1960s initiated a cultural sea change not unlike Shakespeare's dramatic image. The ocean transforms the father's submerged body into coral, his eyes into pearls. This iconic decade and the years that followed initiated changes that are equally "rich and strange." How exciting it was for me to be part of this era, with its vision of a better world! How gratifying to be with others who shared this dream and became actively engaged in making positive changes.

The "Star Trek"[5] mission--"To boldly go where no one has gone before"—epitomizes a feeling many people had in the Sixties. We understood intuitively that our world needed to change. A shared vision of a better world began to emerge, a vision of a world founded on peace, justice, equality, freedom, and love. Some of us began to understand ourselves as co-creators of culture and sought to live

---

5   The original "Star Trek" series aired on television for three seasons, beginning in 1966. The words used then at the beginning of each episode were "to boldly go where no man has gone before." I have chosen to use the gender-neutral term used in later Star Trek series.

that vision in our daily lives, relationships, and work. Not everyone, of course, saw this vision. Among those who saw it, only some took on public roles as culture change agents, but those of us who consciously sought to implement change knew we were not alone. We knew a larger shift was taking place and committed ourselves to live the changes wherever we were.

There was talk of the birth of a new age. Predictions of a new age about to begin can be found throughout history, but I first heard the idea in the 1960s from astrologers I met. They talked about long-term cosmic cycles and said we were living in the end of the Piscean Age, which began with the birth of Jesus, whose symbol, like Pisces, was the fish.[6] We were on the cusp, they said, of the Aquarian Age. This new age would be a time of expanded consciousness, peace, and love. Hence the song from the rock musical *Hair*:[7]

When the moon is in the Seventh House
And Jupiter aligns with Mars
Then peace will guide the planets
And love will steer the stars
This is the dawning of the Age of Aquarius…

Harmony and understanding
Sympathy and trust abounding
No more falsehoods or derisions
Golden living dreams of visions
Mystic crystal revelation
And the mind's true liberation …

We could feel the shift taking place, in ourselves and in the world around us. Realizing I was part of the change felt right, even though I knew we were doing something new and daring. We were changing the rules we had learned from parents, school, and society.

---

6   Each preceding age contributed something important to humanity's collective consciousness and to the civilizations and cultures that evolved out of that spiritual understanding.

7   "Age of Aquarius," *Hair*, lyrics by James Rado and Gerome Ragni, music by Galt MacDermot.

SEA CHANGE: *the unfinished agenda of the 1960s*

As we consciously moved beyond authority and tradition, radically diverging from the way things had been done before, it felt crazy, wonderful, painful, deep, intense, and clearly transformative.

The image of the Sixties era as a hedonistic time of sex, drugs, and rock and roll fails to convey the deeper significance of these cultural manifestations and the larger forces they reflected, as well as the rest of what was going on in that eventful and turbulent era. I hope my stories and reflections will contribute to a fuller awareness of how and why these cultural elements were integral to the transformations of the time and of the wider and more far-reaching meaning of the era itself.

DEFINING THE SIXTIES ERA

Not everyone agrees on the years that constitute the Sixties. At first glance, it may seem obvious. The 1960s is a decade running from 1960 to 1969, and a few writers stick to these years. But it is far more common to extend the era into the 1970s. This wider view makes sense to me, because much of what began in the 1960s continued developing in the early 1970s. This was certainly true in my life.

In this book, I write about the years from 1960 to 1974. When I speak of the decade from 1960 to 1969, I use the terms "1960s." When I want to indicate the full time span, I use the term "Sixties era" or simply "the Sixties."

My personal bookends for the Sixties era extend from the summer of 1960, before I began my senior year in high school, to the summer of 1974 after I ended my six years of public school teaching. Public events that bracket this era were the election of John F. Kennedy as president of the United States in the fall of 1960 and the resignation of President Richard Nixon in the summer of 1974.

MY OWN SIXTIES, BEFORE AND AFTER

I was born on November 20, 1943[8] at Seaside Hospital in Long Beach, California. The hospital sits on a hill overlooking the

---

8   I was born at 9:50 AM. Because of the war, we were on Daylight Savings time.

Pacific Ocean. Born in the middle of the turmoil of war, with ocean waves pounding the shore below me, perhaps I was destined to seek my place in the flow of changes swirling around me. My birth during World War II places me right before the Baby Boomer era. My father worked for an oil company, so his job exempted him from military service. My mother, a registered nurse, wanted to serve and had received a commission to go abroad when she learned she was pregnant with me.[9]

My father's family were Californians, making me a rare breed—a second generation native Californian. My father's mother lived near us and was a loving presence in our lives. We took family trips every year or two to visit my grandfather, his third wife, and my father's brother and half-sisters, all of whom lived in the San Francisco Bay Area. This is how I got to know my Northern California cousins. My dad had to go to work at a young age, so he never finished high school, although he later completed courses at a community college.

My mother came to California from Wisconsin, which we never visited, probably because it was too far to drive. However, since both her siblings lived in southern California, we saw them often, along with my cousin Pat. Pat's mother, my Aunt Willie, had polio as a child and their mother brought her two daughters to California seeking treatment. When Aunt Willie was studying at the University of California in Berkeley, my mother joined her for a year to complete her BS degree. At the time, my mother was working as a nurse in Long Beach, having earned her RN at a nursing school there.

I spent my first seven years in an urban neighborhood in Long Beach, California, where my next two siblings were born, Howard Jr. (known as Howdy), when I was two, and Mary Lou, when I was four. Then, when I was seven, we moved to the suburbs in Orange County,

9	The pregnancy did not come as a surprise, as my parents had been trying to conceive for several years, using the basal thermometer method, which required my mother to chart her temperature and then call my father to meet her when her temperature indicated she was ovulating. When I learned about this as a teenager, I thought it sounded very strange. Now I feel blessed that they wanted me enough to go to all this trouble. I hope it was exciting for them as well.

to Fullerton, where my youngest brother Clark was born, when I was nearly twelve. My father worked at Union Oil and my mother as a school nurse. I was active in Girl Scouts through junior high and the Presbyterian Church through high school. I played tennis and loved to swim, but I was better at schoolwork than sports.

Although my early life shaped me, much of who I am today evolved in the Sixties. I sought a vocation in ministry but found the Church too narrow. My six-month job in a juvenile detention center taught me more than I could handle at the time about how unfair the system is and how it penalizes those who are less advantaged. Through the theater, I saw the potential for consciousness-raising and deep learning. I experienced new forms of relationships, sexuality, and love. Living in an experimental integration project, I faced dynamics and social forces of race and class I barely understood. Participation in an alternative "church without walls" introduced me to new forms of religion. Getting unwittingly caught up in a protest action, I learned how arbitrary and unfair the police can be. As a teacher in an era of educational change and innovation, I brought the emerging values and perspectives of the era into my classroom. As the Sixties evolved, waves of change continued to open my mind and heart and life.

The energy of those waves compelled me on. In the mid-1970s, I lived in a van for a year, journeying across America seeking community. Along the way, I married my traveling companion and we gave birth to a son. In late 1976, we settled down in Austin, Texas, where I played a role in organizing the holistic health movement. When we separated in 1981, I finally came out as a lesbian and helped organize the feminist spirituality movement and a home for women in transition. I discovered Unitarian Universalism and took a seminary course on Women and Religion. In 1983, I left on my second journey in a van, this time headed to the Women's Encampment for a Future of Peace and Justice, where I engaged in anti-nuclear organizing and protest and rediscovered my call to ministry. After four years at Harvard Divinity School, I was ordained a Unitarian Universalist minister in 1988. Since then I have engaged in ministry in congregations and with community organizations, including founding the UU Women's Heritage Society. I edited and wrote several books and co-created curricula for adults. Most recently I joined with several others to create a series of workshops to raise awareness of class issues and encourage class inclusivity, particularly in churches. My spouse (wife) and I have been together for over 25 years and live in Medford, Massachusetts, near Boston, where we are both active with groups and movements working for justice, continuing to envision a better world, and doing our part to make it real. In everything I have done the vision of freedom, equality, justice, love, and peace has inspired and guided me. The Sixties lives in me still.

THE BOOK

This book is organized thematically rather than chronologically. The story starts with my awakening to a sense of self and the realities of the cultures around me in the first half of the 1960s (sections 1-3). The next part describes the ways I engaged with the changing culture, primarily in the mid-late 1960s (sections 4-5). The final part demonstrates ways I sought to implement Sixties values in education in the early 1970s and concludes with observations of culture change in process (sections 6-7). Most sections begin with cultural context, then my story, then reflections on the theme, including what I understand to be the unfinished agenda of the era.

- Section 1, Something Rich and Strange, began with visions from the Sixties and early signs of coming change, and provides background about my life both before and after the Sixties.
- Section 2, Hearing the Call: Awakening to Spirit, reflects on religion in the 1950s and 1960s as a context for my experiences of being spiritually called to live a life of meaning and action.
- Section 3, Culture Shock, Awakening to Cultural Differences, describes the experience of culture shock and my growing awareness of different cultures and choices I could make about how to live.
- Section 4, Dreams of Beloved Community, focuses on my awakening to dynamics of race and class and my growing commitment to implementing principles of equality and justice

in my life and work.

- Section 5, Love Is All You Need, explores love relationships, sex, and lifestyle choices that were part of my struggle for authenticity and living based on ideals of love.
- Section 6, Education = Change, explores influences from emerging and changing culture on the practice of teaching and my efforts to empower students to actualize their potential to learn in freedom and to live in love and peace.
- Section 7, Culture Change: Changing the World, describes examples of culture change, of people living the dream of freedom, equality, love, and peace, and the ongoing struggle to make this vision practical and real.
- At the end of the book, I express my Gratitude to the many people who helped along the way and provide a page of Dates and Milestones to clarify the chronology of my life.

I hope my stories from the Sixties will help those who lived though this era remember their experiences of times when it all came together and we lived ourselves into the new culture. May this book empower all of us today in our continuing work toward creating a better world and inspire us to take concrete action to complete the agenda of the Sixties-inspired sea change.

EDGE OF THE WAVE

"*Admit that the waters around you have grown ... for the times they are a-changin'.*" -Bob Dylan, 1964

In the early 1960s, we were on the edge of a wave, a wave that was the visible form of the Sixties sea change already churning in the depths of our culture. In scientific terms, the leading edge of a wave is known as a wave front or face, but to some of us born in the first half of the 1940s, the early 1960s felt like an edge. I know because I lived on that edge.

In the only childhood dream I remember having dreamed more than once, I am running away from the rising ocean, finding safe places to stay and interesting people to be with. I know when to move to stay safe, and I find places to stay along the way. I am conscious of the force of the ocean, but I am not afraid.

Dorothy May Emerson

By the mid-1960s I began to be conscious of myself as part of a major wave of culture change. As this dream suggests, perhaps I was even ahead of the wave. How did I come to be that way?

2. HEARING THE CALL:
awakening to spirit

"How many days has it been
Since I was born
How many days until I die …

When the baby looks around him
It's such a sight to see
He shares a simple secret
With the wise man

He's a stranger in a strange land
Just a stranger in a strange land
Tell me why."
Leon Russell, 1970[10]

Who am I? Why am I here in this place and time? What is the purpose of my life? What am I called to do?

It was not uncommon for young adults and others in the 1960s to ask themselves these questions. Like me, many people sought answers beyond those provided by the culture of our time. What we discovered changed as we went along, guiding us in becoming our unique selves. In my case, one of the first places I found answers to my questions about life was the Church. Fortunately for me, my church encouraged me to ask questions and seek my own answers. These questions led to my spiritual awakening.

---

10   "Stranger in a Strange Land," composed by Leon Russell and Don Preston, on the album *Leon Russell and the Shelter People*, released 1971.

Dorothy May Emerson

RELIGION IN THE 1950S

The 1950s was a heyday for religion in America, especially for mainline Protestant churches in burgeoning suburban communities, thanks to the baby boom generation. Young families flocked to churches and other religious organizations. Whether they were believers or not, many people considered attendance at religious services a social obligation and many parents considered their children's religious education part of their responsibility. Robert Ellwood, author of The Fifties Spiritual Marketplace, explained: "It was a fine time to go to church. . .and to build. It was a decade when the American family was embraced as an institution by men and women seeking normalcy after World War II."[11]

Many churches expanded and built new facilities to accommodate their growing membership. Churches often had multiple ministers, with one dedicated to serving children and youth. Large youth programs provided religious education and fellowship for teenagers. Robert Ellwood wrote:

On a typical Sunday morning in the period from 1955-58, almost half of all Americans were attending church—the highest percentage in U.S. history. During the 1950s, nationwide church membership grew at a faster rate than the population, from 57 percent of the U.S. population in 1950 to 63.3 percent in 1960. ...

It was a time when religion was powerful in American life – partly because most people believed they needed it and there was seemingly nothing to discredit it.[12]

THE CHURCH DOWN THE STREET

The First Presbyterian Church of Fullerton was an important place for me. There I learned from personal interaction with wise adults that I was a person of value who could think for myself. Our youth ministers and advisors functioned as bridges into the adult world. Often younger than our parents and teachers, they offered

11   Robert Ellwood, The Fifties Spiritual Marketplace: American Religion in a Decade of Conflict (1997).
12   Robert Ellwood, in Carol Taylor, "The 1950s—Powerful Years for Religion," USC News (University of Southern California), June 16, 1997.

alternative perspectives on the world we lived in and served as role models for living engaged, meaningful lives. They respected us as emerging adults with something valuable to contribute to our life together at church and to the world beyond. Being part of the church gave me a place to encounter the sacred, in worship services, in the church community, in the church building, especially the sanctuary, and in myself. Conveniently for me, the church was barely a block from our house.

After getting my brother, sister, and me[13] established in choirs and Sunday school, my parents rarely attended church services, except when we were in special programs. On Sunday mornings, my mother made sure we were all properly dressed and ready for church, and then stood at the door waving goodbye and watching us walk down the block on our own. She must have breathed a sigh of relief and enjoyed the next hour or two of peace before we returned.

I first connected with the meaning of religion though singing in choir. I still remember songs we used to sing. One of my favorites was "I Believe."[14]

I believe for every drop of rain that falls a flower grows.
I believe that somewhere in the darkest night, a candle glows.
I believe for everyone who goes astray, someone will come to show the way.
I believe. I believe.

By the time I was a teenager, the church had become a second home to me. I sang in the Chancel Choir, sometimes at the early service. Although it wasn't required, I usually stayed for the whole service, listening intently to the readings and sermons to find something of meaning for my own life. One year I helped teach Sunday school for younger children, which meant I spent the whole morning at church. Then I came back in the evening for Church

---

13   My youngest brother wasn't born yet.
14   "I Believe," composed by Ervin Drake, Irvin Graham, Jimmy Shirl and Al Stillman in 1953, was introduced by Jane Froman on her television show, the first hit song ever introduced on TV. Troubled by the uprising of the Korean War in 1952 so soon after World War II, she commissioned the song as a gift of hope and faith.

School and Agape Fellowship, our senior high youth group.

AGAPE FELLOWSHIP

Agape, we were told, refers to the highest form of love, unconditional love, the love of God for humanity, the same love we were encouraged to practice towards one another.[15] We embodied agape by beginning our meetings with a Fellowship Circle, where we held hands and welcomed each other, with everyone, including our adult leaders, standing together as equals. After a time of recreation where we played group games, there was generally an hour-long program, followed by a short worship service and refreshments. Our group was an interesting mix of high school kids, cutting across social groups and ages. The usual cliques, so evident at school, were forgotten. While we were together, we were one in the spirit. Nowhere was this more affirmed than in our closing Fellowship Circle, as we sang: "One in service, truth, and love."[16]

Students helped plan and run the Sunday evening gatherings, although the adults usually chose the theological topics. I made note of one of the programs I helped plan. What I said in the worship service provides a window into what I was thinking and learning as the 1960s began.

In my "sermonette" I reflected on the theme "What does it mean to be free?" using words from the apostle Paul: "Plant your feet firmly, therefore, within the freedom that Christ has won for us, and do not let yourselves be caught again in the shackles of slavery." I understood freedom as something we could only attain through faith. "Ideally, if everyone lived completely in harmony with God," I said, "there would be no need for laws." I explained: "Our religion isn't a set of morals. It is a faith, a vital faith in God as a living personality; it is not a strict obedience to laws for laws' sake.

---

15   The statement, "God is love," in 1 John 4:8, uses the Greek word agape to describe God's love.

16   Westminster Fellowship national anthem: "Youth at work are bringing God's glory/ To the earth from heaven above. /Here to set aflame His glory/ One in service, truth, and love. We are striving to be faithful to the Will of God. To the will, the Will of God." Hymn tune: "God of Grace & God of Glory"

This does not mean that we should ignore laws and the right kind of living. It simply means that we don't have to fret about keeping the law to the letter."[17]

One of the primary ideas I remember learning in church is that laws and rules, even the Ten Commandments, are superseded by God's law of love. As a sixteen-year-old, this idea gave me great freedom to ignore certain rules, believing myself not limited by them.

Our minister, the Rev. Herbe Stocker,[18] told me years later that our youth group was unique in the way we bonded and explored together what it meant to be young people of faith in a changing world. Another active member of the group noted that Herbe and his wife Jean "had a genius for involving people the likes of which I have never seen again."[19]

Ironically, considering the conservative reputation of many churches, Agape Fellowship was where I heard progressive ideas, an important counterbalance to the culture around me. Our programs introduced us to a wide range of social issues and challenged us to form our own opinions, applying the law of love to our decisions. For instance, a program on the legalization of gambling led me to oppose the idea and make a life-long commitment not to gamble. A program on conscientious objection to military service led me to conclude that if I were a boy, I would be a conscientious objector and refuse to fight in any war. Later, I supported my brother in his refusal to fight in the Vietnam War. We talked about the anti-communism scare that was sweeping our community. Although the church viewed communism as being in opposition to Christianity, our leaders cautioned us

---

17   Dorothy Emerson, "Christian Freedom," sermonette given at Agape Fellowship, Oct. 9, 1960. Handwritten text. I referenced Ernest DeWitt Burton's description of "Life by the Spirit" as distinct from either legalism or "yielding to the impulses of the flesh," but rather "a highway above them both, a life of freedom from statutes, of faith and love."

18   Rev. Herbe Stocker served as Minister of Christian Education, one of four ministers at First Presbyterian Church Fullerton at the time. We considered him "our youth minister." His wife, Jean, and lay leaders Nat and Ralph Kennedy were also key adult leaders of our youth group.

19   Ann Crutcher Zulliger, email, July 16, 2016.

against getting caught up in fear and accusing people who expressed different views of being communists. Later I encountered the anti-communist movement firsthand and was grateful for the alternative perspectives I had heard.

I learned that this focus on social issues was relatively new in the Presbyterian church, when I represented the senior high youth on the Christian Education Committee. Part of this committee's work was to integrate social education and action into religious education. An article in the church newsletter explained the purpose: "Present-day social issues are so varied and urgent that no church can afford to be complacent or resigned. We, as Christians, must be conscious of the fact that our approach to these problems should consider the human element — effects on the lives of men, women, and children, rather than in terms of any political or economic bias."[20] This emphasis on social issues inspired me and was part of what kept me involved with church over the years. I was learning how to be an adult who cared about the world and wanted to make a difference. The following February 1961, I amplified the theme of love in my Youth Sunday sermon at the adult worship service.[21] How I began reveals what my life was like at the time. "This is a confusing, befuddling world, and the life we live is filled with problems and troubles. We all have to do so many things for which there seems to be no time. Sometimes we feel as if we are being squeezed through a ringer for no reason at all. It becomes often difficult to continue when we feel no purpose in what we do."

God's love, I said, is what gives us the power to go on. "God does not assure us of protection from trouble, He assures us of love and aid in trouble. ... Through God we can gain a new sense of peace and harmony." I needed peace and harmony in my life, and I found it both with the people at church and in the assurance of God's love.

I spoke of a variety of ways people could share the love of God with others, including giving money to the church, taking an active role in church, being sincere and helpful in relationships with others,

20   "Committee on Christian Education," *Kaleidoscope*, First Presbyterian Church, c. Feb.-Mar. 1958 (no date given), p. 6.
21   Youth Sunday service, Feb. 12, 1961. Theme: Into All the World Together.

and "living our lives so they show how Christ's love has changed us. I concluded that the logical course of faith is to love and be concerned for others, and that when we do that "we begin to find that because of our love and concern our lives take on new meaning. ... God gives us a sort of inner reinforcement. He actually lives in our hearts through our faith." And then I repeated what I now understood about rules: "We realize that no longer do moral laws have any significance in our lives, for we know our lives can be better governed by God's love."

These two ideas would carry me through the Sixties and beyond—that God's love supersedes rules and that this love lives in us and through us. These principles freed me to develop my own interpretation of how to live my life.

THE CALL

The youth leaders at church recognized the seriousness of my faith. As we were leaving the church one evening after youth group I stopped Ralph Kennedy, one of the adult advisors.

"Why doesn't our church stay open all the time like my friend Mary's Catholic church?" I asked. "When I need a quiet place to think, I wish I could come to this this church. Our sanctuary[22] is such a beautiful and inspiring place."

"Hmmm," he said, and paused. I waited, wondering if I said something wrong. "I suppose I could show you how to get in. Do you have a library card?"

"Yes, of course," I replied and pulled a small cardboard card out of my wallet to show him.

"Come with me then," he said after looking around to see that everyone else had gone home. He led me to the front door of the church, took me outside, and closed the door. Then he showed me how to open the not-very-secure lock by sliding my library card in the crack and holding back the part that locked the door. I tried it and was amazed at how easy it was to open the door!

"Thank you so much," I said. "I promise I will use it only

---

22   When the church was first built at the end of our street, the campus consisted of offices and Sunday school rooms, plus a large fellowship hall that served as the sanctuary. A new sanctuary was added in 1958.

when I really need it."

"Don't worry," he replied. "You are part of this church, so this building belongs to you. I know you will treat it with respect."

A week or two later when things seemed particularly hectic and contentious at home, I remembered the gift I had been given. I was nervous the first time I opened that big door. It was early evening and there was little light inside, but I managed to find my way across the long foyer into the sanctuary without turning on any lights. That first time, all I did was sit in silence in the back pew, absorbing the inspirational beauty of the place with its simple, modern design, rafters rising into a high vaulted ceiling, and watching the light fade though the frosted white, clear blue, and red glass of the windows. Later when I began to feel comfortable being in that space alone, I walked around the sanctuary, singing my favorite hymn "Be Thou My Vision," softly at first and then with increasing volume and confidence, as I began to recognize this sacred space as my home.

Be Thou my Vision, O Lord of my heart;
Naught be all else to me, save that Thou art.
Thou my best Thought, by day or by night,
Waking or sleeping, Thy presence my light.
Be Thou my Wisdom, and Thou my true Word;
I ever with Thee and Thou with me, Lord;
Thou my great Father, I Thy true son;
Thou in me dwelling, and I with Thee one.[23]

This place became my personal sanctuary, where I could go to be alone and be quiet, to think about what was going on, pray for guidance, and try to find peace in my heart. In the process, I found inspiration for my life.

One evening as I was walking around in the sanctuary singing, I stopped, struck by a terrifying and yet enticing realization. I looked up at the rafters and wondered aloud, "How did Jesus know who he was? How old was he when he first realized the purpose of his life?" My next thought was the scary part. "What if I were

---

23   Attributed to Dallan Forgaill; translated from ancient Irish to English by Mary E. Byrne; verses by Eleanor H. Hull, 1912. At this point, I was unaware of the problem of male language and felt included as a "true son."

someone like Jesus? How would I know who I was?"

I reasoned that since God was fair and considered all people equal (something I learned from my church), then if there were a second coming of Jesus (an idea I heard from friends in other churches) surely this second child of God would be a girl! How would she know who she was, I wondered? What if I were that girl? These questions led me to a new sense of commitment. I resolved to live my life as if I were God's special representative on earth. I felt a special glow as if new light had descended into my soul.

Then I realized I had better get home before anyone started worrying about where I had gone. I did not want to explain to anyone what had just happened. Integrating my experiences at church with my family and school life wasn't always easy. My mother often accused me of coming home from church with my head in the clouds. When I failed to cooperate with her agenda for me, she would say: "What do they teach you at church? Don't they teach you to be nice?"

SUMMER CAMP

Beginning in junior high school, I spent one week each summer at Presbyterian Church camps.[24] These camps gave me an opportunity to meet young people from all over southern California. Although each camp was only a week long, living in community away from family gave me insight into who I was and helped shape me into who I was becoming. Each year for one special week, we were a community of young people of faith. We were also teenagers.

Each day at summer camp began with morning devotions, a time when we went off by ourselves, read the Bible verse of the day, and reflected on its meaning. Then we ate breakfast and attended morning classes, the themes of which differed from year to year. In the afternoons, we participated in the usual camp activities: games, nature walks, crafts, hiking, and swimming. We also had time to

---

24   The first two summers (1956, 1957) I went to junior high camp in Pacific Palisades, a coastal town north of Los Angeles. The next two summers (1958, 1959) high school camp was in the mountains at Big Bear Lake. In 1960, I served as a camp counselor and attended a Commission Conference.

hang out with friends.

In the evenings, we sat around the campfire, singing camp and youth group songs, and telling stories. One year, an adult advisor read to us from a book whose title has stuck with me ever since, *The Salty Tang*. The title is an extension of what Jesus said to those gathered on the hillside in what came to be known as the Sermon on the Mount: "You are the salt of the earth." (Matthew 5:13) Author Frederick B. Speakman interpreted this image to mean "indispensable," relating it to what Jesus said to his disciples: "You are the light history is going to see by, if it ever reads life aright. You are the hope that will always be, in all the death traps of time. ... For there is at work within you now ... a certain flavor of existence which must be so kept that it can be caught and spread, if ever the earth is to discover the livableness of life. ... You alone can flavor the earth with this salty tang of living truth."[25]

At camp for one week each summer, I could see how life could be different than it usually was. Camp was an expansion and a deepening of what I experienced in youth group back home. I knew I wanted to be one of those people who acted from a sense of faith and who made a difference in the world. What I learned at camp, combined with what I learned in my home church, prepared me for the radical ideas I would embrace later in the Sixties.

YOUNG LOVE

I was 14 in 1958 when I attended my first high school camp. That's where I met Carl, who became my most consistent boyfriend during high school. With Carl, I explored sex and struggled to apply the law of love to our relationship. I also began to wonder how a love relationship would fit into my life and affect whatever career path I chose.

On the second day of camp, I walked into the main lodge and heard someone playing "Rock Around the Clock" on the piano. I tried to get close enough to see who was playing. but there were too many people crowded around singing and dancing. When the crowd cleared, I saw a young man with short blond hair, horn-rimmed

---

25   Frederick B. Speakman, *The Salty Tang: Messages for Today*, 1954, 15.

glasses, and a big grin, playing the piano. He's cute, I thought. I wonder what he's like. The next day, I managed to meet him.

Before the week was over Carl kissed me. On my camp name and address list, I connected his name and mine with a heart and the word "Lovers." Even though he had a girlfriend back home, we promised to stay in touch via letters, because long-distance phone calls were considered too expensive in those days. Back home, I ignored the girlfriend part and began writing letters. Eventually he asked me out on a date. He had a car and lived in Burbank, easy driving from my house. We had a great time and met several more times that year.

I was disappointed that he planned to be at a different camp from me the next summer (1959), but his plans changed and there he was. I took this as a sign that maybe we would be together after all. That year a counselor encouraged us to write a letter to ourselves about what we learned at camp, which the counselor would mail to us six months later. In my letter, I described how Carl and I had been visibly together at camp but between ourselves had broken up many times and then gotten back together. "With God's help," I wrote, "I have succeeded in keeping Carl as a friend. Because he is afraid of getting hurt, he hasn't wanted to commit himself or even let himself become involved."[26] Although I knew he had received letters from his girlfriend at home, he also paid special attention to me. But sometimes he would pull back and act as if he didn't even like me. It was confusing, but I never stopped hoping for love.

One evening he said he needed to talk to me. It was a warm evening and we walked down to the lake after the evening program. He told me he got another letter from his girlfriend. She made it clear she considered herself his girlfriend. Even though it was fun hanging out at camp and kissing, he didn't think we had a future together.

I was crushed. I liked him a whole lot, more than any boy I had known. I refused to believe it was over. So, I begged. And then I cried. Carl was comforting me, saying we'd find a way to make it work,

---

26   Letter to self, dated 10:00 PM, Aug. 28, 1959, mailed from Arcadia, CA to author's home, Jan. 29, 1960.

when the voice of the camp dean came over the loudspeaker, calling our names and demanding we report to our cabins immediately.

I ran to the bunkhouse, embarrassed and relieved at the same time, hoping we had worked things out. The turmoil between us continued until the end of camp, but I concluded that we had "come to a wonderful understanding that, through God, we were meant for each other." This would not be the only time in my life when my idealism kept me from seeing how truly tenuous a relationship was.

Ignoring my doubts, I fantasized about a long-term relationship with Carl. I wrote in my letter to myself. "I had wanted to be an overseas missionary, but now I may want to be a social worker, so I can be near Carl. I can't know if I really love Carl, but God willing, we may someday be husband and wife!" Having a partner was part of how I saw my future, so when I thought about my mission in life it mattered who my partner would be. These two themes—partnership and mission—would continue to be important throughout my life.

RELIGIOUS STUDY AND LIFE PURPOSE

Although I imagine there was a range of topics available, the classes I kept notes about were mostly about relationships and sex. For instance, at the 1959 camp, I took a class called "Sex in Christian Life: Building a Wholesome Life." My notes reveal what I was being taught and how I assimilated what I heard in the months before the 1960s began. The focus of the class was on how to have healthy, responsible relationships based on respect and a shared faith in God. Getting married and having a family was promoted as a goal, because we would not be complete alone, we were told. Every family should be concerned not only about themselves but also about the community and the world. This fit in with what I was dreaming about. I wanted love, but I also wanted to make a difference in the world. On a practical level, we learned about different forms of birth control, with diaphragms as the recommended method. Birth control pills weren't mentioned because they weren't approved for contraceptive use until 1960.[27]

---

27   Decision Card, Senior High Summer Program, Aug. 22-29, 1959, signed

SEA CHANGE: *the unfinished agenda of the 1960s*

That year I attended a Commission Conference, designed to prepare us to be future church leaders. With birth control pills now available, the topic of sex took on a new immediacy. What amazes me now looking back on the class I took that year was the teacher's affirmation of sex as an intrinsic part of love.

Martin Fuller, a chemistry professor at Pomona College where I dreamed of going, explained that the Church understood sex as a gift of God to be used or abused. There is no spiritual-physical duality, he said. Sex is not only to enjoy but plays a part in relationships. It is a partial description of who we are. Then he raised the question of who sets our individual standards of behavior. "I am totally dependent on God and totally independent of socially accepted codes," my notes show. "Our relationships are with persons not codes." Our responsibility is to care for others and not hurt them. With such radical thinking coming from church authority figures, it is not difficult for me to see how I came up with the nontraditional ideas and practices I enjoyed later in the decade!

Martin described eleven aspects of the Christian attitude toward intercourse, which I numbered in my notes. What I find most interesting is that his statement, "Marriage is the only context for this union," is number seven, not number one. These statements, among others, came first in his list:

1. The body is to be used for glory and praise of God.
2. Pleasure in sex should be gladly affirmed (also in little intimacies), if we are aware of limitations.
3. In the union of two human beings, each does something to the other. Once done it can never be obliterated.

Right after the statement about marriage came: "Sex is the giving away to another our final secret. Our natures are fully developed in this." Already at sixteen I had the naïve notion that I was ready to be fully developed. For the past year Carl and I had been exploring each other sexually, always stopping before intercourse. But the longing was growing in me for the completion of this act. And here was the promise. Experiencing sexual intercourse would

---

by Dorothy Emerson "Dodi" listing Rev. Hugh Nelson, Director, copy to be sent to Rev. Herbe Stocker at First Presbyterian, Fullerton.

fully develop my nature. Perhaps this was what was required for me to better understand my path in life.[28] At the end of the sex discussion, however, we were cautioned that, when dating, the test of our concern is restraint. In my notes, I asked myself, "Why do I do what I do? Where is my concern?" and then I recorded the warning, "Stop! until you know the meaning of responsibility and detachment."

In another talk about the importance of our responsibilities as students, Martin warned that it was "immoral to waste time or not to do the best possible." It strikes me now as notable that the one time the word "immoral" appears in my many pages of camp and conference notes, it is about school, not sex. I think of the messages others received from their religious training about what is immoral and am grateful that my training was so progressive.

REGIONAL CONNECTIONS AND CONFERENCES
Periodically, members of Agape Fellowship joined with other youth from southern California for worship and conferences. In March 1960, I attended a youth convention at the Santa Monica Civic Auditorium[29] that affected me deeply.

The major speaker was Dr. Ted Stein, then president of the seminary I would attend five years later. The theme, "Foolishness of God—Wisdom of Men" was ironic. Dr. Stein suggested it might be time for some of God's foolishness, such as believing that disarmament was possible and working for peace. Science and religion were not opposed to each other, he said, but science shouldn't be our religion. Wisdom of men can destroy, as in Nazi Germany where educated people used their learning to destroy. True wisdom, he said, requires "using your mind coordinated with your faith. ... With all our knowledge, we know so little of the purpose of life. Have we lost our souls?" I wondered how I would know what my

---

28   The story of my relationship with Carl continues in Love is All You Need, Evolution of a Sexual Revolutionary.
29   Tri-Presbytery Youth Convention, Santa Monica Civic Auditorium, March 25-26, 1960. Theme speaker: Dr. Edward V. Stein. Notes taken in pencil in a small notebook.

life purpose was.

Housing for the convention was at area churches, where we slept on the floor in sleeping bags—not the best situation for a good night's sleep, but exciting to be with others who took their lives seriously and who wondered, as I did, what their life purpose was. The next morning, each housing group heard a different speaker, all on the same topic: "Consider Your Call." The Rev. Donald Hartsock, University Pastor at UCLA, startled us by saying, "Today the best place to hide from God is in religion." If we weren't fully awake, that got our attention. He went on to explain that people tend to be preoccupied with doing, even in church. Doing, he said, is your occupation. What we need to think about here is what our vocation is, what we are called to be. He pointed out, "We don't go to church. We are the Church and we go to worship. Worship comes from an Anglo-Saxon word meaning 'to be.' Worship helps you discover who you are and choose to be in response to your faith." He challenged us to live out of our sense of call, our vocation. What is the world calling you to be? Acknowledging there is no simple answer, he asked us to "Go home and think life through."

When I heard Rev, Hartsock's definitions of occupation and vocation, I knew I wanted a vocation. He defined vocation as responding to the "call of the world" rather than "call from God." This distinction would become increasingly important to me as time went on. I already knew at age 16 that I would follow the call I was hearing, even if I wasn't completely clear yet as to what I was being called to be or to do.

At the closing worship, Dr. Stein spoke on "The Love that Integrates." True religion isn't deep faith, sentiment, or altruism, unless love is there. Love, compassion, should be our guide in action, our reason for courage and intellectual honesty. He claimed something I would hear later in the Sixties in different words and which I took to heart both then and now: "We are either a part of the world's sickness or a part of its cure." To be part of the cure we need to love all things and find God's mystery there, he said.

He talked about the problems of the world we were living in. The "angry generation," which might include some of us, was right, he said, if their anger was against fear and out of awareness that war was wrong. He hoped, though, that anger would lead to love and shift its focus to building a better society. In this, it seems to me now, he foresaw the shift from the Beat Generation to the Love Generation.

Knowing the world's suffering and identifying with it is what Christ did and what we must do, Dr. Stein said. We are called to stand in defense of freedom and fight against evil, to bear the tensions of the world, and wait to see what love can do. I heard this message deep in my heart and resolved to follow my call, wherever it might lead.

BECOMING A CAMP COUNSELOR, 1960

The youth convention program booklet listed different summer opportunities for youth to become more fully involved, including becoming a junior counselor at a camp for younger kids at Pacific Palisades, where I attended junior high camp. I jumped at the chance and applied right away. Although I was still only 16, I was growing up, and nothing proved it to me more than my new status as a counselor.

After a training session for junior counselors, we welcomed the young campers, fifth and sixth graders, to Junior Choir Camp.[30] Having been in church choirs for many years, I was excited about sharing my love for music with others. I was assigned to a cabin where I was responsible for ensuring that my group of girls was safe and having a good time. Although I wasn't good at enforcing discipline, we managed to be one of the most successful cabins, winning the competition for cleanest cabin several days in a row. Being on staff at a camp and working alongside adult staff members reinforced my feeling of being grown up. I had been baby-sitting for several years and had three younger siblings, so I thought I knew what it meant to watch over younger children, but there I learned I was responsible not only for the girls in my cabin but for all the kids at the camp. I was glad I was part of a team of counselors who shared this important responsibility.

Rob was one of the most popular junior counselors. He had

---

30   Junior Choir Camp # 5, July 24-30, 1960, counselor training, July 23.

35

an easy way of being with the kids and yet being responsible. I saw him as a role model and gravitated toward him. I also thought he was cute and was glad when we became friends. He had a serious nature and thought deeply about things, so I enjoyed talking with him.

When that first week was over, I went home to wash clothes and see my family. Then I returned for a second week, this time in the role of Junior Leader for Leadership School,[31] a program with activities for people of all ages. I was assigned to a cabin, but was not solely responsible for the fourth through sixth graders who slept there. This gave me the freedom to be out at night after my responsibilities were finished.

Rob and I took long walks where we shared our evolving understandings about our lives and the future. As youth leaders, we could leave camp and walk to town or to the beach. One night we walked through a neighborhood with beautiful big homes.

"I wish I could live in a place like this," I sighed, looking at a house with a spectacular view of the ocean.

"I don't even dare imagine it," Rob said.

"Why not?" I asked.

"My family is poor. I will consider myself successful if I can afford to buy a house someday, any house."

Although I knew many people in Fullerton with more money and bigger houses than mine and some with less money and smaller houses or apartments, no one I knew was poor. I tried to imagine what that was like.

When we talked about the future, I learned what being poor meant.

"Most of all I want to go to Pomona College," I said, "but unless I get a really good scholarship, I will have to go to a state school, probably Berkeley."

Rob didn't say anything for a while. "Well," he sighed, "you are lucky to be able to think about college. The only way I can get an education is to enlist in the army."

"How can you do that? Don't you think war is wrong? Could you actually kill another human being?" This went against

---

31   Leadership School # 2, Pacific Palisades, Aug. 7-13, 1960.

everything I had learned in church.

"I don't have a choice," he said sharply. "I hope I won't have to kill anyone, but sometimes you have to do what you have to do."

"I'm so sorry," I said with tears forming in my eyes. "I wish things were different for you."

Rob and I continued to be friends throughout the following year, dated occasionally, and wrote each other letters in between. I came to feel real love for him. Although it was different from the way I felt about Carl, I learned from my relationship with Rob that I could love more than one person at a time. Knowing him helped me understand the difficult choices some people are forced to make because of their economic circumstances. I resolved that part of my mission in life would be to make the world more just and fair for all people.

WHAT I LEARNED

My last set of notes from Presbyterian camps, conferences, and retreats is from the annual Agape Retreat of our Fullerton church youth group held in February 1961 at Loch Leven, a camp in the San Bernardino Mountains.[32] Rev. Herbe Stocker talked about theology.

Reflecting now on my notes, I realize I did not think critically about the theology I was learning. Instead I tried to find a way to believe what I heard and figure out how to live that way. In college, I struggled to hold on to my belief in God and Christ, but continued to be inspired by my experiences in church and at camps and conferences.[33] I knew I wanted my life to mean something, and the Church provided a way for me to do that. What stayed with me throughout my life was not the theology but rather the commitment that the Church had to be relevant and engaged with the world. In his historical overview of Presbyterian social witness policies, Dale Irvin, president of New York Theological Seminary, explained that

---

32   Agape Retreat, Loch Leven, February 3-5, 1961.

33   I attended one more church retreat while I was in college, March 23-25, 1962, at Loch Leven, but have no notes from it—and no memories.

in the late 1950s the Presbyterian Church began shifting its focus toward greater engagement with society:

The Church must be relevant to its time, having a clear knowledge of the state and a complete as possible understanding of contemporary social problems. The Church should not simply endorse government policy or dominant cultural values, but be a community that offers alternatives.[34]

My involvement with the Church coincided with this shift toward offering alternatives to dominant social values, contributing significantly to my life-long commitment to social change. I am grateful to the ministers and youth leaders who fostered in me the belief that I could make a difference. I know I disappointed some who hoped I would fulfill my calling as an active leader in the Presbyterian Church, but if any of them read this book, I hope they will see that their teachings mattered and had impact far beyond what they might have imagined at the time.

POMONA COLLEGE AWAKENINGS

Pomona College was a place of many awakenings for me. Not only did I have the opportunity for an excellent education, but being in college provided many opportunities for spiritual exploration.

The stone gates that served as the original entrance to Pomona College framed our education. One gate cautioned new students: "Let only the eager, thoughtful, and reverent enter here." The other sent us on our way with a challenge: "They only are loyal to this college who, departing, bear their added riches in trust for mankind."[35] When the college community gathered each year for the opening Convocation, we often heard the idea that each of us has a unique calling, a vocation. Pomona shaped me in ways I continue to uncover as time goes on. But perhaps its greatest influence was

---

34   Dale T. Irvin, "Social Witness Policies: An Historical Overview" *Journal of Presbyterian History* 57 (Fall 1979): 38990.

35   Quotations from James Blaisdell, who served as the college's fourth president, 1910-27. When I became aware of the importance of gender inclusive language, I wanted to change the word "mankind" to "humankind," but the words are, in fact, set in stone. In my mind, however, when I recall this quote, I make the change.

the challenge its departing gate presented: to do something of significance with the riches college added to my life.

The Church had taught me that God calls us to be people of faith and to serve the world. Pomona College taught me that the world calls us to use our gifts to benefit humankind. Over time, these messages merged.

AWAKENING TO SELF

Among the gifts of my Pomona College education were the small classes and professors who knew our names. Early on this caught me up short. I had stayed up practically all night because I had two papers due the next day—one in philosophy and the other in English. The philosophy paper was the hardest for me so I worked on it first. Around two in the morning I started on my English paper. The next afternoon, I stopped at Edmunds Union for a cup of coffee. To my surprise, my English professor, Richard Barnes, noticed me.

"May I join you?" he said as he sat down, not waiting for my response. "What you wrote in your paper intrigues me," he went on. I gulped because I couldn't remember what I had written! The fact that a professor would talk with me about my ideas awakened me to the realization that maybe what I thought and wrote was worthy of discussion. Later, when I became a teacher, I remembered how this one incident awakened me to my own validity as a person with ideas worth considering, and I attempted to engage my students in similar dialogs.

EXPLORING DIFFERENT FAITHS

During my first year in college, 1961-62, I stopped attending church every Sunday. This was a big change for me. Since I was no longer involved in a specific church community, attendance at worship sometimes took a back seat to other elements of student life. Sometimes I attended the ecumenical College Church,[36] which held

---

36   Although the services were held on the Pomona College campus, they were planned through the chaplain's office at McAlister Center, a central service to all the Claremont Colleges. Ministers from different denominations spoke, offering different perspectives on faith.

services in the music building across the street from my dorm. When a friend invited me to come to a meeting of the Religious Liberals group on campus to help make posters, I met the minister of the Unitarian church. One Sunday I walked over a mile to attend a service there. On a postcard to my family, I described it as "very interesting," especially because the minister defined himself as a social activist.[37] Another Sunday I got up early for a communion service led by the Episcopalian campus group at McAlister, the campus church center. We stood in a circle as communion bread and wine were given to us. Wine, as opposed to the grape juice we used in the Presbyterian Church. That one swallow of wine on an empty stomach on Sunday morning shocked me, in a nice way. I thought, "This must be one of the attractions of being Episcopalian."

After my freshman year, a college friend invited me to visit her in Seattle for the 1962 World's Fair. Besides the excitement of taking my first airplane ride and attending a World's Fair, this was a new experience because Joni's family was Jewish. Before college I hadn't known anyone who openly identified as Jewish. My mother had expressed prejudice against Jews, but after Joni spent semester break with our family, my mother declared, "I like Joni. She's not a typical Jew." Her conclusion was fortunate for me, since it paved the way for my trip to Seattle. Besides, my mother thought it was time for me to have my first experience of airplane travel.

As it turned out, Joni's family was what my mother probably considered "typically Jewish," but I learned it was the opposite of a bad thing. Joni's parents were Reform Jews but not particularly religious. Her father ran a credit jewelry store, where people could purchase diamonds with very little money down. Although my mother might have looked askance at such a store, she probably would have shopped there, as she was an early user of credit to buy what our family needed.

Although the family did not regularly go to Temple, they took me to a service there. It didn't seem substantially different from the church services I was used to, except that the readings were in

---

37   Postcard to family, Oct. 9, 1961. The church had a new minister, Dr. W.E. Cole, who was an outspoken social activist.

Hebrew. There were words of faith and encouragement to live our lives in a sacred way. They talked about being good Jews, just like we talked about being good Christians. After the service, they gathered informally, as we did, only they had more food and served things I wasn't familiar with. With Joni's encouragement and guidance, I tried various dishes and liked most, but I can't say now what they were.

I came away feeling maybe there wasn't as much difference between religions as I had been led to believe. Certainly, the goals were the same, to help people live meaningful lives, encourage them to help each other, and inspire them to work for a better world. Joni's family differed from mine in their much larger and more elegant home, and the fact that Joni's mother did volunteer work and grew bonsai trees, which I had never seen before. Her parents also allowed us to drink alcohol. Joni and I had fun trying out different liquors they had on hand, and we never got drunk. It felt good to be trusted.

Sophomore year I decided I wanted to be part of a church community again, so I joined the College Church Choir.[38] I told my family that getting up early for rehearsal and church was part of my commitment to being organized and getting better grades. My reward for such diligence was that after church I would meet my friends at Walter's, our favorite local restaurant. Most of them ate breakfast and I ate lunch, I explained to justify the expense. I promised I would spend the rest of the day studying.

Later that year, I went back to the Unitarian church. Although it was more than a mile from my dorm, I enjoyed walking there by myself. The low ceilings of the cinder block building built in the 1950s did not inspire me the way my home church did, but there was something about the message that intrigued me. Rather than focusing on the Bible and Christian teachings, they talked about the changing world we live in and how we need to be a part of that change. I noticed that the words of familiar hymns were often changed to focus on people rather than God.[39] This went along with

---

38   I was also a member of the College Choir, for which I receive course credit. The College Church Choir was a smaller, all-volunteer choir.
39   Because many Unitarians and Unitarian Universalists had shifted from

their focus on human responsibility for the future.

I appreciated the liberal and accepting way the congregation and the minister acted. Although this example seems trivial, one thing that impressed me was that people smoked cigarettes at the outdoors social hour after the service, even the minister's son. I smoked at school but would never dare smoke in front of my parents or at any church event. This openness about smoking, I thought, meant that people in that church could be honest about their lives, not pretending they were something they were not. The minister's son and I got to be friends. Several times he gave me a ride back to my dorm, and we sat in the elegant dorm parlor of Mudd-Blaisdell, talking about our lives.

During my senior year in college, my graduate school friend Jerry took me to Sacred Heart, a Catholic mission church in what Jerry called the "barrio." When I wrote home about it, I referred to it as a slum. The people who lived there had come from Mexico to work at the college or in the orange groves. I liked being in that warm and welcoming community and sharing their worship rituals, so different from Protestant churches.

STUDYING RELIGION ACADEMICALLY

At Pomona, we were encouraged to study what we were drawn to, rather than what might be practical for future careers. I as a philosophy major, but ended up majoring in German Literature. I initially chose philosophy because I was interested in ideas, but I struggled with my first class, Problems of Philosophy.[40] I was just beginning to understand one philosopher, when we were on to the next. Because I found something of value in what each philosopher said, I found it difficult to keep track of the differences among them. Getting a B minus was a crushing blow to my confidence in myself as a student.

Not one to give up, the next semester I signed up for Issues

---

theism to humanism by the 1950s, the words of hymns were changed. In the 1970s and early 1980s Unitarian Universalists made another major shift to using gender-inclusive language, and the words of hymns and liturgy were once again changed.

40   Taught by Frederick Sontag.

in Religious Thought.[41] I liked this class better because of the religious content, but had a similar problem differentiating among theologians. When I learned that one of the professors was an ordained minister in the United Church of Christ, I was intrigued with the idea that a minister might be a college professor. Although the assigned readings helped me delve more deeply into questions of faith, by the end of the year I was questioning whether to continue as a philosophy major. I struggled with my own ideas about God. Then I discovered Garcia Lorca's statement: "Quiero querer creer." (I want to want to believe.) I learned it by heart in Spanish and repeated it periodically to myself.

FACING DEATH

Near the end of my sophomore year something happened that drew me more deeply into questions of faith and purpose than anything I experienced either in churches or in the classroom.

A guy I had dated a few times stopped by my dorm one Saturday afternoon.

"What are you doing on this beautiful day?" he asked.

"Studying," I answered, "What else?"

"How about taking a ride with me up Mt. Baldy?" he offered. "I have stuff for a picnic."

Without thinking much about it I said yes and hopped in his car. It was a great excuse to avoid studying on a warm spring afternoon. Driving up the mountain on the winding road was beautiful. Then we stopped for our picnic, but instead of food all he had was a quart jar of fruit punch heavily laced with alcohol.

"Hey, where's the food?" I asked. "I skipped lunch to come with you."

"Who needs food?" he replied. "This is better. I made it especially for you. Try some." I drank out of the jar he held out to me. He drank more than I did. Then he wanted sex. I said no.

He got mad and said, "OK, it's time to go."

He drove back down the mountain like a maniac and lost

---

41   Taught by Sontag and Robert Ferm. Sontag was just completing his first book, *Divine Perfection: Possible Ideas of God.*

control of the car on a curve. As the car veered out over the cliff, I saw myself smashed to death hundreds of feet below. But we were saved -- the car swerved back onto the road and crashed into the cliff behind us. Was it the hand of God or centrifugal force? I wondered. The windshield shattered (in those days before safety glass), and the breaking glass cut across the top of my right hand as I shielded my face. When the car stopped, he asked me to take the booze out of the car and throw it behind the rocks. Only then as blood ran down my face did I realize my scalp was full of glass. People stopped to help, eventually medics came, and the rest is a blur. What stays with me most from the experience is the feeling that I was saved for a reason. I felt the hand of God protecting me for some larger purpose in my life.

The most serious physical effect of the accident was to my right hand. I lost the fingernail on the ring finger and had a protruding scar on my middle finger for many years. The fingernail grew back and now, some fifty years later, the scar has nearly disappeared. Not serious compared to what could have happened, but at the time it meant that my right hand was bandaged and I could not write my finals.

I took my French and German finals orally and my father drove me back to Claremont during the summer to Professor Richard Barnes' house to take my final in Chaucer. That proved to be an interesting meeting. I had wondered what my professor and my high-school drop-out father and would say to each other while I wrote my exam. The professor's credentials did not intimidate my father. He had a talent for observing details and identified an antique clock on the wall as made by Chauncey Jerome, just like the one that hung in our house. Professor Barnes was impressed because he hadn't realized his clock was made by a famous company.

Fortunately, my summer job as at Southern California Edison, the company that was providing my college scholarship, could be adapted to my temporary disability. By July the bandages were off and I was beginning to return to "normal." But the sense that I had been saved for a reason stuck with me, and I moved through those hot summer days with a new awareness of my identity as someone who had a mission in life, even if I wasn't sure what that was.

SEEKING VOCATION, CHOOSING MINISTRY

The idea of vocation was very much on my mind as I approached my senior year. I had to decide what to do when I graduated. What was I being called to do, to be? What were my next steps? I knew I wanted to do something that mattered. I thought about the adults I knew who made the most difference in my life. Although I appreciated the way my professors inspired and guided me, I did not think I was a good enough student to spend the next four or five years of my life earning a master's degree and a PhD. I considered getting a teaching credential as some friends were doing, but I wanted to do something different, something less expected of me as a woman, although I knew teaching was something I could fall back on if other options did not work out. I recognized that I had long felt called to some sort of vocation involving religion, that the people who inspired me most were ministers, so I decided to apply to seminary. Even if I didn't become a minister, seminary seemed the best place to learn about the Church.

Although I sought support from the Presbyterians, they did not require me to go to a Presbyterian seminary. Meeting with the Dean of Students from Harvard Divinity School[42] inspired me to apply there because, as he explained, the students came from many different Christian churches and from other religions, and that the study of world religions was encouraged. I knew immediately that this was the place I wanted to go. I also appreciated the kind letter he sent me later with the names of two women students I might correspond with to learn more about the school. On my application, I stated my understanding that "dialogue among Christians of different confessions, between Christians and non-Christians, and among Christians of different national and historical orientation" existed at Harvard and was a determining factor in my application.

As a back-up, I also applied to San Francisco Theological Seminary (SFTS), a Presbyterian school in northern California. In

---

42   I met with Herbert Long in Nov. 1964, when he visited the Claremont Colleges.

that application, I described my faith journey: "From time to time in college I forgot how important Christianity is, but after each time of forgetting came a time of stronger acceptance. Now is the time for me to decide which of the important factors in my life to pursue, and I have chosen. Exactly how the Church can best use me I do not yet know, but that it can use me I do believe."

On both applications, I wrote about my desire to move beyond facades as part of what drew me to a church vocation. "Because I like people, I dislike facades which hide people from one another. The Church provides at least the invitation for the recognition of facades, and this recognition allows for alleviation of the pain resulting from faith in facades." I applied for the three-year bachelor of divinity[43] degree rather than the two-year master's degree most women chose in preparation for careers in Christian Education. This way my options would be open, in case I decided to become a minister.

The seminary applications expected me to show current involvement in a local church, so I began regular attendance at the Claremont Presbyterian Church. On my initial visit, a year or two earlier, I felt it lacked the spirit I was looking for, but when I went back with seminary in mind, I found the church more to my liking. I began by attending the 11 AM service but then volunteered to teach second grade Sunday school at the 9:30 service, and later to sing in the choir. It wasn't easy to arrange to spend the morning at church, given other college activities and responsibilities, but I managed to be consistent in my participation. However, I saw it more as preparation for seminary than as something I was doing for my personal faith development.

The decision to attend seminary set other processes in motion as well. Choosing a church vocation in the Presbyterian church meant declaring your decision to various church bodies and asking for their approval and support. In October, I was presented to the Session, the governing board of my home church. They approved

---

43   Although it was a graduate degree, it was historically called a Bachelor of Divinity until the mid-1970s, when most schools changed the name to Master of Divinity.

me as a "candidate for full-time professional Christian service."[44] An article, "College Girl Named Seminary Candidate," appeared in the local paper the following week.[45] That made it official.

After local approval, I had to be accepted by the Presbytery of Los Angeles. That was much scarier than appearing before adults from my own church. First, I had to undergo a series of psychological tests. Later I would return to appear before a panel of church leaders who would evaluate my application to become a candidate for ministry. Both times I took the train to Los Angeles and found my way to the Presbytery offices. After the first trip, when I spent over four hours taking tests, I treated myself to a movie. "Becket," starring Richard Burton and Peter O'Toole, told a story that took place in twelfth-century England of the relationship between King Henry II and his long-time friend, whom he appoints to be the Archbishop of Canterbury. In his new role Becket puts service to God above service to the king, which angers Henry and leads to Becket's eventual death. I felt shaken by the story and the reality of what choosing a religious vocation might mean. Later, after the panel approved my application, I wondered if my future status as a church leader would change me the way it changed Thomas Becket.

AMERICAN STUDIES

My decision to go to seminary influenced other choices I made my senior year. For instance, I signed up for a course in American Studies at Harvey Mudd, one of the other colleges in the Claremont Colleges complex. The seminar brought together experts from history, anthropology, sociology, literature, philosophy, religion, and political science to explore the formation of modern American culture. This multifaceted approach allowed me to study religion in a larger context and gave me new insights about culture change and the role of the Church in that process.

Students made presentations each week about people who shaped contemporary American thought. My first presentation was

---

44   "Dorothy Emerson Candidate for Seminary," *Chi Rho*, newsletter of First Presbyterian Church, Fullerton, Oct. 28, 1964.
45   "College Girl Named Seminary Candidate," *News Tribune*, Oct. 31, 1964.

about William Ellery Channing, nineteenth-century minister and one of the founders of Unitarianism, whose religious perspectives I would embrace later in life. I liked what he said about the role of the Church in awakening the soul.

> The great end in religious instruction is not to stamp our minds upon the young, but to stir up their own; not to make them see with our eyes, but to look inquiringly and steadily with their own; ... not to form an outward regularity, but to touch inward springs; ... not to impose religion upon them in the form of arbitrary rules, but to awaken the conscience, the moral discernment. In a word, the great end is to awaken the soul, to excite and cherish spiritual life.[46]

This described what I gained from my involvement in church, and I was grateful for those who awakened me to a spiritual life. I hoped I would discover in seminary how I could best touch those "inward springs" in others.

For my term paper, I chose to study the twentieth-century religious leader Reinhold Niebuhr,[47] whom I had heard speak freshman year at College Church. The title of his book, *Moral Man and Immoral Society*, intrigued me, as did the book's thesis that individuals could strive to be good but society was inevitably evil because of decisions made to protect the self-interest of the group. He claimed: "There is not enough imagination in any social group to render it amenable to the influence of pure love."[48] I wondered what it would take for society to be governed by love. Niebuhr challenged the Church to move beyond its tendency toward self-righteousness and realistically face the social problems of the day, seeking to reduce selfishness and promote forgiveness and love.

---

46 William Ellery Channing, "The Sunday School: Discourse Pronounced Before The Sunday School Society," in *The Works of William E. Channing*, Volume 4 (1841), 361.

47 My paper was entitled, "Biography of an American Churchman," but I no longer have a copy. I used a combination of sources on the internet in writing this about Niebuhr, combined with what I remember and what I later learned in seminary.

48 Reinhold Niebuhr, *Moral Man and Immoral Society*, 1932, chapter 10.

I discovered the newly published book *Courage to Change*,[49] which detailed Niebuhr's engagement with twentieth-century religion, world affairs, and social change. What intrigued me was the way he changed his understanding of right action over the course of his life. He was a pacifist in World War I, but as Nazism began to spread in Europe, he became an advocate of Just War theory and encouraged the United States to intervene. Later he developed a new theology in response to the human evil he saw in the actions of Hitler and Stalin. I could see how the changing times led to each of these shifts. I wondered how my beliefs might shift in response to the times I was living in, and I hoped I would have the courage to change as he did. Niebuhr had been a professor at Union Seminary in New York City, and had he not retired, I might have applied there to study with him.

Learning about these religious leaders and how they interacted with the culture and history of their times helped shape my vision of how my own life and ministry might evolve.

CHOOSING A SEMINARY

I was accepted by both schools and awarded scholarships. Since my family could not afford a trip across the country for me to visit Harvard, my mother suggested I visit San Francisco Theological Seminary (in Marin County) during Easter vacation. "You should see what seminary is like before you decide for sure that's what you want to do," my mother said. I knew the trip would be fun, even though I was sure I wanted to go to Harvard.

San Anselmo is a beautiful town, and the seminary on the top of the hill is impressive. Many students and faculty had recently participated in the Selma to Montgomery March,[50] and there was

---

49   June Bingham, *Courage to Change: an introduction to the life and thought of Reinhold Niebuhr*. Niebuhr is the author of the famous Serenity Prayer used by Alcoholics Anonymous and other 12-step groups. He wrote a somewhat longer version during World War II which was picked up and adapted with his permission. The original prayer spoke of "the courage to change what <u>should</u> be changed. The AA version uses "<u>can</u> be changed."
50   On March 7, 1965, 600 people began a march from Selma, Alabama to Montgomery, Alabama, to demand an end to discrimination in voter registration.

much talk about their commitment to civil rights work. That excited me, as did the presence of a repertory theater company on campus. Toward the end of my visit, the seminary president Ted Gill took me aside, put his arm around my shoulder, and said with a twinkle in his eye, "Don't go to Harvard. You'll like it better here. We're much more sensual." I was surprised at his remark but laughed and was pleased he took a personal interest in me.

I realized that going to school in northern California where I had relatives nearby would be a whole lot easier than going across the country where I knew no one. It would also be much more affordable, a necessity after my father made it clear he would not support me financially beyond graduation from college. "Four years is enough," he said. "We need the money to help your sister and brothers with their education." Shortly after I got home, I reluctantly wrote Harvard a letter, saying I had decided to attend San Francisco Theological Seminary.

SAN FRANCISCO THEOLOGICAL SEMINARY

I chose seminary over traditional graduate school because I wanted to be involved in real life, not just studying all the time. But once my regular seminary classes started, the reality of what was ahead of me for the next three years began to sink in. The seminary was exactly like other graduate schools, with classes, extensive reading, papers to write, and finals. Plus, there was field work, and I needed a job to make enough money to live on. I was truly on my own for the first time in my life, and I wanted to enjoy all the Bay Area had to offer. Just reading about my many activities exhausts me now. I wonder that I had any time to study.

Still I learned a great deal in the short time I was there. One of my most treasured learnings came in the form of a large, expensive

---

At the Edmund Pettus Bridge, state and local lawmen attacked the marchers with clubs and tear gas, driving them back to Selma. Dr. King called for clergy of all faiths to come to Selma. On March 21, 3,200 people marched out of Selma, for under the protection of federal troops, walking about 12 miles a day and sleeping in fields at night. By the time they reached the state capitol in Montgomery, there were 25,000 marchers.

book I had to buy, *Ancient Near-Eastern Texts Relating to the Old Testament*, edited by James B. Pritchard.[51] Studying the different texts used in Genesis opened my eyes to the layers of story embedded in the Bible. I concluded that neither Moses nor the "hand of God" wrote the Bible, as some church people claimed, but rather it was assembled from other sources. I carried this big book with me for many years and still had it when I went back to seminary seventeen years later.

I also had classes in theology and social ethics,[52] but what interested me most was field education at the Presbyterian Church in Novato, with Jim Upshaw, whom I described as "a very freewheeling minister." My assignment was to observe "the inner workings of a church and its component parts," so I attended meetings of the governing board as well as worship services, church school classes, and the women's association.[53] I was also expected to participate in extracurricular activities on campus, so I joined the choir and the committee that was planning a new student-faculty publication, *Challenge*.

LOSING MY RELIGION

Going to seminary ended up driving me away from the Church.[54] It also introduced me to key elements that would shape my life for the rest of the Sixties and beyond. Four encounters and resulting realizations led to my decision to leave seminary five months after arriving.

---

51   The course, History, Literature, and Religion of the Old Testament, was taught by a well-known biblical scholar, James Muilenberg, who had served on the translating committee for the Revised Standard Version of the Bible.

52   Systematic Theology with Arnold Come and Benjamin Reist, and Ethics with Robert Lee, who was the first East Asian professor at an American Christian seminary, hired by SFTS in 1961.

53   "Girl Divinity Student at Local Presbyterian Church," *Novato Advance*. Nov. 23, 1965.

54   I was part of the trend described by Don Lattin: "Millions of Catholics, Protestants, and Jews in the baby boomer generation left organized religion in the Sixties and embarked on a new spiritual search." In *Following Our Bliss: How the Spiritual Ideals of the Sixties Shape Our Lives Today*, 10.

The first encounter was with the belief in the uniqueness of Christianity as the one true path to God. One of the most popular students at seminary grew up Jewish but became a Presbyterian in high school. Everyone liked him, but his conversion to Christianity confused me. "Why did he need to convert to live a life of faith? Wasn't being Jewish just as good?" I wondered. I could no longer accept the traditional theological idea that because if you knew of Jesus and did not choose to follow him, you were damned. By then I knew Jewish people who were in every way as faithful and good as any Christians I knew. Besides, I reasoned, why would God create different religious if there was only one true way?

Second was the job I got as a youth director for a church near Palo Alto, more than an hour's drive from the seminary campus. I was excited at the prospect of working with youth. This was my first real chance to share the inspiration and empowerment I had received in my own youth group experiences. Full of hope and a sense of mission, I drove south through San Francisco into the exclusive wooded community of Portola Valley. Then I met the students. The dozen or so that participated were not happy about being there. Absorbed with their own lives of privilege, their studies, their dates, and their activities, they didn't seem to care about church and had no interest in making a difference in the world or living lives of meaning. They liked the way they were and saw me as an outsider, not part of their exclusive community. This was my first encounter with a church as social club, and I neither understood nor liked it. But I needed the job, and it paid well, so I continued to make the trek there every Sunday evening while I was still in seminary.

My third perspective-shifting encounter occurred when I participated in an international simulation on campus. Held for two days in December, after first quarter classes were finished, the seminary's Academics Commission arranged for this innovative program as "an experiment in learning and an introduction to a possible new method of teaching."[55] Our setting was international relations, with each of us assigned to a different "country." Each

---

55   *Currents*, Oct. 10, 1965. The simulation was held Dec. 3-4, 1965, on Friday afternoon and evening and on Saturday.

country had four decision makers, who needed to consider both domestic and international priorities. Each country also had an opposition leader. The decision-makers could arrange for foreign aid, build nuclear weapons or conventional forces, and suppress rebellion. A team of psychologists[56] from Western Behavioral Institute in La Jolla conducted this complex and detailed simulation. It was an intense experience. I was assigned to one of the smaller countries. After assessing the "world" situation and realizing we were in a difficult position internationally, I joined the delegation from my country that attempted to form a coalition among smaller nations. However, despite our best efforts, the big nations started a nuclear war and the planet was destroyed.

Later we reflected on our experience. While we were engaged in the game, we lost track of who we were in the rest of our lives and acted based on our simulation roles. When it hit me that even members of a seminary community could blow up the world, I wondered if studying for the ministry made any difference at all. Clearly commitment to Christianity and having accepted the call to become religious leaders didn't affect the way we played the game. One student described the experience in the school magazine: "Learning is not information, not technique, not just a body of knowledge. Rather, learning is a dynamic, an excitement too often denied by the inability of a class to allow the learner to be a participant in the process of coming to conclusions. A game comes closer to reality than a class which deludes itself by imagining that no game is being played."[57] I was ready for dynamic, exciting, participatory learning, and I wasn't finding it in my classes.

The fourth and most decisive reason was the hypocrisy I encountered in relation to sexuality. I arrived at seminary having recently acquired birth control pills. I had come to believe that love and sexuality were closely related and that making love was a valid way to connect deeply with another person. As one of a handful of women on campus—and the only one studying for ministry—I

---

56   Hall Sprague and John Razor, two of the three authors, came from project team SIMILE to conduct the simulation.
57   Bob Shukraft, "Simulation as Education," *Currents*, Oct. 10, 1965.

was an easy object for men's sexual fantasies. In my naiveté, I misinterpreted lust for real connection and shared myself sexually with several students, two of whom turned out to be married. As a recently liberated woman, I expected my partners to be open about our relationships and was surprised to learn they wanted to keep what we did "between us." I was confused. How could these men who were studying to be ministers act with such duplicity?

My confusion—and disillusionment—were exacerbated when seminary president Ted Gill[58] asked me to take a walk with him. As we walked away from campus through the neighborhood of well-kept houses and flowering yards, he asked:

"How are you finding seminary?" he asked.

"I'm enjoying it, especially getting to know the other students."

"That's good," he said. "There aren't many women on campus, so I wanted to be sure you felt welcome and included."

"I seem to fit in just fine," I said.

Then, his tone changed and he got a serious look on his face. "Maybe you're not aware, but some of the students are talking about you in ways you might not like."

"Really?" I was surprised.

"It has to do with some of your activities," he paused, lowering his voice, "your sexual activities."

"Oh?" I wondered what would come next.

"You see," he said. "It's not that I want to put a damper on your activities. You have a right to do whatever you choose, but I wanted to give you a word of advice."

I waited for the wisdom of this religious leader.

After a pause while he apparently gathered his thoughts, he said, "Many ministers find it important to follow a general principle: Don't shit on your doorstep."

---

58   Theodore A. Gill was an otherwise honorable and respected religious leader, with many good works to his credit. He was president of San Francisco Theological Seminary from 1958 to 1966. Shortly after our "talk," he left to serve as director of higher education at the World Council of Churches in Geneva, Switzerland. For more on his life and career, see his obituary at www.sfts.edu/about/news_pressRelease_archive.asp.

"Huh?"

"There's nothing wrong with sex, but especially if you're going to be involved with married men, keep it off campus."

I hardly knew what to say. I was shocked on so many levels. "Are you asking me to lie?" It didn't occur to me at the time to ask if he had talked to the men involved.

I was stunned. I had explained in my application essay that I disliked facades, and here he was telling me I needed to create one. I had believed churches were places where people could learn to interact with each other without facades. How could I live a life of integrity as a religious leader if this was the way it was done?[59]

FESTIVAL THEATRE

Fortunately, Festival Theatre provided both salvation and a way out of the Church. This repertory theater company was housed in a large building on campus that had been a gym in an earlier era. When I arrived at SFTS that fall, I discovered the theater building right next to my dorm, so one of the first things I did was to get the schedule and figure out when I could attend the plays. Thanks to a discount for seminary students, I could attend all the productions, some more than once. Some of the actors ate in the school cafeteria when they were on campus rehearsing. That's how I got to know Thomas, the man who eventually became my first husband. He was older than most of the students at seminary, who like me were fresh out of college. He had a sophisticated and urbane manner and always had something interesting to say. Over time I found myself looking for him at meals.

Thomas had been in the play I saw when I visited the seminary that spring. Reflecting on the meaning of that play brought us together six months later. *Cup of Trembling* was a powerful play written by the director of the theater, Elizabeth Berryhill, about Dietrich Bonhoeffer, a German minister who opposed Hitler and was eventually put to death in a concentration camp. I had written about him in a college term paper on the Church in Nazi Germany.

---

59   For more on the larger context of this story, see Love is All You Need, Sex in the Seminary.

That fall the theater produced *Our Town*, by Thornton Wilder. I had read the play in high school but seeing it acted was so powerful I experienced a new awareness of the meaning of life and death, deeper and more profound than what I was learning in seminary. The play's religious implications were presented in a way that was more accessible than most theology, I thought. I began to understand why the seminary had invited Festival Theatre to the campus.

Our Town was the first in a five-year series of plays the theater was planning to "bring to life the journey of the human spirit in twentieth-century America as it has been articulated by our dramatic artists."[60] This unique theater not only produced excellent plays, they also had a mission not unlike ministry, to help people live lives of meaning. Artistic Director Elizabeth Berryhill was largely responsible for this vision and chose people to work with who shared a sense of the larger mission of the theater. Together the company believed that "serious drama ... can provide us with a critical self-awareness and a sense of our individual and collective identity which may help us go forward through the remainder of the century fruitfully and creatively."

I wasn't interested in acting, but I loved the theater, and the plays they chose had important meanings for my life. I volunteered as an usher and helped in the office. Later I helped Thomas run lights and sound. As his partner, I was accepted as a member of the community, and the theater became a spiritual home to me.

MARIN CITY

What I found most inspiring about seminary was the way it served as a place of connection, where people came to share what they were doing to make a difference in the world. That's how I became involved with a community that ultimately took me away from the seminary and into a new life. I learned about Marin City when two ministers—one white and one black—came to the seminary to recruit students as tutors for elementary school students. This mostly black

60   Marjorie Casebier, "Project Five," in Festival Theatre Student Study Syllabus V, 1.

unincorporated area was located on the opposite side of the freeway from Sausalito, a mostly white art and resort community. Although the schools integrated early on, many kids from Marin City were not doing as well academically as their more privileged classmates from Sausalito. The tutoring program helped any students who needed it, but most of the kids served were black.

After I signed up to be a tutor, the white minister, Rev. Don Schilling, invited me to attend services at St. Andrew Presbyterian Church in Marin City. I loved it. It was the first time I was in a church filled mostly with people of color. Don told me about a housing project currently being built there with a new purpose: "to form an integrated community and to involve the residents in community action." This interested me even more than tutoring. If I moved to Marin City, I could be independent and I would have a sense of purpose I wasn't finding at seminary.

I arranged with school officials to move out of Baird Hall at the end of the first quarter, and then wrote a letter to my family enlisting their support on the basis that it was an important aspect of my seminary education. This was my first major independent decision as a young adult, still only 21 years old. Although I knew I would to do it no matter what they said, I hoped for my parents' support, both "technical" (meaning money) and spiritual. Here's how I "sold" the idea: "I have felt very rootless and vague about my life in seminary and just what I'm doing here. I need to feel some action; I need to know that something is being done in such areas of need as Marin City. If the Church is not effective in such areas, then I am going to seminary under false illusions. There is only one way to put my ideas to the test; and that is to confront life squarely—to jump in and live. I need to root myself in a community."
Although my father stuck to his decision not to support my further education, my mother agreed to send $25 a month and sometimes included a little more.

EXPLORING RELIGIOUS ALTERNATIVES

When I decided a month later to leave seminary altogether, I also left the Presbyterian Church. The hypocrisy both at the seminary and in the Portola Valley church youth group sickened me. In contrast, Festival Theatre fulfilled my ideal of a community where people could be honest about who they were and what they were doing. People could even be honest about being gay. As time went on I had less and less desire to be associated with a church. However, I was not yet aware that I was part of a social movement, one that would change the nature of religion and religious institutions for all time. As Don Lattin explained: "Religion … California style … would spread across the country and around the world. It was about workshops, not worship, seeking your true self, not eternal salvation."[61]

A year later a new kind of church was established in San Anselmo, where Thomas and I were living at the time. Open End initially described itself as a church without walls. The founders were an Episcopalian clergy couple, Barbara and Frank Potter, who had participated in weekend workshops at Esalen Institute in Big Sur and valued the transformative personal growth work offered there. They felt, however, that lasting change requires a community where people can share what they are learning and can grow together. The result was an alternative spiritual community based on the new teachings and practices of personal growth and humanistic psychology.

The Open End congregation gathered in small groups that met for six weeks at a time in members' homes, each engaged in a particular practice such as Gestalt therapy, psychodrama, yoga, meditation, and encounter groups. At the end of each cycle, there was a break for community meetings and planning sessions at the founders' house, Saturday workshops, like bread baking and art projects, and occasional group trips. Then a new schedule appeared and sign-ups began for the next round of groups.

During one of the community meetings I spoke up about something I felt was missing: a sense of worship. We were planning a gathering that would bring the whole community together, and I wondered if some form of worship could be part of it. Others agreed but did not want it to be like a church service. Someone had an idea of how to tie the mask-making activity we had already planned

---

61   Don Lattin, 14.

into a ritual at the end of the day. I wasn't sure what that meant but agreed to help plan it. The gathering was held on a Saturday at the seminary, in the same space where I had eaten meals when I was a student. Everyone was invited, including children. We began by making paper-bag masks to represent our inner selves. Then we had a wonderful potluck feast, followed by music, dancing and singing. At the end of the gathering we danced together with our masks on as a way to see each other in new ways, forming a circle to affirm our unity and deep connection with each other as a community. This was my introduction to community ritual as an alternative to traditional worship.

Thomas and I were actively involved in Open End even after we moved to Sonoma County in late 1970, but the drive back to Marin to meet weekly with groups became cumbersome and we stopped participating regularly. I continued, however, to read the newsletter, attended special events, and dreamed about forming an alternative spiritual community where we were. By then I was a teacher hoping to create ways to bring these ideas into the classroom--without calling it religion, of course.

SEEKING A NEW SPIRITUAL UNDERSTANDING
No longer actively a part of a church or spiritual community, I still thought in religious and spiritual terms. Before I began regular journal writing in 1972, I occasionally made small books using odd ends of paper and card stock Thomas brought home from his work as a printer. In one of these,[62] I described my struggle to define a new form of spirituality that would work for the way my life was evolving:

It's a long time since I've believed in ANYTHING. Off and on in my life I've believed in God/Church, but what I really believed in then was how I felt—belonging, people being together, people caring, people being kind, open, honest. IS THAT GOD? Is there a being that makes that happen? PEOPLE MAKE THAT HAPPEN. I want to be with people who are alive and who live with love, who give openly and freely.

Around this same time, probably 1971, I wrote a prayer,

---

62   "Who am I? What do I want to be?" probably written in 1971.

probably in response to the struggles I was having to implement my educational ideals in a less than receptive school environment:

Oh Spirit of Life!

Let me be an instrument of peace and love.

Through me thy goodness may be spread to others.

Help me to work through the darkness without fear.

Give me strength to be amidst hate and still love.

Grant me serenity within myself to know that I can help.

Keep me from becoming angry with the stupidity I see.

Let me show others by my actions that peace is possible.

Don't let me feel threatened by the pettiness of others.

Help me to rise above small concerns and think only of life.

Let me spread life, peace, and love in whatever I do.

The idea of God continued to evolve in my consciousness, although I rarely talked about it with other people, not even with Thomas. A couple of years later I described my understanding of the divine in an angry letter I wrote but did not send to a lover. By then I no longer capitalized the word "god."

Your god is an ugly reality... You seem to have rejected any idea of perfection—that there is a wholeness which underlies everything—and that basically all life is striving to attain some measure of this perfection—that evolution is a constant process of moving closer to the perfection which is possible in our minds. Perhaps god only exists in our minds, but everywhere we see the pattern reflected, so I assume god to be universal.

CONTINUING THE SEARCH

Being an educator began to dominate my life more than religion, but I never lost the sense of being called to a life of purpose and meaning. Whenever I encountered new ideas about religion, I was reminded of the importance of faith in my life, but for over fifteen years I did not have a community with whom to share my spiritual life. From time to time I tried to find or form one as I did later in the Sixties, but without being part of an organized religious community I did not have a way to respond to the call to ministry I felt so clearly in the 1960s.

I finally found my way back to organized religion in 1981, when I joined the Unitarian Universalist church in Austin, Texas. Within a few years at a large gathering of UUs, I once again heard the call to ministry. I answered that call in 1984 by enrolling in Harvard Divinity School, and in 1988 I was ordained as a Unitarian Universalist minister.

RELIGION'S UNFINISHED AGENDA

In the 1950s and early 60s, the Presbyterian church and some other mainline Protestant groups shifted focus to address social issues in the wider world. Black churches provided leadership and gathering places for the civil rights movement. The Catholic church experienced radical change because of what became known as Vatican II, transforming the church to one of intentional engagement with the needs of the world.[63] Progressive Protestant churches provided support and sanctuary for draft resisters. Many people of faith, including both secular and religious Jews, marched for civil rights and to end the war in Vietnam. In most religious communities, however, the changes were gradual, and strong emphasis on personal faith and commitment remained. By the end of the decade my church and others were beginning to lose members.

The commitment to social change that inspired me as a young person became one of the factors in declining participation in mainline religious institutions. The changes that were underway in religion didn't go far enough to engage the social activists but went too far for others. For some, organized religion was too closely aligned with the traditional middle-class values they were rebelling against. Others felt rejected by judgmental attitudes toward the new freedoms people were exploring. I was driven away by the hypocritical attitudes of members and leaders who espoused one

---

63   Known as Vatican II, the Second Vatican Council lasted from October 1962 through December 1965 and instituted many changes in the Catholic Church, including interfaith dialog and calling for peace among nations, in addition to changing the language of the Mass. Because of Vatican II people in religious orders, especially women, began to modify their habits (traditional dress and head coverings) and sometimes wear street clothes.

thing and did another.

Many of us who left our religious homes in the Sixties explored alternative forms of spirituality and new ways to celebrate the spirit. Some people immersed themselves in the human potential movement and others explored earth-based traditions, both pagan and Native American. Teachers and practitioners of Eastern religions began gathering audiences, and some people became devotees or began practicing yoga and meditation. Some African Americans explored Islam as an indigenous African religious alternative and several leaders drew large followings.

At the same time, more conservative religious movements grew both within traditional religion and as new alternatives, gaining strength at least partially in reaction to the radical life-styles of the Sixties and to progressive social activism. Even today, the popular view of religion as a bulwark for what have become known as "traditional family values" obscures the voice of more progressive religious groups advocating for rights of all people. Until recently, that is.

Today among the greatest proponents of a Sixties-style progressive agenda are coalitions of people of faith, such as the Moral Monday Revival movement,[64] started in North Carolina initially to protest restrictions on voter rights. The movement has brought together people from diverse faith communities and others concerned with a wide range of social justice issues, including women's rights and civil rights, climate change, protecting women's right to abortion, and stopping violence and fear-mongering against women, people of color, immigrants, and LGBTQ people. This and other faith-based coalitions across the country have called on the conscience of the nation to do what is morally right for all the people. Although not everyone who participates and supports these efforts is actively involved with religious groups, a significant portion of the leadership is.

In the 1990s, Christian Smith reflected on the role of religion in culture:

---

64   William Barber, *The Third Reconstruction: How a Moral Movement Is Overcoming the Politics of Hate and Fear* (2016).

Religion provides life, the world, and history with meaning, through a sacred reality that transcends those mundane realities. But in so doing, religion establishes a perceived objective reality above and beyond temporal life, the world, and history, that then occupies an independent and privileged position to act ... on the mundane world. That which is sacred and transcends temporal reality also stands in the position to question, judge, and condemn temporal earthly reality. In this way, the ultimate legitimator of the status quo can easily become its ultimate judge.[65]

By reclaiming its historic role as an independent force which questions and challenges those in power to live up to their higher values, religion can be a force for positive social change. But this is only possible when different religious groups fully accept each other and acknowledge the validity of diverse paths to the holy. Religion is at its best when it brings people together and galvanizes action to make the world better, by supporting the inherent worth of all people, protecting the earth as sacred, and making sure that those who struggle economically have the means for decent lives.

Being actively engaged in the world is not only essential for organized religion to survive, but also, I contend, such engagement is necessary for the unfinished sea change of the Sixties to reach its full potential. Religion needs to reclaim its role in promoting equality, justice, peace, and love.

---

65   Christian Smith, "Creating a Curious Neglect, or Bringing Religion Back in," in *Disruptive Religion* (1996).

3. CULTURE SHOCK:
awakening to cultural differences

"Toto, we're not in Kansas anymore."
Dorothy, in *"The Wizard of Oz,"* 1939 movie

In the early Sixties waves of change began to build that would soon become the widespread culture changes that made the era famous. People began waking up from the complacency and seeming security of the 1950s with a sense that something was missing. The decade began with television images--like Ozzie and Harriet's[66] sanitized white suburban family life and Amos and Andy's[67] slapstick comedy about lower class blacks—projected into homes on black and white televisions. What moved us from these artificial worlds into civil rights, women's liberation, and other movements for equality and freedom? What awakened people to the need for change? What made things change?

By the mid-1950s we already knew change was in the air. Images of the Montgomery bus boycott in 1955-56 on the television news showed us that people could take action to create change and that they could succeed.[68] The civil rights movement in the South

---

66   "The Adventures of Ozzie and Harriet" aired on American television from 1952 to 1966. The sitcom starred the real-life Nelson family.
67   "Amos 'n' Andy," aired on television from 1951 to 1953, with black actors playing stereotypically demeaning roles. Syndicated reruns were broadcast through 1966. The show began as a nightly radio serial (1928-43) and continued to be played through 1960. Developed for radio by white actors out of the minstrel tradition, the show achieved great popularity with primarily white audiences and regular protests from black groups such as churches and the NAACP.
68   The bus boycott campaign lasted from December 1, 1955, when Rosa

inspired many people to believe in the possibility of full citizenship for other marginalized people.

The new spirit of leadership ushered in by the 1960 election of John F. Kennedy as president helped awaken many others to previously unarticulated possibilities. These famous words in his Inaugural Address still inspire me: "The torch has been passed to a new generation of Americans, born in this century, tempered by war, disciplined by a hard and bitter peace, proud of our ancient heritage, and unwilling to witness or permit the slow undoing of those human rights to which this nation had always been committed, and to which we are committed today at home and around the world."[69]

Before he spoke these words, he reminded us that we held in our "mortal hands the power to abolish all forms of poverty and all forms of human life." This awesome responsibility reverberated throughout the decade to follow and remains a challenge for us today.

Nine days later, President Kennedy highlighted the disturbing state of the economy in his State of the Union Address. Those who remember the 1950s as a time of easy prosperity have forgotten the 1958 recession, higher than usual unemployment, rising prices, "seven years of diminished economic growth, and nine years of falling farm income" that preceded his presidency. After outlining his ambitious plans, he ended on a hopeful note: "Life in 1961 will not be easy. ... There will be further setbacks before the tide is turned. But turn it we must."[70]

How did this turning of the tide play out in individual lives? How do new ways of thinking and being come into our shared cultural life, and what is the process by which some of us adopt them and make them our own? Each person's story is unique both in its awakenings and in the changes we sought to create, but common

---

Parks refused to surrender her seat to a white person, to December 17, 1956, when the United States Supreme Court upheld a district court ruling, Browder v. Gayle, and declared segregation on Montgomery and Alabama buses unconstitutional.

69   John F. Kennedy, Inaugural Address, January 20, 1961.

70   John F. Kennedy, State of the Union Message, January 29, 1961. A month later, on March 1, he proposed the Peace Corps to Congress.

threads of collective consciousness raising run through our stories. I can see how small awakenings grew into the wave of change that swept me into becoming a very different person from what my parents and upbringing might have predicted. There were many others whose experiences, although different from mine, had similar results. By the end of the decade the world we inhabited had changed in significant ways. Like me, many born during World War II or before were old enough at the beginning of the 1960s to participate in the changes as they happened throughout the decade. Some of us even became catalysts for change, working in small and large ways to apply principles of equality, freedom, peace, and love wherever we were engaged.

Just as the culture changed in radical ways, I changed more than might have been expected in some other era. Writing this book has led me to consider how those changes happened in my life and cultural location and seek to understand what drew me then and still draws me into engagement as an active agent of culture change.

WHAT IS CULTURE?

When I was growing up in the 1950s, my mother talked about "culture" as something we needed to get—by taking piano and dancing lessons, by reading good books, by using proper table manners, by going to classical music concerts, and by going to church and later to college. These activities would make us "cultured," we were told.

In a college German Literature class, Professor Karl Baumann made a clear distinction between high and low culture. He talked about "gesunkenes Kulturgut," the corruption of cultivated tradition—how the lower classes adopted the forms and manners of those above them and in the process perverted these cultural assets, which then "sank" into kitsch. The literature we studied and the culture it grew out of was high culture, the only culture worthy of study in the opinion of most professors. I accepted this idea and didn't think much about how it might apply to my life and my family of origin. If anything, Baumann's attitude reinforced my interest in classical music and opera, foreign films, and learning about art.

It wasn't until 1967, when I went back to school for my teaching credential, that I encountered a different view of culture. In a course on the American novel, we used a text called *The Popular Book: A History of America's Literary Taste.*[71] I was fascinated to learn about the books that interested the majority of people and surprised to discover that most of the "classics" we studied in German literature were only read by a small elite group of people. What was popular was often entirely different and rarely made it onto reading lists for college literature classes. If we wanted to understand the culture of a given time, however, we needed to look at what was read by large numbers of people. This was an awakening moment for me. I began to see myself and my own culture from a new perspective and to realize that my personal tastes were a mix of high and low culture.

It dawned on me that the concept of culture can be understood in more than one way. Bringing the two ideas together can enrich our understanding of what culture means. As one of the founders of the new field of cultural studies, which developed in the 1960s, explained: "We use the word culture in these two senses: to mean a whole way of life—the common meanings; [and] to mean the arts and learning—the special processes of discovery and creative effort. Some writers reserve the word for one or other of these senses; I insist on both, and on the significance of their conjunction. The questions I ask about our culture are questions about deep personal meanings. Culture is ordinary, in every society and in every mind."[72] This more holistic way of viewing culture became my new lens, and I began to see culture as a composite of how we live, our values, beliefs, patterns of behavior, customs, social norms, symbols, and rituals, as well as the literature, music, and art we produce and enjoy. Those who are preparing people for study or work in other countries define culture as "an integrated system of learned behavior patterns

---

71   James D. Hart, *The Popular Book: A History of America's Literary Taste,* 1963.

72   Raymond Williams, "Moving from High Culture to Ordinary Culture," in N. McKenzie (ed.), *Convictions* (1958), posted by the National College of the Arts, http://www.nca.edu.pk/cultural/culturedemocracy/downloads/Culture%20Handout.doc

that are characteristic of the members of any given society. Culture refers to the total way of life of particular groups of people. It includes everything that a group of people thinks, says, does and makes—its systems of attitudes and feelings."[73]

Culture is like the air we breathe, the way we orient ourselves in daily life. It is what we pass on from generation to generation, almost without realizing we are doing it. At the same time, culture is changing and evolving, even as we are immersed in it and interact with each other within it. Soon I would find myself immersed in the culture change of the Sixties and became an eager participant in creating new culture.

WHAT IS CULTURE SHOCK?

I first heard the idea of "culture shock" in 1963 when I was preparing to spend a semester in Germany during college. Culture shock may be defined as "the psychological disorientation a person may feel when experiencing an unfamiliar way of life due to immigration or a visit to a new country, or to a move between social environments."[74] The term was first used only a few years before[75] to explain the responses people often have when visiting or moving to another country. But I realize now that I had similar experiences when I moved from one environment to another within my own country. A mild form of culture shock accompanied each crossing, even though I didn't realize it at the time.

What causes culture shock is the experience that our usual "cultural clues, the signs and symbols which guide social interaction, are stripped away."[76] This stripping away isn't necessarily a bad thing, although it can be initially incapacitating. For me the initial shock

73   L. Robert Kohls. *Survival Kit for Overseas Living* (Maine: Intercultural Press, Inc. 1996), 23.
74   John Macionis and Linda Gerber, "Chapter 3 – Culture," *Sociology* (7th edition ed. Toronto, ON: Pearson Canada Inc., 2010), 54.
75   Kalvero Oberg, "Cultural Shock: adjustment to new cultural environments," *Practical Anthropology* 7: 1960.
76   Piet-Pelon & Hornby, 1992, quoted by the Center for European Studies and Architecture at Virginia Tech, www.oired.vt.edu/cesa/currentstudents/cs_culturalshock.htm

of difference became a source of motivation to learn about the new culture and about myself within it. Ultimately the experience of adapting to the new culture brought positive change into my life and expanded both my sense of who I was at the time and my capacity to appreciate and engage with all kinds of people. For me culture shock served as a catalyst for awakening new consciousness.

CROSSING CULTURES

My first experience of culture shock happened in 1951 when I was seven years old and my family moved from our urban neighborhood in Long Beach to the suburban community of Fullerton. Although I was too young to understand how different these communities were, I knew something important was changing in my life. Because it was the middle of the school year, I had to complete three readers and workbooks on my own to "catch up" with where my new class would be. I was told it was a "more advanced" school. Since I was a good reader, I thought the school work was fun, and I looked forward to my new class. It would take me several years to realize I had left behind the diversity of my former city school for the almost exclusively WASP[77] environment of my new upwardly mobile community.

The only real loss I felt at the time was moving away from my best friend, Diane.

My next culture crossing came when I finished sixth grade at the school across the street from my house and had to take a bus to the junior high school a few miles away. Instead of being in one classroom with one teacher for the whole school day, we moved from room to room, from teacher to teacher. There were many students I didn't know who lived in different parts of town, so I had to learn how to interact with new people and how to make new friends. After school I continued to do things primarily with my friends from grade school, since we rode the bus together and often went to each other's homes because they were nearby. Until the end of eighth grade, we had our Girl Scout Troop, so we continued to be together as a group.

---

77   White Anglo-Saxon Protestant, a derogatory term used to indicate what was then considered the dominant social group in America.

Thus I only partially crossed over into the new culture.

In 1957 I began high school, with its larger version of junior high culture. The Class of 1961 was the last in Fullerton to be all together in one school.[78] Over 600 of us graduated. It became clear there were different groups, subcultures I might call them now. There was no way I could relate to the whole student body, so I had to figure out my place, my group. I no longer saw my grade school friends daily, since some of them had different classes. I tried unsuccessfully to fit in with the "popular" kids but failed. I had been assigned to accelerated English and history classes and began to realize that my real friends were those who also got good grades and were planning to go to college. A bunch of us, mostly girls, started identifying ourselves as a "group." I felt more at home in my high school culture after finding my group. I also began to see myself as an individual, with my own interests, because I took classes none of my friends were in and grew more confident navigating the challenges and opportunities of a large high school.

At the same time, throughout both junior and senior high school, I experienced a different culture at church. There all types of kids were together in one group. Because it was church and we were supposed to accept everyone as equal, we did. It was a big relief from the competitiveness of high school. I got to know kids I would not have spent time with at school, and I learned the value of diversity and inclusion. Some of the ideas we learned at church were different from those of the dominant culture. We were encouraged to think for ourselves when it came to social and political concerns and to evaluate what we heard in terms of how it meshed or didn't mesh with our faith. That's why I was so upset when I encountered the Christian Anti-Communism Crusade.

---

78   With the rapid growth of Fullerton and the entry of the first baby boomers into school, a new high school, Sunny Hills, opened in 1959, two years after I began at Fullerton Union. Since we lived closer to the new school, my brother was in the first class there, but my class continued through graduation at Fullerton Union.

ANTI-COMMUNISM CRUSADE

In early 1961 Herbert Philbrick[79] came to town. We were excited because his experience investigating communism as a counterspy for the FBI was the basis for a popular TV show, "I Led Three Lives." Who wouldn't want to meet this famous man? He was scheduled to speak at a special program in a hotel during the afternoon of a school day. A friend's mother who was active with the local Republican Party arranged for several of us girls to be invited. We got permission from the school to leave, and although our absence was technically "unexcused," our teachers encouraged us to go.

After our arrangements were made, a big rally in a football stadium was announced for later that same afternoon. The school decided to let all the seniors leave early to attend the rally. The fact that the rally was sponsored by a pseudo-religious organization, the Christian Anti-Communism Crusade, didn't seem to bother anyone in those days. We heard that the school figured students would cut to go so they might as well make it legal. I suppose our absences were also made legal by this decision.

We were excited, though, to be attending a smaller program where we might get to see Herb Philbrick up close. Dressed in our Sunday clothes we arrived with our friend's mother at the Disneyland Hotel. The room where the program was being held was full of adults, no other kids as far as we could see. At the back of the room I noticed a row of nuns in their traditional black habits.[80] I hadn't seen many nuns and was fascinated but tried not to stare.

That day I was introduced to the game of democracy versus communism. The program seemed more like a football pep rally

---

79   Herbert Arthur Philbrick was a Boston-area advertising executive who was paid by the FBI to infiltrate the Communist Party USA between 1940 and 1949. His autobiographical book, *I Led Three Lives: Citizen, 'Communist', Counterspy* (1952), was the inspiration for a television series, "I Led Three Lives" (1953-56).

80   Prior to Vatican II (1962-65) the traditional clothing worn by nuns varied depending on the order to which they belong, but all habits were long-sleeved, floor-length black or white robes, with head coverings that completely covered their hair and necks, leaving only their hands and faces visible.

than a presentation of information. Fred Schwartz, the organizer of the Crusade,[81] spoke first. He explained how communism was at war with both democracy and God and that the communist goal was to destroy our country and all forms of religion. Communists were bad people, whether they were in Russia or the United States, so we had to fight them in every way possible. He set a sort of rah-rah atmosphere by encouraging the audience to cheer democracy and boo communism. Then he introduced Herbert Philbrick as a man who had confronted communists personally and knew how bad they were.

Philbrick began by describing communists as people who can lie with a straight face. "Nothing is a lie if it helps the Communist Party," he said, describing "how they thought about things."[82] They use underhanded tactics to lure innocent citizens into their groups, he said, by calling them names that appeal to Americans. He called them "dirty," claiming they started race riots, but mostly he called them "Godless," which he found to be "the most frightening word of all because it accounts for every other bad word that describes them." Life under communism was the most terrible thing we could imagine, so we must watch out for communist infiltrators wherever we were because they wanted to take over this country too.

The rah-rah atmosphere failed to impress our small group of high school girls. It was weird seeing this whole group of maybe 100 adults behaving like kids at a football game. At the break, we found our way into an alcove where we could compare our impressions. Mostly we felt confused by what we were seeing and hearing. Several nuns followed us and asked why we weren't cheering. They wanted to know where we went to school, and when they found out, they said we had a really bad world history book and a teacher who was a

81   Frederick Charles Schwarz was an Australian physician and political activist who founded the Christian Anti-Communism Crusade. In 1960 moved his base of operations to California and published *You Can Trust The Communists (to be Communists)*.

82   This and other statements are based on notes about a film, "What is Communism?" presented by Herbert Philbrick, produced by Jerry Fairbanks, www.holology.com/se.html. These notes helped me remember the sorts of things that were said that day.

communist sympathizer. We had better watch out, they warned us, or we would be misled.

We were shocked at being spoken to in such a way. We had learned in our history class that the communists were accepted in Russia because their policies improved life for most people, especially those who had suffered under the dictatorship of the czars. Our teacher confirmed what the book said that although communism did not allow people the kind of freedom we had here at least they had greater access to basic needs, like food, health care, and housing. Democracy wasn't always able to provide this, so we could learn from what Russia was doing.

After the break, we discovered that Herb Philbrick had left to go speak at the big rally our classmates were attending. We wished we could leave, too, but we were trapped on the side of the crowded room farthest from the door. Besides we feared that if we left we would be accused of being communists. The rest of the program presented specifics "proving" that communist ideas and systems must be destroyed for democracy to survive. At least the rah-rah atmosphere was toned down. On the way home, we agreed that it was not like a pep rally, because we did not usually boo the other team. We realized, though, that these people were completely serious. They truly believed what was being said. We were more scared by them than anything that had been said about communism.

Later I thought about the experience and talked it over with my minister. I realized that part of what upset me was that they claimed to be doing this in the name of Christianity, yet their approach seemed anything but Christian. They accused others of being evil, dirty, Godless liars, worthy only of destruction. They could not see them as their neighbors with even a bit of God-given worth and dignity.

This awakening was the most traumatic culture shock experience of my growing up years. Finding myself in a group of people from my own community and yet feeling like a complete outsider was uncomfortable, confusing, and disorienting. The fact that they were adults and I was only 17 years old meant I should have been able to trust them, but I could not. I have rarely felt so ill at ease anywhere, even in a country where I did not speak the language.

POMONA COLLEGE EDUCATION

Winning the scholarship that made it possible for me to attend Pomona College still seems like a miracle for which I am eternally grateful. The four-year scholarship I received was sponsored by the Southern California Edison Company. In addition to the scholarship, they offered me a summer job that paid better than most jobs college students were otherwise able to get. Before the announcement of the award, I expected to go to a state university because that was what my parents could afford.

But Pomona was my first choice. In 1961, it was rated 10th of the Top Ten Liberal Arts Colleges in America by Newsweek magazine. When I first visited the campus, I fell in love with the way the college blended into the town of Claremont that surrounded it. Within a block or two of campus were a movie theater, a coffee shop, a bank, and stores that sold practical and unique items, everything a college student might need. Other colleges I visited in southern California had campuses that were separated from the towns they were located near. I loved the way the campus looked, too, with its ivy-covered walls and classic-looking buildings.

Founded in 1887, the college was formed by people from New England who had their schools in mind when they designed Pomona, but unlike those older colleges, Pomona was open to women from the beginning. By the time I was there, the founding philosophy of educational equity was being extended to students of different class backgrounds through scholarships. Racial diversity was not yet a major goal, although there were a few students of color. In 1961, there were 94 faculty members and 1,099 students. Tuition was $1,250, and my $1,000-a-year scholarship was just enough to make it possible for me to attend.

Besides its setting, what made Pomona unique were its small classes, excellent professors, top notch students, and visionary leadership. The curriculum was based on a four-course system, different from the unit system common in most colleges. All courses were of equal value and four courses were considered a full load. We could choose our courses, but the first semester we were assigned two basic courses: Introductory English and History of Western Civilization, which all students were required to take. I ended up with the worst possible schedule, six 8:00 AM classes!

CULTURE AND CLASS DIFFERENCES

One of my first realizations as I got to know the other students was that they were all at least as smart as I was. We were assigned far more homework than I ever had in high school. I struggled to find time for it and was often distracted by the many exciting things to do on campus and off. I thought I was keeping up well enough, but when I received my first-semester grades I was shocked, and so were my parents. Two Cs. I never even had a C before and only an occasional B. I had to face the fact that I wasn't going to get mostly As the way I had in high school, and I would have to work hard to earn a B average.

I learned that some of my classmates graduated from private schools that specialized in rigorous preparation for college. Plus, some students were quite simply brilliant. I heard about kids who received almost perfect scores on their college entrance exams. My scores were good, especially in English, but I was far from a top-notch student compared to many at Pomona. Realizing this was my first major adaptation to the culture shock of being at one of the best small liberal arts colleges in America. I knew I could improve my grades by studying more, but I also wanted to enjoy other opportunities Pomona provided. Throughout the remainder of my four years at Pomona there would be constant tension between wanting to get good grades and experiencing the rest of college life.

Getting to know other students was one of the joys of my college years. Although some students were from southern California, many more were from elsewhere in the country and a few from abroad. Even the ones from nearby lived in communities different from Fullerton, and it was interesting to compare notes on our high school experiences. But before long, those stories faded from our conversations as we immersed ourselves in our new lives in college. We fell naturally into groups of new friends, some of whom are still friends today.

Every now and then, our differences would reemerge, like the time it snowed. It almost never snows in southern California, so those of us who had rarely or never seen snow falling ran outside and danced around in the lightly falling snow. When we came back inside the dorm our friends from the Midwest and Northeast laughed at us. "That little dusting hardly counts as snow! See, it's already stopping." We were crestfallen, as we had been hoping to make snow people later in the day. We could drive up the mountains not far from campus if we wanted to play with snow, but snow falling on us was new and we were secretly pleased at the experience despite the jaded remarks of our classmates.

The real difference that separated me from most of the other students took a while to sink in. It was the fact that they came from more well-to-do families than mine. I later learned only ten percent of the students were on scholarships. How the others lived intrigued me, but sometimes I felt I wasn't good enough to be at Pomona. More than once I wished my family had more money.[83]

My first-year roommate, Julie, seemed to have lots of money to spend, at least at the beginning of the month. Later in the month she sometimes borrowed money from me until she got her "allowance" for the next month. I, on the other hand, knew I had a certain amount of money and had to make it last, although I sometimes had to beg for more from my parents when I ran low at the end of the year. Julie shopped for clothes in a way that was foreign to me. For one thing, she never once looked at a price tag. Once she found something she liked, say a skirt, she would find a blouse and belt and accessories to match, never asking the price of any of it until it was time to pay the bill. I had been taught to look for good buys and sale prices. One day Julie ordered a blouse with her name embroidered on the collar and encouraged me to order one as well. I decided to splurge and treasured that blouse for many years, keeping it even after it was too small for me to wear.

Julie had a drawer full of cashmere sweaters. Sometimes when

---

83   For more about class differences, see Beloved Community, Experiencing Class Differences.

she wasn't there I opened the drawer and ran my hands lovingly over the soft wool. I have never yet been able to afford even one such sweater. Julie had lots of other nice clothes, and yet she usually just dumped them carelessly in a pile on the one comfortable chair in the room. Eventually I would get frustrated with the mess and hang them up so I could sit in the chair.

One weekend, she invited me to go home with her to visit her family in Redlands. Her parents seemed unaffected by living in what looked to me like a mansion. It was only after I was there a while that I noticed a difference, when her father mentioned that he didn't have to follow the ban on daytime lawn watering because he "had a lot of influence in the town."

After seeing the rest of the house, I wasn't surprised that Julie's room was large and beautiful. When we got ready to go to bed I noticed she threw her clothes on the floor, but when we got back from breakfast the next morning, the clothes were gone. Later in the day they came back washed and ironed and I found out they had a maid. I guess I was lucky that in our room at school she at least put them on the chair!

Besides visiting my richer classmates' homes from time to time, I had other experiences that reminded me of my comparatively lower economic status. During school vacations, some students went snow skiing and to resorts my family could never afford. During summers, some went to Europe or spent time at beach houses, water skiing, or sailing. The last summer of college, several students volunteered for voter registration drives and other civil rights activities in the south, and more than anything else I wished I could have done that. But even if I could have afforded the trip, I had to spend nearly the whole summer earning money for the next year at school.

One further difference was in the gifts my more privileged friends received from their families. I dreaded the inevitable question each January, "What did you get for Christmas?" How could I compete with the fancy new Polaroid camera Julie got which we all enjoyed using? Or how about the brand-new blue Volkswagen bug she got for her birthday, which we also enjoyed. There were definite advantages in having rich friends, if I could just keep my feelings of unworthiness at bay.

My awareness of class and economic difference, begun as a subtext earlier in my life, became more nuanced the longer I was at Pomona, but it wasn't something I would talk about or understand until many years later. What I did realize at the time was that by being at Pomona I had entered a world of greater privilege than I had known before. I recognized that I had been given a special opportunity by being allowed to go there. I felt a responsibility to do something with my life to help others, which is part of what led me to ministry as a career.

CHOOSING A MAJOR AND A SEMESTER ABROAD

My confusion about what major to choose was solved with an opportunity I neither anticipated nor sought. My sophomore-year roommate Tanni (Ruth Crowley) was applying to go to Germany during the fall of our junior year. The study abroad program had been instituted the year we arrived at Pomona. Rather than establishing programs in other countries as Stanford and other colleges did, Pomona chose to work with the Experiment in International Living, which arranged homestays and student housing in different cities, enabling students to create individualized programs. Because the program was new, it was undersubscribed and they had space for one more student for the fall semester. Would I like to go? I had been thinking about majoring in German, but I would need to decide for sure before applying for this trip. I had taken the first two years of German language as required for the philosophy major but now I would need to take a lot of other German courses. The courses I would take while in Germany would be a good start. I would learn how to speak the language better than I could any other way. How could I say no?

Certainly, my parents could have, but my mother convinced my more fiscally conservative father that this was an opportunity of a lifetime and I should go. They checked to make sure my scholarship could be used in this way, but since the money was still paid to the college, it was fine. After applying, it seemed like forever before we were accepted and learned where we would go. Finally, we found out that Tanni was going to Munich and Jeri, another German major, was going to Tübingen. My destination was Marburg, in the state of Hessen, in the center of what was then West Germany.

We would each be required to complete three courses for college credit that semester. One was Advanced German, which we would be learning every day just by being there. The second was Classics of Eighteenth Century German Literature, which included reading plays in German by Goethe, Schiller, and Lessing, and writing a paper on them. Then we each needed to choose an elective. I chose Philosophy of Religion, which involved a long reading list in English and a term paper.

VISITING THREE AMERICAN CITIES, 1963

To get to Germany, I was sent a ticket on a ship sailing from New York. In finding out about cross-country flights, we learned that many stopped in Chicago. My mother got the idea for me to stay over there with my aunt and uncle and then go to Washington DC. Although these visits were short, friends and family helped me experience firsthand places I had only read about. The culture crossings along the way to Germany kept me disoriented, but in a fun and exciting way, so by the time I arrived at my destination, I was wide open to my new cultural home.

Enduring memories from my brief stay in Chicago are examples of culture shock awakenings. My aunt took me to the Chicago Art Institute. I was fascinated with the gigantic stone lions guarding the steps and asked her to take my picture with them. I had not previously been to a large art museum and knew little about the history of art, but right away I was attracted to impressionism. I stood for a long time transfixed by a huge painting of the crucifixion that covered an entire wall. I wondered what it meant to be martyred for a cause, what I would suffer in my life for my beliefs. I could see the importance of art both for me and for the world and resolved to learn more.

My other memory is more profane. We were getting on a highway and had to practically stop because a street sweeping machine ahead of us was moving very slowly as it cleaned the entrance road. The vast Midwest landscape and the highway that at the time was practically empty of cars reminded me that I wasn't in southern California anymore. I had time to get out of the car to take a picture.

My next stop was Washington DC. In the 1960s, we had to get off the plane via stairs. Immediately I noticed a strange, unpleasant feeling as sweat began to pour down my face and arms, soaking my short nylon travel dress Growing up in California without the constant weather reports we have today, I had no concept of humidity. I thought something was horribly wrong, except that everyone else was walking around like nothing had happened. I was relieved to find my friend Sue, because I was starting to panic.

"Look at me," I said. "I'm dripping wet. What happened here to make the air so damp?"

She laughed. "This is the way it is in the summer in DC! It's called humidity, silly."

Sue took me to some of the most famous sites: Arlington Cemetery, Mount Vernon, the Washington and Lincoln monuments, and the National Zoo. That night we heard two excellent folk singers at the Cellar Door. The next day Tanni and I visited the Pentagon where her father worked. We went to the National Art Gallery, where I found the British and American art "cold and dull" compared to impressionism. After visiting these historic sites, I wrote to my family, "I am imbued with Americana and it is a fine feeling to be so proud of my country and the people who have kept its past alive."

The following day I visited the Supreme Court, the Library of Congress, and the Capitol building, with Jeri, who was also going to Germany. I felt like I was walking on hallowed ground to be in the center of where our government functioned, but the highlight of our visit was lunch in the Senate dining room. Jeri's mother had arranged for us to sit at Senator Jackson's table. He wasn't there, so we had the table to ourselves. We caught a glimpse of two famous Kennedy brothers, probably John and Robert, but what I wrote on a postcard was that Marlene Dietrich was sitting at the next table! I could hardly keep from staring at her. Being so close to famous people made me feel special.

Then we met Tanni and went to the Smithsonian where we saw the Hope Diamond, a mummified bull, a restored dinosaur, and the first airplanes. Later we took a bus to Georgetown to Francis's Goat and Compass Pub. At age 19, it was legal for us to drink beer. These sites and experiences in our nation's capital filled me with images to carry with me as I embarked on my journey to a more radically different culture.

But first we had to fly to New York City, where we would get the ship that would take Tanni, Jeri, and me to Europe. Barry, a college friend, met us at the airport and acted as our guide for a whirlwind day and a half tour of Manhattan. We checked into the Henry Hudson Hotel near Times Square, walked to the Guggenheim where we saw an exhibit of Cezanne and modern expressionism, walked along Fifth Avenue, saw Central Park, and visited the United Nations. We were especially impressed with the beautiful assembly halls and speculated about what took place there. That night we ate at Mama Leone's where they served family style at long tables, and we sat with people we didn't know. Here, too, we could drink legally— carafes of wine on the table, all we wanted. New York night life was like nothing we had ever seen, so many people up late at night out in the city, with bars and clubs staying open until 4 AM. No curfew like there was back at the college dorm. No parents to monitor what we did. We enjoyed our newfound freedom!

Already within my own country I was observing significant cultural differences. Had I stayed in any one place longer than a few days, I might have experienced greater culture shock than I did. But on this whirlwind trip of three major US cities, all I felt was euphoria, except perhaps for the humidity in DC.

The next day was our last full day in the US. We visited Riverside Church, Columbia University, and Union Seminary in the morning. Then we took the subway to Greenwich Village for lunch, rode on the Staten Island Ferry, bought shoes for the boat, went into the Stock Exchange on Wall Street where we could look down at the trading floor. We had dinner at Fedora's and cognac at the Limelight—all in the rain! We heard a fantastic concert of Kurt

Weill songs by two German singers, Martha Schlamme and Will Holt, at One Sheridan Square. The perfect transition to our voyage to Germany!

VOYAGE ACROSS THE SEA

The next morning the hotel forgot to wake us up and we were almost late getting to the ship, but thanks to Barry we made it. Along with 800 other passengers, we boarded the SS Groote Beer, a Dutch ship used in World War II which had been converted to a student ship with more dormitories than cabins. Since all the tickets cost the same, they randomly assigned passengers to all the decks. I lost out and ended up on the lowest deck in a narrow dorm room with eight bunk beds. My biggest complaint was that there was no place to open my suitcase, so I wore the same clothes for most of the week-long trip.

Jeri, Tanni, and I made a pact not to get seasick and learned what we needed to do to avoid the curse. Eating saltine crackers seemed to help and we managed to be among the twenty-five percent who did not get sick on the rolling seas of our passage. In a letter to my family I described the boat as "'full of movement'—the engines shake the whole boat and there is an almost constant sway from starboard aft to port fore—kitty corner, in other words."[84]

I loved standing on the deck and seeing the vastness of the ocean. Days went by without seeing land or other ships. We were truly on our own, our little community of eight hundred students. Anything could happen, which was both exciting and terrifying. I had always loved the ocean but being in the middle of it was a different experience. It reminded me how small we as individual human beings are. What do our lives matter in the larger scheme of things? What would change if our ship disappeared?

During the crossing, we were immersed in international culture, with a multiplicity of languages around us. We tried to communicate, sometimes with few words in common. Knowing some Spanish and French in addition to German helped a great deal. In my journal, I tried to capture the experience of being on a

---

84   Letter written Wed. Sept. 18, 1963, mailed on board the Groote Beer.

ship with hundreds of other people for a week. "What can I say that would explain these wonderful days? A boat is like a little world in itself. It is self-sufficient, but more than that. Everything happens on a boat that happens elsewhere. But, of course, it is terribly unreal. You begin believing that it is a world, and that perhaps you need never get off—and then the trip must end or you will go crazy."

I was ready to fall in love in Europe and started right off on the way there! I made friends with Stefan, from Bad Salzuflen. He was 23 years old and a student at the University of Bonn. Our last night on the ship, we stayed up until dawn.

To my family, I described all the other people I met. "There are about two hundred kids on board who were counselors at camps in the US for the summer," including the seven others in my cabin (six from England and one from Flemish Belgium). "I met lots of nice Germans—one boy who studied in Marburg and has told me about the school and the town. There is a group from Millersville State College in Pennsylvania who will spend the year in Marburg, so I won't be the only American in town.

FIRST STEPS IN EUROPE

We entered our new European world at 4 PM on September 22, 1963, at La Havre, France, and took the train to Paris. We waited several hours for a representative from the Experiment in International Living to meet us, but no one came and we didn't know where we were supposed to stay. Eventually, the leader of the Pennsylvania group made a call, found out we were staying at Hotel Sevres, and helped us get there. Compared to American accommodations, the place was old and a bit creepy. We had a bidet in our room, but we had to go down a flight of stairs to use the toilet. Showers were out of the question.

We didn't have any French money, so we had to convince the hotel to accept a traveler's check, which they were reluctant to do until they realized there was no other way for us to pay them. On the way to the train station, our cab drove past the Eiffel Tower, but that was about all we got to see of Paris. Tanni and Jeri took trains to their cities, while I took the one going to Frankfurt, where I would change trains to Marburg.

It was only when I was on that train by myself that the enormity of what I was doing hit me. Here I was, a vulnerable 19-year-old, traveling all alone in a foreign country. I could make myself understood in German, but it was difficult to understand what others said to me.

The trains themselves were different from American trains. Instead of seats lined up facing one direction, there were compartments, with seats facing each other and corridors that ran along one side. At one point, I was standing in the corridor looking out the window at the passing countryside, when I was surprised to hear English being spoken. I hadn't paid much attention when the two soldiers walked by. I was intent upon the scenery and didn't smile at them or notice they were Americans.

Then I heard one of them say sarcastically, "Well, she's really friendly."

I had to respond. "Yes, and I'm also American." Were they ever embarrassed! We talked for a few minutes. One was from southern California.

For the second part of the eight-hour trip I was in a train compartment with a girl about my age and an older couple with a "darling" dog. "We laughed about the dog," I wrote home. One of the advantages to the arrangement of seats in European trains was that you faced those in your compartment and could develop a sense of connection, especially on long trips like this one. I felt comfortable to be with these people "although I didn't say much." As we were getting off the train, the girl saw the Paris stickers on my luggage.

"Are you from Paris?" she asked.

"No, I'm American," I said, "from California."

"Oh, that's so exciting. I want to go there someday. Would you please, please, please send me a postcard from California?"

She carried one of my suitcases to the other train and gave me her address. Frankly, I don't know how I would have made it without her help. I suppose there were porters, but I had no idea how to find one. I mistakenly got on the wrong car and had to pay a few marks extra for first class, but the seats were more comfortable and I was exhausted after the week on the ship and a restless night in Paris. I felt isolated and alone. Tears pushed for release, but I didn't want to cry in front of strangers. Could I hold it together a few more hours?

I was never so relieved as when I finally got off the train in Marburg at 7 PM and found my host brother, Friedrich-Karl, waiting for me! We drove straight to the Bartuzats' home, where I would stay for the first month of my time in Germany. Frau Bartuzat greeted me warmly and right away I began to feel at home. She recognized how tired I was and showed me to my room, brought me a snack, and said we could get to know each other after I had a good night's sleep.

LIVING IN GERMANY, 1963

The Bartuzats lived on the southern edge of Marburg in what was known as a *Flüchtlingswohnheim*, refugee housing. Before the Berlin Wall was erected in 1961, refugees had been fleeing west ever since the Soviet army invaded Germany during World War II. The government built he housing to accommodate the influx of two and a half million refugees. Women headed most of the families, because so many men had been killed.

The apartments were in large complexes, four stories high. Each unit had a balcony that looked out on open space between the buildings. I was impressed that there were no fences between the different properties but rather shared common space to be enjoyed by all. Nestled into this open space were community gardens where people could grow their own food. Across the expansive landscape, I could see a green forest out of the window in the room I stayed in. It was new to me to be in a major city and see so much green space.

Inside, the apartments were small by California standards, but people furnished them with lovely furniture, often precious family heirlooms they managed to bring with them when they fled. Compared to similar apartments I would see later, the Bartuzats' place on the third floor was large and comfortable. Friedrich-Karl, age 21 and known as Fritz, slept in one bedroom and I stayed in the other. I didn't realize until later that the room I was in was not a guest room but belonged to Fritz, who was sleeping in Jochen's room. Jochen, age 20, a two-week holiday in Italy with his class and would sleep in the attic when he returned. Frau Bartuzat slept in the living room. It was common practice for one family member, often the mother, to sleep in the living room and for others to switch rooms around to accommodate guests.

Being in Germany was the first time I was truly on my own. Although Frau Bartuzat was helpful and provided guidance, it was not her job to watch over me, set limits on what I did, or make sure I got home safely at night. There was no school with rules about my behavior. My mind was constantly expanding by my immersion in a new culture, a new language, a new community, a new way of life. Everything was new. Everything was different. Who was I in the midst of all that was new to me?

One of my first observations about difference was the weather. At home in late September it was likely to be warm, even hot. In the first letter from my parents they wrote it was 106 degrees! I wanted to share this information with the Bartuzats but I did not know how to convert Fahrenheit into Centigrade. In Marburg, it was cool and rainy and in my first letter home I asked my mother to send my warm clothes. It rained nearly every day, so I had to buy an umbrella and carry it with me. Before long, I had to buy a wool winter coat, something I had never needed in California.

Culture shock occurs when you realize you don't know the basics of the place where you are. For instance, I had to find formulas to translate temperatures, distances, and weights from US to German measurements, which my otherwise informative travel journal failed to provide. It's also a form of culture shock when you encounter prejudice about your home culture.

The Bartuzats had many friends and enjoyed entertaining. The Esse family came to visit soon after I arrived. They lived on a farm in Westfalen where the Bartuzats stayed when they first arrived from the east. They were friendly people but I was taken aback when they began telling me what they believed about life in America. I wrote home, "They are every bit as wrong as our misconceptions about Germans are." For instance, "they think Americans are unhealthy because we eat white bread" and that "American women are lazy" because they serve food out of cans. "I am doing my best to tear down that picture." I also tried to correct misconceptions I thought my family might have about Germans.

I noticed many differences between our two cultures, but for the most part instead of finding something negative about them, I enjoyed them. "It does seem that many things are different," I wrote, "in fact many things are opposite, but it doesn't mean that the opposite way is wrong. The Germans are just as concerned for cleanliness, healthfulness, and education, as are the Americans, it's just that they clean things differently, think different things are healthy, and educate their children in a different manner." I noted a tendency in the way people evaluate foreigners.

They think I am a good person (or that anyone they meet is such) but they are still willing to lump the rest of "America" in the same misconception they previously had. I think this is much the same way we look at other countries. We tend to like the foreigner we meet, but what we don't like about him we attribute to his "different" upbringing, instead of understanding what this difference means—and that perhaps they might have a point after all.

CULTURAL DIFFERENCES: FOOD AND MEALS

Food and practices around meals provided a fertile context for my developing awareness of differences in cultures. Most obvious was the Germans use of eating utensils, with the fork in the left hand and the knife in the right and both hands above the table throughout the meal. After I got used to this, I realized how much more sense it made. Our American practice of only putting the fork in the left to cut meat and then putting that hand in the lap seemed awkward by comparison, so when I got home I continued eating the German way—to the horror of my parents, who considered it a serious breach of manners. My father reminded me, "You're back in the United States now, and you need to eat the correct way." If they understood the concept of cultural relativity, they didn't let on. Their goal was to shape me into a proper young American lady, a goal at which they largely failed.

When we ate and what we ate differed too. At home, we ate

cereal and fruit, toast, and sometimes bacon and eggs for breakfast. In Marburg, *Brötchen* (bread rolls) were delivered every morning. These rolls, crunchy on the outside and soft inside, served as the basis for every breakfast. We split them open and put on butter, jam, and sometimes meat or cheese. I learned to eat a soft-boiled egg in an egg cup, tapping the top of the egg and carefully peeling off enough of the shell to insert my spoon to remove a bite of egg. Remaining in the shell until eaten kept the egg warm, as opposed to taking off the whole shell at once and putting it in a bowl the way we did at home. I gave several family members egg cups, but I couldn't convince them to try using them.

The main meal of the day was at noon, whereas at home ours was in the evening. We were at school at noon and ate sandwiches we bought with us or cafeteria meals. Our dinners didn't vary much: meat, potatoes, and a vegetable, usually canned or frozen. In Marburg, stores and businesses closed for two hours so workers had time to come home to eat. The family always sat together at the table and talked about whatever was on our minds that day. Most days we ate ragout or sauce with meat and vegetables, usually over potatoes. The potatoes were served in a large bowl in the middle of the table. Each person took several potatoes, stuck a fork in each one, peeled it, and then smashed up the peeled potatoes to serve as a base for whatever else was served. Sometimes noodles replaced the potatoes, but potatoes were by far the most common in the homes I ate in.

Meat was almost never served separately from sauce. I learned why one time when I decided to cook an American meal and wanted to serve steak. We went to a German meat market but all I could find was what they called Bifstek, much thinner than the steaks we had at home. Nevertheless, I bought several pieces despite the high price but was disappointed at how tough it was when cooked. My attempt to share my favorite meal failed as cuisine, but instead became an occasion for laughter and good spirits.

Desserts were usually something the women had made themselves, often a pastry tart with fruit on top. Sometimes we ate fruit with *Quark*, a type of curd cheese also used in main dishes. I often found myself eating something I did not recognize, so meals were a daily cultural adventure. Most of it tasted good and I was hungry, so I ate and enjoyed what I was served.

After the main meal, everyone went to their rooms for a nap or quiet time. They claimed it was good for digestion to rest after a meal. I rarely slept, although I did lie down. Usually I read. Sometimes I wrote letters home. I grew to like having quiet time for myself, as strange as the practice seemed to me at first.

For *Abendbrot*, literally "evening bread," we sat in the living room and ate on trays or on our laps. A variety of foods were served, and we could choose what we wanted to eat. Typical meals included: one or more kinds of dense wheat or rye bread, with meats, cheeses, tomatoes and other sliced vegetables and mustard. They had a firm rule that you buttered the bread first and never put both meat and cheese on the same piece of bread, which was sliced at the table.

"Do you ever buy bread that is already sliced," I asked.

Frau Bartuzat was shocked. "It wouldn't be fresh! Do you eat sliced bread in America?"

"All our bread is sliced," I admitted, "and it seems fresh enough."

Frau Bartuzat was doubtful. "Slicing bread is a skill women must learn before they get married." She showed me how, but I wasn't very good at it.

Particularly with *Abendbrot* but also sometimes when afternoon tea was served, we drank schnapps of varying flavors and types. Wine and beer might be served in the evening but not usually midday, unless it was a special occasion. Nearly every night before bed, Frau Bartuzat and Fritz drank a shot glass of cherry schnapps, which I liked, or vermouth or gin, which I didn't. On no occasion did I ever see them or most anyone else in Germany drink too much, as was common at home, especially among my college friends.

GETTING ORIENTED IN A NEW CULTURE

The day after I arrived in Marburg, Frau Bartuzat took me into town. When we walked to the bus stop two blocks away, I learned they did not own a car, although now that Fritz had his driver's license they could occasionally rent one, as he did the night before when he picked me up. Most often they rode the bus or walked. As we rode into the town center Frau Bartuzat proudly pointed out the sights that made Marburg unique. The most prominent feature was a beautiful early Gothic church, built in the thirteenth century in honor of St. Elisabeth, with dual spires reaching high into the sky. The impressive old university building, built in the sixteenth century, rose next to the bridge across the Lahn River. Up on top of the biggest hill is the Marburg castle, built in the eleventh century as a fortress. These historic buildings were intact because Marburg was not viewed as a strategic target during World War II and escaped the bombing that damaged or destroyed so many other buildings in Germany. Blending in with the historic were more modern buildings, especially those of the university which expanded after the war. The market place where we did our shopping was framed by more old buildings and narrow cobblestone streets. In the center was a fountain that served as a common meeting place. I realized I was seeing streets and buildings that had looked much the same for centuries. I could spend my whole time here without running out of places to explore.

Frau Bartuzat went shopping nearly every day, because they had only had a small under-the-counter refrigerator and a cooling closet that opened to the outside for use in cold weather. There were no supermarkets, so she went to different small shops to buy meats, breads, vegetables and fruits, and dairy products. The shops wrapped some of the food in paper but did not put it in bags, so you carried your own bags. I still have the string bag I bought to use for shopping.

The next day I learned there were problems with the arrangements that had been made for me to stay in student housing after I left the Bartuzats. So in the midst of the culture shock of being in a new country and speaking another language, I was forced to be responsible for myself in ways I had not expected. Fortunately, Frau Bartuzat was able to help me. She found another family I could stay with, but I had already decided I liked the idea of the student house. I persisted and finally succeeded in making the arrangements. In the process of securing my room, I was directed to an office at the university for foreign students. It required a mental shift for me to think of myself as foreign, but that was my new reality. Resources and supportive allies are essential to successfully entering a new culture, I learned.

I had expected to enroll in the university and get a student Ausweis (identification card) which would qualify me for student rates and advantages, but I discovered the card would cost 200 marks. Even though that was only $50 it seemed too expensive since I would only be there a couple of months. I hoped I would still be able to attend classes and that no one would ask for my ID.

NEW FRIENDS AND EXPERIENCES

Frau Bartuzat knew from the materials that introduced me to her that I played bridge, so she arranged for me to participate in a bridge club that met in a private dining room at the train station. I wasn't sure either my German or my bridge skills were good enough, but I figured it would be interesting to try. On my third day in Marburg, I learned to play duplicate bridge in German. It was a challenge to keep up with the bidding when I barely knew the names of the suits, but I did well enough to be invited back.

Another new activity I was introduced to right away was taking walks. At home and at college I was used to walking sometimes a mile or more to get places I wanted to go, but the idea of taking a walk for exercise and enjoyment was entirely new to me. These walks were often in the woods I could see from the window in my room. I was fascinated at all the different kinds of trees and tried to learn their names in German, but what amazed me most was the different shades of green. Nature was more diverse and beautiful than I had realized before. Walking in the woods was a common German activity and the wide, well-worn paths made walking easy. People of all ages took walks, often after the midday meal on weekends and holidays. I was told that it was good for digestion.

During that first month, I was in a German conversation class where I met other American students on whom I depended for company. However, after I got more comfortable there, I chose to spend most of my time with my new German friends. I wanted to think in German and switching back to English interrupted that focus. I still used English when I wrote letters, although as time went on I found myself using German sentence structure in writing English. If my family thought it odd, they were kind enough not to mention it.

Writing letters home was one of my important occupations while I was in Germany. Although I also kept a journal where I wrote down appointments and activities each day, along with private thoughts and experiences, the letters became my official record of what I was learning. My mother thought the letters were so interesting and informative she shared them with her friends and our extended family and even took a few over to Pomona so some of my friends could read them. Since my mother had gone out on a limb to convince my father I should go, I was glad she was getting something out of it.

The Bartuzats loved to go places in the country, usually in a rented car with Fritz driving. I learned how diverse just this one area of the country was, and how beautiful. Our first trip was to the Lenz *Künstlerhaus* in Erdhausen. Karl Lenz was a well-known painter of landscapes and farm scenes. After he died, his wife and daughter opened their home as an exhibition of traditional farm life in Hesse, with a shop and a coffee house. Frau Lenz made pottery and the daughter made gold jewelry, which they sold along with hand-woven cloth, carved items, and paintings. I bought a few small pieces of painted pottery for gifts.

When he came home from his school trip, Jochen introduced me to his friend Rudolf Spalke, who lived in a nearby section of refugee housing. The Spalkes became the other family I spent a lot of time with. First, they invited to me to a party, hosted by Rudolf and his older brother Gottfried. There I met the third brother René and his wife Erika, plus many friends of one brother or another. I don't know that I ever described a party at home to my family, but I described this one because it was so different. "I got to talk and dance with every one of the guys instead of being matched up one and one. Much fun, but what really surprises me is that these students, mostly 24-27 and very intelligent, don't act or look any older than my Pomona friends!" I was still 19 at the time.

A few days later Gottfried, Rudolf, and Frau Spalke took me on a drive through several small towns, including Frankenberg and Mellnau. We visited a twelfth-century church where the ceiling had been painted white. In an old book, the people learned that an intricate mural had been painted on the ceiling, and volunteers were carefully chipping away the white paint and discovering its hidden beauty. I was fascinated that even in Germany with its appreciation for the past something as amazing as this painted ceiling could be lost for centuries.

Although Marburg was still recovering from the war and relatively poor compared to other cities in Germany, it remained a center for culture in terms of the arts, literature, and music. I had many opportunities to enjoy excellent performances of all sorts, including plays. At first it was difficult to understand the dialog, especially if there were many words spoken quickly, as in the first play I saw just a week after I arrived, Moliere's *School for Wives*. The next week I saw Beckett's *Das letze Band* Krapp's Last Tape which I understood better, since the dialog was sparse with silence in between the lines. By the time I saw Albee's *Who's Afraid of Virginia Woolf?* in Munich a month later, I was delighted to report I understood "almost all of it."

Germans loved classical music and many played instruments well. Sometimes Rudolf and Jochen played together for whoever happened to be around, Rudolf on piano and Jochen on flute. I could listen to them for hours. We also attended wonderful concerts, often with well-known musicians, such as the Zürich Chamber Orchestra and the Hungarian Philharmonic. One highlight was hearing a woman pianist, Elly Ney, play Beethoven sonatas, but my favorite was Bach's B Minor Mass.

Movies were another favorite activity for both my American and German friends. After tennis and a bike ride with Fritz, we went to my first German-made movie, the newly released *Der Fluch der gelben Schlange* Curse of the Yellow Snake, a mystery I found easier to understand than the more philosophical movies and plays I had seen before. Rudolf took me to my next German film, *Das*

Glas Wasser, the last film starring one of the most famous German actors Gustaf Gründgens, who had just died. A few days later I saw *Faust,* in which he played Mephistopheles. This movie was especially helpful, because I would be studying Goethe's *Faust,* when I got back to Pomona.

I was especially glad to see German-made movie versions of classics like *Faust* and *Die Dreigroschenoper* Three-Penny Opera. But I saw many more American-made films, because that is what most of my German friends wanted to see. Some favorites were *Tender is the Night, The Apartment, Lawrence of Arabia, and Robin Hood.* After President Kennedy's assassination, newsreels about his life and death preceded every movie. I found it ironic that I learned more about Kennedy in Germany after his death than I had back at home when he was alive.

Going to church had been one of my usual activities at home, but I learned this was not common practice for most Germans. People still considered churches important and paid taxes to maintain the historic buildings and staff to keep them open. In each German state, taxes supported either the Catholic or the *Evangelisch* (Protestant) church. Marburg was in the Protestant state of Hesse.

The first Sunday I was in Marburg, Frau Bartuzat took me to the university church for what they called a *Stunde der Besinnung* (hour of reflection) rather than a *Gottesdienst* (worship service). I described it in a letter: "Not a regular church service but more of a chapel sort of service—a sermon-lecture plus music." What I found most inspiring, though, was "to sit in such old buildings and think about the wars they have withstood and the famous people that have probably been in them." After that first Sunday I continued to go sometimes and joined the choir that sang for special programs.

Overall there was much about German culture I admired and even grew to prefer over my own. I wrote, "I am really excited about the German way of life. I don't think they get old here so quickly ... The country is prosperous enough. The combination of this prosperity with the German attitude is quite ideal, I find. One takes enough time to live. A day is not so packed full of events that one hasn't time to relax and think a little." In response to a letter my father had written apparently expressing concern that I wasn't doing any studying, I said, "I can't feel that the time I spend other than in studying is a waste. In fact, that is what I've really learned here—that it is impossible for time lived to be wasted." I encouraged them to "be a little European and don't worry about me too much."

ABOUT THE WAR AND THE EAST ZONE

In going to Germany, I wondered if I would meet former Nazis and what people's attitudes might be about Nazism and World War II. Most of what I knew came from popular culture resources rather than academic study. I had seen the movies *Diary of Anne Frank* (1959) and *Judgment at Nuremberg* (1961) and *Life* magazine photos of concentration camps. In preparation for the trip, I read William Shirer's *The Rise and Fall of the Third Reich*, a best-selling book published in English in 1960.

I would hear critical discussion of Nazism among the students, but first I learned about the impact of war on individual families' lives. The Bartuzats were better off than other refugee families I met because the father had been an officer in the Nazi army. This meant Frau Bartuzat received a widow's pension plus a stipend for each child up to age 25 while they were in school. Because Jochen was studying for the *Abitur*[85] and Fritz was taking private classes in English and Spanish in preparation for a career as an export merchant, both qualified as students.

Frau Bartuzat never talked about the Nazis or the war, and I was afraid to ask for fear it would damage our relationship. She did, however, talk about what it was like to live in the East Zone under communism. Her parents still lived there, so she was personally aware of the ongoing situation. She regularly sent packages because "they can't get much fresh fruit or vegetables" unless they pay "exorbitant" prices on the rare occasions when produce is available. "Chocolate, coffee, and cigarettes are out of the question—also medicine…and

---

85   The German school system consists of thirteen grades, making it a year longer than American schools. The *Abitur,* required for graduation from the *Gymnasium,* is a prerequisite for university entrance. The exam consists of written and oral tests in four core subjects.

wool and cloth are hard to get. Of course, the people can't leave." However, she could occasionally visit them.

Frau Bartuzat left her home in the East Zone before moving was restricted, but she could only take with her a few of her most precious things. She showed me the pieces of Meissen china she had managed to save from the large set her family prized. Sometimes I would see her holding the one cup lovingly, perhaps remembering all she had lost or in gratitude for having survived with this piece of her past intact.

She was proud of her present ability to live well and offer housing to students like me. I wondered if it was her way of atoning for whatever her husband did in the war. She made it clear we did not need to scrimp on heat or warm water. I would learn later that some families only had heat in one room, and water was heated on the stove or only turned on weekly for bathing. "In fact," I noted, "Frau B. has to scold me when I am hesitant about turning on the heat. She doesn't want me to catch a cold!"

Frau Bartuzat was able to hire Frau Braun to come once a week to clean house and wash our clothes. Frau Braun was fascinated with me and invited us to visit her family in Dreihausen to meet her children, since they had never seen an American. The small village was charming. I was intrigued with the large wood-fired *Backofen* (oven) in the village center, where the women still baked bread in the traditional way. Herr Braun was a laborer, but the family had their own home with a lovely garden. I loved the bridge and small stone house Herr Braun had built in the backyard for the children. The family was considered poor, but "instead of living in a slum or a cheap house in a city," they lived in the country where they could survive well "by the fruits of their labors."

In contrast to the Bartuzats, the Spalkes lived in a smaller apartment in refugee housing not far from the Bartuzats. The father had been a minister who resisted the Nazi takeover and worked against them during the war until he was killed, so Frau Spalke received no government assistance except the student stipends her sons shared with her. Their place had only one heat source, a coal stove in the main living area. Rudolf still lived at home and had a small bedroom. His oldest brother, Gottfried, had recently moved back home, so Frau Spalke slept in the living room. When the grandmother arrived, she slept in the kitchen, which she said she liked because it was warm.

Gottfied, age 28, had completed medical school and was doing his residency. Although he had finished school before they left the East Zone, he had to pass the *Abitur* before he could enter the university, because Russian-dominated education was considered inferior. René, age 26, and Erika had two children and lived in a very small place above a flower shop. He had nearly finished his studies in theology when his questions about faith caused him to decide to become a teacher instead. He had to start his new course of study at the beginning because work for one degree did not transfer to another. Rudolf, age 20, had just passed the Abitur and was deciding what he wanted to study.

Frau Spalke had been a concert pianist, but since moving west her life focused on her children. As I got to know her better, I wrote, "She is typical of many women who had beautiful lives, handsome husbands and newly born children. And then came the war that killed their husbands. And then came the communists who killed the beauty." I found myself imagining what it would be like to have lived her story and it made me want to cry. "It's really sad, not for the kids—it's been a good experience for them to see, so that they know what to fight for—but for the mothers who lost their men. They still laugh and enjoy life, but it could have been so much better, and that they know and must accept."

It was hard for me to understand the impact of a whole generation of children growing up without fathers or what it would be like to flee from your home and start all over in a new place, often with practically nothing. About the Spalkes I wrote, "It's a lot to face—but the good thing is that they still think well and are always moving up and improving themselves."

Each day the new places I visited and new people I met increased my awareness of the culture I was becoming part of. "By now," I wrote a mere ten days after my arrival in Marburg, "the people are somewhat more real to me. I mean, I can see how they live and how it would be good to live here. It's hard to explain, because it's such a non-concrete thing—this development of an understanding and appreciation for other people—but it comes, and talking about differences helps."

WALDORF SCHOOL

The Spalkes and the Bartuzats came to West Germany when Jochen and Rudolf were in their early teens. Because their education in the east was different from the west—for instance, they learned Russian instead of English—and they missed some school while they were in transition, they were not prepared to enter the regular German high school, the *Gymnasium*. Instead the boys went to the Freie *Waldorfschule* (Waldorf School) in Marburg. Learning about this innovative form of education, inspired by the work of Rudolf Steiner,[86] introduced me to the existence of alternative educational theories and practices.

Even though the boys had now graduated, the families still participated in the Waldorf community. We visited the school one day when Frau Bartuzat and Frau Spalke went there to help make things for an upcoming bazaar. I had time to wander around and explore the uniquely designed building and observe the students. Rather than the square or rectangular rooms found in most schools, this one had odd nooks and crannies that were said to foster creativity by providing places students could go individually or in small groups to talk, think, write, draw, or make something. The day I was there, some groups were meeting with one teacher or another, but other students were using the various spaces the building provided. Nobody seemed to be "supervising" the students who were working on their own, but I could feel the excitement of learning going on. Was it my imagination or was this a new school culture?

At Christmas time, the school presented the most unique holiday pageant I had ever seen—with Adam and Eve and gods and

---

86   Rudolf Steiner (1861-1925) was an Austrian philosopher, social reformer, and architect, who founded the esoteric spiritual movement anthroposophy. His innovative ideas about education led to the founding of the first Waldorf school in England. There are now approximately 1000 Waldorf schools world-wide.

goddesses along with the traditional story of the birth of Jesus. The pageant made use of a form of dance developed by Steiner, called Eurythmie, with long flowing costumes and gentle movements combined with words read by a narrator. The overall effect was mystical and strange. I was entranced as I felt my mind opening to new ways of understanding religious stories. Later I discovered a Waldorf school in Los Angeles and attended several programs. I was eager to learn more about this unique form of education.

ON MY OWN AT BETTINAHAUS

On October 21, a month after my arrival in Marburg, Fritz and Rudolf helped me move into Bettinahaus, a rooming house for thirty women students. I shared a room with Petra, from Stuttgart, who was studying English and French. The housekeeper Frau Jacobi was in charge, along with the head resident Evelin. There was a large living room on the main floor and a shared kitchen in the basement where we could cook and store food.

In our shared room, we each had a narrow bed with a foam mattress, a small desk, and an armoire for clothes. I quickly discovered I had too many clothes to fit in the space I had been given. I had never thought of myself as rich, but in terms of clothes, I certainly had more than my roommate, who often wore the same clothes several days in a row, something I had been taught never to do.

Since I was no longer eating regularly with the family, I had to figure out how to feed myself, something I had not yet been responsible for doing regularly at home or at college. I relied on foods like soup and bread and cheese that were easy to prepare and often ate my midday meal at the Mensa, the university cafeteria and student center. Once, Petra and I made potato salad for supper with Rudolf and her friend Siegfried. She showed me how to make the German style and I showed her the American version. The guys liked both equally well.

Because I ate out a lot, I had to find places I could afford. A favorite was the place next door to where Rudolf's brother lived, a café featuring Schaschlik, an Eastern European meat dish (kabobs) cooked in a spicy sauce and served in a roll. I learned to appreciate a wide range of German foods, such as Knödel (dumplings of many different variations), many types of Wurst (sausage), Rotkohl (red cabbage with apples), Spätzle (egg noodles), Hering in Sahnesoße (herring in a cream sauce with apples and onions), Grünkohl (kale usually with potatoes), Sauerbraten (marinated beef pot roast), and Sauerkraut (pickled shredded cabbage). Although I was learning to eat less meat, when I got hungry for something familiar I went to a place with racks of rotisserie broiled chicken in the window.

One of the advantages of Bettinahaus was its central location, making it easier than before to explore Marburg. I discovered that the university museum had an exhibit about the Grimm Brothers who had studied at the university. I loved their stories as a child and now I had a new reason to feel connected through my personal past to the city that was fast becoming home to me.

Rudolf took me to many places in town, several of which became our favorites, such as Café Vetter for coffee and Club Maxim for dancing. I also spent time wandering the streets and watching the people. I loved looking in stores and finding little things I could afford for gifts for people back home and for the people I was coming to love in Marburg.

One of my first challenges, assigned by my mother, was to get a flu shot. I was sure Germany wouldn't have anything like that, since the shots were relatively new in the US, but she insisted I ask. I finally found the university medical office, spoke with a doctor, and learned that they gave the flu immunization in pill form. "I must get a paper from one office, have a doctor sign it, and then I can get the pills from the pharmacy," I explained. "So, we'll see how it works with German doctors!" I sent the prescription home in a subsequent letter and complained that it cost 14 marks, about $4.00.

I finally began thinking seriously about studying. Because I was alone in Marburg, I had no support for studying and many more interesting activities to engage in. I justified my choices to myself and to my family by explaining that all of what I was doing was educational. Earlier Frau Bartuzat observed, "Du macht alles mit," meaning that I participated in everything. Her observation proved to be accurate. Every time there was an invitation to do something new, I chose that over studying.

SOUTHERN TRAVELS

I was just getting oriented to life in Bettinahaus when I left for a ten-day trip. I had been invited to attend a conference of women students in Heidelberg and decided to go on from there to travel around southern Germany. I figured it would be a good opportunity to see more of the country and to visit Tanni in Munich. Thirty women students and ten leaders came to the conference, held in a youth hostel where we stayed. I found it odd the meeting was held there, because they not only had a strict curfew, they also turned the lights out at 10 PM, much too early for someone like me who would have enjoyed seeing the night life in Heidelberg. I concluded that youth hostels must be primarily for younger travelers and was glad I hadn't invested in a hostel pass.

The International Federation of Women had been formed to support women students at universities. At the time, there were no women's deans or counselors and women students could spend years studying without finding a clear direction. Many failed to graduate and ended up getting married and foregoing their dreams of a career. The same questions women students had been struggling with in the US for years were discussed as if they were new dilemmas. Do women lose their femininity if they have education and careers? How can women balance marriage and career, especially when they have children? In a letter, I noted that "the conference was a little bit funny to me, because it seemed as if I knew all the answers already, or at least knew how things must eventually work out."

Nevertheless, the discussion inspired me to reflect in my journal:

The question is whether to live for yourself or for others … It is not that I am afraid of losing friends but that I feel myself fulfilled by making others happy. The difficulty is that others do not know what they want from me. Therefore, I must justify my life first for myself. …

We have the capacity to be so many things and when called

upon to be something new, when one feels the call within strongly enough, there is no stopping you. How can one ever know what is best to do? One can merely try and if it gives a satisfactory feeling and makes other people smile and reaches other souls—then it is good!

Earlier I had contacted my shipboard friend Stefan, who was on break from the university and agreed to meet me after the conference and travel to Munich where he had studied and where my friend Tanni was staying. Although I had originally told my family I would be traveling by train, he suggested hitchhiking since it would be much less expensive. Knowing my family would be worried, I offered this explanation about who usually picks up hitchhikers:

Mostly it is students or people who were recently students and who probably hitch-hiked themselves and men alone who pick you up in order to have a little company for the trip. [I am amazed at my naïveté in thinking "men alone" would alleviate my parents' fears!] But we also rode with a very well dressed family in a beautiful new Mercedes who actually crowded their car to give us a ride and went twenty miles out of their way to take us where we wanted to go! Sometimes there's no explanation—the people just want to be nice!

Our most unusual ride was with a married Army couple and friend. When their 1956 Chevy broke down on the way from Tübingen to Munich, I wrote, "we found out how helpful the Germans can be, even with an American car." Stefan was surprised that the people who stopped knew how to fix it.

I became an instant convert to hitchhiking because it put us in direct contact with people we would not have otherwise met. It also meant we sometimes ended up going places we hadn't planned, because we could get a ride there and not where we originally wanted to go. For instance, on our way from Heidelberg to Munich we got stuck near Stuttgart and decided to go to Tübingen to spend the night. Wherever we went, we saw castles, universities, historic town plazas with cafes and open-air markets, and, when there was time, museums with paintings by famous artists. Stefan was a great tour guide, making sure I saw whatever was most notable in each city, like the famous Glockenspiel, a huge clock on the city hall in Munich with figures that turn around as it chimes each hour.

I had to explain to my parents about hotel arrangements. "I do hope you trust me. But even if either Stefan or I had dishonorable intentions, the German laws are so strict and fines so heavy against hotels that rent double rooms to unmarried people—or who allow unmarried people in the same room—that the hotel people are always very careful to give us separate rooms on separate floors and then they watch us carefully too!" I added another sentence, though, that reading between the lines affirms my memory that we did find ways to get together. "I hope you trust me enough to know I wouldn't do anything unless it were right." I managed to find an acceptable version of the truth to tell my family!

As I traveled, I noticed cultural differences within Germany. At the conference, the women spoke Hochdeutsch, High German, which is what I had learned, but each region of Germany had a different dialect, some of which I could barely understand. The buildings were different, too. But most notable to me was that the meat I was missing in Marburg was available and affordable. In Heidelberg, I enjoyed a steak and in Munich I discovered an appetizer of thinly sliced very rare roast beef with horseradish. I also learned to eat steak tartare, freshly ground raw beef steak.

It was great to see Tanni and compare her situation to mine. She lived with a family in Pullach, 20 minutes from Münich, and invited me to stay there. The family was very cordial and even invited me to stay after Tanni left on a previously planned trip to Berlin. Tanni took me to an amazing museum, the Pinakothek, one of the oldest art galleries in the world, where we saw paintings by Rubens, Rembrandt, Dürer, and El Greco. We also saw a modern art exhibit of Georges Braque. Since my visit to the art museum in Chicago, I was getting a crash course in the great art of the western world. I wondered how all these museums could have such great paintings.

Munich was in the Catholic state of Bavaria, with its ornate and flamboyant style. Although the Bavarian Catholics did not celebrate Halloween, the first two days of November were celebrated as All Saints and All Souls Days, a time to go to church, honor the dead and decorate graves. We did not, however, join in. Instead Stefan and I met Tanni and her French roommate in the famous large hall at the Hofbräuhaus. We learned that this hall was a favorite of tourists but that locals tended to prefer the smaller room upstairs. We knew we would be asked if we went there when we got home, so we stayed for a while and then went on to Schwabing, a section of Munich known for its night life. At a popular club called Babalu, we danced and drank Schampers, beer mixed with champagne, the cheapest thing on the menu, to make our cover. I described the club in my journal as having "horrible loud music and a crowded dance floor."

On the way home, Stefan and I went to Würzburg, "one of the most beautiful places I've been." I liked this smaller city better than Munich. "It seems to hang together more as far as style and attitude." I was amazed that it only cost $7.00 to stay at the Hotel St. Joseph for three nights. The city featured a famous "residence" built by two prince-bishops in the early eighteenth century. Severely damaged by the bombings, it was in the process of being rebuilt when we were there. We could only see the spectacular gardens and certain rooms, but what we saw was amazingly expansive and ornate. I shared my thoughts with my family on a postcard:

One wonders if something is wrong with our modern life that we are content to make things so simple in style and to live with such mobility when earlier details were so important that one never perhaps moved very far. It's a question that one can easily overlook in California, but even in Washington DC I was beginning to wonder about whether all this tradition and earlier way of life had any point or any importance in our life today, and now in Germany I am meeting the same question again.

Because Stefan needed to meet several people in Würzburg, I had time to sit in a cafe, reflect on my journey, and write postcards. On a series of postcards cards, I noted: "All these cards I've been writing have been in restaurants! After eating one may sit at the table for hours and talk or read and write and no one throws you out! Very nice and a good way to relax–a good chance to catch up on affairs." After his meetings, we went to a carnival that was in town. I laughed when I saw a vendor with Zuckerwatte (cotton candy), which I had to try. So many things are different in our two cultures, but some things are the same!

Although I enjoyed my travels with Stefan, I no longer felt the same attraction to him as on our trip across the ocean. While I hitchhiked alone on the last part of the journey back to Marburg, I realized our relationship was not going to develop into the great love of my life. It had been a wonderful shipboard romance and he was a great traveling companion, but that was all.

LOVE BLOOMS AND GROWS

Back in Marburg, I settled into my life at Bettinahaus, where I continued awakening to new aspects of German culture. That first night Rudolf took me to the Spanish National Circus and soon became my frequent companion. One day he told me the story of how his family left the East Zone and explained why they were unable to bring anything with them. I was so moved I shared what I learned in a letter.

His family is listed in the Communist Party's black book of political flee-ers from the Russian zone. His older brothers … had been working in resistance groups and they had many friends who were captured and imprisoned for their attempts against the communists. Their family was lucky enough to hear they were being sought and so they had time to flee … Now they can never go through the East Zone again, even by train to Berlin. Can you believe it?!

Although I had already heard bad things about the communist regime at home and from Frau Bartuzat, this story touched me like no other. Ever since my experience with the Anti-Communism Crusade, I held on to the belief that there must be redeeming qualities in communism, but Rudolf's story raised questions for which I had no answers.[87] The letter continues:

---

87   My undergraduate education did not include any study of communism either as a philosophy or as a movement. In reading related to the writing of this book, I have learned a great deal about others in my generation who were friends or members of the Communist Party in the US. I have great respect for their

From the end of the war the East Zone was treated just like a good communist state—perhaps even more organized than Russia since it's smaller and since Ulbrecht was a good friend and follower of Stalin.

I was appalled at what he told me about East German schools and the controls the government imposed on what people read and thought.

The schools were immediately rearranged along party lines. The children learned to shoot guns—using human figures named "Capitalists" as targets. Of course, they are too young to really be able to distinguish such fun and games from propaganda. Rudolf was lucky that his mother was so strong and so careful to train her children to understand that there was another world—a free world—where one could say things against the government and not be imprisoned, where one could read any book, where one could choose friends, etc.

What if no one had told them about this other world, I wondered? I could hardly imagine what it would be like to grow up not knowing there were alternatives. I thought about the children of Rudolf's age still in the east who may have heard stories from their parents, but, I wondered, how would they be able to convey to their children what they themselves had never experienced?

I had great admiration for the Spalke family for being able to construct a new life in a new place with nothing from their past to serve as a foundation except their memories. "Not everyone in the East Zone can do that." It was sad, I thought, "that many people in West Germany pay no attention or do not realize how it is for those others. When Rudolf first saw … the children in the schools he could only think that they had no idea of how their neighbors suffered and are suffering under the yoke of communism!"

I was surprised when Rudolf's grandmother arrived from the East Zone later that month, since I had understood that no one in the family could leave. Apparently, though, she had special status because her husband was part of the famous piano manufacturing

---

motives and initial faith in communism as a viable alternative to capitalism. Their stories are also an important part of what shaped Sixties culture change.

family of August Förster. She was even allowed to bring many things with her to the west, which greatly enhanced the Spalke home and lifestyle.

Before long I found myself in love with Rudolf and grew comfortable in our relationship.[88] He had dark brooding eyes that drew me in and a serious, thoughtful attitude toward life. He was a wonderful companion and showed me many different aspects of cultural life in Marburg. Each of these places and experiences deepened my understanding and appreciation of German culture.

I started going to the university with Rudolf, to a class he was taking on French Impressionist Art. I had attended a few classes earlier, but couldn't follow the lectures well enough to make it worth going. I already knew I liked impressionist paintings, and in this class the professor showed slides while he was lecturing so it was much easier to understand. I learned how the different artists and their styles evolved over time and grew to love the art of that period even more.

On the night before my twentieth birthday, Rudolf took me to Maxim's where they had a band. We could dance only until midnight because November 20 was a solemn holiday of thanksgiving and no one danced, not even in their homes. The next morning, my roommate Petra treated me to a plate of special pastries. The Spalkes invited me for the midday meal and I had Abendbrot with the Bartuzats. After we ate, they invited me to sit at a table they had set with twenty candles. They gave me gifts, small but precious things. Then they brought out a Feuerzangebowle (literally, fire tongs punch), a red wine punch over which a block of sugar soaked in 100 proof rum was lit on fire and allowed to caramelize and drip into the bowl of wine below. As I described in a letter, "All is blue flame and beautiful against the red wine." Once it burns down the sugar is mixed in and the punch continues to glow, kept warm on a burner. "You sit in the dark with the glowing red wine. It's freezing cold outside, but you glow inside, because the people are so wonderful." The honor of this celebration touched me deeply.

---

88   For more about my relationship with Rudolf, see Love is All You Need, Falling in Love in Germany.

In addition to Rudolf, the other Spalke I grew closest to was René. We shared a special connection because of our mutual sense of call to ministry. The story of his crisis of faith made me wonder about my own relationship to religion. His warmth and cordiality toward me made me feel immediately accepted, not as a love interest, since he was married, but as a sort of older brother. So, I was delighted when he invited me to participate in a ritual called Brüderschaft trinken. This was an invitation to use the familiar form of "you," a convention we do not have in English, celebrated in some cases such as this by interlocking our arms and drinking beer. I loved the acknowledgement that we were now siblings.

THE ASSASSINATION

Perhaps my most dramatic experience of culture shock came about because of something that happened in the US which made me question the culture I came from. On November 22 at around 8 PM friends at Bettinahaus barged into my room, where I was talking with a visitor from Fullerton who had just stopped by. "Your president has been shot!" they cried.

We dashed to the living room where both the television and radio were on and stood in shock as the story unfolded. Tears flowed all around the room, as we held each other and tried to grasp the enormity of what was happening. It was fortuitous, I thought, that Dave, whose parents had been advisors for my youth group at the Presbyterian Church, happened to visit that day. Since he only knew a few words of German, I wondered how he might have fared had he not been with someone who could translate and explain what was going on

Late that night I wrote to my family, "I just heard a concert of mourning music. And now all the political leaders are reporting over radio and TV to the German people the sorrow of the German government at the loss of their friend." The next day, Sunday, was a traditional day for honoring the dead and I was going to the annual concert of Bach's B Minor Mass. I knew the concert would be sold out, especially now.

"I can imagine it must be really something in America! Or

was he so much more respected here?" I wondered what the reaction was at home, especially in Republican Orange County. I wasn't certain what my parents' reaction would be since I knew that my father was a strong Republican and not a fan of the president, so I added, "You don't realize how important a president is until you get out of the country and find out how much he represents the country to the rest of the world." Later my sister Mary Lou challenged my doubts about the shock and sadness they were feeling. I explained, "I didn't mean that I didn't think you cared, but we heard here that in the south some bars stayed open all night rejoicing in the death of the 'nigger-lover!'" I was relieved to know it wasn't that way in California.

The impact of Kennedy's assassination was huge all over Germany. On television and at the movies, there were many newsreels of his speeches and stories about his life. The favorite of all, though, was his speech at the Berlin Wall earlier that year on June 26. To emphasize the support of the United States for West Germany, he made two statements in German, something no other American president had ever done: "Ich bin ein Berliner"[89] (I am a citizen of Berlin) and "Lass' sie nach Berlin kommen" (Let them come to Berlin).

TRIP TO BERLIN

For some time, I had been planning a visit to Berlin. I had been invited to stay with an American from my German class in Marburg. My parents, however, were very worried about my trip, since they heard much negative news about the dangers of crossing over into East Germany.[90] Originally I had wanted to take the train, but I decided to fly instead since, as I pointed out in a letter, "The air route connecting West and West belongs to the West!" Because

---

89   Some people joked that he had made a grammatical mistake, referring to himself as a type of local pastry, but he had spoken correctly since he was not technically a Berlin citizen but rather using the term symbolically. Germans loved fact that he even tried to speak their language.

90   Although a significant portion of Berlin, known as West Berlin, was officially part of West Germany, the city was in the middle of East Germany.

of their concern, I promised not to go to East Berlin or to have any contact with East Germans or East Berliners. Although my intentions were good, I did not keep this promise.

A week before I planned to leave, Rudolf decided to come along, particularly so he could see a long-time friend. I knew this trip could be dangerous for him but since I had already decided to fly it was possible. He did not, however, want to tell his mother where he was going, because he knew she would worry. Jochen helped by providing a suitcase. Although Frau Spalke found out about the trip from the Bartuzats, she didn't try to stop him from going.

On November 29, we took the train to Hanover and flew to West Berlin. We rode the bus around Berlin to see the horrible Wall and beautiful new buildings like the Philharmonic and Congress Hall. We learned that after the war Berlin had attracted the best architects in the world to help rebuild the bombed-out city. The Kaiser Wilhelm Church especially impressed me, because the partially destroyed walls of the old church were left in place with a new, modern building rising from the ruins, connecting the history of Berlin with its present and future.

We enjoyed walking along the wide main avenue, the Kurfürstendamm, lined with cafés and large elegant department stores, where we window-shopped. Some cafés featured heated terraces so we could sit outside and observe the street life. At night, we went to clubs to hear music and dance, like Riverboat and Big Apple. Riverboat was a big dance hall with three bands playing mostly American hit tunes. "The people danced about like they did in Southern California this summer," I wrote home. "Elsewhere in Germany, the dancing is a little less up-to-date. The twist is still being done everywhere. But this place was really Californian—in the sense that the people had more of a big city awareness in their attitudes."

At the museum, we saw many famous paintings and the bust of Nefertiti created over three thousand years ago. I stood looking at it realizing it was undoubtedly the oldest object I had ever seen. Going to an art museum with Rudolf was a new experience. Since he was studying art history he knew a lot about the paintings and saw them with "sympathetic eyes. I'm trying to develop that for myself,"

I wrote home.

My mother had suggested contacting the daughter of one of her Fullerton friends. When we got together, she took us to a beautiful lake called Tegelsee. I was impressed that this amazing city had lakes where people could go to the beach and swim in the warm weather. I had only met her once before, but she knew many of the same people I did. Although I enjoyed hearing what was going on with folks at home, I realized I no longer felt a strong connection to my home town. What was more interesting to me was that she had gone to a Waldorf school.

Of all the cities I visited in Germany, Berlin was the most fascinating, but I was nervous when we neared the Wall. This was where I faced a new level of culture shock: fear. We stopped at the Brandenburg Gate, which was now behind the Wall. The large carved stone arch had long been an important icon of Berlin, and because of that was used as a Nazi party symbol. Originally built as a symbol of peace, it was restored after the war as a joint project of the governments of both East and West Berlin. Before the Wall was erected on August 13, 1961, vehicles and pedestrians could pass freely through the gate. I tried to imagine what it looked like before the Wall was there.

For Tilo the Wall had special significance. We were having coffee at Café Zuntz on the Kurfurstendamm, after visiting the Wall, when he told us the following story.

TILO'S STORY

"Building that damn wall tore families apart," he sighed.

"Like my friend, Hans. He lived in East Berlin and spent the night at my house after a party. The next day we woke up late. When we saw my mom she had a horrible look on her face."

"They're building a wall," she said.

"Huh?" We had no idea what she was talking about. "Who's building what wall?" we asked practically in unison.

My mother explained the East Germans had closed the border, torn up the street, and were building a wall all to keep people from leaving East Berlin.[91] "I guess they're losing too many people. I'm not surprised."

We sat in silence trying to take it all in. Finally his mother broke the silence: "So Hans, you have a big decision to make. Are you going home? If you do, you may never be able to come back. You can stay here for a while, if you decide not to go home."

I wondered what I would do. I was pretty sure I would choose freedom over my family. There had been times I wanted to escape from my family, but certainly not forever.

"What did he decide?" I asked.

"He stayed in the west," was all Tilo said. I wanted to ask more about what happened but decided not to press the subject, which I could tell was still very difficult for Tilo to talk about.

I was surprised the next day when Tilo asked me, "So when do you want to go to East Berlin?" He assumed I would want to go.

"Uh, well, I promised my family I wouldn't go," I said without much conviction.

"Why? Don't they know it's perfectly safe as long as you're not on some list like Rudolf is? I'll go with you and show you around. I go over all the time."

"Well, maybe," I said as I was thinking about it. The story that got my parents so upset was about college students who hid someone in their car and got caught. I certainly would not do that.

"You really should see for yourself what it's like. Then you can tell people in America. They need to know why Berlin is so important and they need to help the people in East Germany. Besides, you'll be sorry if you miss this chance to go," Tilo said. Rudolf nodded in agreement.

It was probably that last point he made that pushed me over

---

91   The first version of the "wall" was 96 miles of barbed wire fence and stacks of paving stones. Because people were still managing to escape over it, in 1962 they began building a second fence, 100 feet inside the first. The space in between was left as a buffer zone and guards were told to shoot on sight anyone who tried to cross over. The actual wall was built in 1965 and then a more sophisticated one in 1975. What I saw in 1963 were the stacks of pavers, the death zone, and the roles of barbed wire fence. www.berlin-life.com/berlin/wall

the edge. I hated to miss anything. On December 2, Tilo and I went to East Berlin. I felt safe enough as long as Tilo was with me, but when we got to the border the guard told us we would have to get in different lines because I was American. Then I got very nervous. I was directed to go into a small building and almost changed my mind, but I figured I had come this far and needed to follow through.

The room was simple and clean, but everything looked old, except for the young man sitting at the desk. He stood up and asked for my passport. My hands were shaking a bit as I handed it to him. I didn't even look up.

He studied my passport. Then he looked at me and said, "This girl isn't you."

Oh my God, I thought. This is it. They'll take my passport and never let me leave.

Then he laughed and said, "The girl in this picture is smiling."

I laughed, too, and saw that he was really cute, even in his severe haircut and drab uniform.

"Have a good day," he said waving me through.

I was relieved to come out of the guard station and see Tilo waiting for me. When I looked around to see where we were, I noticed all the buildings seemed to be the same brownish-grey color. On the other side of the Wall, there was lots of color. Many people were walking around, talking, and laughing. Here it was quiet and somber and few people were out and about.

We walked around for a while. Tilo pointed out famous buildings and told me about the architectural details he was studying. He was particularly interested in buildings built in the nineteenth century. After a while, we found a restaurant and realized we were hungry. When we tried to order we were told, "We don't have that today." We finally asked what they did have and ordered that. The saddest thing I saw, though, was when I went to the rest room. An old woman was sitting there tearing up newspapers. I realized that was what they were using for toilet paper, so I gave her a few pennies and she gave me some. After about three hours we came back to West Berlin. East Berlin wasn't dangerous, I later told my parents, just sad.

On our last evening in Berlin we ate at a Chinese restaurant, Lingnan, one of the very few "foreign" food places I had seen in Germany. Then we went to see *Annie Schiess Los!* (Annie Get Your Gun) and later to Cabaret Dorett, which had a floor show that I explained to my family was "very sweet and harmless." We flew safely home the next morning.

LAST MONTH IN MARBURG

With little over a month left in Germany, I tried to focus on all the work I was supposed to do for my classes at Pomona. My lack of experience with "independent study" meant I had not considered how I would get my course work done. Although I had learned a great deal, little of it "counted" toward the credits I needed, except for Advanced German. I knew my speaking and writing skills had improved significantly. Philosophy of Religion required reading in English, which seemed like a real distraction from the opportunity to practice and develop my German skills and understanding, so I decided to work on that course last and write the papers after I got back home. That left Classics of Eighteenth-Century German Literature. I had bought the books early on and started reading, but even when I went to the Mensa to study, I was easily distracted, particularly by my developing relationship with Rudolf.

After Rudolf and I came back from Berlin, I finally figured out the perfect way to work on my German Literature course. Since most of what I needed to read were plays, Rudolf and I began to read them aloud, each of us taking different parts. "It's great and I learn so much more background and hidden-type meanings which I could never figure out myself," I explained in a letter. "Besides, when I don't understand something, then he explains it to me—in German, of course—so it's much better than translating!" In one activity I accomplished three important goals, improving my German skills, deepening my relationship with Rudolf, and learning about German literature. Too bad I didn't discover this solution sooner.

Then it was time for the holidays. On December 6, Saint Nicholas came to the Spalkes. I realized it was time to find gifts for a Christmas package to send home and for my friends here, so the next few days were filled with shopping and sending. In addition, I was invited to give a short talk about American holiday customs for the church women's group I had attended with Frau Bartuzat. This was my first "public" presentation to adults, and I did it in German! Fortunately, they were an appreciative audience.

At the same time, I had to deal again with issues concerning my room at Bettinahaus. This time I felt confident to handle the negotiations myself. University timing was the problem, namely the question of when another student would arrive and move into my space.

Coming from southern California I was hoping it would snow before I left, so I was delighted one day in mid-December when the snow began. I described it for my family because only my mother had ever lived where it snowed. "There is beautiful snow everywhere! People had been telling me that some years it doesn't snow until January, and I was getting to believe that I wouldn't get to see any snow at all. Then one day it came—and it's beautiful! Even if it is a bit uncomfortable at time, I love it! The whole sky is so thick with snow that you can't even tell where the sun is. It's really exciting, and it's so cozy to sit inside and see the beautiful white land out the window."

CHRISTMAS

If you can't be at home for Christmas, I thought, there is probably no better place for an American to be than Germany, since many of our customs and carols came from this land. I was fascinated to learn the German versions of my favorite traditions. Nevertheless, I also felt homesick, as I wrote to my family in a letter I hoped they would receive on Christmas Eve. "Everyone here is excited with family plans, and is of course really good to include me too, but it's not the same as being with your real own live family. In fact, it makes me think how hard it must be to start a new family after living so many wonderful and important years with your own. Everyone must grow up sometime, and this is for me a real step to be away from you all at such a time."

The Bartuzats invited me to stay with them for three nights

over the holidays, since Bettinahaus would be closed. I arrived at noon on Christmas Eve. After the midday meal, I was invited to bathe and then take a nap. They expected to be up late that night. After our naps, we drank coffee and burned the advent candles for the last time.

All stores and businesses closed early in the afternoon and the buses stopped running at 5:30, so we took the last bus into town for the Christmas Eve service at St. Elisabeth's Church. This is one of the few times of year when many Germans attend church, so the sanctuary was filled. There were two huge Christmas trees on the altar and many candles all around the large room. The service included readings of the Christmas story from the Bible and unison responses from the congregation interspersed with songs. The minister gave a short homily and led prayers, spoken and silent, concluding with the Lord's Prayer, which I had learned to say in German. An offering was collected "for the daily work of love in our community, especially for the children and elders, those who are alone and sick."[92] Since we were in a thirteenth-century church, I figured the very oldest songs were appropriate. The only thing I missed was the lighting of hand-held candles row by row as we did at home, but walking home through the snow and delivering flowers to friends along the way made up for it.

When we got home, we had supper while Frau Bartuzat disappeared into the "Christmas Room." No one had been allowed in the room for several days while she decorated it and set things up. We sang carols with Jochen's accompaniment on the flute and then she dramatically opened the door. The first thing I saw was the beautiful Christmas tree lit with candles and decorated with hand-made ornaments, apples, and walnuts. We each had a place where gifts had been set out for us, by the "Christmas man" or the Christ child or both, depending on your story. "It is a delightful idea," I wrote, "that Santa Claus speaks always of the Christ child. They are somewhat closer together in German stories, more like partners in the giving of gifts." My gifts were on a small table: two books, an angel candle holder, a Marburg letter opener, a small pocket calendar

---

92   Translated from the program for *Christvesper am Heiligen Abend,* 1963.

for women, a Marburg dish, candies, fruit and cookies, plus letters from my mother and friends at home. I was especially moved by a folder of pictures of Barlach sculptures Frau Bartuzat's sister sent me from the East Zone, because I knew how little money she had. I had only a few gifts for the Bartuzats, because the box my mother sent from home had arrived after the customs office closed. Fortunately, I had an apron my Grandmother had made and wooden salad forks to give to Frau Bartuzat.

Then we ate our second supper of sausages, potato salad, and champagne. We read poems and stories to each other and sang more carols before retiring to our rooms to look at our new books, or in my case, to write a letter.

With such a great Christmas Eve, I imagined Christmas Day would be a let-down, but I was wrong. We slept late and then had an unusually big breakfast, with special foods eaten only on that day—like smoked eel and grapefruit, along with the usual egg and toast. Then we went for a walk in the woods while the goose we would have for midday meal was in the oven. This was the one day of the year that featured meat as the central focus of the meal. The goose tasted like the turkey I missed having at home for Thanksgiving. Although the accompanying dishes were different—red cabbage and fresh pineapple, in particular—the scope and special nature of the meal felt the same.

Later I went to the Spalkes for coffee and a special holiday treat, *Stollen*, a sweet-bread baked with dried fruits and nuts, similar to fruit cake but lighter in texture and color. Then I tried to teach them to play poker, but realized midway into it that I didn't know all the rules. We made up our own and had a great time.

That evening I went back to the Bartuzats for a supper of wurst, pickles, and beef broth. It was a great day for eating and socializing and would have been more than enough celebrating for me, but there was more to come.

December 26 is celebrated as the second Christmas, in memory of Adam and Eve. In the past, the Germans understood the story of creation and the first "sinning" to go hand in hand, with redemption and return to paradise made possible by the birth of Jesus. We spent two hours at the breakfast table, talking and laughing. Then we played games until our midday meal. Rudolf came to pick me up and take me to his house where we had coffee and played Scrabble. Then we visited another family where we watched a television program from Vienna, one of the few times I watched a TV show in Germany.

The next day I went back to Bettinahaus and shared holiday stories with my roommate, Petra. I finally heard I would be allowed to stay there until January 6, but then I would need to move out. This meant I had to find another place to stay my last week in Marburg. The final holiday activity happened the following day when the box my mother sent arrived and the Bartuzats opened their gifts from my family.

Writing to my sister Mary Lou a few days later, I reflected on my holiday experience.

Even though I had so many new things to do and see I still kept missing all the things that were always a part of our wonderful Christmas. It's sort of ironic, but I just happened to be hearing "Puff the Magic Dragon" where they sing "Dragons live forever but not so little boys..." And it's true. Christmases live forever, and the Christmases we have lived together remain forever in our memories, even much longer than our Christmases together will last. I mean, next year we'll probably both be home, and maybe the next, but then who knows where our lives will take us?

THOUGHTS ABOUT GERMAN CULTURE, THEN AND NOW

Throughout my four months in Germany in the fall and early winter of 1963-64 I was intrigued by cultural differences and shared many of my observations with my family. I noted that Germans seemed to have a more cohesive culture in that they dressed "with approximately the same good taste" and have "much more similarity in moral standards and in ideas of what good in general is." Raising children was also "a community project." I saw the community as united "not through superficially imposed ideals, but through common ideals which have naturally developed through generations of community living." I appreciated the way people at least outwardly behaved in a considerate manner, even those who had new, modern, and even rebellious ideas. When times of traditional or declared days of mourning occurred, such as happened on my birthday or after Kennedy was assassinated, the public standards were universally respected. No one danced, even in private parties or bars. Quiet music was played and parties postponed until another time. Even the radio played "only thoughtful music." I was impressed with this unanimity which I did not think possible in the US.

The country was still recovering from World War II, which had left behind devastation from bombing and families without fathers. Among the students who were born during the war as I was, there was a great deal of conversation about the role of Nazism and the responsibility Germans needed to accept for the aggression against other countries and the atrocities against Jews, resisters, and others. Those I encountered who were adults during Hitler's rise to power and the war were reticent to talk about it, and I did not push them. Of greater concern to them now, especially among the refugee community, was the effect of the Soviet take-over of East Germany, which had disastrous results on the economy and divided families.

Choosing to study German Literature meant I had to confront Germany's role and responsibility in both world wars and in the rise of Nazism. I wanted to understand how a formerly admirable people could be duped into acceptance and even support of Hitler's leadership and actions. Germany clearly had a rich cultural tradition in art, literature, music, and religion. Yet that culture did not protect them from succumbing to the false and dangerous promises of totalitarianism. This is a topic I would explore in my later college studies.

Completing this book now in 2017, I am aware of parallels with our own time, as the United States adjusts to a president whose popularity draws on dissatisfaction, fears, and prejudices reminiscent of those that led to Nazism's rise to power in the 1930s. This reality makes this book even more relevant, I believe, to the present moment. Recalling and remembering into being the visions, hope, and promise of the Sixties may well be a significant antidote to the culture of hate and exclusion that gives rise to totalitarianism.

Because of my prior engagement with religion, I was concerned that regular participation in church was not a feature of German life. Because the people were nevertheless considerate and caring, I started thinking that maybe the Church was not as important as I had once thought. René's experience of preparing for ministry and then having a crisis of faith and changing direction made me doubt the viability of going to seminary and possibly becoming a minister. That idea "is now about as far from my mind as it was before I thought it," I noted. Instead "what I have seen is a land for whom the Church is a staid institution, a taken-for-granted part of growing up, but there exists no necessity of living with the Church as a thoughtful and thinking person. Religion is more a part of daily attitude, therefore one does not need to go to church" or to see oneself as a member of a church body. The fact that Germans seemed to behave responsibly in general tended to eliminate the need for a specific religious connection. "One responds," I continued, "to all the thoughts and calls of society in general, and needs no special group" for encouragement. I wondered why it was so different in America, where the Church seemed to be necessary "as a crystallizing agent for thought and as a moral basis for faith and life in general." My questions eventually led me to seminary.

At Pomona when I studied Nazism, I learned that the German Church had done little to stop Hitler's rise to power, except for a small group of clergy and lay people who actively resisted. I wondered how this might have affected later church participation. Did people feel betrayed by the Church? Certainly, there are lessons here for faith communities today. How do people of faith take effective action to stop tyranny and injustice in all its manifestations?

ATTITUDES TOWARD ALCOHOL AND CIGARETTES

One of the stereotypes Americans had about Germans was that they drank beer all the time. I certainly drank my share of beer while I was there, but not nearly as much as at college parties. At my first party at the Spalkes I noted that no one got drunk, as was common at home. Later Rudolf took me to a party in an unusual place, an old tower with one room on each floor. I drank a lot of wine, and that's when I realized I would have to pee outside because there was no bathroom. While I was outside squatting down, I realized I was getting drunk. How embarrassing, I thought, I'd better watch myself because I would have been highly embarrassed for them to have noticed. At parties, the hosts made sure no one left until they were sober. Towards the end of the party the lights often came up and coffee and perhaps salad were served. Even then, no one would drive a car. In Germany if you were caught driving under the influence, you lost your license forever. So different from home where I never even heard of anyone getting stopped for driving drunk. Learning a more responsible approach to alcohol was probably one of my most valuable personal lessons, although I can't say it carried over into my behavior when I returned home.

Perhaps because there was no age limit on drinking, many Germans learned to drink at home and to do so responsibly. I wrote, "Good wine belongs with a good meal and if you are old enough to eat a good meal then you are old enough to 'appreciate' the wine that goes with it, the cigarette which is smoked after the meal, and the conversation that goes with social intercourse." Although I smoked cigarettes at college, I never did so in front of my parents. I pointed out that most Germans smoke less regularly than Americans do and only with other people. Both smoking and drinking seemed to be understood as a part of traditional life, with customs to guide their use rather than as habits or sins as they were sometimes judged in the US. "The idea is that alcohol is an old custom and a part of enjoying life, and when the younger people can enjoy life with the older ones then they are allowed a little to drink along." Ironically, though, the first indication I had that smoking might be bad for one's health was seeing the cover of a German magazine showing a skeleton with a cigarette.

NEW CULTURE EMERGING

Based on my observations of cultural differences, I concluded that each country developed the ways that worked for them and supported their ideals. Yet for me personally, I felt the need to choose which I felt most at home with, the ways of my family and heritage or the ways of this new country I could imagine making my home. "It is a question of choosing between different aspects of right and goodness. But in any case, one should recognize at least that different aspects of 'right' exist for different people." The idea that what is right is relative has stuck with me ever since.

As I contemplated the differences between Germany and the US and wondered where I would most like to be, I happened to hear a song one day in a bookstore. It's one of those moments I remember with crystal clarity. I can still feel myself bending my head as I went through the low door into the old bookstore a few steps down from street level. I see the table full of books with their spines up where I was browsing when the song came on the radio. The first notes of the song caught my attention, and I walked over to the radio so I could hear it better. There was something about the music that was different from anything I had heard before. The song described a place where "there's no sorrow," where there will be "no sad tomorrow."[93] That place was in one's mind. I was already feeling sad about leaving, so I found the song strangely comforting.

"Do you know what this group is?" I asked the shopkeeper.

"I think it's that new group from England," he replied. "The Beatles, I think they're called." I had never heard of them.

The song offered a vision of possibility, that maybe there could be a new culture that would combine the best of cultures that currently existed. The idea of creating a new culture was swirling around in my mind. In one of my last letters home I wrote," I think it would be nice to be able to travel around and pick the best parts out of every beautiful land and way of life and then somehow be able to put them all together and give them to your children."

HOW BEING IN GERMANY CHANGED ME

In addition to observing and seeking to understand cultural differences, I also saw changes in myself, changes I partially attributed to "a natural growing up process, which is crystallizing here partly because I am in such new surroundings that all things come newly

---

93   John Lennon and Paul McCartney, "There's a Place," first recorded in 1963.

into focus." I needed to integrate what I was learning into the person I was in the process of becoming. "One grows into a new life. You don't notice how you react to changes until you change your whole situation in one fell swoop the way I have done in the last months. I have in the process become extremely aware of all the consequences of my actions and attitudes, as well as how much my life and existence means to me and can mean to others."

I knew I was growing up and that meant growing away from my family. I had two new families in Marburg who accepted me as at least a temporary member, and both treated me more like an adult than my family did at home. I wanted to prepare my family to accept me as an adult, even though I had nearly a year to go before I would turn 21. Yet I also knew I wasn't completely ready to be an adult. I reflected on this dilemma in a letter written as I was preparing to leave.

I'm really glad that I was exactly as old as I was when I decided to come to Germany and that I didn't come earlier or later because I never could have understood it the way I do now. But yet in a sense, there are some things I was too young for—too young in the sense that I have the responsibilities of youth still around me and am not free really to be accepted as an adult or to even want to act like one (in the eyes of society)—and yet I feel so completely ready to take my own life in my hands and live it day by day, according to my own best judgment.

Leaving Marburg and the life and people I had grown to love weighed heavily on my mind and heart. "I could build a whole happy and satisfying life here," I wrote home, "and this realization makes me sad that I must go away and perhaps lose a part of that life." I consoled myself by believing that I would return before too long. I did not, however, come back to Marburg until ten years later.

I needed to go home both for practical reasons and because it was the next step in my growth. "I need the more distant and objective evaluation of this experience which can only be made from the standpoint of my earlier life and situation." I summed up what I had learned and wondered how my family would react to the new person I had become as a result of my experiences, "It took so long to grow into the country, the people, the attitudes. Most of it was personal growth ... and therefore somewhat difficult to explain. I wonder if you will think I am changed when you see me, or if you find a change or development in what I have written in letters." I also wondered what it would be like to go back to where everyone was speaking English!

RE-ENTRY

Before we left for Germany we had been warned about the potential culture shock of being in a new country, but I was unprepared for the culture shock of returning home and readjusting to life in America. The trip took longer than we expected because of travel delays. Tanni, Rudolf, and I danced until 4 AM the night before she and I left on the train for Luxembourg. We expected to leave Europe that afternoon, but our flight was delayed a day. As we sat in a café waiting for news about our flight, I decided to send one more letter home and invited Tanni to add a note. She described her "mixed feelings" about the last four months and our return home. "Thank goodness we both have much work, so that we won't sit and pine for Europe the whole time till next semester starts!"

Arriving home and moving back into the room I shared with my sister felt both familiar and strange. I had truly missed my family and was glad to see them all, but now I missed my German families and friends, especially Rudolf.[94] I wondered how they were doing, if they missed me as much as I missed them, and when I would see them again. In the meantime, my sister was full of questions and fascinated with my stories and the things I brought home with me, as were others in the family. I enjoyed telling them about my experiences, but I began to feel frustrated when they couldn't seem to appreciate the nuances of cultural differences I tried to explain. Mostly my parents' attitude was that I was home now and needed to go back to the way things were at home. I knew I was different and that I could never go back to the way I had been, but I couldn't explain that to them.

---

94   For the rest of the story of my relationship with Rudolf, see Love is All You Need, Falling in Love in Germany.

I couldn't worry about it, though, because I had so much school work to complete in just a few weeks. The whole process is a blur, but I managed to finish what I needed to do and was ready when classes began in February. Tanni and I moved into German House, a large older house set back in the trees at the end of the row of dorms other women students lived in. Although still on campus and subject to dorm rules, there was no one on site to enforce them, so we had more freedom than in the dorms. We spoke German as much as possible, which helped us stay connected to our memories and kept our language skills active. We hosted the campus German Club for fun evenings where we sang German songs and told stories.

Walking around campus, I found I was seeing it with new eyes. I suppose part of what I was feeling was the culture shock of re-entry. I could tell I had changed. I was more introspective, at least for a while, and I felt a strong pull to know students from different cultures.

STUDYING GERMAN CULTURE AND LITERATURE
ACADEMICALLY, February 1964-June 1965

Three of my four courses for the spring semester were on German literature, mostly conducted in German. This helped me develop a deeper understanding of the culture I had been immersed in and further enabled me to develop my language skills. The classes were all held in the same few rooms where the German department was housed. In addition to instructors who taught beginning and intermediate language courses, the department consisted of three professors: Karl Baumann, Dian Lindberg, and Hans-Dieter Brueckner. These rooms and the professors' offices were my home base for the next year and a half. I saw many of the same students in my classes as well, particularly the seven German majors in the class of 1965.

In the Conversation and Composition class we read plays, often radio plays that had been popular in post-war Germany. We soon noticed a pattern. In one way or another, each of the plays dealt with the question of German guilt,[95] which was often broadened to

---

95   Carl Jung wrote about this concept in 1945 and in 1946 Karl Jaspers

include a more diffuse concept of collective responsibility for all that happens in a society. This idea was foisted on the Germans during the American and British occupation, through a publicity campaign featuring posters with pictures of concentration camps and such slogans as *"Diese Schandtaten: Eure Schuld!"* (These Atrocities: Your Fault/Guilt).[96] Before long we students felt like we were carrying the weight of that guilt and responsibility on our shoulders and began to complain, "No more plays about guilt! We're getting too depressed. What are we supposed to do? We weren't even born yet."

The young people I had known in Germany carried this same weight of guilt and responsibility, but because they were Germans, they felt even more implicated in Nazism, although they were only young children at the time. How could they atone for what happened? How could they make sure something like that never happened again? How could I?

This realization reinforced in me the commitment to learn more about how Nazism had gained power, how Germans like the honorable people I knew in Marburg could have been duped into following a leader like Hitler. I was taking Sociology of Religion to better understand the way religion functioned in different cultures, including our own, so I decided to study the institution I thought should have been active in stopping the madness: The Church. In his comments on my paper, "The Church and its Struggle with Nazism," Professor John Thomas suggested I might want to follow up with "a study of the historical factors of German religious life that made Nazism possible, e.g. the long history of anti-Semitism and the nationalistic element in Lutheranism." I did that the following year in a paper for Modern German History, "Inevitable Conflict: Hitler and

---

gave a series of lectures to students in Heidelberg that were later published as *The Question of German Guilt*. He outlined "four categories of guilt: criminal guilt (the commitment of overt acts), political guilt (the degree of political acquiescence in the Nazi regime), moral guilt (a matter of private judgment among one's friends), and metaphysical guilt (a universally shared responsibility of those who chose to remain alive rather than die in protest against Nazi atrocities)." www.amazon.com/ Question-German-Perspectives-Continental-Philosophy/dp/0823220699

96   Jeffrey K. Olick, "The Guilt of Nations?" *Ethics & International Affairs*, September 2003, 109–117.

the German Church." The importance for me of grappling with the Church's engagement with Nazism became clear later in the Sixties when I had to decide how to respond to what my government was doing in Vietnam, in the 1980s anti-nuclear movement, and now as we struggle to prevent a descent into totalitarianism.

In my two German literature classes, the professors lectured in German about the social, political, and historical context within which the literature we were studying developed and evolved. I began to understand the relationship of the surrounding culture to the work of individual authors, as well as the relationship of literature to music and the arts. We also learned about the authors' lives and how their experiences informed their writings. Learning how historical change affected the literature of the times and how different authors changed in response to both societal change and changes in their individual relationships and circumstances helped me formulate ideas about how and why culture changed. I was particularly intrigued by the way one movement in literature morphed into another, and how changes in literature could inspire changes in the larger society. An individual author's work both influenced and was influenced by culture change. These ideas about culture change would stay with me as foundational for the rest of my life's work.

SENIOR YEAR, 1964-65

My senior year I lived in Wig, the newest dorm on campus. For the first time since I was a baby I had my own room. It took getting used to, going to bed in a room all alone, but I grew to like it. I could do exactly what I wanted with my room, and I could stay up as late as I wanted or go to bed early. My friends were just down the hall if I wanted company, so I was never lonely.

By now I had fulfilled basic requirements for my major and could take courses in other fields. This enabled me to continue learning about different cultures, sometimes in our own country. For instance, in an anthropology course, The Human Condition, the professor Charles Leslie, talked about a student research project on why bidets were not found in American homes, the way they were in Europe, especially France. Since the primary manufacturer of bidets was Crane, an American company, the students wondered why Crane didn't sell bidets in the US. They constructed a survey to investigate what the response might be if bidets were marketed to Americans. Most people they interviewed didn't even know what a bidet was. I remembered our hotel room in Paris, which was the one time I saw one and tried to use it. When people found out what they were, many were horrified and indicated considerable disgust. Professor Leslie went on to talk about Americans' puritanical attitude toward sex as the reason bidets were not in use here. I wondered at my own feelings toward sex and why I had missed adopting that attitude. This, I realized, was yet another way I was moving away from the culture I was raised in. Maybe I belonged in Europe after all.

In a course on Social Welfare with professor Jean Barrett[97] that included field trips, I was introduced to people and institutions I knew nothing about. We visited a progressive reform school, the California Junior Boys Republic, operated on a trust system run by the boys themselves, supervised by adults. The director told us about a famous person who once lived there, the popular actor Steve McQueen.[98] He was sent there just before his fifteenth birthday and rebelled immediately. He escaped twice but was quickly caught. After that he was abused by other boys, because his escapes caused them to lose privileges. Forced to dig ditches as punishment, he finally got support from a school superintendent who saw all boys as redeemable and helped him see the good in himself. Over time he managed to become a model of good behavior and earned the right to leave. In the subsequent class discussion, we wondered how many other people who had been at such schools managed to achieve the success he had.

We also visited two minimum-security state prisons in Chino, one for men and the other for women. We were invited to return to the men's prison a few days later for a play being presented

---

97   This was my first course with a woman professor. Ms. Robertson taught beginning German language, but she only had Instructor status and the course catalogue did not even list her full name.

98   Marc Eliot, *Steve McQueen: A Biography*, 2011.

there, The Andersonville Trial,[99] about the trial of a man who worked in a Confederate prison and whose negligence led to the deaths of thousands of Union soldiers from malnutrition, exposure, and disease. When he defended himself by saying that he was only following orders, the prisoners with whom we watched the play booed loud and long. The play had a lasting impact on me both for the horror of the images of so many men dying and for the experience of sitting with prisoners.

In class, we discussed major social problems of our time, what caused them and what might need to change in our communities to improve things. We reflected on our visits to institutions, the extent we thought they were succeeding in improving people's lives and what they might be doing differently. We questioned whether prisons promoted the social welfare of the prisoners or only protected the community from them. The course left me with more questions than answers, but what was most valuable was the window it provided into lives and situations I had not encountered before.

This questioning shaped my research project, the major requirement for the class. After considering homosexuality and finding no resources in 1965, I chose to study alcoholism. Part of my interest came from growing up with an alcoholic uncle and part from my experiences in Germany. My initial research led me to the recently popularized disease concept of alcoholism,[100] identifying biological and genetic factors as predisposing certain people toward the disease. There seemed to be growing scientific agreement that there was no cure, but alcoholics could live normal lives providing they never drank alcohol again, which is what Alcoholics Anonymous had been saying for years. There were few treatment facilities available at the time and none in my area, so I visited a halfway house and attended several meetings of Alcoholics Anonymous.[101] I had a visceral reaction to both the halfway house

---

99   Saul Levitt, The Andersonville Trial, produced on Broadway in 1959 and adapted for television in 1970 by Hollywood Television Theatre.
100   E.M. Jellinek, *The Disease Concept of Alcoholism*, 1960.
101   In the mid-1960s there were few alcohol and drug treatment and rehabilitation centers, none in my immediate area of southern California.

and the meetings, a feeling of hopelessness and amazement that this was the only alternative. Although these visits helped me understand why my uncle was the way he was, I wondered if there was another way. As an avid researcher, I kept looking.

Then I found a book (whose title and author I cannot now locate) that offered a different perspective. The author was a psychiatrist who worked with people he claimed were successfully cured of alcoholism. What made this possible was deep and intense personal self-examination through therapy leading to a transformation of the individual's personality and self-understanding. The author stressed that the goal was not social drinking and that most people decided it was better not to drink, but the fact that they could meant they had been cured of alcoholism, something common wisdom said was impossible. I liked the idea of the impossible becoming possible. It resonated with the experience of religious awakening.

I wrote my paper about the two divergent approaches to alcoholism treatment, and clearly stated my preference for the latter. I wondered what my professor would think of a student challenging the accepted solution to a social problem. Apparently, she approved, because I got an A in the course.

SUMMER OF 1965

After the excitement of graduation, including a wonderful party my family had for me, I found myself alone in the apartment of family friends, who invited me to stay at their place and "take care of things" while they were away on a month-long cruise to Alaska. This enabled me to stay in Claremont for the summer to take Biblical Greek in preparation for seminary. Living by myself in a whole apartment felt like real luxury and another step toward independence. Although I was still in the town where I had spent most of my time for four years, it had become a different world. The college was still there, but the people I knew were gone. Now I was with different people and needed to learn to live in new cultures with new rules.

My Greek class at the Claremont School of Theology on Foothill Boulevard was separate from The Claremont Colleges and about a mile from where I had spent most of my time at Pomona. Its modern building felt different from Pomona. Except for attending class at 9:00 AM, Monday through Thursday, I spent very little time there. Because of the class, though, I needed something other than a 9-5 job so I would have money to take with me to seminary. Working at a restaurant, as I had done the summer before college,[102] made the most sense, and I was fortunate to find a waitress job at Robbie's.

WORKING AT ROBBIE'S

Robbie's was located twenty minutes from Claremont in West Covina, right off the freeway going toward Los Angeles. There I needed to learn new skills and cultural norms. The front part of the restaurant was a coffee shop where I learned to make milk shakes, malts, sundaes, and root beer floats. It was a fun place to work, but the tips weren't as good as in the middle, a dinner restaurant. There I learned the proper way to toss salad, putting the dressing in the bottom of a wood bowl, then the lettuce, using tongs to toss the salad for at least a full minute before serving. Occasionally I worked in the bar in the back, but only when no one else was available. At 21, they thought I was too young for that job. Besides I had no knowledge of most drinks people ordered, and I was supposed to remember them, since they didn't use order pads as we did in the other parts of the restaurant.

I soon learned how different the culture of restaurant workers was from college culture. This was not a summer job for them. It was how they supported themselves and their families. They worked hard, and when work was over they either went home or out for a drink or to eat. Since the coffee shop didn't close until 4:00 AM, by the time we got things cleaned up and ready for the morning shift, it was time for breakfast. Some of my favorite memories of that summer were the hilarious conversations we had in other restaurants as we gorged ourselves on greasy breakfast food and criticized the restaurant and its workers.

---

102   Summer of 1961 I worked a waitress at the famous Chicken Dinner Restaurant at Knott's Berry Farm. I was only 17 but my mother told them I was 18. This was my only other experience of working in a restaurant.

Other than hanging out with co-workers from the restaurant, I didn't have much of a social life that summer, since my friend Dave had left for a job on a ranch in Wyoming. One day, however, I ran into a favorite professor who invited me to a party that introduced me to a life-style I would soon come to embrace in the San Francisco Bay area.

The party was already in full swing, when I got there. People inside the house were dancing to loud music or engaged in intense conversation. There was an unusual scent in the air I thought was incense but realized later was marijuana smoke. I walked out on the deck and discovered that most of the people in the large swimming pool below were nude. Surprised at first, I realized this was yet another opportunity to explore a different culture. I grabbed a drink and walked down to the pool. Since I hadn't brought a suit, I took off my clothes and climbed in. This was the first time I swam nude with men and women I did not know. Before long one of the men came up and began touching me, and I realized that more was going on in that pool than swimming. Since I was not averse to playing around, I joined in.

Another experience with new culture happened that summer at Robbie's, in the coffee shop. A group of people around my age sat down in a booth in my station. Before I had a chance to greet them, another waitress said, "Lucky you. You know who they are?" I shook my head. "They're the Rooftop Singers. They come here a lot."

Their hit song, "Walk Right In," was one of the few popular songs I paid attention to during college. I waited on them several times during the summer. They seemed as interested in me as I was in them, and I realized under other circumstances we could have been friends. I especially liked the one woman in the group, Lynne Taylor. This song reflects the attitude I sought to adopt as I proceeded on to my next adventures in life.

Walk right in, sit right down
Daddy, let your mind roll on
Everybody's talkin' 'bout a new way of walkin'
Do you want to lose your mind?
Walk right in, sit right down

Daddy, let your mind roll on[103]

AWAKENING TO CULTURAL DIFFERENCES: TODAY'S CHALLENGE

In the Sixties, many college students spent a semester or a year in another country. Other people experienced immersion in a different culture through the Peace Corps or VISTA (Volunteers in Service to America). Still others were active in the civil rights movement, often taking them to areas of this country they would not otherwise have encountered. This immersion in different cultures likely opened their minds and hearts the way it did mine to acceptance and appreciation of cultural differences. Many of us who shared such experiences realized that since there are already different ways to be in community with other people, then we can change the practices in our own culture that no longer work according to our evolving ideals. We can invent ways to be together that reflect the values we seek to promote. In other words, we can change the culture we have inherited.

The problem we face today is that not everyone has had the opportunity for experiences that might lead them to develop an appreciation of cultural differences. Instead too many people experience fear or even hatred when they encounter people and communities that are different from themselves. A song from the musical *South Pacific* sheds light on the problem.

You've got to be taught to be afraid
Of people whose eyes are oddly made,
And people whose skin is a diff'rent shade,
You've got to be carefully taught.
You've got to be taught before it's too late,
Before you are six or seven or eight,
To hate all the people your relatives hate,
You've got to be carefully taught![104]

---

103   "Walk Right In," written and recorded by Gus Cannon, 1929, adapted by Erik Darling, Willard Svanoe, Hosea Woods, 1963, for the Rooftop Singers.
104   Richard Rodgers and Oscar Hammerstein II, "You've got to be carefully taught," *South Pacific*, 1949. The movie version came out in 1958. The song title is

Long-held prejudices are difficult to break through, but it is possible. Consider the shift that has taken place in public awareness of lesbian, gay, bisexual, and transgender people. Changing attitudes eventually led to the acceptance of marriage equality, something that was impossible to conceive of two decades ago.

Today's challenge is to figure out how to break through other prejudices that are keeping us from working together to solve the problems our country and world faces. There are no easy answers, but where will we be in another two decades if we back away from this challenge?

---

referred to in "Hamilton," 2015.

Dorothy May Emerson

4. DREAMS OF BELOVED COMMUNITY

"Memoir: the intersection between story and reflection.
Official history is penned by power brokers, but the real stories
are lived on the ground by ordinary folks. Memoir is the ultimate
multicultural act."
                    -Faith Lisabet Adiele[105]

The idea of Beloved Community is ancient. People from many cultures and times have dreamed of a peaceful, cooperative society. The Bible tells of the Kingdom of God, the New Jerusalem. For Quakers, it is the Peaceable Kingdom or the peaceable home. In Buddhist circles, they say "may you go as a Sangha," meaning may you travel not simply as a lone pilgrim, but as a participant in Beloved Community.

Dr. Martin Luther King Jr. spoke often about Beloved Community as the goal of the civil rights movement: "The end is reconciliation; the end is redemption; the end is the creation of the Beloved Community. It is this type of spirit and this type of love that can transform opposers into friends...It is an overflowing love which seeks nothing in return. It is the love of God working in the lives of [people]. This is the love that may well be the salvation of our civilization."[106]

The formation of Beloved Community was one of the dreams of the Sixties. We didn't all call it by the same name, but the idea permeates much of the cultural development of this era. Each of us

105   "Faith Adiele: My Life in Black and White, Why memoir is the ultimate multicultural act," *Yes! Magazine,* March 4, 2010.
106   Martin Luther King, Jr., *"The Role of the Church in Facing the Nation's Chief Moral Dilemma,"* 1957

brought our own awareness into the mix. My journey from insulated white culture into multicultural community has taken many twists and turns, but through it all runs a consistent spirit of openness to diversity, commitment to fairness and equality for all, and a longing for greater connection with people of many colors and heritages. I know I'm not alone in this longing for Beloved Community.

BECOMING AWARE OF RACE

My first conscious memory of racial awareness and its potential implications happened when I was in sixth grade: the Supreme Court decision ending school segregation.[107] I remember seeing a picture of Linda Brown on our 9" black and white television and thought she looked about my age. They told how she had to walk several miles, past a school that was only for white children, so she could go to a Negro school. I was shocked and upset that a child would not be allowed to go to the school in her neighborhood because of the color of her skin. I asked my parents, "So what if she's a Negro? Why does that make a difference?" I don't remember getting an answer. When I saw a picture of her in Life magazine, I noticed that the coat she wore was like the one I had that year. Except for the color of her skin and her hairstyle, she looked a lot like me! We could have easily been friends. Then I wondered why our school only had white kids. Were we segregated, too?

Years later, when my mother found pictures of my kindergarten and first grade classes in Long Beach, I learned that I started school with kids from different racial/ethnic backgrounds: Asian, Mexican,[108] European, and African American. That's the way it should be, I thought. In the process of writing this book, I

---

107   The decision in Brown v. The Board of Education (Topeka, Kansas) was announced May 17, 1954, declaring state laws establishing separate public schools for black and white students unconstitutional. Linda Brown was the poster child for the suit. Her father, a welder and a minister who served as lead plaintiff, attempted to enroll Linda in the nearby white school in the fall of 1951. When she was refused admission, the NAACP filed the class action lawsuit including 12 similar defendants that ultimately led to the end of segregated schools.

108   In the 1940s, most Latin Americans/Hispanics in California were of Mexican descent. Many had lived in the area for generations.

discovered the "baby book" my mother kept of my first five years of life. She noted that my first friend in kindergarten was a "Negro girl." I'm guessing that at the time, skin color had no significance to me. My mother, who was certainly aware of race, found my choice of a friend worthy of recording but did not indicate any objection, for which I am grateful. I wonder now to what extent those first years of school shaped my understanding of race.

At Presbyterian summer camp when I was in junior high, I became friends with a Japanese-American girl from Pasadena. Her name was Pamela, but she went by the nickname, Pamper.

"What a neat name," I said. "I wish I had a nickname, but the only one that goes with my name is Dot, which sounds stupid."

"I made my name up," she explained. "You could too."

"How would I do that?" I wondered.

"I have an idea." She rustled through her things and found a fancy pen and paper. "I've been taking Japanese lessons and learning to write the characters."
I watched as she made strange marks on the paper.

"Here," she said, handing me the paper. "This is the character for the sound 'dough' and this one is 'dee.' You could be Do-dee."

"Perfect," I said with a big smile. I finally had my own name.

For years, I carried her drawing of the characters with me. When I got home, I asked my family and friends to use my new nickname, which I eventually spelled "Dodi." Although I stopped using this name when I was in my thirties, my family, high school and college friends still called me by that name, so when I needed a name my young grandson could say I suggested Grandma Dodi, reconnecting me with my earlier self.

Pamper and I didn't talk about racial differences, but later that week the topic of race came up. Besides the usual camp activities of crafts, games, nature walks, hikes, and swimming, we learned what churches were doing to address problems of our society. To highlight the issue of race, they showed a film called *The Broken Mask*. This 30-minute documentary, filmed the year before at our campgrounds, dramatized how hard it can be even for well-intentioned white people to truly accept people of color. I sat there watching this film with Pamper, hoping we would always be friends.

Another time I remember being aware of differences occurred in my high school driver's education class.[109] The few people named Dorothy I had met were older, never my age. So when the teacher called another girl Dorothy I took notice and wanted to meet her. After class I caught up with her,

"Hey, we have the same name." She paused, carefully choosing her words.

"My real name is Dorotea, but the teachers can't pronounce it right so I go by Dorothy. We speak Spanish at home, and I'm called Dorotea everywhere but school."

"That's nice. I'm taking Spanish. Now I know how to say my name. Thanks ... I mean, Gracias!" I think she smiled.

Realizing she was Mexican American made me wonder why there weren't others in the rest of my classes. My father explained that I was in advanced classes and "they" didn't qualify.[110] That's when I became aware of his prejudice against Mexicans and Mexican Americans, whom he blamed for all sorts of social and economic problems.

My parents' prejudices were selective and limited. My father particularly admired his Chinese American co-worker and was fascinated by the differences in his culture and values. Dad told the story of the day they walked by an olive tree and Dr. Chin noted that he had never seen an olive tree. My father jokingly suggested he try a fresh olive right off the tree, which he did. Raw olives are exceedingly bitter, but Dr. Chin ate the whole thing and pronounced the flavor "interesting." My father was impressed with his fortitude in not spitting the olive out in disgust as most anyone else would have

---

109   Driver's Education was a one-semester class that included two weeks of practice driving, in addition to learning driving laws, and safe driving practices. We also saw scary movies about mistakes people, especially teens, make that cause accidents.

110   It was common practice to group students together who scored well on standardized tests or who came from schools known to have high achievement levels. I later learned students from Golden Hill Elementary School, where I attended, were generally tracked into the highest-level English and Social Studies classes. Students of color were rarely tracked into accelerated classes.

done. He realized Dr. Chin was more concerned about my father's feelings having suggested he eat the olive than he was with his own comfort. Dad was very impressed with the man's dignity.

My mother's primary prejudice seemed to be against Jews. This first came up when she objected to my brother's choice of a date for a school dance. "You don't want to take her. She's Jewish," my mother said with an almost imperceptible sneer. My brother had to go along with my mother's wishes.

My mother seemed to have an uncanny sense about who was Jewish. During my freshman year in college, I wanted to invite a friend named Joni Raphael to visit. My mother's immediate question, "Is she Jewish?" surprised me. I had no idea and had to ask. My mother was right, but she said Joni could visit anyway. Fortunately, my mother liked Joni and we had a pleasant visit. Later Joni invited me to visit her in Seattle.

I wondered where my parents' seemingly selective prejudices came from. Was it because of something that happened when they were young? I couldn't get either of them to talk about it, so I discounted their attitudes because they made no sense to me. Instead, I resolved to be friends with all people.

One other experience in high school highlighted attitudes toward race that shaped me. One of the most popular students was Brig Sanders, a star football player who went on to play pro-football. Even though he was African American, no one I knew thought it was unusual when we elected him Prom King. What I learned at my 50th high school reunion, however, surprised and saddened me. School officials objected to him dancing with the Prom Queen, as was the tradition, because she was white and interracial dancing was frowned upon by the community. Four years later the same thing occurred at Pomona College, when the students elected an African American Prom Queen. This "generation gap" in attitudes toward race was one of the most significant social factors of the Sixties. Change was coming, but the resistance was there too.

Church provided me with an opportunity to learn more about race and the reality of racial injustice. In youth group we learned about the largely Mexican farm workers' struggle in California, the civil rights movement in the South, and prejudice against people of color in our own community. We studied the example of Jesus who treated people who were different from him with respect and love. Using role plays we practiced how we would respond when we heard prejudiced remarks.

One evening we learned about de facto segregation, how communities were kept all white by denying mortgages to people of color. The church was located in an all-white part of town, so most members were white. I had wondered why our neighborhood wasn't more diverse, but learning it was intentional shocked me. This experience of cognitive dissonance was mind-opening. How could something so obviously wrong and unfair be accepted? Who came up with the idea, and why was it allowed to continue? Surely there was something inherently undemocratic about this practice. This was not what I had learned America stood for. What about "liberty and justice for all," the words we said practically every day in school when we pledged allegiance to the flag? Something was very wrong, but other than the discussions in church, nobody around me seemed to notice or care. Something in me shifted as I filed these questions away in my mind and heart and continued with my life and education, but I could never go back to believing that adults were trying to do good all the time.

When our youth group joined with other youth in southern California for worship and conferences, we learned that other churches, especially those in the Los Angeles area, were more diverse than ours was. Once we went on a mission trip to San Francisco to the oldest Asian church in the United States, located in an area known as Chinatown. Until then I had never been in a large immigrant community. I was impressed with the way that church served both its members and this wider community, many of whom did not speak English. The trip opened me up to a new world both in the new culture I encountered and in showing me how a church might engage with the world around it. The wonderful meals cooked by church members introduced me to food that was very different from what my family ate. At the time I had not yet encountered Chinese restaurants in southern California. Eating this new food gave me

Dorothy May Emerson

direct experience of a different culture.

When I was in college, I remember hearing about a controversy at my home church. I was glad that the church leaders had finally decided it was time to integrate the congregation. They invited several black families from a nearby community to worship and to consider becoming members of the congregation. They came and were welcomed by most people, but a few members quit in protest, some of whom usually made large financial contributions. But the leaders held their ground. The idea that the church should take the lead in addressing social injustice by taking visible action was deeply impressed on my young mind. I admired the ministers for doing the hard thing, for risking their own positions for the sake of what they knew was right.

DYNAMICS OF RACE AT POMONA COLLEGE

My growing awareness of racial and cultural diversity continued in college. At Pomona almost all of the students were white, with one Mexican American whose family had been in California for generations and a few Asian Americans, one of whom I dated freshman year. There had only been a couple of African American students ever at Pomona. The year I arrived, Willie Boone was about to graduate in the spring. Jeanne Martin was a member of our entering class.[111] She was a celebrity, having been part of a singing group that had cut a record. I would have liked to be friends with her, but she was usually surrounded by the most popular girls and I didn't fit in with that crowd.

Later two students from the historically black Fisk University were with us for a year. We also had several students from Africa. They were part of a national initiative to bring students from the new African nations to American colleges to study.[112] This was a time of major change in Africa, with seventeen countries having become self-governing in 1960. In addition, Pomona had recently joined the

111   After I graduated, Myrlie Evers, widow of slain civil rights leader, Medgar Evers, entered Pomona and graduated in 1968.
112   Sponsored by the newly-formed Agency for International Development and the African Scholarship Program of American Universities.

141

national Operation Crossroads Africa program, founded in 1958 by the Rev. James H. Robinson. Pomona's Crossroads Africa program enabled a few selected Pomona students to spend summers there as part of work project teams, working alongside their African hosts digging wells, building schools, planting crops, teaching children, or whatever the people deemed most necessary and useful to the community. President Kennedy considered the program, which continues to this day, the "progenitor of the Peace Corps."[113] To educate students about Africa, a campus committee, with support from local Claremont citizens, arranged guest speakers, seminars, concerts, and library displays. My favorite was a concert by Martha Schlamme, the German singer I first heard in New York. She performed international folk songs, including many songs from Africa.

Intrigued with difference, I took advantage of opportunities to meet and talk with the African students. From each encounter, I learned something new about people and cultures I knew little about, since the classes I took focused on "Western Civilization." When I read what one of my African friends wrote in our senior yearbook about the impact of African students at Pomona, I realized my experience was not unique.

Not only has he brought with him ideas about his or her own country, which were not easily available to the American student, but he also has successfully bridged that gap of personal knowledge of African affairs that is ever-lacking in many an American student. Africa ceases to be one vast jungle. The constant questions about the jungles and tree huts give place to consideration of national units, the individuality of each person. ... Only one major problem of major consequence faces the African student; that of reconciling his particularism and his role as a representative of his country.[114]

We were fortunate to have these students as classmates. Few

---

113   According to Operations Crossroads Africa website, http://operationcrossroadsafrica.org/index.php#div[content]=1202
114   Enoch M. Munemo, "The African Student," 1965 Pomona College *Metate*, 140.

people in the United States at that time had the opportunity to meet people from Africa.

When I arrived in Germany in the fall of 1963, the Germans I met were aware of the US civil rights movement. The first movie my host family took me to see was *To Kill a Mockingbird*.[115] The German soundtrack was so well synchronized that if I didn't watch the actors' lips carefully, I would have thought Gregory Peck was speaking German! After the movie, my new German family wanted to know what I thought of das Negerprobleme, (the Negro problem). I tried my best to respond, but my German wasn't good enough yet to understand all the nuances of the story. Besides, I wasn't sure what to say because I knew very little at the time about the realities of racism in the South. Later I introduced my host family to Professor Bailey, who coordinated the Experiment in International Living program in the area. When he invited me to coffee on my birthday, Jochen and Frau Bartuzat asked to come along because they had never seen a black professor.

In my German conversation class in Marburg, I got to know Inez, an African American graduate of Fisk University. She was a Fulbright scholar but wasn't staying in town long because her goal was to go to Japan. Tall with light brown skin, her biggest fear about being in Japan was sticking out because of her height, not the color of her skin. We both laughed about this. We shared many similar interests and went to plays and museums together. I wished she would stay longer because I felt we could have become good friends.

When I got back to Pomona, one of the first major events the second semester of my junior year was the student-sponsored Conference on Civil Equality, coordinated by the newly-formed Human Relations Council.[116] It was a big deal with nationally

---

115   The German title of the movie was *Wer die Nachtigall stoert*, because mockingbirds are not generally found in Germany.
116   Conference on Civil Equality, held at Pomona College, February 28-29, March 1, 1964. Speakers included Louis Lomax, James Farmer, John Doar, John A. Morsell, James Forman, John Buggs, and SI Hayakawa. The conference brochure describes the Human Relations Council, part of the Associated Students of Pomona College, as "a civil rights group dedicated to the extension of equal opportunity to all" which had recently begun doing support work for the Student Non-

known speakers and students from a hundred West Coast colleges, who brought sleeping bags and slept in student dorms. They each paid $10.00 for three days of meals in our dorm cafeterias. I was a bit removed from some of the excitement because I was living in German House that semester, but I attended the major programs and began to realize how little I understood about race relations in my own country.   I was particularly impressed with the opening keynote speech by Louis Lomax, author of *The Negro Revolt*, who talked about race fear based on sexual, moral, and religious grounds. He contrasted white philosophers who were at the time focused on existentialist issues of futility, emptiness, and non-being, with Negroes who were speaking of struggle, freedom, pain, trial, and happiness, which he called "words of life." "Perhaps there is in the Negro a vitality, an aliveness, which can rejuvenate and save our country and even our whole culture." Despite the potential renewal a more inclusive culture would bring, he warned, "Negroes have become increasingly convinced that the white power structure will not yield willingly."[117]

James Farmer, national director of CORE (Congress on Racial Equality), echoed this theme later in the day. He stressed how important it was for white liberals to "no longer expect to run the show." The work ahead needs to be on the Negro's terms. There is no time to go slow, he said, as he warned against "false partial support."[118] SI Hayakawa, noted semanticist and professor of English at San Francisco State College, gave the final address on "Communications: Interracial and International."[119] In the weeks following the conference, there were many articles in the student

---

Violent Coordinating Committee. Conference sponsors included the Rosenberg Foundation and other charitable funds, plus the Social Action Committee of the Claremont Church and the Claremont Council of Churches.

117   Louis Lomax, "Where Are We?" Feb. 28, 1964, Conference on Civil Equality.

118   James Farmer, "Where Do Whites Fit into the Civil Rights Struggle?" Conference on Civil Equality.

119   Hayakawa went on to become president of San Francisco State during the time of student protest (1968-73) and later served as senator (Republican) from California. I am indebted to articles by Rob Cooley in *Student Life*, March 5,

newspaper debating the ideas presented at the conference. The entire program was rebroadcast on the student radio station, KSPC, in April.

During my senior year, I was fortunate to become friends with several Asian graduate students. Although Pomona College was an undergraduate school, it was part of a five-college complex that included a graduate school, where the Asian men I met were studying. They lived in Blaisdell House, a center for international students not far from Honnold Library where I spent a lot of time studying and worked during my senior year. Since someone was almost always at the house, I often stopped by after studying or when I needed a break. Whoever was there would invariably invite me in for tea and sometimes offered rice, which they cooked in a small electric pot that sat on the kitchen table. I was fascinated with the idea that rice was so important that it had its own cooker which could not be used for anything else. At that point in my life, I rarely ate rice, so theirs became a model for me of what rice should be. They taught me to eat with chopsticks. Chinese restaurants were just becoming popular and, once I developed the skill, I would ask for chopsticks and show others how to eat with them. I loved being able to share a new cultural practice I had just learned.

Several of the students were from Japan and one from China. Other than my Jewish friends at college, they were my first non-Christian friends. We had fascinating conversations about religion. Although their religions—Buddhism, Shinto, and Confucian—were different from mine, I could see they were equally valuable and inspired them to live lives of integrity and truth. I learned more at that house about the value of religious diversity than in any college or seminary class during the Sixties.

When Ikuno, one of my Japanese friends, was going back home at the end of his studies, he asked me for a ride to the local airport nearby, since I happened to have a car on campus at the time. While we were waiting for his plane to Los Angeles, he had an idea.

"I have to wait six hours in LA for my flight to Tokyo. Why don't you come with me? I'll buy you a round-trip ticket. We

1964, for his reflections on the conference and quotations from the speeches.

can have drinks in that bar that turns around," Ikuno said with a twinkle in his eye.

"But I have to study, and besides I'm not wearing any shoes." This was the year I decided to go barefoot much of the time to toughen up my feet for summer.

"Come on. I'll get you some shoes at the airport." How could I resist?

At an airport shop Ikuno bought me a pair of thongs, which he pointed out were like traditional Japanese shoes. Then we went to the circular restaurant and had fruity drinks until it was time for my return flight. It was a great adventure. When I got married the following year, Ikuno sent me a set of Japanese dolls he said were a traditional wedding blessing. I kept them for years, long after the marriage ended.

Shortly after I arrived in San Anselmo for seminary, another of my Japanese friends, A´be, called and invited me to spend an evening with him in San Francisco. He took me first to a Japanese restaurant where we sat at a bar in front of a display of raw fish, which I later learned to call sushi. He chose items he thought I would like, and I drank Scotch to mask the strange flavors. Then we went to Fisherman's Wharf and had abalone chowder and lobster Newburg, much more to my liking. Later A´be took me to a club called Bocce Ball, where people came to sing opera. Some were professional singers, and others were amateurs but equally good. Even the waitress and bartender sang! It was a treat to hear such powerful music up close and personal. I realized later how ironic it was that my best introduction to "the City by the Bay" was with my Japanese friend from Claremont!

EXPLORING LOS ANGELES

Southern California in the Sixties had no local public transportation besides buses, but we lived near the train that went along the coast from San Diego to San Francisco. When I was in high school, my parents allowed me to take the train to Los Angeles to go to Olvera Street, right across from Union Station. Known as the oldest street in the city, this colorful market place with its kiosks, restaurants, and small stores is a bustling place filled people speaking both English and Spanish. One of my goals in going there was to practice speaking Spanish, even though I knew Mexican Spanish was different from what I was learning in school. It was difficult to make myself understood and to understand what people said to me in return, but at least I tried and gained a sense of what it might be like to be in another country. What I liked best, though, was buying my family inexpensive but unique items for Christmas and birthdays.

After I came back from Germany, I took the train to Los Angeles to go to Olvera Street and a German Bookstore that turned out to be several miles away. I had to walk through a run-down neighborhood where groups of Mexican-American men hung out on the sidewalks. I made eye contact with a few of them and smiled but kept walking. I wondered, though, if I was in any danger. When I finally got to the bookstore, I was immediately transported back to Germany helping me remember my life there.

Later, when I lived in the San Francisco Bay Area, people often complained about Los Angeles, saying it was boring, a cultural desert. I disagreed, remembering my trips on the train to places where I could speak Spanish and German. I also remembered the many musical performances I heard and the plays I saw. I told them, "LA is full of culture. You just have to know where to find it."

When I was home from college in the summer, one of my favorite things to do was to look through the Calendar section of the Sunday *Los Angeles Times*. When I was able to borrow the family car, I drove to performances, like the one that changed my world-view. *Blood Knot*, a play by white South African playwright, Athol Fugard, was so controversial it was shut down after its premier performance in Johannesburg in 1961. Produced Off-Broadway in 1964, which is probably when I saw it in Los Angeles, the play highlighted the world of everyday life during apartheid. Set in a one-room shack, half-brothers Morris, who could pass for white, and dark-skinned Zachariah dream of a better life and are saving money to buy a small farm. The limitations of living under apartheid become glaringly apparent when the woman Zach has been corresponding with turns out to be white and says she is coming to visit. The "blood knot" that unites them as brothers begins to unravel as they face this crisis.

The performance took place in a small theater with the two actors on the floor with a simple set and the audience on risers on two sides of the stage area. Stark lighting highlighted the dramatic impact of the story. The night I saw the play the audience was small, maybe 25 at most. As one of the few white people there, I felt a sense of shock and shame I had never known before. I knew very little about South Africa and apartheid, which was one reason I wanted to see the play, and what I learned shook me. Racial hatred was far worse than I could have imagined. I wished I had not come to the play alone, because how could I talk about it with anyone who had not seen it? I left more determined than ever to take whatever opportunities might come to me to build bridges with people no matter what their color. My first real chance to practice that new resolve came the following summer, after I graduated from college.

RIOTS OF 1965

Working at a restaurant the summer after college, I had my first direct experience with overt racism. At Robbie's, the food for both the coffee shop and the dinner restaurant was prepared in a central kitchen. While we were at work, we could order any meal (except steaks) from either menu. Restaurant staff ate in the staff room next to the kitchen. Getting to know the cooks was important, because then they would make your food just how you liked it. Joe was my favorite cook. He was close to my age and we hung out together on breaks. The fact that he was the only black person working there seemed to matter little to anyone, until the Watts Riot[120] broke out. The day after the rioting began I went to work in the late afternoon. When I saw Joe he looked sad and anxious.

As usual, I said, "Hi, how're you doing?"

He almost broke into tears. "I've been here since this morning

---

120   The Watts Riot (Aug. 11-17, 1965) began in the commercial section of Watts, an impoverished African American neighborhood in South Central Los Angeles, and spread to a 46-square mile section of the city, resulting in 34 deaths, 1000 reported injuries, and over $40 million in property damage. Civil Rights Digital Library, http://crdl.usg.edu/events/watts_riots/?Welcome

and you're the first person to speak to me all day other than to give me an order." We both knew why.

"I am so sorry," I said as I looked around. No one was nearby to hear the conversation, but it made me wonder about my co-workers. "Do you know anyone who lives in Watts?"

"My family lives there and I'm really worried about them," he said.

It was time for me to start work, but I made it a point to check in with him again before he left for the day and to talk to him every day after that. The scariest time was when we heard rumors of snipers on the freeway, but not as scary, I thought, as it must have been for the people in or near Watts.

At this same time, my mother was in a hospital in Los Angeles, having an operation on her ears to improve her hearing.[121] When I went to visit her after the operation, she was in the midst of a lively conversation with her roommate. She introduced me right away to Mrs. Evans and told me what she was learning about what life had been like in Watts before the riots. I was impressed that she wasn't the least bit intimidated by having a black roommate and instead took it as an opportunity to learn about another person's life. Despite the ways I thought of myself as very different from my mother, this experience made me realize our similarities.

EXPERIENCING CLASS DIFFERENCES

The focus of much of Martin Luther King's work towards Beloved Community was on racial justice, but he was also concerned about economic justice and was well aware of how race and class intersected and supported each other to deprive people of civil rights. Whereas I learned about race through key experiences that awakened me to the realities of racial injustice, class differences were more apparent to me all along and played a role in forming my

---

121   The operation was a stapedectomy, a relatively new procedure at the time in which the innermost bone (stapes) of the middle ear is removed, and replaced with a small plastic tube surrounding a short length of stainless steel wire (a prosthesis). This was done to correct my mother's progressive hearing loss, caused by otosclerosis, by improving the movement of sound to her inner ears.

attitudes and approach to life.

When my family moved to Fullerton, we managed to achieve a marginally middle-class life by building our house on a street designated for multiple-unit housing. We lived in two of the apartments. My clever father designed the units with a door between them and the plumbing for the unbuilt kitchen already in the wall of what served as our dining room. The front unit was rented to others. In addition, my mother worked outside the home.

In contrast, almost all the kids in my grade school were more solidly middle-class than we were, and some were even upper middle-class. I didn't have the language to understand class, but I knew our family was different, and I often wished we lived in a "real" house. I was glad, however, that my mother had a job, even though none of my friends' mothers did. This meant that my grandmother was often there, or that I got to be "in charge," since I was the oldest.

In high school, I began to have friends from other parts of town. Charlotte's family was rich and lived in what seemed to me like a mansion, located all by itself on top of a hill with both a swimming pool and a tennis court. Her family had servants and she was given her own car as soon as she could drive. She had a great deal of freedom to do and buy whatever she wanted. I loved going to her house on the few occasions when I was invited, but we never became close friends.

I also had friends who lived in less affluent circumstances than our family. Donna was in my history class and we worked on a project together at her house. I noticed it was smaller and more crowded than mine, but her family welcomed me and often invited me to stay for dinner. My mother, however, discouraged our friendship and didn't want me to be at her house after dark, because she didn't think the neighborhood was safe.[122]

Even after more experiences with class in college, I had still never talked about the subject until I received a surprise invitation. My first weekend at seminary, a graduate student I had dated when he was a student in economics at Claremont Graduate School called

---

122   For experiences with class in college, see Culture Shock, Culture and Class Differences.

me up. Jerry invited me to join him at his family home in Pittsburg[123] for his last weekend before leaving for the Peace Corps. I liked spur-of-the-moment invitations, so I said yes, packed a small bag, drove across the Richmond-San Rafael Bridge, and found my way to his home. That weekend with his family gave me a new understanding of class cultures and insights about my own class background. I was so impressed with the experience that I shared it in detail in a letter to my family.

I began by explaining that Jerry and I discovered that what he wanted to accomplish in the Peace Corps, still a new program at the time, was much like my goal in working with the Church. Then I described Pittsburg as a "mostly lower class or lower middle-class, partially dying community on the river," dying because the shipping business had long since gone. What was left was work in factories or small construction businesses. Jerry took me aside when I first got there and explained, "My relatives and friends are mostly lower-class people."[124] I wasn't sure what to say, but I realized he assumed I came from an upper-middle class background, like many students at Pomona.

For him the class distinction is not so much based on salary bracket or type of work as it is on style of living and attitudes toward life and people. His father runs a steel construction business—sort of an original small businessman. His mother is a second-grade teacher in a local Catholic school. ... I can't contrast the family very well with our own, because we are not so entirely middle/upper-middle class as we sometimes would think. But I can contrast them with some of the general attitudes of Fullerton society (or southern CA suburban life) ...

The biggest differences would be in such things as family importance. The family comes first for Jerry's family (not just the nuclear family but all the aunts and uncles and grandparents too). I do get the feeling that some of our biggest problems in suburbia

---

123   Pittsburg is an industrial city in the East Bay region of the San Francisco Bay area, at the time about 20,000 people, with a small downtown section.
124   I would now describe them as working–class, but Jerry called them lower-class.

are caused by the separation of families from older and younger generations. I know it is a feeling of some that their parents, sisters, aunts, etc. are not worthy of being in their homes. For instance, if one part of the family has moved far ahead economically and socially of the rest, then it may choose to ignore them! A regard for all members of the family is a very important kind of social security—much more important than a good life insurance policy.

I described the lavish meal Jerry's mother and extended family prepared: "barbequed chicken and steak, spaghetti, ravioli, green salad, fruit salad, garlic bread, beans, some other vegetables, fruit, and ice cream," and commented: "It's one of the important ideals that food be enjoyed and enjoyable as a social function."

I was also impressed at how I was immediately welcomed into the family and put to work "cleaning up, running errands, amusing kids, etc."

I noticed how friendly everyone was—open and natural, with a sense of propriety learned more by living rather than learning rules. The younger children especially are so much more friendly and accepting of others. There is no clinging to mother's dress in this family; there is no reason to distrust other people. This is the crucial difference. The children have been exposed to different kinds of people—so there is no reason for them to stay away from new people. This is perhaps my biggest reason for telling you all this, because I am concerned about our loss of such important human values as friendship, acceptance of all kinds of people, family ties, etc. And these people of Jerry's renewed my faith in the working possibilities of such values. These people do not need psychologists—the health of their society is built in. They are able to take care of themselves; they learn to build houses and pour cement, fix radios and drive trucks; and these are perhaps more valuable in the long run than learning German or History.

As much as I admired them, what I perceived as the limits of their "lower-class" culture concerned me. "They have no drive to do anything else in the world except to live as they are living." I had inculcated the middle-class value of ambition, the drive to better one's lot in life. I could not understand how Jerry's people could be satisfied with how they lived, no matter how happy and well-adjusted they seemed. Ironically, I would soon be invited to celebrate holidays with my father's Bay Area family and would realize they were more like his family than my southern California relatives.

I concluded the letter by bringing it back to the desire we shared to create a better world.

The problem which Jerry and I have is that we appreciate and love the values of such living, but we have been trained to see the injustices in life as well. It is, in fact, social injustice which Jerry is fighting in the Peace Corps and I am fighting in the Church. ... The Peace Corps tries to help people determine what they need and to teach them how to go about accomplishing it. I'm trying to figure out what the Church does which is comparable. The Church today is, in fact, searching for ways to help people on their own ground and according to their own needs.

At least, that's what I thought the Church was doing at the time. As I explained earlier in "Hearing the Call," I would before long discover holes my idealistic vision of what the Church was doing.

A fortuitous connection I made at Jerry's party was with Bea, a social work student at College of Holy Names in Oakland. She shared her excitement about going to the upcoming Monterey Jazz Festival and invited me to come along.

BEING IN THE MINORITY

The last weekend in September, I drove to San Francisco to meet Bea and three other women (a teacher, teaching student, and a dietician at Mills College). We all piled in one car and drove three miles south to Monterey. We went directly to the Festival for the afternoon concert, where we heard Harry James performing with drummer Buddy Rich and singer Anita O'Day. I thought she was fabulous! Then it occurred to me that she was probably about my mother's age.

After the concert, we checked into our motel in Salinas and had dinner on Cannery Row in Monterey. I wrote to my mother that I had turtle soup, cheese fondue, prime rib, and cheese cake. At the evening concert, we heard Dizzy Gillespie and Duke Ellington.

These musicians had been around a long time, but I hadn't heard much of their music although I knew of them, especially the Duke, who had recently hit the popular music charts with his version of "Hello, Dolly!" Most intriguing to me, though, was vibraphone player Cal Tjader. His music brought together Asian, Afro-Cuban, and Latin themes, all featuring the vibraphone with other percussion instruments, some I had never seen before. I fell in love with the vibes that day.

Sitting in the same row with us were several probation officers and social workers who worked with Bernice's aunt in Sacramento. They invited us to a party after the concert in 17 Mile Drive Village, one of the ritziest communities in the area. Most of the people at the party were professionals, and well over half were African Americans. It was my first experience of being a minority. I was fascinated to meet black doctors, lawyers, social workers, and even a realtor. The women I came with wanted to leave early, and I wanted to stay, so I found someone who agreed to give me a ride back to the motel. I had a great time drinking and dancing. After a while it seemed like I was the only white person left. This only enhanced my excitement. I was doing something I had never done before, and I liked it. Dancing in the middle of the floor, I became aware that others were watching me. I wondered if this was how black people felt when they were the only one in a sea of white.

The next morning, we went to Mass in Salinas, since the others were all Catholics. After spending the middle of the day in Carmel, I made it back to San Anselmo by 7 PM, just in time to get ready for classes on Monday. What a great weekend! I loved the whole adventure of it.

Both that weekend and the one with Jerry's family expanded my vision of Beloved Community. I began to realize that community existed in many forms, some built up over generations, like Jerry's family and friends, and others that come together for a short time, like the jazz festival. I still hoped the Church was another place where Beloved Community was possible, but it was good to know there were alternatives.

Dorothy May Emerson

DISCOVERING BLACK LITERATURE

Festival Theatre, on the seminary campus, provided many awakening experiences for me, one of which was *The World of My America*, a one-woman show with African American actress Pauline Myers. She brought to life the poems of Langston Hughes and Paul Lawrence Dunbar and the speeches of Sojourner Truth, none of whom had I ever heard of before. I thought the show was "absolutely fantastic" and wondered why I hadn't learned about these famous people in any of my previous education. I realized I knew very little about the realities black people faced historically and now, and I wanted to learn more.

Once again it was clear to me that the theater had a potentially transformative power to awaken people to truth and inspire them to live lives of integrity and right action. Could the Church do anything comparable?

DISCOVERING MARIN CITY, 1965

After these direct encounters with class and race within my first month at San Francisco Theological Seminary, my classes seemed the least interesting aspect in my life. Nevertheless, I had come to seminary to study, and I did my best to pay attention and learn what the professors had to teach me. However, what interested me more than my studies was learning about the world around me. I volunteered to be a tutor with a student from Marin City and soon decided to move there. This reflected a growing shift in how I viewed my life's work. As I learned more about the community, the possibilities intrigued me.

Marin City was established in 1942 as temporary housing for 1500 ship builders and their families brought there by the federal government during World War II. The community that formed for this purpose was unique in all the country in its diversity: approximately 60% percent white, 40% black, mostly from the South, with a few other ethnicities as well.[125] With 6000 residents in 1943, Marin City was "lauded as a model development," a largely

---

125   Harman S. Dillon, "Citizens in Search of a City," Marin Tenants Council Report, 1958.

peaceful, multiracial community.[126] After the war, it became one of the few places in Marin County where people of color could live. Businesses begun during the war grew and a permanent community was established.

The 2500 mostly black residents who remained in Marin City after the war did their best to stabilize and weatherize the temporary shacks built during the war, but the housing was still clearly inadequate. The low-lying area where the shacks were built tended to flood and whole area was sometimes very muddy. Those who could afford it built houses on stilts up against the hills. In the late 1950s, apartment buildings were built with government funding. The residents at the time praised the five-story pink concrete buildings as beautiful and safe, a big improvement over the shacks. By the mid-1960s, however, the complex had gained as reputation as unsafe, because of the supposedly less than savory people who hung out there. Most of the students who needed tutoring lived in the apartments or in one of the remaining shacks.

Being a tutor turned out to be more challenging than I thought it would be. We were told our job was to help the kids with their reading and math skills. I was assigned to tutor a black boy in third grade. When I arrived, the project coordinator took me to meet Michael, who was on a swing in the play yard at his school in Sausalito.

"This is your new tutor," she said, and left me there to fend for myself.

Michael didn't seem interested in my help and continued swinging. I thought maybe if I joined him it would break the ice.

I sat on the swing next to his and swung for a few minutes. When his swing slowed down and it looked like he was about to get off, I stopped mine and said, "Hi, Michael. You can call me Dodi." He still said nothing. In retrospect, I realize I didn't understand the barriers to communication he must have felt. I imagine he was suspicious of this do-gooder white woman who was trying to make him do schoolwork he did not want to do.

"Why don't you show me your school books?" I asked. Another

---

126   "The Marin City Ghetto," *San Francisco Chronicle*, Dec. 19, 1965.

minute went by. "Please show them to me." I was begging now, getting desperate. Finally, he pulled one out of his bag.

"This is my math book," he said. "I hate math most of all." I could see that his workbook was full of red marks.

"Maybe I can show you how to do one of these problems," I said. Math was never my strong subject, but this was pretty basic so I thought I could help. He watched patiently while I tried to explain how to do the problem he had missed. Then I asked him to try it, but he still couldn't do it. I felt like a failure as a math tutor.

The next time I came I asked him to read to me, but he wasn't very good at that either. So, I read to him. He didn't seem to be particularly interested, but I kept reading, because that way I felt I was doing something. When I told the person in charge about the difficulties I was having, she said not to worry too much about actual schoolwork. What was important was to help the child feel more confident in his ability to learn and to relate better to adults (white adults, I assume now, like virtually all his teachers). I kept going to our tutoring sessions and kept trying to connect. I suppose the best thing I did was to be consistent about showing up. I wonder if the experience benefitted him and what he's doing now.

Shortly after starting to volunteer as a tutor, I learned about a new integrated housing project in Marin City and was intrigued. Here was an opportunity to put my faith into action by being with people who were asking for my support and involvement. I wrote to my family: "Daddy is lucky that there aren't any good slums around, because I would probably want to live there! (But I would be scared!!) This is anything but a slum…"

My understanding of my call to ministry was shifting from church to community. Although to others this may have seemed like a radical change from my former path, to me it felt not only right but also a direct application of what I was learning and consistent with how I was growing both in faith and in life. The seminary considered me courageous and planned to use me as an example to others. In my letter home, I explained: "The community here is interested in my actions—for after all, this is the decisive factor. We can talk about love, but if we do not love we have said nothing in our lives." In a newspaper interview about my internship at the Novato church, I was quoted as saying: "For me the church is nothing if it's just for the people in the sanctuary on Sunday mornings. It must be involved in the world. The call of Christ is the call to respond to all of life. At the seminary, we call it 'authentic humanity.'"[127]

The apartment complex I would be moving into as soon as it was completed was set up as a cooperative. Much smaller than the five-story "projects" on the other side of town, this two-story complex had twenty units, all in one building. It was built on stilts on one of the lower hills, with parking spaces for each unit underneath. One-bedroom apartments were $92 a month, plus a $270 investment in the cooperative, returnable when we moved out.

I flew home to Fullerton for Thanksgiving, packed several boxes of things I would need for the apartment, went back to the seminary, and moved out of the dorm at the end of November, expecting to move in to my new apartment in December—only to discover it would not be ready for several weeks, maybe a full month! My car became my home, or at least my closet. My clothes were hanging on the rod my father put across the back seat when I was coming to seminary, and that's where they stayed for a month.

I stayed at various places that month, sometimes with relatives who lived in the area, sometimes in San Francisco with my new boyfriend, Thomas, and sometimes with people I didn't know who offered to put me up when they heard about my situation. One night I even stayed at the Mill Valley Motel, a big splurge for a student on a tight budget. Because of my new connection with the black community in Marin City, I was invited to stay for a week in a house in Mill Valley to take care of the child of a musician who was going to be away on tour. I never met Richie Havens, but I certainly enjoyed staying in his house. It was the most elegant and beautiful house I had ever been in.

That month I was still in seminary, finishing papers and then beginning a new semester. I tried to keep up with classes and

---

127   "Girl Divinity Student at Local Presbyterian Church," *Novato Advance*, Nov. 23, 1965.

homework, but my interest was clearly waning. Finally, the time came to move into my apartment. Thomas helped by "loaning" me some furniture. He stayed that first night and often thereafter. In early January, after I was finally settled in Marin City, I made the decision to drop out of seminary on the last date to withdraw without penalty. I told the seminary I needed to take a leave of absence, but in my heart I knew it was unlikely I would return.

WORKING AT JUVIE, 1966

Leaving seminary meant I needed to find a job, but what sort of job? What did my degree in German Literature prepare me to do? I didn't want to be a translator, the only job I knew my education qualified me for. Since I had never needed to look for a professional-level job before, I had no idea how to begin.

Fortunately, I happened to find a job in an easy and unexpected way. I was in a bar having a drink and talking about needing to find a job. A man at the bar told me about a job opening at the county juvenile detention facility where he worked. The only requirement was to have graduated from college. They needed a woman to go to work right away in the girl's unit. I called the next day, went in for an interview, and despite my lack of experience and qualifications, they hired me on a six-month trial basis.

That's how I became a "group counselor" at the Marin County Family Rehabilitation Center, described in their brochure as "a new kind of program for older adolescents requiring institutional care." Billed as an alternative to the California Youth Authority which served "sophisticated delinquents from all over California," the Family Rehabilitation Center provided was designed to provide programming which substituted "individual, group, and staff control, to a large extent, for fences, locked doors, and restricted movement." This was the theory. However, before I could go to the girls' unit to which I was assigned, I was outfitted with a belt to which was attached a ring of keys and told never, under any circumstances, to take the belt off while I was at work. Because I mostly worked the evening shift, from 3 to 11 PM, Tuesdays through Sundays, I rarely experienced the "programming" that occurred during the day, although occasionally I was asked to lead a group counseling session for which I had no training. For the most part, though, my job was more custodial than anything else.

Almost everything about this job was new to me. My least favorite responsibilities were locking the girls in their rooms when told it was time to do so and then watching them on monitors in the office that showed us what they were doing in their rooms. When they were out of their rooms, my responsibility was to make sure they were behaving. The best way to do this, I was told, was to engage the girls in activities and conversations. Sometimes we watched TV in the evening. Other times we played games. I enjoyed getting to know the girls, hearing their stories, and encouraging them to learn from their experiences, even here in this program.

At first the girls didn't seem much different from kids I remembered growing up with, but it didn't take long for me to figure out what the real differences were—mostly factors beyond their control, like money and education. My family didn't have a lot of money, but we had enough to live in a decent house in a decent neighborhood with good schools. My parents both had steady jobs and earned better than minimum wage. We kids were sometimes home alone in the afternoon, but never at night. We had books in our home, and our parents encouraged and supported us in our education. We all liked school, enjoyed learning, and most of the time didn't object to doing our homework.

Some of the kids in "juvie," as they called it, came from single-parent families, usually with their mothers working in low-paying jobs sometimes at odd hours, which meant they were often home alone, even sometimes at night. If their fathers were around they were often out of work, making their financial situation precarious. The girls went to school, but it didn't click for them. It wasn't that they weren't smart, but either their classes were boring or they hadn't figured out how to succeed in school, and so they rebelled.

When I found out what most of the kids had done to get them into juvie, I was surprised. Only a few had done anything that would be considered a serious crime. Mostly it was things like cutting school too often, stealing candy or clothes from stores, or minor acts of vandalism, like tearing up a neighbor's flowers. What got them sent away was their parent's failure to rescue them and make apologies and sometimes amends. Their other "crime" was that many of them had brown or black skin.

Were they bad kids? For the most part I didn't think so, although occasionally there were girls who scared me, as did some of the bigger boys on the few occasions when I worked in the boys' unit. I figured what they needed most was for adults to listen to them and trust them. Which is what got me into trouble and led to the eventual decision not to give me a permanent contract after my six-month trial period.

The girls knew I didn't like locking their doors, so one day a small group of them challenged me. I was down in the hall where the girls lived in groups of two to four in small rooms with bunk beds, a sink, and a toilet. Although nicer than most jail cells, the effect was similar since they were locked in.

"Hey, Dodi," one of the older girls said. "Why don't you let us lock you up so you can see what it feels like?"

I knew it was a bad idea, but before I could respond, she grabbed my keys, pulled my belt loose, pushed me into the room, and closed the door. In retrospect, I should have yelled for help, but instead I went along with it, because I didn't want the girls to get into trouble.

"OK, that's enough," I said.

"No, I have to lock the door for you to feel the full effect." I waited while she fumbled with the key.

"OK, now let me out!"

"So, how does it feel? Do you like being locked up?" she asked.

"Of course not!" I declared. By now a group of girls were staring at me through the small window in the door.

"I get it. I feel trapped, helpless. It's no fun at all to be locked up."

That must have been what she wanted to hear, because she then unlocked the door and handed me back my keys. I got out of the area as quickly as I could. I was scared but relieved that other counselors were unaware of what had just happened.

However, the girls talked and the staff heard, so my bosses found out. They called me in and reprimanded me. They pointed out what a serious violation it was. The girls could have taken my keys and escaped. I had to admit that thought had not crossed my mind. Whether it crossed the girls' minds, I don't know, but I believe not. However tenuous, there was a certain level of trust between us and they were sharing their experience with me in a visceral way. They were teaching me a lesson, a very powerful one, about authority and power, about human rights and feelings, and about justice. I have never forgotten the experience. In fact, because of it I chose never to do civil disobedience. I don't ever want to be locked up again.

THE TRANSFORMATIVE POWER OF THEATER

While I was working at the juvenile hall, Thomas was in production or performing in plays at Festival Theatre. My job was in Novato at the northern boundary of Marin County, and we lived in Marin City at the southern end. When I got off work at 11 PM, I often stopped in San Anselmo, halfway in between. I could generally find actors and crew members at the local bar. It was a great way to unwind after a hard day.

As with the plays I saw earlier, each play in 1966 broadened my understanding of life and my role in it. No other play, however, became a central part of my thinking the way Arthur Miller's *All My Sons* did.[128] Set in the Midwest right after World War II, the story takes place one Sunday with Joe Keller's family and friends, when the consequences of a decision he made during the war come to a crashing climax. The play explores the relationship between individual actions on behalf of one's family and the impact of these actions on the larger family of humankind. Joe Keller's tragic mistake is allowing airplane parts he realizes are defective to be shipped from his factory to the military, justifying his actions as essential for the support of his family and the continued financial success of his business. Joe's limited moral and ethical sense have disastrous results that eventually hit close to home. After the parts fail and cause deaths, he regrets his actions, but never so much as

---

128   "All My Sons" performances at Festival Theatre, Feb. 11-Mar. 20, 1966.

when he discovers one of his sons killed himself when he learned of his father's role in providing the failed parts. Ultimately Joe realizes that those who died because of his faulty parts are, as he says, "all my sons."

In a letter to local churches, Marjorie Casebier wrote that in his plays Arthur Miller affirms "the possibility that the dramatic experience can...through heightened awareness and increased sensibility, enable us to be more human."[129] This wider awareness of each individual's responsibility to the larger society was coming to the fore as the Sixties proceeded. At what cost did our leaders decide to send the military to fight wars? How could anyone claim civil rights that were denied to others because of the color of their skin? Even if we act without malicious intent, if the consequences cause harm, are we innocent? I thought about the Germans who witnessed the Nazi takeover of their country and felt powerless to do anything. Were they innocent? Was I innocent if I did nothing while wrongs were being done in my name? What is my responsibility to the rest of the world? And what does this have to do with Beloved Community? These big questions have stayed with me throughout my life. Inspiring people to ask big questions was the prophetic ministry of Festival Theatre.

REALITY SETS IN

As it turned out I wasn't very realistic about what it would mean to live in Marin City. Because of my participation in the mostly black Presbyterian Church there, a local newspaper reporter interviewed me and about my plans to move to Marin City. I was quoted as saying:

I've found people there are very apprehensive of white people, and it's a difficult situation. I'm not idealistic about it. By being open and friendly I've received the same reaction from them, although they indicate they don't quite understand me because I really accept them.[130]

---

129   Marjorie Casebier, All My Sons Study Guide, 1966.
130   "Girl Divinity Student at Local Presbyterian Church," *Novato Advance*, Nov. 23, 1965.

Because we lived in a cooperative apartment complex managed by the residents of the apartments, there were meetings, dinners, and other opportunities for residents to get to know each other. The problem was that these almost always took place in the evenings when Thomas and I were both at work. I participated in the few gatherings that took place on Sundays, one of my days off, but for the most part I was unable to become as involved in the community as I had expected. I did my best to get to know my neighbors whenever I encountered them, but it was hard to feel part of the community when we were so rarely there.

However, I could see what being a resident of Marin City meant to the outside world. Sometimes I had to pass through a police blockade to get home. With only one road in and out of Marin City, it was easy for police to block access whenever they deemed it necessary. Sometimes there were altercations, particularly in the "project" area where people were suspected of drug trafficking. The first time the police stopped me, I was scared.

"What are you doing here, young lady? Don't you realize that it's nearly midnight and this place is dangerous?" the burly white policeman said.

"I live here. I'm going home," I said nervously.

"Let me see your driver's license," he demanded. As I got out my license, I realized I had a problem.

"This says you live in Fullerton. Where's that?"

"This is my parents' address in southern California. I just moved here," I explained.

"So how am I supposed to know you live here?" he said suspiciously.

"I live in the new apartment complex, over that way. My address is 919 Drake Avenue," I said.

He took my license and left to consult with the other cops. When he came back, he said, "Well, we'll let you go this time, but you'd better start carrying something with your address on it. There will be other times like this."

"Thank you," I replied.

"Now be sure you go right home!" he admonished as I drove off.

I started listening to the radio on my way home and could predict whether I would be stopped. I carried an electric bill in my car to prove residency.

This was my first indication of the difficulties of being white in a black community. I wondered then, if the sounds I had been assuming were of a car backfiring, might be gunshots. I still felt safe though, because I was confident that whatever was going on did not involve me, but then one night we came home to find our apartment door open.

It had been a lovely evening. Thomas and I had gone to Palo Alto for dinner with friends. After dinner, we all went to a play by Bertolt Brecht, *The Good Woman of Setzuan*, performed by the Stanford Repertory Theater. On the way up the stairs at home, we were debating the question raised by the play, whether it is possible for a person to be good in an evil world.

"If it's so hard to be good because the world is evil, then good people need to change the world," I contended.

"Good luck!" Thomas responded with a sarcastic laugh.

"Speaking of good, we should be quiet. It's late," I said as we reached our landing on the second floor.

"Did we leave the door open by mistake?" he asked.

I rushed inside, saw that my stereo was gone, and shouted to Thomas, "Oh, no! We've been robbed. They took my stereo."

Once inside the apartment we realized they had taken our new television as well. We called the police, who seemed to take forever getting there. Having watched crime shows on TV, we expected them to look for fingerprints, but all they did was take a report about what was stolen and tell us we had little hope of getting our property back.

Not one to accept bad news without a fight, when I got to work a couple of days later, I told the kids from Marin City what happened. They gave me more support than the police. Later one of them told me she knew where my stereo was. It could be easily identified by the Monterey Jazz Festival sticker on the front. I let the police know, but they refused to go get it, and I didn't have the nerve. By then Thomas had set up his stereo, which was better than mine anyway.

The TV was a different story. Credit cards were not yet common in 1966, but banks offered programs where you could buy something "on time," as we called it then, to establish credit. The bank provided the $100 cost of the TV and gave us a coupon book with ten $10 coupons to be paid monthly. We paid a small fee for the service and went to the bank to make the monthly payments. For nearly a year we were reminded of the night when our apartment was robbed, when we went to pay for a TV we no longer owned.

I knew I would have to tell my parents what happened, and I could hear my father's reaction. I explained that "the robbery could have happened anywhere." That assertion proved true several years later, when we had another robbery at our upscale apartment in Terra Linda and on a separate occasion Thomas's bike was stolen. What we learned from our first robbery was the importance of having renter's insurance, which we signed up for right away.

Before the robbery, we were already considering moving. Our commutes had always been a problem, especially since Thomas didn't drive. If I couldn't give him a ride, he had to take a bus. But the main reason was that the cooperative had been asking us to sign a new lease ever since we got married. We would have done it sooner, except that with my job we made too much money to qualify for the subsidized rent. Ironically, once we let them know we were going to move, I found out that I was not going to be hired on a permanent basis, although I would still be on call to fill in as needed. By then, though, we had found an apartment in San Anselmo near Festival Theatre, and the idea that Thomas could walk to work overrode any hesitation about leaving Marin City.

I was sad to leave Marin City, especially since I had been unable to fulfill the purpose that had inspired me to move there. Getting married changed things for me and I immersed myself in my new life with Thomas. I learned to cook, using my shower gifts, *The Better Homes and Gardens Cookbook* and my favorite, the *I Hate to Cook* book. Our new life together focused on entertaining friends and enjoying the rich art and culture of the Bay area in the second half of the 1960s.

I still dreamed of the Beloved Community. Festival Theatre and Open End provided some of what I imagined, and eventually the Sixties vision of love and peace merged with my earlier vision. A few years later when I became a teacher, I tried to implement that vision in my classroom by teaching that love is not only possible but also practical, the best way for us all to live together in peace. I still believe this is true. Remembering this vision and seeking ways to implement it is one of my reasons for writing this book.

BELOVED COMMUNITY: POSITIVE CHANGE AND
UNFINISHED AGENDA

Making Beloved Community real is necessary work that remains to be competed as part of the unfinished agenda of the Sixties. Twenty-first century trends are causing some people to wonder if it is possible to have a truly just and equal society where people of all races and diversities are not only accepted but respected. Is the American dream of equality, freedom, and justice for all possible?

We can take heart by noting the positive changes that have occurred in the past fifty years. Affirmative action policies made a significant difference in the lives of many families of color, opening doors for achievement and advancement. Although not all have benefited equally from increased access, people of color now fill many professional and political leadership positions. Movies and television feature many well-known actors of color. Interracial families appear in programs and commercials as normal and fully acceptable. Music and sports have produced many superstars. The election of an African American president in 2008 would not have been conceivable without the changes set in motion in the Sixties. Younger people, especially now, see racial diversity as a given.

Not everyone is happy with this movement toward racial equality, however. Even though demographic changes make clear that the United States is becoming increasingly diverse in terms of race and ethnicity, the white backlash has struggled to hold on to power and influence elections. Laws to restrict voting rights are used as allegedly legal means to keep people of color from having full voice in choosing political leaders. Challenges to affirmative action laws have resulted in fewer people of color having access to jobs and education. Racial profiling, the targeting of young black men as potentially dangerous, and unequal sentencing practices for drug-related offenses have filled prisons with a growing population that is disproportionally people of color.

The civil rights movement demanding racial equity and justice, like the abolitionist movement a century earlier, inspired other groups to advocate for their rights. The women's liberation movement was the next and most visible in their demands for equality. Results included the legalization of abortion in 1973 by the Supreme Court and Title IX of the Education Amendments of 1972, signed into law by President Nixon. The text is short, but the implications were far-reaching: "No person in the United States shall, on the basis of sex, be excluded from participation in, be denied the benefits of, or be subjected to discrimination under any education program or activity receiving federal financial assistance." This policy brought major changes in educational institutions at all levels, including the expansion of women's sports in high schools and colleges. Despite the positive changes, growing backlash requires us to make sure this progress is not eroded.

In 1972 the Equal Rights Amendment, originally proposed in the 1920s, passed both houses of Congress and was submitted to the states for ratification. Its text was also short but with widespread implications: "Equality of rights under the law shall not be denied or abridged by the United States or by any State on account of sex." Although it failed to receive ratification by the required number of states, working on this amendment was part of a new consciousness-raising movement for women across the country. Since then women, too, have benefitted from affirmative action policies and an emphasis on diversity in the workplace, but we still have a long way to go to achieve gender equity in Congress and other governmental bodies and on corporate boards and leadership positions in major companies.

The Stonewall riots in New York City in 1969 catapulted the issue of gay rights into public awareness, and the advent of Gay Pride celebrations each year after that increased the visibility of gay people in communities across the country. Before that, the topic of homosexuality was rarely discussed. The medical and psychological establishment labeled homosexuality a mental disorder. It wasn't until 1973 that the American Psychiatric Association rejected that view and called for homosexual rights. Since then the movement has grown as lesbians, bisexual people, and later transgender people have become visible activists working for equal rights in employment, housing, adoption, and the right to marry. One state after another affirmed equal marriage, beginning with Massachusetts in 2004, and in 2015 the Supreme Court removed all restrictions to equal marriage.

Expanding Beloved Community to include diversities other than race was not always easy, but in the twenty-first century that broader vision is finally taking hold. Poet activist Audre Lorde often talked about the three diversities she embraced—being female in a sexist world, African American in a racist world, and lesbian in a heterosexist world. She taught: "It is not our differences that divide us. It is our inability to recognize and celebrate those differences."[131]

Building coalitions and movements that reflect this diversity is still a work-in-progress and remains one of the challenges for the unfinished agenda. Developing an understanding of intersectionality is key. This requires recognition of how one oppression, such as race, intersects with others, such as class and gender. It is essential for different identity-based groups to fully understand and respect the differences in how each system of oppression functions. Growing coalitions, such as the Moral Monday Revival, succeed when they focus on common needs and goals.

Dr. King's often repeated "I have a dream" vision, articulated at the 1963 March on Washington, catapulted the civil rights movement into the nation's consciousness. Similarly, two statements by Hillary Clinton at United Nations' gatherings brought the necessity for intersectionality into world-wide cultural awareness.

131   Audre Lorde, *Our Dead Behind Us: Poems*, 1994.

"Human rights are women's rights, and women's rights are human rights," she declared at the UN Fourth World Conference on Women in 1995 in Beijing, China, when she was First Lady. Later, as Secretary of State, she took that statement a step further. At the United Nations celebration of International Human Rights Day in 2011, she asserted: "Human rights are gay rights, and gay rights are human rights."[132]

The reality that growing numbers of people understand the intersection of oppressions can be seen today in the massive protests, such as the ongoing struggle at Standing Rock in North Dakota in support of indigenous people who are fighting an oil pipeline that endangers their water supply and sacred lands, as well as the Missouri River. This movement has brought together people of faith, young people, environmentalists, climate change activists, military veterans, native people from all over North America, along with thousands of supporters all over the country who could not make the trip to rural North Dakota. This ongoing protest began in April 2016 and continues in 2017, making it the longest protest in American history.

A second massive protest took place in many communities around the world the day after the presidential inauguration in 2017. Called the Women's March and organized by a grassroots coalition of diverse women, the marches drew as many as five million people worldwide and is said to be the largest protest in American history. These massive peaceful protests of people across the spectrums of gender, class, race, immigration status, and other diversities expressed support for a wide range of inter-related causes and opposing restrictions on immigration and rights of all sorts.

Making connections between movements and people with diverse identities is key to the completion of the unfinished agenda of creating Beloved Community where all are respected and have equal opportunity to thrive and fulfill their potential. This work is well underway but requires constant vigilance to make fully real.

---

132   Dates of these two speeches are September 5, 1995 and December 10, 2011.

Dorothy May Emerson

5. LOVE IS ALL YOU NEED

"What the world needs now is love, sweet love
It's the only thing that there's just too little of
What the world needs now is love, sweet love,
No not just for some but for everyone."
      Lyrics by Hal David, Music by Burt Bacharach
      Hit record by Jackie DeShannon, released April 15, 1965

THE SWINGING SIXTIES

My 1960 high school yearbook called the new decade "the swinging sixties." Later the term came to mean the relaxation of social taboos, especially those relating to sexual mores and practices, but for our high school yearbook staff the term probably referred to the new music and dances of rock and roll.

Rock and roll had been developing throughout the 1950s with roots in even earlier music. Many of us who grew up in that decade first heard this new music on the radio or on the coin-operated music boxes in soda shop booths where we gathered after school. My family only had one record player and it only played old-fashioned 78 rpm records.[133] We also had a radio, but I had to ask permission to listen to the station that played rock and roll. My mother didn't pay much attention, but if my father came home while the radio was on he would say, "Turn that noise off. It's not music. That guy can't even sing."

---

133   In the 1930s and 40s music was played on 78 rpm shellac and then vinyl records. In the 1950s two new speeds were introduced, 45 rpm and 33 1/3 rpm. 45s were primarily children's and popular music, and 33s were primarily classical, jazz, and musicals. New record players were needed to play the new speeds. Our family finally got one in 1959.

SEA CHANGE: *the unfinished agenda of the 1960s*

After I got my driver's license in late 1958, I volunteered to run errands for my parents partly so I could listen to the car radio in our new 1957 Chevrolet. When hand-held transistor radios became available, I asked for one on every wish list until I finally got my own in 1960. The sound quality wasn't very good, but at least I could choose for myself what I wanted to hear.

Along with the new music came new dances and eventually entirely new ways of dancing. Throughout junior and senior high school, I attended a ballroom dancing program called Cotillion, held at the local Ebell Club.[134] Getting ready for Cotillion meant dressing up in party clothes and wearing our best shoes. At first, I worried about learning the dances and finding dance partners, but we were not permitted to choose favorites, so we learned to dance with anyone. I discovered I loved to dance, especially with a good partner, but when my partner was unsure of himself, I tended to lead, something girls were not supposed to do. In addition to the box step, foxtrot, waltz, and tango, we learned cha-cha, swing, and bop. By the time the 1960s began, our teachers had taught us several rock and roll dances, like the Stroll and the Twist.[135]

Later in the Sixties, especially in the big rock venues in the San Francisco Bay Area where I was by then, dancing became more spontaneous and freestyle. Specific dance steps gave way to free expression, as we moved our bodies in response to the music. Party clothes of the early 1960s gave way to flowing garments or jeans. The freedom of rock and roll dancing meant I could dance with a partner, move around on the dance floor and exchange partners, or even dance alone. Twirling around the dance floor, feeling the music deep inside, and enjoying the feeling of freedom, I realized how much I had changed from that nervous girl who had to get "dressed up" for Cotillion.

---

134   Taught by Mr. and Mrs. Gollatz from Pasadena.
135   Vera Wilson, *The Girl's Book of Ballroom Dancing* (Roy Publishers, 1959), 117, 118, describes rock and roll dancing as "performed without undue tension, the body and legs being flexible, so that there may be a physical rhythmic expression of co-ordination with the beats of music ... a dance which leaves much scope for personal expression and interpretation in style, movement, rhythm, and even in the manner in which the figures are constructed."

As the dances changed, so had I changed, probably more than anyone would have anticipated in 1960. Apparently, this was not the first time in history that new dances were signs of culture change. Nineteenth-century polite society objected to the waltz because men and women held each other face to face, which had not previously been allowed. Ironically, rock and roll dancing was criticized for its lack of direct contact, also seen as threatening to the status quo.[136]

Calling the new decade "the Swinging Sixties" indicated that at least some people at my high school knew change was in the air. Music and dancing were facets of change. Love, sex, and relationships were others.

POPULAR SONGS REFLECT CHANGING RELATIONSHIPS

Popular songs often illustrate attitudes toward love, sex, and relationships. Two songs highlight differences between the sexuality of the Sixties and previous eras.

"When I'm Not Near the Girl I Love"[137] from the 1940s is written from a man's perspective and tells of his inability to control himself when he is around women, any women, even though he loves a woman who is not with him at the time. The song is a sort of confession in which he admits being fickle while bragging about his ability to connect with whatever women "let me choose 'em."

"Love the one you're with,"[138] from the end of the 1960s, implies gender equality in relationships. On the surface, this song tells a similar story of loving someone absent and loving the person who is near, but this time it is without the guilt and confessional quality of the older song. Proper action, the song says, is to love whomever one is with, regardless of other relationships, thus avoiding confusion and unhappiness. If everyone loved the people they were with, then no one would be lonely or alone.

---

136   See, for instance, Richard Powers, "The Life of a 1950s Teenager," https://socialdance.stanford.edu/Syllabi/fifties.htm.

137   "When I'm Not Near the Girl I Love," by E.Y. Harburg and Burton Lane, 1947.

138   "Love the One You're With," by Clifton George Bailey and Stephen Stills, on solo album "Stephen Stills," 1970.

The two songs view the same activity—loving someone you just met—in very different ways. In the 1940s this activity is considered illicit, a result of men's inability to control their sexual desires and some women's apparent willingness to fulfill those desires. It is one-sided, with men needing and women responding. The late 1960s song invites us into a new way of viewing loving relationships—being open to the love that potentially exists between all people, with both men and women equally wanting to express and enjoy that love. This section describes my attempts to put that philosophy into practice.

Sexuality in 1950s was defined in rigid terms with marriage considered the only proper context. Before marriage, holding hands and kissing were permitted, and women were supposed to remain virgins until their wedding days. Sex outside of marriage was taboo, and alternative choices such as same gender relationships were considered deviant behavior. Although Alfred Kinsey's research[139] showed that the reality of American sexuality was much more diverse and active than anyone realized, the idealization of the nuclear family and strict limits on sexual expression continued.

Just as I was finishing college in the spring of 1965 one of the most popular songs was "What the World Needs Now."[140] Sung by Jackie DeShannon, a little-known, pretty, blond singer, it was framed as a heartfelt prayer. "Lord, we don't need another mountain/ We've got mountains and hillsides enough to climb/ Enough to last/ Till the end of time/ What the world needs now is love." The more I learned about the world the more I wanted to believe in this simple idea.

Just two years later the world was much more complicated, and love was needed more than ever. With the war in Vietnam raging and the antiwar movement growing, an historic television

139   Alfred Kinsey was an American biologist, professor of entomology and zoology, and sexologist who in 1947 founded the Institute for Sex Research at Indiana University. Ground-breaking publications include *Sexual Behavior in the Human Male* (1948) and *Sexual Behavior in the Human Female* (1953), also known as the Kinsey Reports.
140   "What the World Needs Now," lyrics by Hal David, music by Burt Bacharach, hit record by Jackie DeShannon, released April 15, 1965.

show featured another important song about love. On June 25, 1967, "Our World," the first live television show broadcast by satellite, was viewed by 400 to 700 million people in forty countries. The British Broadcasting Company produced the program, with segments filmed in Canada, the United States, Japan, Australia, Sweden, Italy, and eight other countries. The show featured opera star Maria Callas, artist Pablo Picasso, the Vienna Choir Boys, media philosopher Marshall McLuhan, Mick Jagger, Marianne Faithful, and the Beatles. Asked by the producers to compose a song with a simple message that could be understood by all nationalities, the Beatles premiered "All You Need is Love." They were accompanied by a studio orchestra and surrounded by other British pop stars who sat on the floor and sang along on the chorus. People wearing sandwich boards saying love in many different languages walked through the studio audience. A perfect conclusion to an historic event, the message of this song resonated with people all over the world: "Love is all you need."

LOVE AND SEX IN THE 1960S

How and what people did sexually and how society viewed these actions and practices changed significantly during the Sixties. Practices that had earlier been kept behind closed doors began to be discussed openly. Premarital sex, same gender sexual relationships, free love, open marriage, and group sex were not invented in the 1960s, but people were increasingly open and honest about engaging in these activities.

To some who observed the changes from the outside it looked like the same old story—people having sex who weren't married to each other. They called it promiscuity or having affairs or adultery (if one of the partners was married), but we who were involved didn't see it that way. We knew what affairs and adultery were, if not from direct personal or family experience then from novels, plays, and movies. We knew these practices were common and inevitably surrounded by secrecy and shame. That's part of what we objected to and sought to change by being honest and open about our sexuality. Sharing our separate experiences was an essential aspect of my open relationship with Thomas.

The idea that women as well as men sought and enjoyed sex became a popular topic of discussion, particularly after the 1962 publication of Helen Gurley Brown's *Sex and the Single Girl*. She articulated what many women were already thinking and doing and shocked polite society into waking up to the reality of women's sexuality. She recommended that women be prepared to support themselves and not expect marriage to mean security forever after. I had already learned this from my mother who worked and insisted that her daughters as well as her sons prepare for careers. "You can't count on a man," she warned my sister and me.

As the war in Vietnam became an increasing focus of concern, "Make Love, Not War" bumper stickers and buttons became popular. First appearing at an antiwar demonstration in April 1965, and then popularized by the distribution of buttons at the Mother's Day March in Chicago the following month, this slogan has continued to be used ever since.[141] The sentiment is simple: If people stopped hating and killing one another, the world would be a better place.

The act of making love became a lifestyle choice, affirming life over death, love over hate. The availability of birth control pills made this choice safe by preventing pregnancy. The only possible physical consequence was an occasional bout of gonorrhea, easily cured with antibiotics. Some sexual adventurers carried the idea of the healing power of love further by engaging in love-making with multiple partners, as one way to spread the power of love and counteract the hate that resulted in the culture of war.

Note that in the Sixties we generally talked about "making love," as opposed to simply "having sex." This was more than a euphemism, as the author of a book about the sexual revolution points out: "Love was the central tenet of the counterculture— love of nature, love of life, love of oneself, love of love. Sexual intercourse was merely a way to communicate with, and express love for, another person."[142] Those of us who were engaging in this new sexuality sometimes called our openness to making love "free

---

141   http://en.wikipedia.org/wiki/Make_love,_not_war
142   David Allyn, *Make Love, Not War: The Sexual Revolution, An Unfettered History*, 2000, 101.

love," meaning there were no strings attached to the physical sharing of sexual relations and no expectation of an ongoing relationship. The primary motivation was to connect deeply and intimately with another human being. Sex became a vehicle for the expression of the love that potentially exists between all people.

Practicing free love did not mean that you necessarily acted every time you felt loving feelings or a physical attraction toward someone, but some readily took the opportunity to express those feelings physically. Because sex connected us more deeply and immediately than almost anything else, it was a way to be vulnerable with each other, opening to the experience of love as real and alive, even if only for the time of shared lovemaking.

Although free love practices may have benefited men more than women, my experience as a liberated woman meant I enjoyed the freedom to use my body any way I chose, including making love with whomever I chose. The emphasis was on choice, which meant any type of forced sexual activity such as rape was antithetical to freely given and received love. As the Sixties progressed I became increasingly aware of the importance of choosing relationships where love and respect were present.

I know I would not be who I am today without my sexual explorations in the Sixties. Although I did some things I would not recommend to others, especially given the circumstances and understandings of today, I am grateful for all my experiences because they contributed to the person I have become.

EVOLUTION OF A SEXUAL REVOLUTIONARY

To understand how I arrived at my sexual practices in the later Sixties, I need to go back to how I first learned about sex. Personal values evolve over time and are influenced by many factors. In my case, a series of influences moved me from the values of the 1940s and 50s I was raised to think were right, to the values I came to espouse during the Sixties. This transition didn't happen all at once. As the decade developed so did my understanding, beliefs, values, and practices about sex, love, and relationships.

Growing up we didn't talk about sex at home, although my mother in her role as school nurse showed a Disney cartoon[143] about menstruation to various groups I was part of in grade school. The cartoon explained about eggs and sperm and diagrammed how they got together to create a baby, all without ever showing actual bodies or sex organs. That's why I had to read *Peyton Place*[144] before I understood what intercourse was. I waited my turn to read the well-worn paperback copy that circulated around our junior high school, read it only at night after everyone else was asleep, and hid it in my closet during the day, because I knew my mother would take it away if she found it.

In addition to books and songs, I also learned about boy-girl relationships from movies. That's where I learned how to flirt. Going to the movies on Saturday afternoon was one of the first things my girlfriends and I did our own as young teens.[145] Our parents had to approve our movie choices, but I doubt they realized the subtle messages even innocent-sounding movies contained.

Movies taught my generation of girls how we were supposed to act around boys, even animated Disney films like *Cinderella*, and *Lady and the Tramp*, and musicals—*Oklahoma*, *The King and I*, and *South Pacific*. Sometimes the female leads resisted male attention at first, but ultimately, they all succumbed and started acting girly and sweet, tilting their heads as if to say "I'm available. You can kiss me." When I was in high school, I saw more sexually explicit movies like *The Pajama Game* with Doris Day, *Gigi* with Leslie Caron, and *Some*

---

143   "The Story of Menstruation," a ten-minute animated film by Walt Disney, sponsored by Kotex Products/Kimberly Clark.

144   The 1956 novel, *Peyton Place*, by Grace Metalious sold 60,000 copies in the first ten days and eventually over ten million. The story dramatized the hypocrisy of American sexual attitudes and secrets in a small New England town.

145   We had two movie theaters in Fullerton, one showed first-run movies usually within a month or two of their premieres in nearby Hollywood and the other showed popular movies on their second or third runs a year or two later. This meant if we were too young to see them the first time around, we could see them later when we were considered old enough. This access to movies was important because it wasn't until 1966 that the first full-length feature movie was shown on television. In those days, theaters only had one screen and the movies changed frequently.

Like It Hot with Marilyn Monroe. These and other actresses became role models for how to act. One movie provided two different models for female behavior. In *Raintree County* Eva Marie Saint played the blond good girl and Elizabeth Taylor played the dark-haired vamp. I wanted to be both.

In high school, sex education was part of our health education class. We learned specifics about male and female genitalia and reproductive systems, and about gonorrhea and syphilis, the only sexually transmitted diseases common in those days. The subject of homosexuality was not mentioned. In addition to the regular class, there was a one-day-only sex education program which required parental permission slips. That day we were given a numbered information booklet to use during the class. No discussion was allowed. Because we had to return the booklets, I don't know for sure what information was presented, but I suspect that is when we learned about birth control, which would have been considered very progressive at the time and was likely why we needed parental approval.

At church, we learned about love as a religious principle. We were introduced to three Greek words representing different kinds of love. Eros, passionate love, which may or may not be sexual, attracts us to each other but can also refer to the love of beauty and other ideals. *Philia*, the love of friendship and caring, is what we feel for our family, friends, and our community. The third, and highest form of love, we were told, is *agape*, unconditional love, the love of God and with which God loves us. When relationships are very strong and commitment is high, then *agape* love can be expressed between two people. When a church functions as a loving community, agape love prevails. Our senior youth group was called Agape Fellowship in recognition of this ideal.

When it came to boy-girl relationships we learned that equality and mutual respect are essential for healthy relationships, both for dating and later when choosing a marriage partner. Marriage was idealized as a potential context for *agape* love, a special and unique way we could experience God's love in human form. I dreamed of finding a special person with whom I could share this kind of love.

One summer at senior high summer camp we learned specifics about birth control in a class on Christian Marriage. The leaders explained that the rhythm method favored by the Catholic Church was not reliable. Condoms, they warned, were only partially reliable, so diaphragms were recommended as the most effective way to prevent unwanted pregnancy. Birth control pills were not yet available. Although the teachers seemed to expect we would only use this information once we were married, they wanted us to know we could and should make decisions about if and when to have children. A subtext came through as well. If we were going to be sexually active before marriage, we would need this information.[146]

Back at my home church, our youth minister introduced the concept of situation ethics. He and his wife had graduated from Princeton Theological Seminary where they had learned about this newly evolving[147] perspective on morality, which asserts that the law of love is primary and supersedes the Ten Commandments. What love required might vary in different situations. If one's intent was to act out of love, then what one did could be considered moral. The primary rule was to love one another, as God loves us, and to allow the law of love to guide us in our actions. In my life, I have often reflected on this teaching and tried to apply it. A friend in that same group remembers the message as "Love God, and do as you please." One of my first applications was in making decisions about sex.

Another important influence was the family for whom I

---

146   The National Council of Churches issued a statement "endorsing family planning and advocating population control through voluntary contraception." *New York Times*, Feb.24, 1961.

147   Herbe and Jean Stocker studied with Paul Lehrmann, a primary advocate of situation ethics, while he was developing the ideas in his book, *Ethics in a Christian Context*, published initially in 1963. An online description of the book states: "Lehmann argues that while principles for moral action can be rules of thumb, there are no absolute moral norms beyond the general norm of love. Lehmann contends that Christians are to act in every situation in ways that are consistent with God's humanizing purposes, but what that means changes from context to context and requires strong, faith-shaped discernment." www.amazon. com/Ethics-Christian-Context-Paul-Lehmann/dp/0060652314

regularly babysat, the Eschners. Meg and Al became role models for me of adults who were happily different from everyone else I knew in my community. Meg had long hair she often let hang free down her back, not tied up in a bun like my mother's. The house they designed themselves was what we now call open concept, with one room flowing into the next, generally without doors. A wall of windows faced an arroyo left natural in its vegetation. In front of the windows was a grand piano, a rarity in houses I visited as a teenager. They were the first people I knew who did not consider themselves Christian. I knew they were good people no matter what their religion, and I was curious about what they believed. I took care of their four children while they attended concerts and plays and participated in the Vedanta Society[148] in Los Angeles.

Once the kids were asleep, I liked to wander around their house exploring their unique furnishings and artifacts. There was a calm, almost spiritual quality to the space. One night I discovered a book on a bedside table, *This is My Beloved*. I went back to that book many times, often reading the poems aloud and dreaming of a day when someone would see my body in the beautiful way the poet describes his lover. I longed to be treated with the loving tenderness he described.

I memorize you ... walking as if to music. Your dress lies
against the cheeks and hollow of your thighs like running water.
Your breasts nod yes each step,
your slow involute hips cradle the eternal synonym for God.[149]

I read these love poems at the Eschners while Carl[150] and I were experimenting sexually. He and I agreed that we would not "go all the way," as we said in those days, and managed to find other ways to express physically the love we felt for each other. Until one night

---

148   Founded by Swami Vivekananda after his appearance at the first World Parliament of Religion in 1893 in Chicago, Vedanta is one of the orthodox schools of Indian philosophy. Practices include meditation, breathwork, yoga, and education in Hindu principles.
149   Walter Benton, *This is My Beloved*, 1943. The poems have been compared to "Song of Songs" in the Bible.
150   How I met Carl and the beginning of our relationship can be found in Hearing the Call, Young Love.

when I let my virginity go.

The setting was less than ideal for this momentous event. We were in Carl's green and white Nash Metropolitan parked in our favorite place on the edge of a cliff where we could see the city lights sparkling below. After watching the lights and talking we moved into the tiny back seat. Although there wasn't much room to move around, we had already spent hours there doing everything short of intercourse. As before, we began passionately kissing and touching each other. Usually we both stopped before intercourse, even though we clearly wanted to complete the act. What changed that night? Partially it was my realization that Carl and I would not last as a couple once I left for college. I wanted to experience what I had heard the previous summer at a church conference: "Sex is the giving away to another our final secret. Our natures are fully developed in this."[151] We had been working up to this for several years and this might be one of my last chances to experience it with the one I loved.

I barely remember my feelings at the time, but I know I was happy we had finally carried our sexual exploration to its conclusion. When I got home I discovered a fair amount of blood on my clothes. My mother had taught me how to get menstrual blood out using cold water, so I did the best I could. In the morning when she asked about my wet clothes hanging in the bathroom, I explained that I had an "accident," implying that my period had started unexpectedly. She did not pursue the matter any further.

I felt good about my new status as a non-virgin. It made me feel grown up. This was one thing I would not have to face in college, I reasoned. I didn't worry about being pregnant, nor did I feel any conflict with my religious values. This was done out of love, so it was OK.

SEX AT POMONA COLLEGE

As my Pomona College roommate and I were getting to know each other, Julie asked me,

"Are you a virgin?"

---

151   Martin Fuller, Commission Conference #1, Camp Sturtevant, Aug. 29-Sept. 3, 1960.

"Well, no," I responded, surprised at the directness of her question, "How about you?"

"I lost my cherry riding a horse. You know how hard saddles can be!"

I didn't know much about horses and saddles but I nodded in agreement, realizing we weren't exactly on the same track with this. Later we were having hot fudge sundaes with two other freshman girls at Walter's, the restaurant in town that became a favorite place to go when we got tired of cafeteria food. Julie took the cherry off her sundae with her spoon and reached it across the table to me saying, "For the one you lost." So right from the beginning I was "out" as a non-virgin, unlike most of my new friends at Pomona College, it turned out.

During my freshman year, I kept a detailed calendar of my activities to show my mother what I was doing. I made note of concerts, lectures, movies, plays, dances, parties, dates, and more. I had many "coffee dates" and, on several occasions, two in one evening. According to my calendar, I dated more than fifteen different boys that first year. Several boys were steady dates but none became what I would call a "boyfriend" that first year.

I had one special friend, though. Tall, dark, and handsome, Pat had a car and we often drove out in the country. Having lived in the Seattle area all his life, he complained about the brown California hills, even though, as I pointed out, they would be green in the winter when it rained. He was a great dancer and one night he surprised me by picking me up and swinging me over his shoulder! Our relationship took the usual course, with kissing and after a while increasingly heavy petting. Occasionally we went all the way. I loved his gentle spirit and felt good about nurturing him with physical love. I'm not sure why our relationship didn't continue past that first year.

I didn't yet have a philosophy about sex, but I enjoyed kissing and what we called petting and only occasionally went further. Like many college students both then and now, I drank a fair amount of alcohol at parties, so sometimes what happened was less a decision and more a response to the situation. I tried to be careful by paying attention to where I was in my menstrual cycle, and sometimes the boys had condoms. I knew neither rhythm nor condoms were entirely safe but I hoped the combination would be OK—that and a lot of luck!

Mostly I enjoyed my relationships in college, both those that involved sex and those that did not. Two difficult things happened, however. In my sophomore year, I was date raped, and in my junior year I got pregnant. I only realized I was date raped many years later when I saw a made-for-TV movie about the subject. Until then, that fateful night remained one of my most painful and embarrassing experiences. Once I had a larger perspective in which to understand what had happened, I could forgive myself.

Lonny was the older brother of a Pomona student. We dated during the summer after my freshman year. His family had a funky cottage on Balboa Island where their small sailboat, a nine-foot sloop, was docked. We sometimes sailed through the harbor into the ocean past much bigger boats. People waved at us and laughed in amazement at our daring to sail out so far from the safety of shore in such a small boat. I had no fear because I was a good swimmer and Lonny had been sailing all his life, but in retrospect I might have been more cautious, especially since we were also drinking beer.

Sometimes we stopped at a tiny undeveloped island called Little Balboa, sandwiched between the one where his cottage was and the mainland. We had picnics there, drank beer, and played around sexually on the sand. It was a daring adventure to be nearly naked on this deserted island surrounded by civilization. We could see and hear the cars going by all around us, but no one could see us if we were lying on the sand behind the scrub brush.

The next year Lonny showed up at school and invited me to a drive-in movie. He had brought a mixed drink which he offered me in a paper cup, but when I drank it I started to feel woozy. The next thing I remember was waking up in the middle of the night on a mattress on a floor somewhere. I looked at the clock and freaked out. "This clock must be wrong. It can't be 4:00 AM already! Don't you know I'm supposed to be back in the dorm by 2?"

He didn't say much but quickly helped me get my things

together and took me back to the dorm. The police were already out searching for me.

The housemother came out to greet me, "I'm glad you're OK. We were worried. What on earth were you doing?"

"Uh, I fell asleep," I stammered and walked quickly past her to my room, hoping she couldn't smell the alcohol that must have been on my breath.

The next day, I was informed, I would have to talk to the Dean of Women and then go before the women's judiciary, known as Girls' Court. This student group would decide my punishment for this serious transgression of dorm rules.

Lonny sent me a dozen pink roses, but I never wanted to see him again, although I wasn't sure at the time it was entirely his fault. Maybe I because I hadn't eaten dinner the alcohol hit me too hard. We had sex before, so that wasn't unusual. Maybe we had really fallen asleep. Maybe he didn't realize I had to be back by 2 AM. But why couldn't I remember what had happened? I wondered.

My meeting with Dean Walton was the worst experience of my life at that point. Although other students considered her one of the most supportive adults on campus, my only encounter with her did not go well. She was unwilling to accept my explanation that I accidentally fell asleep. "What were you doing in a bed in the first place?" she wanted to know. When I confessed to not being a virgin, she stated primly and unequivocally, "You aren't supposed to be having sex until you get married. Pomona girls aren't like that."

The fact that I admitted to having sex and drinking alcohol meant the whole thing was my fault and there could be no mitigating circumstances. She could not understand that I felt OK about having sex with guys and even thought it was a positive thing to do. She decided my transgression was so serious and embarrassing she did not recommend my appearing in person before the judiciary. At our 50th reunion, a friend who was on that judiciary told me she doubted the dean had brought the case before them. Whether my peers would have understood my perspective, I will never know. The dean soon informed me that I was to be "campused" for two months. This meant I had to be in by 9 PM every night for the first month and by 11 PM for the month after that, even on weekends.

Years later, when I saw a movie about date rape, I realized it was highly likely I was drugged that night.[152] That possibility helped me remember other things. I had plenty of other experiences with alcohol both before and after this incident, and this was the only time I ever lost consciousness. The fact that I remember feeling woozy and did not wake up until at seven hours later indicates the likelihood there was something other than alcohol in that drink. The other indication was that about a week after the incident I was shocked to discover a tampon had been pushed deep inside me. No way would I have not taken it out had I been conscious!

Being "campused" made dating difficult. Fortunately, I began hanging out with Lew, who was amazingly understanding about the situation. He helped me feel OK about myself again. We had long discussions, kissed, and petted, but he never asked for more.

Lew was one of the more conservative students in our class. One time we walked by a group of students standing with signs on the steps of Bridges Auditorium. Having never seen a protest before, I wondered what they were doing. He scoffed at them, calling them peaceniks, and showed me a political button with a silhouette of a B-52 bomber that looked like a peace symbol turned on its side. The dots underneath the plane were supposed to be bombs. The words said: "drop it." This was my introduction to the peace symbol, which the protestors displayed proudly. I was so politically unaware, I thought his button was funny.

FALLING IN LOVE IN GERMANY

Lew gave me a nice respite and helped me heal, but we weren't in love. Summer came along and then I went to Germany. I complied with my German professor's recommendation and fell in love with Rudolf Spalke.[153] I saved the love story for this section.

---

152   Robin Warshaw, *I Never Called It Rape*, 1988, helped raise awareness about non-stranger sexual assault after which the terms "acquaintance rape" and "date rape" became popularly understood and policies developed on campuses and elsewhere in response.

153   For more on my relationship with Rudolf, see Culture Shock, especially

Dorothy May Emerson

Rudolf initiated our relationship by inviting me to go dancing and to movies, plays, and concerts—all of which I loved. After I moved to student housing, we were together frequently. He showed me his favorite places in Marburg and introduced me to aspects of German culture I might otherwise have missed. In early November, he wrote me a letter about how beautiful we were together, like children enjoying our play time. But, he continued, our minds and bodies are adult and even if we might not achieve the dream of a "snow white house by the sea" we still have now and that is enough. I realized I was in love with him and resolved to enjoy whatever time we had together, but I could not forget the fact that I would be leaving in a couple of months.

The love I shared with Rudolf was beyond anything I had previously experienced. Although I felt love toward both Carl and Rob in high school, it was with Rudolf that I first experienced the feeling of being deeply "in love." Because Rudolf had been raised in East Germany where they learned Russian, he didn't speak much English, and I was forced to communicate with him almost entirely in German. We spent many hours talking about our lives and analyzing our experiences together, including the plays and movies we were seeing. This level of discourse was not easy for me as a nonnative speaker, but my desire to communicate as accurately as possible helped me learn more German than I might otherwise have been inclined to do. My professor was right about falling in love being an excellent way to learn the language!

Making love with Rudolf was special in a way I had not yet experienced. He was very gentle and loving and always wore a condom, because he wanted to be sure I did not get pregnant. In this Germans were ahead of Americans. Because few Germans got married before they were in their 20s, when they had sex they took precautions. They also had strict social codes. For instance, we were not supposed to display affection in public. Once when we were standing on a street corner kissing, a man yelled loudly from an apartment above, telling us to stop.

Finding the right place and time to make love was tricky.

For one thing, his bedroom and bed were very small, and the room was cold because the primary heat source in the apartment was a coal stove in the living room. For Christmas I bought Rudolf an oil heater for his room. Once we were in Rudolf's room, thinking his mother would be away for several hours. When she came home unexpectedly, I had to quickly dress and climb out the window, come around the building to the front door, and enter as if I were just arriving! Occasionally Rudolf's married brother, Rene, let us use the bedroom in his apartment, which was a real treat.

In December, we decided to exchange rings to indicate we were serious about each other. We had them engraved with our initials and wore them on the ring fingers of our left hands. I liked the idea that in Germany both men and women wore commitment rings, often the same rings they would wear when they married, when they moved the rings from their left to their right hands.

It was nearly impossible to say goodbye. As January began and I knew my time in Marburg would soon end, I tried to be brave and confident that we would see each other again soon, but I found myself in tears many times. I hadn't expected to fall in love, but I was glad I did.

TIJUANA ABORTION

Leaving Rudolf in Germany was bearable for me because I naively believed it would be possible for him to come to America within the next year. Surely love would find a way. I thought. We both wrote long letters almost every day, in German of course, declaring our love and promising to stay together. In the meantime, I had to finish writing papers for the courses I had taken while in Germany and then begin a new semester at Pomona College. I focused on studying and mostly only went out with girlfriends. This worked for a while.

Right away I began trying to figure out how Rudolf could come for a visit in the summer and enlisted my mother's support, but I kept running into roadblocks. The reality of his limited financial resources (and ours) and the time commitment required for his own studies began to sink in. I grew discouraged at the prospect of not seeing him again.

Then Tim, whom I dated earlier, asked me to a frat party. In a moment of weakness, I agreed to go, thinking it was about time to have some fun. I drank too much beer and before he bought me home, we stopped to make out. We had enjoyed playing around sexually before, but this time one thing led to another and he was inside me before I realized it. When I got back to my room I looked at my calendar. "Oh no!" I said to myself. "This is exactly the wrong time of month and he didn't wear a condom." I jumped in the shower and washed like I'd never washed before, but it was too late. If only we had morning-after pills back then!

Sometimes my life coincides with contemporary social issues in mysterious ways. A few weeks earlier, I heard two of my friends discussing abortions. I wasn't sure what an abortion was until they explained. Mary's boyfriend, Hal, knew where to get one in Tijuana, Mexico. Supposedly this was a decent place, not like the back-alley abortions they also knew about. It was all new to me, and I filed the information away in my mind, just in case I ever needed it. A month later I did. Knowing that option existed, I never seriously considered having the baby. It would ruin my education and I wasn't ready to be a mother. I went to a doctor to be sure, and he declared me officially pregnant. Thanks to that conversation about abortion, I knew what I needed to do.

Tim reached out to Hal, who agreed to help me get an abortion. Hal made the arrangements and planned to drive us to Tijuana. The cost was $300. Tim had enough money in his checking account at school to pay for it, but he would have to ask his parents to replace the money. He wanted to wait until after the abortion, so they wouldn't try to talk us out of our decision. I agreed to go with him when he told them so they would see I was a decent person. I did not, however, plan to tell my parents about the abortion either before or after. Instead I told them that a group of us were going to Tijuana for the day, to sight-see and buy souvenirs.

During the time between getting pregnant and having the abortion, I started hanging out with a graduate student, Dave, who was getting his PhD in Economics. His graduate school friends were a welcome alternative to missing Rudolf and to my worries about being pregnant. When my plans were set for the abortion, I decided to tell Dave. He convinced me I needed to tell my parents before the operation, just in case anything happened. I could hardly imagine facing them, but it turned out to be a pivotal point in my separation from parental authority and becoming an independent young adult.

I wanted Dave to go with me to talk with them, but after we talked about it I realized this something I needed to do by myself. I had the family's old car, a 1960 Chevy, so I could make the trip on my own. I first drove to see my father at work, at the Union Oil Research Center in Brea. I called his lab from the lobby and asked him to meet me in the car, parked out in front.

After a few pleasantries, I came straight to the point. He knew something was up, since I had never b stopped in like this to see him at work.

"Dad," I said, "I'm pregnant and I'm getting an abortion."

Ignoring the second half of my sentence his immediate response was, "When are you getting married?"

"I'm not," I said patiently. "I'm getting an abortion." I explained when and where and that it was safe, because it was in a clinic.

Finally, after many probing questions, he accepted my decision and said he was glad I told him.

Then I drove to our house in Fullerton to talk with my mother. Since the other kids were there, we went into her bedroom. When she heard the news, she turned away from me. I think there were tears in her eyes. "I understand," she said softly. "I had one too, before I met your father."

Thankfully they were both supportive. We never talked about it again. I noticed, however, a subtle shift in their attitude toward me. I was an adult now, able to make important decisions on my own, even though I had not yet turned 21. I only learned recently that my mother called Tanni and put her on the spot about the situation.

The day of the abortion, we left early in the morning for the three-hour drive to Tijuana. This was my first trip to Mexico—and my only trip there for many years. Hal drove the car and Tim came along. Border crossings were easy in those days and by 9 AM I was standing in a parking lot waiting to be picked up. We had been told I must be alone or the people from the clinic would not meet me, so my friends had to leave me there. Abortions were illegal in both countries, although they were readily available in Mexico, especially in border towns. This was supposed to be one of the best clinics, run by licensed doctors, or so I was told.

Finally, after what seemed like forever, a car stopped and asked if I was Dorothy. Several American women were already in the car, so I felt safe getting in. One of the women laughed at my nervousness. "It's no big deal," she said. "This is my third one. It will be over before you know it." I cringed.

The building where the clinic operated looked more like an apartment complex than a clinic. I learned later they moved the location every few weeks to avoid getting caught. There wasn't much furniture, but the place looked clean. The prediction about time turned out to be an exaggeration. The waiting seemed to go on forever, so I had plenty of time to get nervous, but the die was cast and I knew I would go through with it. Finally, it was my turn.

The operation took place in what was probably supposed to be a bedroom, but there was a medical table covered with a white sheet, a cart with surgical instruments, a woman who appeared to be a nurse, and a man who appeared to be a doctor dressed in white hospital garb. They gave me a local anesthetic to numb the pain but did not completely put me out. It hurt. The nurse, who spoke English with a strong accent, told me to remember the pain and not come back again. The operation didn't take long, but I had to lie there awhile before I was allowed to get up.

Then I had to wait in the outer room until the others in my group were ready to leave. They took us back to a different parking lot, where my friends were thankfully already waiting. As I got out of the car, the driver said cheerily, "*Hasta la vista!* See you again." I resolved this would be my one and only abortion, and it was.

Dave let me stay at his place while I recovered, so I didn't have to be at school. I had been told: "no sex, no alcohol, and no physical activity for two days." Dave made sure I followed the instructions. By the time Monday came, I felt OK and went back to my usual activities.

I was relieved it was all over and never doubted my decision. Only years later when I read a book about Wilma Rudolph, the famous Olympic runner, and learned that she had given birth as a teenager to a child her mother raised, did I wonder what my child might have been like, if my circumstances had been different. I realized I didn't even know if it had been a boy or a girl.

Once I recovered from my abortion, I was determined to find a doctor who would prescribe the newly-available birth-control pills.[154] Because I had heard they only gave the pills to married women, I lied and said I was about to get married and wanted to be prepared.

PLAYBOY PHILOSOPHY

Knowing I was trying to figure out how to move forward after my abortion, Dave suggested I read a series of articles in his *Playboy* magazines. At first, I was resistant, thinking the magazine was only for men. I found the airbrushed pictures of nude women disturbing yet strangely intriguing, but the articles on "Playboy Philosophy" were definitely thought-provoking. They provided new perspectives both on my own experiences and on the way attitudes toward sex were changing. The fact that I could read these essays and apply them to myself indicates that they pointed to a larger truth, though couched in masculinist and sexist terms.

Hugh Hefner, publisher of *Playboy* magazine, wrote the editorial essays called "Playboy Philosophy" over the course of four years, from 1962 to 1965. Dave had kept the older issues so I could start at the beginning. I read most of the series over the year and a half we dated. Hef (as he was called) felt the need to explain to "friends and critics alike—our guiding principles," and to offer "a few personal observations on our present-day society and *Playboy*'s part in it."[155]

154   The first birth-control pills were developed in 1957 and licensed by the FDA in 1960; however, the America Medical Association did not recognize the legitimacy of any form of contraception until 1965, the year I graduated from college.
155   Quotations from Hugh Hefner are taken from Carrie Pitzulo, "The

The basic thesis was that people were sexual beings and that sexuality could be a positive aspect of one's life, if it was given free rein of expression. Instead society and religion tried to control sexuality by confining it to marriage, which clearly didn't work. Look at the ubiquitous practice of infidelity, often leading to divorce, he wrote. If instead social strictures against sexuality were removed, sexuality could be expressed and engaged in openly, and marriages could be built on love and mutual understanding, instead of possessiveness, suspicion, and jealousy.

I agreed. I had already come to understand sex as good, as a gift of God. What was bad were all the rules people claimed to believe in but didn't follow, like the rule that said people weren't supposed to have sex outside of marriage. I respected people who acted in accordance with their beliefs. Integrity has always been a high priority in my moral understanding. I could see from my own experience how easy it was to love more than one person at once, and I could see no reason to hold back that love. I became convinced it was unhealthy to do so and a waste of the God-given impulse and instruction to love one another.

Dave and I continued to date, and I often hung out at his apartment, even when he wasn't home. We agreed to have a nonexclusive relationship, and sometimes I dated his friends. I liked this arrangement.

SEX IN THE SEMINARY

When I got to seminary I felt like a liberated woman. Now that I was taking birth control pills I could engage in sexual relationships without fear of pregnancy, so there seemed to be no negative physical consequences for having sex.[156] The invention of the pill and its availability changed life for millions of women and ultimately for the whole culture.

My openness to sex, however, got me in trouble with the seminary president. After a couple of months, he took me aside

Playboy Philosophy Turns 40," *The Brooklyn Rail*, July-August 2005, www.brooklynrail.org/2005/07/express/the-playboy-philosophy-turns-40
156   AIDS and HIV were still fifteen years away.

and warned me that people were talking about my sexual liaisons. I was surprised, since the men involved asked me not to tell anyone. Although the president acknowledged that there was nothing wrong with sex, he asked me to keep my activities off campus.[157] I was disillusioned to realize that people at seminary were still operating according to old ways of hiding their true sexual natures and practices. What I was not aware of at the time, however, was that the seminary president was already in hot water for raising the subject of changing attitudes toward sex.

The year before I arrived, the students invited the president and two professors to speak at a forum to discuss changing views of premarital and extramarital sex, homosexuality, and obscenity. Earlier the president of the seminary had stated in his inaugural address:

> Penicillin and oral contraceptives are stripping us of the real sanctions that have always put order in our sexual ethics. Abruptly we are confronted with the fact that it was not so much the law of God or the love of Jesus that inhibited Christians as it was fear of pregnancy and communicable disease ... What might happen if energies and attentions and imaginations so long tied to knots in our minds could finally escape their ages-long captivity.[158]

An article in the seminary magazine[159] about the forum was picked up by the *Presbyterian Journal* and spread around the denomination as an "exposé," resulting in condemnation of the seminary by conservative Presbyterians and the withdrawal of much-needed financial support by some donors. The discussion of new morality had begun, though, and would continue to be debated for years to come. Then I arrived and put the new ideas into practice. No wonder people on campus were talking about me!

Once I realized how my actions were being perceived, I became uncomfortable with what felt to me like a serious lack of

---

157   For details about the conversation, see Hearing the Call, Losing My Religion.

158   Ted Gill, Inaugural Address, quoted in *Currents*, "Editorial: The Recurring Sex Theme," May 18, 1965.

159   Tom Towle, "Sex and Love," *Currents*, Sept. 24, 1964.

integrity at the seminary. From my perspective, I was acting in harmony with my beliefs. I believed in love, that our attractions were gifts leading us to make deep connections with each other. I believed the love we shared increased the amount of love in the world and was a good thing. Although I was unaware of the larger context and naïve about relationships and families, I was trying to be authentic in how I acted.

At that point, I backed off from relationships with students who might be married. I had already been enjoying my mealtime conversations with Thomas. I enjoyed his stories about life at Festival Theatre. Another seminary student, Kevin, was also interested in theater and began to hang out with us at meals. Kevin was tall and blond, and had the good looks of the quintessential surfer. We were all attracted to each other, and one night after dinner we ended up in the room where Thomas stayed when he was at the theater. We drank wine and all danced together. One thing led to another and with mutual attraction and alcohol leading the way, we ended up in bed together.

When we saw each other afterwards, we all grinned. We had done something perhaps only Thomas had ever heard of before— and we loved it. The three of us were now connected in a special way. We got together a few more times, but it was never quite as magical as the first. However, Thomas and I continued to develop our relationship.

LOVE AND OPEN MARRIAGE

When Thomas and I began our relationship, I was still only 21 and he was 28. I was intrigued with his sophistication and his life as an actor and artist. He had a unique face, partly because the lupus he contracted as a child had left his nose scarred. The fact that he had physical limitations because of the accompanying rheumatoid arthritis only added to his uniqueness. He made good use of his physical conditions in his work as a character actor.

Thomas introduced me to the world of theater and the arts in San Francisco. He also took me to gay bars and told me about his interest in men. I was fascinated to learn about this new life style

I had tried unsuccessfully to research for my social welfare class. Thomas had been married to women twice before but his attraction to men had caused conflict. I enjoyed the gay men I had met thus far, including several at Festival Theatre. I loved to dance and didn't mind an audience. The gay men cheered me on and I thrived on the attention, as did Thomas.

I was curious about lesbians. At the bars, the women usually sat off by themselves, huddled together in a corner or around one end of the bar. I thought they might be watching me, but they never said anything, which was fine with me since they kind of scared me. Most of them wore plaid flannel shirts and jeans while I tended to wear pretty dresses and high heels.

Thomas had a studio apartment in the North Point section of San Francisco near North Beach and Fisherman's Wharf. A large room with a bath, it was filled with amazing things, including some that were former or potential props for plays. But there were no kitchen facilities except a hot plate he wasn't supposed to have. After I moved out of the dorm and while I was waiting for my apartment in Marin City to be ready, I stayed with him off and on. When it was time to move in, Thomas loaned me a few pieces of furniture and helped with the move. By the time we finished it was late, so he spent the night and often stayed over after that, since he didn't have a car and depended on the bus to get around.

During the next few months, we spent a lot of time together, either at his place or mine. Gradually we brought more of his things to my place, since I had a full kitchen and a larger living space. When my mother announced she was coming to visit, we faced a dilemma. We could not tell her we were living together, since I was sure my parents would be horrified. Either we had to move his things out— or we could get married! It seemed like a crazy idea at first, but the more we thought about it the more sense it made. By then we were not only in love but also each other's best friend. We shared a similar life style and both believed in free love. We were intrigued with the idea of open marriage and agreed from the start that would be our way of being together. We felt a deep commitment to each other but no need to put limits on each other's activities, sexual or otherwise.

It was an ideal situation for me. I would have the respectability and security of being married, with none of the limitations. I had not expected to get married so young, but being in an open marriage wasn't like being married in the traditional sense, so it seemed like a perfect compromise. For Thomas, this was a chance to explore his homosexual side and still have a relationship with a woman he loved to come home to.

So, we announced we were engaged and picked a wedding date in March. Since this meant my mother had to prepare, she postponed her visit until after we were married. Problem solved.

A SIMPLE WEDDING

Although I didn't realize it at the time, my mother hired a wedding planner. We wanted a small family wedding at home, but my mother wanted to have a big reception, so she could invite our extended family, friends, and people we knew in Fullerton. We agreed, even though Thomas wouldn't know anyone. The wedding planner figured out how to set up the house for a large reception. This involved moving lots of furniture, decorating, arranging for food, and providing people to help with the reception.

We did not want a traditional invitation with the parents' names coming before our own, so Thomas designed a unique invitation and we had it printed by friends of ours. We chose a quotation from Kahlil Gibran's *The Prophet*: "And in the sweetness of friendship let there be laughter and sharing of pleasures." Below that the invitation stated when the wedding would take place and invited people to "share the pleasure" at an open house reception. My parents' names came at the end as hosts. The invitation was printed in dark green ink on tan card stock and had an earthy feeling. After the event, however, my mother had more traditional wedding announcements printed to send to other friends and family.

Rev. Bob McLaren officiated. He had become a minister at our local Presbyterian Church while I was in college, so I did not know him well. Before the ceremony, he met with us and asked us to take a personality inventory.[160] The results showed that we were

---

160   Johnson Temperament Analysis Profile, 1945 version.

very different. I scored high on "gay-hearted" and active, whereas Thomas was somewhat depressive and less active. I was much more cordial than he, and he was more sympathetic than I. I scored high on aggressive, but Thomas was clearly submissive. Bob pointed out that it would take a lot of love and understanding for our marriage to work. Ultimately these differences would matter, because I advocated for what I wanted and Thomas felt forced to acquiesce. But at the time, we were confident our love our love was stronger than our differences.

My high school friend, Janna, was my maid of honor. Thomas chose my brother, Howdy, as best man, because he would be the one person there Thomas knew. I wore a white silk boucle suit with a dark orange shell underneath. The brunch beforehand was hosted by Janna's mother and Mrs. Crutcher, mother of my childhood friend, Ann, who was unable to come. The guests stood or sat in a semicircle around us while Thomas and I exchanged traditional vows. Then more than a hundred additional guests arrived for the reception, bringing so many gifts we barely knew what to do with them all.

FREE LOVE AND OPEN MARRIAGE: IDEAL VERSUS REALITY

As our married life evolved, so did our experiences and ideas about free love and open marriage. Two books were key influences: Gavin Arthur's *Circle of Sex* and Robert Heinlein's novel *Stranger in a Strange Land*. Both had cult followings at the time.

Gavin Arthur, grandson of the twenty-first president and a popular figure in the Bay Area gay community, believed that birth control would free people from traditional sexual mores and enable them to express their true sexual natures. Kinsey had already shown that a large percentage of the population did not practice monogamy or exclusive hetero- or homosexuality. As an astrologer, Arthur put Kinsey's sexuality rating scale into a circle with twelve categories to describe a range of possible sexual orientations. He chose different figures from history and mythology to exemplify each of the twelve categories, bringing them to life in a unique way. We liked the idea that there were many ways to express one's sexuality and that all had positive role models. In describing the different ways of expressing sexuality, Arthur theorized that the lines between the categories were more fluid than the usual descriptions of gay, bisexual, and straight. This idea appealed to us because we saw the fluidity in our own experiences and we observed it in our friends.

To my surprise, the questionnaire in the book placed me as well as Thomas in the category ambigenic. Gavin preferred this term to bisexual for people attracted to both men and women, because he pointed out that the more common term incorrectly combines Greek and Anglo-Saxon roots. Answering the questions made me aware of my attraction to women and cut through my resistance. I wondered how and when I would have a chance to explore that attraction.

In 2012 the Library of Congress named Robert Heinlein's *Stranger in a Strange Land* one of the 88 "Books that Shaped America."[161] In the 1960s it was a cult classic that coined a new word, grok, now found in most major dictionaries. Grok can be defined simply as "to understand profoundly and intuitively,"[162] but in the novel, the meaning is more complex. A Martian word, grok means literally "to drink," and by extension "to be one with." To grok something indicates that it is now part of you and you have entered its spirit and worldview. As one of the characters explained: "Grok means to understand so thoroughly that the observer becomes a part of the observed—to merge, blend, intermarry, lose identity in group experience. It means almost everything that we mean by religion, philosophy, and science—and it means as little to us (because we are from Earth) as color means to a blind man."[163]

The novel challenged the sexual mores of the time and the narrowness of religion that sought to limit love. Thomas and I resonated with many of the book's ideas, particularly the notion of God as being in all people. "Thou are God," was how people in the book learned to greet each other when they became "water

161   "Library of Congress reveals the 88 books that shaped America," *Daily Mail Reporter*, July 17, 2012, www.dailymail.co.uk/news/article-2175188/The-Library-Congress-reveals-88-books-shaped-America.html
162   "Grok," Merriam-Webster online dictionary.
163   Robert Heinlein, *Stranger in a Strange Land*, 1961.

brothers." We liked the idea of "water brothers," which referred to both men and women with whom one was connected spiritually and sometimes sexually. (I was not yet aware of the problem with sexist language.) Although the story did not include same-gender sexual relations, we appreciated the way it acknowledged that one could love more than one person, justifying this love through theological reasoning based on key tenets from world religions.

Reading this book added to our consciousness of what we were doing and became part of our vocabulary and lifestyle. We often felt like strangers in a strange land, because the way we were choosing to live and be in relationship was different from most other people. Although the book was clearly sexist when judged from today's perspectives, at the time I appreciated the strong, dynamic women characters and the central roles they played in the story, not generally the case in the fiction of the time.

Although we became increasingly committed to the ideas of free love and open marriage, we engaged in relationships with others primarily when the opportunity happened to cross our paths and a strong attraction was present. Sometimes, however, we chose to be in situations where this was likely to happen.

Thomas's extramarital activities usually involved going to gay bars or gay baths. San Francisco was noted for its bathhouses where gay men could meet each other and engage in relatively anonymous sex in private rooms.[164] Thomas's bisexuality expressed itself in his periodic need for male bonding and sexuality. He preferred the baths, since they seemed easier, safer, and more directly in line with his needs.

My open marriage activities were occasional encounters with someone I met socially when Thomas was elsewhere. We agreed that if either of us was going to be away for the night, we would call the other to say where we were and when we would be home. I especially enjoyed the moment when I would call my husband to tell him, with the guy standing by terrified that he would come after them. I had to laugh, because Thomas wasn't about to get into a fight with anyone,

---

164   Allan Berube, "The History of Gay Bathhouses," *Journal of Homosexuality* 44: 3, 33-53 (2003).

especially not the bigger and stronger men I was often attracted to. Afterwards I would tell him about my encounters. Full disclosure was an important aspect of our open marriage agreement and often led to great sex.

I often wished there were a place I could go like Thomas's gay bars and baths, because if I didn't have some other activity planned or someone I wanted to be with, his leaving was difficult for me. One time I followed him to the bus station and sat in my car crying because he was leaving me alone, even though I knew it was just for one night. Feelings of jealousy and abandonment arose in me from old programming. Intellectually I knew being alone for the evening was a small price to pay for the freedom I enjoyed and the energetic sex we would have when he came back, full of male energy that seemed to be recharged by his encounters with men. But I was not in full control of my emotions.

After I became a teacher in 1968, my opportunities for interesting sexual encounters increased when I began attending teachers' conferences. I found myself especially attracted to men who were organizational leaders or conference speakers and wished I could get to know them better. I discovered I could choose someone I wanted to get together with and attract him to me. I learned a great deal from making love with these men with these men. After sex, I could ask them anything I might be wondering about their work and how they got their ideas. I discovered that even supposedly great teachers had their doubts and struggles as well as often unexpressed hopes and dreams.

Because I connected in this way with several of the organizational leaders, they allowed me to participate in late night "bull sessions" in hotel rooms where they planned strategy for implementing their ideas in the meetings that were part of the conferences. What I learned about running organizations from these men helped me develop my own leadership abilities.

Although this was personally gratifying for me, I realize now how self-centered I was in my approach to free love. I focused on the mutual attraction with my partners, but I failed to understand or care about the impact my relationships with other men might have on their marriages or how it might affect the larger community. I knew Thomas was fine with what I was doing, and I figured what my partner was doing was his responsibility. However, several uncomfortable situations forced me to consider the wives' point of view. One time I met a man's wife when she came to pick him up from a flight home from a conference. We hadn't made love, but sitting together on the plane we played with each other's' hands in a sexually arousing way. I was still aroused when we got off the plane and he introduced me to his wife. I suspected she could tell that something had been going on between us. Another time I shared a hotel room with a man I worked with locally and was not involved with sexually. His wife didn't like me, though, because she could tell he was attracted to me. These encounters made me uncomfortable and should have, perhaps, been indications that there was something off about my approach. For the most part, though, I ignored the signals and went right on as I had before, firm in the belief that what I was doing was right and moral, based on principles of free love and open marriage.

Our approach to open marriage worked well, at least for the first few years. Although Thomas's sexuality with me seemed to go in cycles, when we made love he was always sensitive and considerate. He introduced me to my clitoris and tried to make sure I felt as satisfied as he did. There were times I wished we could make love when he wasn't interested, but overall our sexual relationship was satisfying. We enjoyed our open life-style almost all the time. Our friends loved hearing about our arrangement and admired us as one of the most stable and loving couples they knew. As an attractive, sexually active woman in my twenties, this arrangement was indeed the best of all possible worlds for me.

MY FIRST TRIP, 1968

In early September 1968, Thomas and I were still living in our apartment in San Anselmo and I was just about to start teaching, when my brother Howdy invited us to go with him to the Renaissance Faire. Our friends had been talking about this unique festival for the past few weeks and we were excited to participate. When Howdy and his girlfriend arrived at our apartment, however, something extra was added to the plans for the day.

Howdy announced he had a surprise for us. He opened a small leather pouch and took out some tiny blue pills.

"Do you know what these are?" he asked, and after a pause added, "LSD."

"We've heard of it," I said, "but haven't really thought about taking it."

"I brought some for you," he said. My brother, who lived in Berkeley in the middle of the hippie and student protest culture, knew about all the latest cultural innovations.

"You don't have to do it, of course, but it might be fun. Anyway, we're going to take some now and get ready to experience the Faire in a special way," he said as he put the tiny pill in his mouth and swallowed.

Thomas and I looked at each other. We had already tried marijuana and enjoyed the way it made us feel, so why not try LSD? In unison, we reached out and took the pills.

"Let's go!" Howdy said, and we piled into his car and drove to the Faire. We were starting to feel the effects as we arrived at the gate, fumbled a bit getting our tickets, and walked merrily into a wonderful new world.

The Faire was a magical place whether you were on drugs or not. So much to see! An entire village had sprung up in the woods, small wood enclosures or brightly colored tents serving as shops, costumed musicians wandering through the crowds playing medieval music, magicians and mimes gathering small audiences as they perform spontaneous acts, food vendors hawking their wares, in the distance a small stage with actors performing a scene, dancers weaving through the crowds as they sing merry tunes from long ago. It was like being on the set of an historical movie as part of the scene, not knowing exactly what to do but getting caught up in the spirit and finding ways to participate. Everyone was smiling and swirling around. It was hard to tell how much was the drug and how much was real.

I lost track of the others, but everyone else was so friendly I felt safe and surrounded by love. I was drawn to the crafts and could spend what seemed like hours looking at a single glass jar, or a necklace, or a painted wood panel. After a while I noticed a row of portable toilets and realized I needed to use one. I was sitting inside when someone knocked on the door. It was such an amazing sound that I sat there listening to the reverberations. Then I heard someone yell, "Is anyone in there? Are you OK?" I mumbled something and got out as quickly as I could. When I stepped into the bright sunlight, all I could do was smile. The woman waiting smiled back, perhaps knowing.

I didn't get very far before I realized I felt unstable on my feet, so I sat down by a small bridge built over a shallow ravine, where I could watch what was going on around me. Everyone who came by smiled and some said hello. Something about this environment made people happy and friendly. I felt at home in this world in ways I didn't usually feel in other places, at peace with myself and at one with my surroundings. I could stay this way forever, I thought to myself. I didn't ever want to leave.

An interesting looking young man in a leather shirt came across the bridge and seeing me said hello. I wasn't into talking so I just smiled at him. He said, "I've been where you are," and sat down beside me, smiling too. We sat there looking deeply into each other's eyes and smiling. Then he got up, reached for my hand, "Come, I want to show you something." He took me to the booth he shared with his partner Kie, introduced us, and showed me their leather work. She offered me a glass of water and a place to sit, which I greatly appreciated. I enjoyed watching as they interacted with people looking at and buying their belts and bags and other wares.

I was spacing out in fantasies of living in a place like this when I heard a familiar voice. Thomas was negotiating with David to buy a hanging candle holder. I got up, went over to them, and gave Thomas a big hug. "I knew I'd find you someplace!" he said. "Let's look for Howdy."

I thanked David and Kie for taking care of me. They laughed and said in unison, "Anytime!" Then David said, "If you want to stay after the Faire closes, you're welcome to spend the night in our booth. It gets pretty interesting around here when it's just the Faire folks." I hurried off to catch up with Thomas, but the idea had been planted in my mind. Later in the day when it was time to leave, I told Thomas about David's invitation to stay. He said it was OK and left with Howdy and Sue.

When they got home, they were still high on acid, so they decided to hang out and listen to a new record we had just bought, Jefferson Airplane's *Crown of Creation*. What happened next is one of those uncanny instances of synchronicity that seemed to happen frequently with LSD.

The phone rang just after Thomas heard these words in the song that was playing: "Your mother's ghost stands at your shoulder. Got a face like ice—just a little colder. Saying to you, you cannot do that it breaks all the rules."

It was my mother! Thomas stumbled through a greeting and managed to make up something about why I wasn't there. Then he handed the phone to Howdy and said, "Here, you talk to her."

After Howdy got off the phone, Thomas said, "We've got to play that weird song again." The song was "Triad," by David Crosby. His own group at the time, The Byrds, had rejected the song for release as being too risqué. The song tells of a person in love with two others and asks, "why can't we go on as three?"

You know we love each other it's plain to see
There's just one answer comes to me
Sister lovers—water brothers
And in time maybe others
So you see what we can do
Is to try something new—that is if you're crazy too
But I don't really see, why can't we go on as three

While this was happening, David and I were roaming around the Faire. The same place that had been filled with hundreds of people hours earlier had become a community of craftspeople and performers, sharing stories of the day, eating soup they shared with those who passed by, and making music, not as a performance but for themselves. It was magical, like a village from medieval or Renaissance times. I felt privileged to be invited to be there.

Kie indicated that she was going to bed early and seemed fine with whatever David and I did. The magic and the music continued late into the night. When it came time to sleep, David shared his sleeping bag with me. I felt good knowing that Kie knew what was going on and apparently approved.

MÉNAGE A TROIS AND GROUP SEX

The next week David dropped by our apartment at dinnertime and we had a chance to live out the story in the song "Triad." Thomas was uncomfortable at first, since he rarely had to face men I had slept with, but David's open friendliness and excellent pot helped break the ice. We ate dinner, drank wine, and sat around with brandy and smoke talking about the Renaissance Faire, comparing theater and crafts, and dreaming about possible futures.

Eventually all three of us ended up in bed together. Like our ménage a trois partner in seminary, David thought of himself as fully heterosexual, and yet when we were all together and Thomas touched him, he responded. Sex was sex and bodies were bodies. Discovering he could be turned on by a man as well as a woman was a revelatory experience for David. We grew close all three of us, the bond of pleasure uniting us.

But I was worried about Kie. David assured us she was fine with our relationship, but I wasn't convinced. The next weekend we drove into San Francisco and visited them at their leather shop in the Haight-Ashbury, the center of hippie life in 1968. The shop was their Faire booth writ large. One of the first things I noticed was a sign they had made, "Work is Love Made Visible," a quotation from Kahlil Gibran's *The Prophet*. I could feel the love that went into their work and permeated their space and wondered what it would be like to be able to see my work as an expression of love. I spent time with Kie, getting to know her and learning about her part of the business. I bought one of her beautiful carved leather hair pieces, perfect for my hair which I was letting grow long. She seemed just as happy to see us as David was, no trace of jealousy or suspicion, even when David's visit to us was mentioned. "Next year you'll have to come to the Faire again," Kie offered. "You can both stay with us and help in the booth."

We were hooked, both by the Faire and by this openly loving couple. We spent many hours together both between the Faires and during them. When it came time for bed, David usually slept with us and Kie slept alone, assuring us that was what she wanted. Their invitation to us to join them at the Faire led in a couple of years to Thomas's decision to become a weaver and have a booth of his own.

With two positive experiences with group sex it seemed natural to seek more. We became aware of couples who got together to swap partners and invited one of them over. The evening felt awkward from the beginning, knowing we were meeting to have sex rather than as friends with other common interests. In the previous situations sex evolved out of our interactions with each other, but this time our interactions were merely a prelude to sex. In a strange accident of timing, my college friend Tanni was there too. I was more interested in talking to her than getting to know the couple we were entertaining. When it came time to go to bed, I tried to get Tanni to join us, but she was not interested. Thomas wasn't interested either. We learned that this sort of planned sex would not work for us, and we never tried it again. Nor did we ever go to sex parties, common at the time, where couples switched partners sometimes on a random basis.

The threesome became our ideal group arrangement. Thomas wasn't interested in other women but he loved demonstrating to straight men that they could respond sexually to him as well as to me. Here and there throughout the rest of our married life a few occasions presented themselves, but none were as successful as our first two. I, however, had more opportunities, several times with two men and once with a man and a woman.

MOVING TO THE COUNTRY, 1970

By 1970 life in San Francisco was beginning to unravel for many people we knew. The Haight-Ashbury was being flooded with hard drugs like speed and heroin. Those who were not caught up by this began to look for ways to continue their peaceful, loving lives in the country. Some talked about buying land in remote rural areas and creating self-supporting communities. Although we lived a half hour north of the city in a more suburban area, Thomas and I decided to look for a house near where I was teaching in Sonoma County, another half hour north and definitely more country than where we lived in Marin County.

Moving to Cotati meant Thomas was now further away from San Francisco and the urban life he had been living before we got together. His work at the theater had ended and his job as a printer at the Marin County Civic Center was less than satisfying. For me the move meant being closer to my work. We used money he had inherited from his family for the down payment on a two-story farmhouse on three acres of land in Cotati, about an hour north of San Francisco. Although the property backed up to Highway 101, which meant we could hear trucks and cars going by, it was a beautiful place with an established rose garden, apple and plum trees, and a 100-foot tall redwood tree, plus a barn/garage and another small building, unfinished on the inside. A row of eucalyptus trees separated the property from the cow field next door, and a seasonal creek ran across the east side. We decided to call our new home "The Fertile Delta," inspired by a song by Leon Russell.[165]

Naming our place is an example of how music was woven into our lives. We played Leon's song, "Delta Lady," when we first moved. The song highlights the contrast between the "dirty" city with "concrete mountains" and the "soft and fertile" country, using female images to represent the contrast. The imagery combined our appreciation of sexuality with our hopes for our new venture in country living.

Woman of the country now I've found you
Longing in your soft and fertile delta
And I whisper sighs to satisfy your longing
For the warmth and tender shelter of my body

Living in the country changed both our individual lives and our relationship. The school[166] where I taught was only a mile from

---

165   The song, "Delta Lady," was written by Leon Russell and recorded on his 1970 solo album. The first hit recording of the song was by Joe Cocker in 1969.
166   More about the school and my approach to teaching in Education =

our house. Instead Thomas had to commute to Marin where he continued to work part-time as a printer. Inspired by the Renaissance Faire, his dream was to become a craftsperson. He had majored in art in college and while his life until then had been focused on theater, which he also loved, it was time to make a change. I supported him fully in this. We had both fallen in love with the Faire, which we expected to be a primary outlet for his work.

After trying several other crafts, he settled on weaving, bought a loom, set it up in the dining room, and began producing cloth in a variety of traditional patterns. He made beautiful wall hangings, pillow covers, shawls, vests, and bags. His unique sense of color enabled him to create a modern look using traditional patterns. I was in awe of his ability. I had fallen in love with him as an actor, but now I had a new man to admire as an artist. Initially this gave new life to our relationship.

The early 1970s were exciting years, as ideas from the 1960s began to be applied to new settings. We were conscious of our participation in a continually evolving alternative culture. Despite emerging conflicts between us, Thomas and I were still each other's best friend. We loved many of the same things and could talk for hours about experiences, ideas, and possibilities. We attended many concerts—both rock and classical, as well plays, movies, dance performances, and art shows. Our house became a gathering place, where people just showed up, having heard about us from mutual friends. We often had guests who "crashed" at our place, staying for a night or longer. We generally welcomed them and valued the opportunity to share our lives. People called our house a "happening place."

We decided to fix up the small building on our property as a studio for Thomas's weaving and a place where guests could stay. With the help of friends, including several of my students, we put up sheetrock, built a sleeping loft, and installed a wood-burning stove. One of my students brought us a phone he had acquired and hooked up an "unofficial" phone line.[167] The fact that there was no

---

Change.

167   In those days, phones were sold and installed by the phone company.

running water or bathroom in the "little house," as we called it, didn't bother us. We could pee outside or go down to the main house to use the bathroom. However, before Thomas had time to set up his studio, Jack, a bass player in a band called Horsefeathers, showed up needing a place to stay because he had just separated from his wife. He became our little house's first resident.

Jack and Thomas became good friends and this helped Thomas feel less isolated. He had known in advance that moving so far from San Francisco would cut him off from much of his previous life, but as the reality of it set in he became increasingly dissatisfied. He clearly had the talent and skill to be a successful weaver, but he struggled to maintain the motivation and physical energy required to produce enough products to build a successful business. He also lacked his past opportunities for easy sexual connections with men, unless he drove over an hour to get to the city.

At the same time, I became more involved in teaching. When we moved on Thanksgiving weekend 1970, I had just launched my first Experimental English and Social Studies class. Over time a few students became friends and came to our house to work on projects or just to talk about what was going on in their lives. The following year I held evening classes once a week at the house for students from the first and second experimental classes. Although Thomas tried to be polite, I could see that the presence of the students disturbed him. He considered it an invasion of his privacy, while I defended my right to choose how I would use our shared house.

All this put stress on our relationship and we found ourselves arguing frequently, picking on each other about minor irritations which began to significantly affect our ability to be together in loving ways.

EXPLORING LOVE WITH WOMEN

When I came out as a lesbian in the early 1980s, I wondered about earlier experiences with women that might have been precursors to the lifestyle I would eventually embrace. With greater awareness of same-gender attractions, I remembered several incidents. At slumber parties when I was in junior high, my girlfriends and I would "practice" kissing with each other. Later, when a girl in high school wanted to snuggle in bed, it confused me and made me feel uncomfortable. But the most confusing to me was in college, when an older girl befriended me.

Joan was the teaching assistant for my Introduction to Music study group freshman year. One day she invited me to her tower room in Mudd-Blaisdell, a dorm where older students lived. There were only three tower rooms and they were highly prized. Her room was different from any other dorm room, with its exotic pictures and colorful fabric draping the walls. We sat on her bed and she lit incense, something I had not previously experienced. She asked my birthday and seemed pleased to discover I was a Scorpio. I wasn't sure what that meant.

Joan's brother was my favorite English professor. She invited me to come with her to babysit for his kids. I loved their house up in the hills with its Spanish-American style furnishings, including a massive library table in their dining room. Since it was getting late, she suggested we go to bed until the parents got home. I thought this was strange but went along with the idea. We were just getting comfortable when they drove up. I wonder what would have happened if they had come home later. When she took me back to the dorm, she kissed me on the mouth and I responded. Then I blushed and ran inside. When I got back to our room, I told my roommate, "She kissed me like a boy!"

After college, my primary attractions and relationships were with men. Men were the interesting ones, with ideas and plans. Most women I met seemed pale by comparison. Often when we had group dinners, I would be in the living room with the men smoking pot and envisioning alternative futures, while the rest of the women were in the kitchen talking about food and babies (or so I assumed). The first time I experienced a strong attraction to a woman it took me by surprise. Our friends Danny and Karen, artists and dancers who lived in San Francisco, had come to Cotati to go with us to our favorite local music venue, the Inn of the Beginning. They brought some pills they described as "horse tranquilizers." What the heck, we thought, and took them.

The group featured that night was one of our favorites, Joy of Cooking, with two female singers, Terry Garthwaite and Toni Brown. As they sang, "Sometimes like a river you touch my life and I can feel you flowing down into my soul," Karen and I looked at each other and smiled—and couldn't stop smiling as we connected first with our eyes and then with our hands. The drug wasn't like the mind-altering ones we were used to, but instead produced a body high, opening me up to a physical attraction I might have otherwise ignored or resisted.

A few weeks later, Karen invited me to come with her to a performance art experience she and her friends were doing at the park near Coit Tower, atop Telegraph Hill in San Francisco. The two-hundred-foot tall concrete tower with its panoramic view of the city and surrounding water is a favorite sight-seeing location, but I had never been there before.

The view was spectacular! Surrounded by lush vegetation and kissed by fresh ocean breezes, we could see the sparkling lights of San Francisco spread out below. All kinds of people, dressed in a wild array of colors and costumes, were in the park that evening. When the dance began, everyone was invited to participate, even tourists and those who came to watch the dance. We began slowly following the leaders, weaving in lines amongst each other, then dancing faster and faster as the drums increased in intensity. It was exhilarating and new. I loved being part of the whole scene.

After this inspiring and exciting evening, Karen and I went back to her place and got in bed. We kissed but the passion we had felt earlier didn't come.

"What do we do now?" Karen asked.

"I'm not sure," I answered.

Neither of us had been with a woman before and we didn't know what to do. We laughed at ourselves, cuddled, and fell asleep. The next day I shared what had happened with Thomas. His wise observation was "When it's the right time and the right person, you will know what to do."

That right time was in the summer of 1971 at a weekend class called American Writers and the Environmental Crisis in

Mendocino, a small art town on the ocean. I was attracted to the class both because of the location and the subject matter. I drove our VW van north for two hours up Highway 101 and then another hour down a winding road out to the coast. The long drive by myself gave me a lot of time to think about where I was in my life. I knew things were not going well with Thomas and I wondered what the future might bring.

As soon as I saw the professor, I felt attracted and wondered if he would make love with me. The only problem was Lisa, another woman in the class who had the same idea. It seemed silly to compete, so Lisa and I joined forces. After class one day, we planned to invite the professor to go to a nearby beach with us for dinner. We divided up responsibilities. I got the food, and she succeeded in getting him to go with us. The rest was easy and later that night all three us ended up in the bed in the back of my van. Finally, I had the opportunity to discover what Thomas had helped our male partners learn. Indeed, I was as turned on by her touch as by his.

A NEW FRIENDSHIP

I met Ruth Miller at Sonoma State College.[168] It had been a long time since I had a close woman friend, which is what she soon became. Ruth had an amazing mind and an even more amazing ability to connect people and ideas. Her study of biorhythms brought her into contact with others who were studying cycles, symbols, ancient wisdom and healing systems, and psychic phenomena. She saw connections in these diverse systems and encouraged cross fertilization among people who were exploring them. I loved hanging out with her and sharing ideas with others who were attracted to her energy.

When we weren't together, Ruth would often call me up and talk at length on the phone. We were both having adventures with different men, and we shared our hopes and frustrations along the

---

168   Sonoma State College, located in Rohnert Park, was renamed California State College at Sonoma, referring to the county not the city where it was located. Later it became Sonoma State University. I refer to it by its original name, Sonoma State College.

way. Sometimes she would call up with a last-minute invitation to meet someone, go out to eat, or hear music. I tried to never say no, because I knew whatever she wanted to do would be interesting.

Ruth's house in Santa Rosa was a popular gathering place. I never knew whom I might meet there or whether it would just be Ruth and me—and her six kids! The adults sat around the dining room table, drinking tea and smoking cigarettes, often with one or more of the kids playing underneath the table. Ruth didn't try to keep her children away from the adults. If they had questions or needed something, she took care of it right away, rarely missing any of the conversation. When it was bedtime, they often slept in sleeping bags under or near the table. I admired her easy, comfortable way with her children, a new model for me of parenting.

We grew close as we shared adventures and worked together on projects. At one point when we were both without any potential relationships with men, I took a daring step. I declared my desire to make love with her. I wasn't so much in love with her physically as I was emotionally, and I thought the idea of our being together might appeal to her. It didn't, and my request ultimately drove a wedge between us, although we continued to be friends and work together.[169]

I felt like a failure as a lesbian and didn't seek any other opportunities to explore my emerging interest in women. Perhaps if I had looked further and found someone I might have come out much sooner, but life had other things in store for me first and it would be nearly another decade before I finally and happily came out. In the meantime, my sexual fantasies became increasingly focused on women.

THE DREAM IS OVER

In 1970 the Beatles broke up. It took Thomas and me several more years before we admitted to ourselves and each other that we were moving in different directions and needed to separate. The change in our relationship didn't happen all at once and even in retrospect it is difficult to pinpoint exact causes. Changing desires

---

169   See more about Ruth in Culture Change, Synthesis.

and needs related to love and sexuality were part of it. Other factors were work and finances.

Being in Cotati only a mile from the school where I taught in Rohnert Park meant that I sometimes came home for lunch or if I needed to get something. Some version of the following scene occurred more than once. I would come home and discover Thomas at the dining room table drinking his morning coffee at noon and reading the newspaper.

"Are you just getting up?" I asked in an accusing voice. "I've been up for hours and worked hard today. How come you get to laze around like it's your day off?"

Thomas sighed. "I need to ease into the day and give myself time to get the creative juices going."

"Well, maybe if you got up earlier your juices would be flowing by now!" I said sarcastically.

I tried to be patient, but this difference in our work styles ate into our relationship. I knew nagging didn't work, but it was hard for me not to feel resentment when I was working so hard and providing most of our money. He also nagged me when I didn't do something he wanted me to, like cook dinner. Rather than defend my right to pursue whatever I was doing, my response was to feel guilty, apologize, and then feel bad about myself.

It was 1972 before Thomas was ready with enough products to have his own booth at the Renaissance Faire. By then he was no longer working as a printer, so our financial stability depended on how well he did at the Faire. Our relationship was already coming apart, but we were still living in the same house and operating as a family unit. That spring, however, we had decided to try a partial separation. We moved our king-sized water bed into the living room and made that my space and he moved out to the little house. I invited several people I knew to move into the empty rooms upstairs to help with expenses.

In the summer, while Thomas was making final preparations for the Faire in September, Jack invited me to go with him in his van on a trip to southern California. He had been more Thomas's friend than mine, so I was surprised at the invitation, but I figured with me gone Thomas would be better able to focus on his work, so I said yes. Besides I almost always enjoyed trips—of all kinds.

The trip got me thinking in new ways about relationships. We stayed with several couples who had very close, loving relationships. One couple in particular impressed me. Adam and Beth were living in Newport Beach, working on boats. My brother Howdy and Adam were childhood friends. Earlier, when they shared a house in Berkeley, Adam and I made love one night. That gave me a special feeling for him and I was impressed by his present commitment to his wife.

It looked like a great day for sailing so they invited us to come with them on their sail boat, and we headed out into the Pacific Ocean. Adam and Beth were excellent sailors and we all had a wonderful time talking, swimming off the side of the boat, and lying in the sun on the broad shiny wood bow of the boat. But part way back, the wind died. Adam skillfully maneuvered the boat back and forth down the long bay to their berth, trying to catch enough wind to get us home, but no luck. As dusk fell they decided to dock until the next morning and spend the night on the boat. That night under the moonlit sky on a boat gently rocking in the water, new questions formed in my mind and new dreams emerged in my heart. I imagined being with someone I loved so much I never wanted be with anyone else. I could feel that kind of love between Adam and Beth and wanted to feel that way myself. Could Thomas and I ever have that kind of relationship?

The next morning Adam and Beth talked about having children someday. Thomas and I shared a fantasy of adopting children of different colors and nationalities, but we both knew he wasn't cut out to be a father. Would I be missing something if I never had a child? At age 28 my biological clock was ticking, although I didn't think of it that way. A few years earlier, I argued with one of my professors at Dominican College[170] about whether women needed to have children to be completely fulfilled as women. I still believed the answer was a resounding no, but what about my own life? Did I ever

---

170   I attended Dominican College in San Rafael, CA, in 1967-68, to earn my teaching credential.

want to be a mother? I wasn't sure, but I was beginning to desire a closer, perhaps even monogamous relationship with Thomas. Was that even possible given that we had already partially separated?

I was anxious to get home and share my new insights and ideas with Thomas, hoping maybe we could get back together, but when I arrived I discovered that while I was away he became involved with a beautiful young man, James. Up until then, our liaisons with others were secondary to our primary relationship. Beginning to separate meant that principle no longer held. It hurt to see him in love with someone else, and I didn't handle it very well. "What horrible timing!" I thought. "If only I had come to this realization earlier. Would it have made any difference?"

I pitched in to help prepare for the Faire and had plenty of work of my own to get ready for the beginning of another school year. There were strained conversations with Thomas, but for the most part, I tried to put my feelings aside and deal with the tasks at hand. That fall I would be at a new junior-senior high school and was excited about the opportunity to work with older students.

Over the next year it became increasingly clear Thomas and I would not be getting back together. There were moments when we communicated and shared the love we still felt for each other, but more often than not we fought. I had hoped the people I invited to live in our house to help with expenses would come together as a supportive community, but I failed to articulate my vision when I offered to rent rooms to them. Although occasionally we connected in meaningful ways, for the most part having additional people in the house just added to the confusion. To complicate things further, I was hosting meetings at the house of a new group working on a self-directed master's program.[171]

Later Thomas asked me to move to the little house so he could move back into the bedroom upstairs. Changing spaces helped for a while, but we realized the dream was over. Our final break came in April 1973. That same day I bought a plane ticket for Europe for

---

171   The Humanistic Psychology Institute was an independent program housed at Sonoma State with support from many of the professors in the psychology department. HPI sponsors the master's program.

the summer and agreed to move to an apartment in town when I got back. Because we owned the house together, we did not think we could get divorced.

Living in an apartment in town allowed our friendship to continue. Now and then we felt flashes of the old love we had felt for each other, but these never lasted long. In May 1974, Thomas directed *Tale for a Deaf Ear,* for the College of Marin Opera Workshop. We both knew this one-act opera from its Festival Theatre performance years earlier. I loved the chorus and remember the words still:

A seed may fall on stone, but the winds will come
And gently move it where the earth is warm
Though seeming death may cloud the sky above
The only death in life is the death of love.[172]

When I went to see the performance, I cried and cried. Could our love be dying?

Periodically we reconnected but our timing was invariably off. Finally, we had to admit it was time to formally separate. By then we had learned that unmarried individuals could own a house together and that no-fault divorce had been possible in California since 1970. The process of dividing our resources, deciding who would keep which things, and filling out the papers we needed to file was mostly amicable. Friends came with us the day we took the papers to the courthouse and we shared a champagne toast, offering some to the clerks, too.

Over the years we stayed in touch and I occasionally visited him when I was in Sonoma County, where he still lives. But writing this book has caused what may be an irreconcilable split, because he objects to my sharing intimate details about our lives. I have tried to be kind and fair as I wrote about our life together, but he has refused to read any of it or even to speak with me for the past several years. However, I still refuse to admit that the love between us is dead.

SOMEDAY MY PRINCE WILL COME

To better understand what was happening in my life, I began

---

172   *Tale for a Deaf Ear,* music by Mark Bucci, based on a short story by Elizabeth Enright, performed at the College of Marin, May 23-26, 1974.

writing down my thoughts and feelings, but I didn't begin a formal journal until 1972. Writing helped me sort out what was going on and find my own voice. Writing about my inner life instead of sharing everything with Thomas helped me separate myself from him emotionally.

As the reality that my marriage was ending sank in, I learned how one life change leads to another. Without the protection of a primary relationship, my practice of free love changed. I no longer enjoyed spontaneous liaisons as I had in the past, because I kept hoping that this time making love would lead to a long-term relationship. I lost the ability to be present in the moment of connection and instead kept getting attached to the outcome. This raised the stakes and my search for love took on a desperate quality. Earlier in my life, relationships came to me relatively easily, but now that I was actively looking for a new life partner, it was harder than I ever imagined it would be. I could still attract men, but I had difficulty discerning who was seriously interested in a relationship with me and who was only looking for sex.

My journals are full of hope and possibility when I met someone new. I tended to fall in love easily and pour everything into the new person I met. I went on for pages describing what a perfect person he was and how wonderful our life together would be. Then reality set in, my hopes were dashed, and I was miserable. I seemed to have an uncanny ability to choose men who were already committed to someone else, or who turned out to be emotionally unavailable in other ways. Was this karmic payback for my earlier involvement with married men? I think about this now but at the time my primary feelings were disappointment and loss. At least I had my journal to comfort me, if only as a place where I could spill out my emotions.

As my frustration grew, there were times when I settled for sex without love, justifying it to myself by saying, "I seem to need that kind of relationship. Sex is a part of life's energy forces. I skipped around today full of new vitality." This seemed more like the old-style sex game, not our idealized free love. I consoled myself with the thought that this was different because a woman was initiating the game, not a man.

Through all the highs and lows of seeking love I held on to the faith that if I kept love as my primary guide I would find the love I needed. When I was ready for a new relationship, I believed the right person would appear. In the meantime, I felt like a silly teenager dreaming of the day my prince (or princess) would come. I even found myself singing an old song from my childhood:

Someday my prince will come, someday I'll find my love

And how thrilling that moment will be

When the prince of my dreams comes to me.[173]

LOVE AND SEX IN EUROPE, 1973

When summer came, I made my second trip to Europe. I was ready for adventure and decided to hitchhike as my primary mode of transportation. I discounted the potential risk involved because I needed to keep expenses to a minimum. Plus, I felt like putting myself out on the edge and seeing what would happen. This was the last summer of my twenties. In November I would turn 30, the age above which some said one could no longer to be trusted.[174]

I recalled my experiences in Germany in 1963. Those four months changed me in significant ways, and I was ready for another big change. I didn't necessarily expect to fall deeply in love the way I did the first time, but I was open to whatever came my way. I brought with me addresses of several people I hoped to visit and arranged to attend the Montreux Jazz Festival, but other than that I didn't have an agenda. My plan was to go back to Marburg, Germany, and visit the other German-speaking countries in Europe, Switzerland and Austria, but the cheapest ticket I could find was on Sabena Airlines, flying into Belgium.

My adventure began on the way to the San Francisco airport, when my friend's car broke down on the freeway. Fortunately, we were close to the heliport in Sausalito. While I was waiting for my

---

173   Words and music by Larry Morey and Frank Churchill, from the 1937 animated movie *Snow White and the Seven Dwarfs*.

174   One account of the origin of the phrase is given in "Don't trust anyone over 30, unless it's Jack Weinberg," *Berkeley Daily Planet*, April 06, 2000.

first ride in a helicopter, I started my travel journal by reflecting on the ending of my relationship with Thomas. "I know that I am separate from the reality we once had together. I know I have much to learn about my own reality. This trip is an attempt to uncover the lost regions of my soul and to develop the reality that is individual to me."[175]

Then, on the flight to New York, I discovered an intriguing observation in the in-flight magazine: "Change hurts us into art. Because we dread to lose what must be lost, we stuff novels and poems with loved places, people, unforgettable days."[176] Maybe that's why I felt it was important to record my observations and feelings in my journal. I hoped perhaps the changes I was in the midst of would lead to something worthwhile. I reflected: "I have left behind the life I once knew. Accepting the future without fear is a bit beyond my grasp as yet. I still worry about what I will encounter when I return, but for now I am on my way—wondering what I will find."

When I got to New York I learned the flight to Europe was delayed for several hours. Never good at waiting, I wandered around the airport, checked in the bookstore, and discovered the *Underground Travel Guide*. Then I looked around to see if there were any interesting men I could meet. By the time the flight left, I had hooked up with Tom, whom I described as "tall, ruffled, curly hair, dark, slightly babyish face, casual clothes, jeans worn in all the right places—a rather striking figure for sure—soft spoken, gentle, friendly, and a little shy." I reflected later that "I could have been reading, writing in my journal, or even sleeping—but turning on to a man is much more enjoyable! I wonder about myself sometimes! This is one of the things I'm trying to learn on this trip—to be self-sufficient and not need a man—so how am I starting? Falling into the same pattern I have always chosen!"

When we got on the crowded plane, Tom asked if it were possible for us to sit together. The stewardess announced that we were engaged and people were happy to change seats for us. When

---

175   This and other quotations in this section are from my 1973 Journal. Some quotations are translated from German.

176   *American Way*, June 1973.

we arrived in Brussels, we used my new travel guide to find a centrally located hotel, in Rue de Marche, and discovered we could share a room since we were both over 21. After Tom showed me some of the city's sites, we parted ways the next day and I hitchhiked to Cologne, a city I had wanted to visit but missed on my previous trip.

Since I was starting late in the day, I only made it to Liege the first night, got a room by myself, and slept for 12 hours. So far, so good, I thought. The next day I got a ride with a German couple, who took me to lunch and to *Phantasialand*, a theme park like Disneyland only based on German fairy-tale characters. I was struck with the similarities and differences between cultures, something I noticed throughout the trip. The couple drove me to Cologne and located a hotel for me. When I found out how much it cost, I decided not to stay there and went looking for another room, but the next place was even more expensive.

While I was standing on the street wondering what to do, a man came up to me and offered me a free room, I asked what he wanted in exchange and he assured me he wanted nothing. I doubted that was true but was curious as to what would happen, so I went with him. As soon as we got to the room, he tried to overpower me. When I said no, he left, but he took the doorknob with him, so I was trapped. I screamed for help and kept screaming until he let me out and I ran away. After running for a block or so, I realized he was right behind me. He apologized and offered to buy me dinner. When we got to a pub, I decided to eat with him. I figured if we were in public I was safe. He kept trying to convince me to stay with him and wouldn't take no for an answer, so I after I ate I got up suddenly and walked away. I saw a table with a bunch of young people and sat down with them. Gunter immediately started talking with me and finally the other guy gave up and left.

Gunter listened to my tale of woe and said I could stay with him. He even said we didn't have to have sex unless I wanted to. I was grateful for the beneficence of the universe and amazed at how different two men in the same city could be. By the time we went to his place, though, I was ready to have sex with him. He was surprised to learn I was using a diaphragm. All the German girls, he said, took the pill. I explained that American doctors had discovered the pill had bad side effects, so I had stopped taking it to give my body a rest.

I spent two nights with Gunter. During the day, he showed me around Cologne, took me to great places to eat, and paid for everything. I enjoyed being with him but when I woke up on the second morning, I knew it was time to move on and have other experiences. Besides the Jazz Festival in Montreux would be starting soon. Gunter made me promise to return at the end of my trip, maybe even to stay for a couple of weeks, and offered his address for people to send me mail from home. "I wish I could understand all he said," I reflected at the time. "My German is slowly getting better but he speaks fast and with a dialect. He is interested in parapsychology and has many ideas."

Although it was a frightening experience to be locked in a room and almost raped, I realized I had learned something important about myself: "I must have control over whether or not to have sex. I'm happy to give love but I need to give it. No one may take it away from me by force. I wonder why this happened to me, why I encountered this man. Are there so many sex-hungry men in Europe? Or why are they so forward with me?"

Despite this experience, hitchhiking still seemed to be OK. I headed toward Switzerland with a man from India who spoke English. Along the way, he wanted to visit American friends in Bonn and invited me to eat with them. I enjoyed our meal together, but when they were going on to someplace else, I realized I preferred to be on my way, so I got a ride to the Swiss border in a truck. The truck driver invited me to sleep with him in his truck, but I declined and crossed the border into Basel with a Swiss man who left me at the closest hotel to the highway.

The hotel-keeper smiled when he saw I was a woman traveling alone and immediately offered to share his room with me. I was taken aback at his forwardness and said no. But the room I was given was right on the highway and so noisy I couldn't sleep, so I called him up to complain. He came up to my room and surprised me by entering my room with a pass key. He said all the rooms were noisy but maybe if we shared some wine he had brought with him I would relax and be able to sleep. I knew it was a come on, but I gave in. The next day he took me to a swimming pool and then to the train. When I realized I left my wallet behind, he bought my ticket to Montreux. (Fortunately, my traveler's checks were not in my wallet!)

It was a relief to travel on the train. The scenery through the mountains was spectacular and the towns we passed though historic and beautiful. Arriving in Montreux on the shore of Lake Geneva I felt as if I were in a fairy tale and wondered what new adventures awaited me here. I was supposed to stay with my sister's friend Philippe, whom I met when he visited my family in California, but he was away so I was stranded. Two Italian men who lived in the same building rescued me. The three of us ended up sleeping together that night.

The next morning Philippe returned and brought me to the school where he was a teacher. I found it remarkably like my own school. Philippe taught his all-girl English class the song, "Mary Hamilton," which he accompanied on guitar. The girls were entranced and so was I. I could see why my sister was attracted to him. He was disappointed that she refused his offer of a long-term relationship.

That night Philippe and I slept in the same bed, since it was the only one in his small apartment, but we did not make love. I found this most disconcerting and reflected that in the past few days I had said no to several men, and now a man was saying no to me. The next morning, I wrote in my travel journal: "Falling in love is always so exciting to me. And knowing that isn't possible puts strange vibrations in the air. I feel quiet this morning—subdued."

When it was time for me to move on, I decided to hitchhike toward Zurich. This time, though, I had to wait a long time and finally ended up taking a ride to Bern with an Italian truck driver. We came to a deserted place where we stopped for lunch and he tried to get me into the back of the truck, where the food supposedly was. I was determined not to oblige. He kept trying but I ran away and asked a young man who had stopped to see the view to give me a ride to the highway. He explained he was driving his first car and was very proud of it.

Later, after a brief stay in a rural village, I had to wait a long time to get a ride because there were few cars on the road. As I stood there waiting, I realized how alone I was. What if something happened to me out there in the country? Who would know? I could disappear and my family and friends would not know where to begin looking for me. It was a scary thought, but also empowering. I saw it as a unique opportunity to reinvent myself. I needed to find out who I was without Thomas. I wanted to find a new love, but I also wanted to be my own person. Only I wasn't yet sure who I was now. I hoped this trip would help me begin that discovery.

On my way to Vienna, a seven-hour journey, I started out with several short rides, one with a man who bought me a meal but wanted more and I said no. I was proud of myself for being able to discern who was safe to ride with and who was not. Finally, a young couple with a child gave me a ride. Once again, I felt longing to be part of a family: "I miss so much being a part of someone. Is it just that I want to be dependent? Perhaps I prefer to think that it is more to do with my need to exchange energy. Sharing releases my own flow."

It was late in the day when I arrived in Vienna, so I reluctantly paid for a hotel room that seemed overly expensive. I was exhausted but couldn't fall sleep because of the noise outside on the street. I got dressed again and went to find some schnapps. I noticed happy people in an open-air beer garden and was drawn to an interesting looking white man with frizzy hair similar to the "afros" some African Americans were wearing at the time. Wolfgang and his friends lived in Vienna and were going to the movie *Cabaret*. He invited me to have a beer with them and come along. I noted in my journal that he did not pay for the beer, which was fine with me, since it meant I didn't have to play the dumb woman role. Although I had already seen the movie, this time it was in German, except for the songs. The scenes with Nazis were especially chilling in German. After the movie, we drank a Viennese specialty, new wine, and I went home with him, never spending the night in my expensive hotel room.

FALLING IN LOVE AGAIN

It didn't take long for me to fall in love with Wolfgang. He lived with his mother in the flat where he grew up but was independent from her and had no compunctions about bringing me home. I was nervous about meeting her that first morning, but although she was distant at first, she seemed to accept me after Wolfgang told her I was staying for a few weeks.

Wolfgang had a large comfortable bedroom, but only a narrow bed. After all my traveling, it felt good to have a place to stay for a while and someone to relate to on an ongoing basis. We had wonderful, fun sex, so sleeping close together was mostly a real joy. The one downside to the arrangement was the fact that when he was at work I needed to be out of the house. This gave me plenty of time to explore Vienna on my own, but I felt sleep-deprived, since we often stayed up late.

Sometimes as I walked through the streets of the historic city, I had the feeling I had been there before, maybe in a past life. I dreamed several times of being buried in a tunnel while escaping from the Nazis and then learned that Vienna was one of the places where tunnels were used for just such escapes. It gave me an eerie feeling that I had some special reason for being in Vienna and I started to imagine what it would be like to live there.

Wolfgang had lived in Vienna all his life and had a good job working for an advertising company. We spent a lot of time with his wide circle of friends, going to movies, concerts, and gathering at their favorite outdoor beer garden. Wolfgang spoke some English and wanted to practice it, but I wanted to speak German, so we went back and forth in our conversations. I could only barely understand the Viennese dialect, so he translated for me, sometimes into English and other times into German.

I still wanted to go back to Marburg, so after a couple of weeks I told Wolfgang I was leaving. He begged me to stay, or at least to come back. It was a long trip each way, but I agreed and even left some of my things there to make sure I would return. He didn't like the idea of my hitchhiking alone, but I was insistent and promised to be extra careful.

RETURNING TO MARBURG

I spent a week in Marburg, walking in familiar streets, visiting places I had been before, reconnecting with Frau Bartuzat and the Spalkes. The first night I stayed in Bettinahaus, where I had lived ten years earlier, and arranged to stay in another student house for the remainder of the time. I reconnected with Rudolf's brother, Rene, his wife Erika, and their three girls. In addition, I met several men who expressed interest in connecting with me, especially one with whom I had several deep philosophical conversations. Although it was a new experience for me, I said no, knowing I was going back to Wolfgang. After one such encounter I wrote: "I feel the drive within me to be with him, but I did get out of the car—slowly. Wolfgang, if you could only know how difficult and how unusual this is for me!"

When I saw Rudolf and met his wife, I realized that although the attraction was still there, I was glad I had moved on. "We could look into each other's eyes and see the past love we had shared," I wrote, and then turned it into a poem.

Looking into your eyes
    I remember
Loving you still forever
    I remember
The past is always a part of what we are now
    I remember

Being in Marburg helped me make peace with my past relationship with Rudolf. He seemed happy with his present life, but there was a moment when he speculated about what might have been. Frau Bartuzat mentioned an American woman who had taken her German friend with her when she went back home, and Rudolf said with a sigh, "You see! It would have been possible!" But I knew it wasn't possible for us, financially if for no other reason. I wanted to talk with him further about his leftover feelings of disappointment, but we didn't get the chance.

I learned from Erika and Rene that Rudolf's wife tended to dominate him and that he wasn't motivated to pursue a career. He had worked at various jobs, but his wife's income covered most of their expenses. I had felt bad about the way our relationship ended with my pregnancy and abortion, but now I could see that we would not have made it anyway, so I felt relieved. I had felt similarly relieved when I visited Carl some years after our relationship ended. He had given up on music and taken a mundane job. I thought, too, about Thomas, and how difficult it seemed to be for him to pull his weaving work together into a business that could support him. It made me wonder why I fell in love with people who had difficulty fulfilling their potential in life.

With Erika and Rene and their children, I experienced once again the strength of a loving family. We shared similar interests and dreams for the future, and they encouraged their girls to get to know me. They accepted me as a family member and I so wished I could have been one. I wrote:

> We shared views on life and love and meaning. They would agree in basis with Wolfgang that only a deep, long-lasting relationship with one person carries the kind of love I am seeking. I spoke of not wanting to be dependent, but they see the dependence on a partner as an essential part of love. They don't expect to be close to many people, which is one reason I am somewhat surprised at their openness with me and value our contact very highly.

Because I stayed in Marburg longer than planned, I decided to take the train back to Vienna. I had a lot to think about on the long train ride. I realized how strong my longing was for a family, "the being part of I have waited for, for a long time." The visit inspired me to reflect on what remembering the past meant. I felt the past pressing in on me and wrapping me up in memories and concluded that this process was at least in part why I was on this journey: "Remember: to put together all of what went before and what is now and what will be." That's what writing memoir is about as well.

LIFE WITH WOLFGANG IN VIENNA

My reunion with Wolfgang was wonderful. It felt good to have been missed. I was very happy, happier than I had been in a long time. I didn't understand why, but I decided it must be right to be here and enjoy this time of love. Now that I was back at the Krammers, Wolfgang's mother took a greater interest in me. She showed me how to prepare some of their favorite foods and I helped her wash dishes. Letting her teach me something was a way for us to relate.

Wolfgang and I began to have serious talks about our lives and about the future. He accused me of thinking too much, but I was keenly aware that I would be leaving again in less than a month. He said he didn't expect to live long and imagined committing suicide at age 38 so he would not have to grow old. That terrified me, but what emerged as more problematic was something he had done in the past.

Several years before, Wolfgang had traveled through Asia, carrying only a backpack and walking much of the way. In Thailand, he had fallen in love with a young woman named Khae. Before he left he promised to marry her if she would come to Vienna, and they exchanged rings. When he first told me about this, he presented it as something that was unlikely to ever happen.

"She's never going to have the resources to come here, so there's nothing to worry about," he explained.

"But what if she does? Suppose she just shows up here one day?" I asked, worried nevertheless.

"I doubt she'll ever be able to leave Thailand, because I'm supposed to send her father dowry money before he will let her go. Besides, even before I met you, I realized I don't love her anymore," he assured me.

I was sufficiently in love with him by then to ignore the danger signs. Yet occasionally he would receive a letter from her, and I could see it was still a live option for him.

At the same time, our love-making progressed in wondrous directions. I realized I had never been with a partner who completely satisfied me. With Wolfgang, I was finally learning how to have orgasms. I could imagine if I were with him I wouldn't need anyone else. This made it doubly difficult to be objective about the future.

However much I sought to stay in the present and enjoy my life with Wolfgang in Vienna, thoughts of the future kept pressing in. I reflected, "What sense does it make when I know too well the pain of our parting? It is sweet to live a few weeks in love, but what then?

After August, an ocean and a continent will come between us." One day when I visited the beautiful castle and grounds at Schönbrunn by myself I wrote:

Opening an orange that is
Rotten in the core
Hoping for peace but
Finding only war
Beginning a love that can
Only end in pain
Sitting in the sun but
Waiting for the rain.

As with any relationship, there were conflicts. Ours dealt mostly with practices of daily living: diet, health, and cleanliness. Wolfgang had strong feelings about what was right and so did I. While frustrating, these conflicts gave me an opportunity to assert myself rather than take criticism to heart and punish myself with it. Knowing at least part of the conflict was cultural helped me stand up for myself. I noted, "This confidence to defend myself I've been lacking for a long time. Wanting and needing always to be accepted and appreciated I allowed sex to substitute for full acceptance as a person. Now perhaps I can learn to accept myself and not need such assurance from others." I appreciated what Wolfgang helped me learn about love and about myself.

Wolfgang's big dream for the future was to buy a Range Rover, drive it from the United States all the way to the tip of South America, and then ship it back to Vienna. I bought into his dream and extended it. We could buy crafts along the way and open an import shop for hand-made goods from both North and South America, something that didn't yet exist in Vienna.

CELIBACY AND A VIBRATOR

Despite Wolfgang's potential marriage to Khae, when it came to the possibility of my involvement with anyone else, he was jealous. For instance, when I received a love letter from Gunter, the man I stayed with in Cologne, he was upset and fearful he would lose me. What I would later come to understand as male possessiveness, I saw then as love.

When it was nearly time for me to return home, Wolfgang challenged me,

"The only thing you haven't tried sexually is being celibate."

"I suppose you're right," I laughed, wondering if it would be possible.

"Tell you what," he said. "I'll take you to buy a vibrator. That way you can enjoy feeling sexual and think of me."

I had never masturbated, so this was a completely new idea for me, and it intrigued me enough to agree to try it. But then I wondered, "Where would we go to buy such a thing?"

"To a sex shop, of course," he responded, surprised at my naïveté. Europeans were considerably more advanced than we were in the US, I thought.

I accompanied Wolfgang on a business trip to London and then he accompanied me to Cologne. I needed to meet up with Gunter to pick up mail and say goodbye. Wolfgang wanted to be sure I wasn't tempted to stay with him. We found a "sex shop," picked out a vibrator, and that night in a hotel we tried it out. Indeed, I returned from Europe with a new love and two new sexual practices: masturbation and celibacy.

Deciding to be celibate and changing the way I encountered men turned out to be two different things. My first test came in Marburg where I stopped on my way back to the airport in Belgium. One of the men I had met on my visit the month before came over to Rene's and Erika's where I spent the night. He came on to me right away, started touching me, and wanted me to go to a bar with him, even though I was already yawning and said I was tired. I later wrote, "The funny thing was that although I knew exactly what he wanted from me and although his hands were soft and gentle, I felt no desire or obligation to respond—Wolfgang, you have freed me!" Erika laughed and said, "You just can't say no," but I did, and he went home. I was proud of myself and hoped I could keep it up when I got home.

Once I got home I was too busy to worry about much of anything except getting settled and starting school. I decided to concentrate on connecting with people I already knew with whom I hoped to develop deeper, non-sexual friendships, rather than seeking to meet new people. In situations where I would have earlier been looking to connect with a man, I held back instead and watched the sex games. This holding back changed the way I was in groups, and I wasn't sure I liked it although it gave me a different perspective. For instance, at a gathering of psychology students and professors, I observed that "psych grad programs are so full of [sex] games, all in the name of openness, freedom, and flow. Now I have the strength to see that I wasn't gaining anything by playing that role." I was disappointed, though, that because I wasn't putting out sexual vibes, most men simply ignored me.

I tried using the vibrator but didn't find it very satisfying, especially at first. Eventually I managed to make it work, but it was never an adequate substitute for sex with a real person. Better than nothing, though.

In October Wolfgang came to California. I was ecstatic but still had to work, so this time he was on his own during the day. I struggled to maintain myself at school, with my heart and body back in my apartment with Wolfgang. He came to school with me a couple of times and for months afterwards the kids asked about him. Making love with Wolfgang on my king-size water bed was even better than before. Our fulfilling sexual relationship gave me great hope that we would be together eventually and blinded me to the reality of his other commitment. We imagined buying that Range Rover he dreamed of and making the trip to South America together.

It ripped my heart out when he left as planned three weeks later. I had hoped he would be so happy with me he would decide to stay. When we got to the airport and discovered his flight was delayed for several hours, I thought it was a sign. We found a quiet place to lie down together and fell asleep, but he woke up just in time to catch his plane. On the way home "Midnight Train to Georgia"[177] came on the car radio and the song spoke directly to me: "I'd rather live in his world than live without him in mine," I sang along as I

---

177   "Midnight Train to Georgia," by Jim Weatherly, recorded by Gladys Knight and the Pips in 1973.

bawled my eyes out.

Two weeks later, Khae arrived in Vienna. Even though Wolfgang had been unable to send the money her father demanded, she came on her own. Nevertheless, our exchange of love letters and occasional expensive phone calls continued for six more months.

In the meantime, I was learning what it meant to be celibate, unavailable to other men. On New Year's Eve, I decided to go hear music and walked over to the Inn of the Beginning a few blocks from my apartment. I had never gone there by myself before. Most of the evening I danced alone, but I had several encounters with men who assumed I was there to pick someone up. It was hard to explain that I wanted to be alone. One man wouldn't take no for an answer and followed me back to my apartment. I got the key out before reaching the door, managed to get inside, and slammed the door in his face. It felt good to say no. But then I realized I was alone and cried myself to sleep, missing Wolfgang. The vibrator helped, but not enough.

Receiving and writing letters kept me going. In every letter Wolfgang wrote of his love for me and how much he wanted to return to California once Khae left. I wrote twice as many letters to him because the act of writing allowed me to feel close to him. I vacillated between dreams of the day we would be together and fears that he was choosing Khae over me and had never really loved me. I based my happiness on whether I got a letter, although as time went on his letters frustrated me with their mixed messages—assurances of love along with requests for more time to figure things out. I knew I was crazy to believe in our love, but couldn't stop myself. Our love for each other felt so strong, so real, and the sex had been so good, like nothing I had experienced before. That had to mean something, I reasoned in my despair. But Khae didn't leave, and eventually they got married. My heart broke.

While I waited anxiously for letters, dreaming the impossible would become possible, another dynamic was taking place. I was figuring out how to stand on my own and how to love myself. My journal is filled with contradictions as these two sides argued with one winning for a while but then the other coming back strong.

DISCOVERING FEMINISM, 1973-74

Before my summer trip to Europe, at the 1973 conference of the California Council for the Social Studies (CCSS),[178] there was talk about doing something on women's studies the following year. I was asked to help. Since I didn't know much about the subject, I asked each of the publishers exhibiting at the conference what they had in terms of curriculum and resources for the possible program. Most agreed to send me samples of what they had available. When I moved into my apartment in town I was hoping my brother Howdy would share it with me, but things changed for him and he only stayed there briefly. Instead the second bedroom began filling up with packets and boxes from the conference publishers. Then in January 1974, I met with CCSS leadership and agreed to coordinate the program.

My salvation from the pain I felt nearly constantly from my impossible long-distance relationship with Wolfgang came through discovering feminism. While many women joined consciousness-raising groups in the early 1970s, my opportunity to learn what being a feminist meant and how it applied to my life came through reading books in preparation for the conference. What I learned helped me gain perspective on my tendency toward dependence on men. I wanted to become a truly independent woman, but I wasn't sure how to.

I was fascinated with the variety and scope of the essays in the thick paperback anthology, *The Feminist Papers: From Adams to de Beauvoir.*[179] I hadn't realized how far back in history the struggle for equality went and how persistent the resistance to change was. From Robin Morgan's *Sisterhood is Powerful* I learned about the development of the modern women's liberation movement. Reading the justifiably angry essays fit right in with how I was feeling about

---

178   "Breaking Down Walls: the social studies in an integrated curriculum," CCSS annual conference, March 16-18, 1973, Oakland Hilton Inn.

179   *The Feminist Papers: From Adams to de Beauvoir,* edited by Alice S Rossi, 1973. Robin Morgan, Sisterhood Is Powerful: An Anthology of Writings from the Women's Liberation Movement, 1970. Betty Friedan, The Feminine Mystique, 1963.

Wolfgang and helped me come to terms with the failure of marriage to Thomas. I finally read Betty Friedan's *The Feminine Mystique*, which had seemed irrelevant to me when it came out ten years earlier, because I didn't think I needed liberating. But now that I was struggling with relationship issues, it made a great deal of sense.

By the time of the conference in March 1974, feminism was becoming essential to my thinking. I was still going back and forth between believing that Wolfgang and I had a future and knowing the dream was over. In a letter written a few days before the conference, I described "the frustration of having my life tied to something I'm not sure I believe in anymore. The pain caused by your dual life with Khae makes me seriously wonder if love can be real under those conditions. ... I won't suffer any more for you. It's not worth it, because it destroys the love."[180] Then I responded to his diatribe against feminism in a previous letter.

Your views on women's liberation are typically and predictably male and narrow-minded. ... I've learned a lot in the last few months and think quite differently about the subject than I did before I began to see the amount of cultural bias which influences all our beliefs about men and women and the so-called natural order of things. I could have easily expressed your views some years ago, but now I see them as dangerously in the way of evolution.

While the reading and the conference inspired me and opened my eyes to how much sexist culture had instilled in me an "insecure image of myself," the intellectual recognition of this barely touched my usual emotional responses. I explained to myself and to Wolfgang: "I have put a lot of energy into being strong in certain ways, and that drained a lot of inner resources, which need to be replenished by love. I'll always be a love freak, I know!"

FINDING HOPE AGAIN

During this same time, I was taking classes at Sonoma State College and continuing to work on my self-directed master's degree.

---

180   Letter to Wolfgang, March 11, 1974. Carbon copy on the back of flyers for "The Female Principle."

What I was exploring and discovering contributed to my recovery from the pain of lost love, both with Thomas and Wolfgang. Two professors helped me find new ways to understand myself in relation to male-female dynamics.

Chuc Kemesu, assistant professor of psychology, taught courses in Man-Woman Relations and Cross-Racial and Cross-Cultural Relations. An attractive man with light brown skin about my age, we acknowledged the sexual vibes between us, but he was clear in choosing to avoid such relationships in the school setting. In this he differed from other professors at the time, one of whom had a big bed in his office which he invited others to use when he wasn't there. I wrote in my journal: "It's been a long time since I've been responded to so honestly and non-manipulatively. ... We [are] attracted to each other, enjoy talking sexy, but he doesn't take advantage of my vulnerability. Nor does he avoid responsibility for his own reality. I wish a man like that would fall in love with me."

We spent time together in his office and off campus, talking about the dynamics of sex and love and the culture changes we were part of. I noted in my journal that he was helpful with personal advice, "thinking through sex roles, black-white roles—an old subject I've never worked through." This was my first opportunity to reflect on my experiences in Marin City.

Chuc enabled me to explore my conflicting feelings about sex and love and the role sex played in my life. I told him about my experiment with celibacy.

"I find it de-sexes me in my relationships with men, so we can be friends," I explained. "I can be a person first, rather than a sex object."

"I still think you're pretty sexy," he said. "I know what you mean, though. There are plenty of students who would like to get me in bed. That's why I've decided not to go there."

David Thatcher, assistant professor of education, had just published his first book, *Teaching, Loving, and Self-Directed Learning*,[181] which became an important reference as my own approach to teaching continued to develop. When I first got to know

---

181   David A. Thatcher, *Teaching, Loving, and Self-Directed Learning*, 1973.

him, he was married with three children, but after a few months I learned his marriage was ending and he was on his own. I described him as "very nice to talk with. He's so friendly and open, non-threatening, no fear, lots of touching." I wasn't particularly attracted to him, though, so this time I was the one who set boundaries. We became good friends and he became an advisor to me in my work as a teacher. He was always kind, someone I could seek out when I was troubled either about relationships or about my teaching. He would help me understand what was going on and figure out how to move forward.

In the meantime, I continued friendships with several former students from my first experimental class. By then they had finished high school and were living on their own. One day two of the boys invited me to their apartment in Santa Rosa. Now that they were on their own, we began a new phase in our relationship. Love was the theme of the class their experimental class chose as its primary focus, and since then I had occasionally felt what seemed to be mutual sexual attraction, particularly with one of them. We even kissed a few times. Being in their apartment that day, though, I sensed a shift. They were young men now and they treated me as a woman. I was not displeased, but I remained cautious. Over the next few months, though, the barriers we had often talked about breaking melted, and both approached me with invitations to make love. Eventually I accepted the offer, and their tender young love contributed to my recovery from the love I was losing with Thomas and Wolfgang

In the years since then, I have reflected on these relationships in terms of today's understanding of sexual abuse. In writing this book I considered omitting this part of the story but decided to do so would be inauthentic. Instead I took the occasion to speak openly with each of them about it. They each separately assured me they did not feel abused and even thought they were the initiators. Nevertheless, I acknowledged my role as the older adult who had been their teacher and apologized for my actions. I was relieved to learn they felt no negative results in their lives. Making love was an extension of the love we shared in that first experimental class and an affirmation of the love we believed would heal the world.

Although I had returned to my former practice of being open to making love and I still hoped my prince would come, my idealism about love began to shift from the personal to the collective. Ruth and others were talking about finding land to start a community. Frustrated with the lack of acceptance of the changes I worked hard to bring about in education, I decided to take a leave of absence from teaching and focus on creating a new form of community. I offered Water Road as a temporary place to gather and talked with Thomas about my moving back there, at least temporarily, once school was over.

A year later I was caught in a dilemma. Despite my vision and work toward building community, I missed having a partner and kept hoping for a lasting relationship that might include the possibility of children. Although I wanted to be independent, I had trouble seeing the future alone. In my private moments, I imagined my own version of Wolfgang's dream: buying a van and traveling around the US looking for a community where "we" could make a new life. It was always "we," as I could not imagine doing this alone. In November 1975, just before my thirty-second birthday, a man showed up at Water Road who helped me fulfill that vision. But that's another story.

LOVE'S UNFINISHED AGENDA

On the plus side, the Sixties initiated a sea change, moving the culture towards greater honesty about sexuality and enabling people to live in ways that more closely coincided with their stated values. Opening the culture to the many varieties of love made it possible for interracial and same-gender partners to acknowledge their relationships, live together as families, and care for their children. Acceptance of sex outside of marriage has enabled marriage to become a choice based on love and a status sought after by people who were denied access in earlier eras.

I still resonate with the Sixties mantra "Make love, not war" and continue to believe in the possibility of a world where love is stronger than hate. However, I realize that our experiments with free love did not necessarily accomplish what we imagined they would. Our experiences were often not as different from the past as we would have liked them to be, partly because we had not evolved emotionally. Our ideals about open, loving relationships did not eliminate feelings of jealousy and abandonment. As committed as I was to open sexuality, love, and caring relationships, my actions sometimes failed to match my ideals. If only I had understood the concept of right relations.

The ethical principles of right relations (or right relationship) began to develop in the 1980s and are still not widely known or practiced beyond faith communities and justice-making organizations. These principles shift the emphasis in moral decision-making from rules to relationships. What is essential is for people to take into consideration both the person with whom one is directly involved and the larger community within which the relationship exists. People are encouraged to "understand relationships as expressions of value, commitment, purpose,"[182] and "to make ethical decisions that give expression to one's values in relationship, to consider what is expressed in relationship and not just, for example, rights or fairness or equality."[183]

This is what I and others too often failed to do in the Sixties. Engaging in free love without awareness or concern for other relationships sometimes caused complications and even pain, both for me and for my partners. This failure to be aware of the impact of individual relationships on others continues to plague our culture's ongoing efforts to get right with sexuality as an expression of love. Understanding and practicing right relations needs to be incorporated into our culture as essential to the completion of the Sixties sea change.

The advent of AIDS in the early 1980s put an end to the era of relatively safe and easy exploration of open sexuality. Although safe sex tools and practices developed in affirmation of the continuing value of sexual freedom in people's lives, not everyone made use of

182   Deborah Pope-Lance, "An Ethic of Right Relations," in *Creating Safe Congregations: Toward an Ethic of Right Relations*, 1999, edited by Patricia Hoertdoerfer and William Sinkford.
183   Deborah Pope-Lance, email to Dorothy Emerson, Nov. 17, 2015.

the tools that were available. The fact that the disease continued to spread even after public education campaigns about safe sex is part of the ambivalence some still feel about their sexuality and self-worth, and in some cases about the rights of women to control their own bodies. Becoming responsible about sexual relationships remains a challenge for Love's unfinished agenda.

Sex remains a powerful physical drive often accompanied by equally powerful emotions. Still today in far too many situations, sexual feelings draw people into relationships that end up causing pain both to those directly involved and others with whom one is in relationship. The principles of right relations would go a long way towards completing the unfinished agenda of the Sixties and making possible a world based on love and mutual respect.

Ending rape, domestic violence, and abuse is also essential. Growing awareness of sexual and relationship abuse can be directly linked to the feminist awakening that began in the late Sixties, when many women participated consciousness-raising groups and talked openly with each other about their experiences of rape and domestic violence. In 1975 Susan Brownmiller published *Against Our Will*, which drew widespread attention to the issue of rape. In 1976 *Ms. Magazine* published a story on domestic violence with a cover showing a woman with a bruised face. Public awareness grew during the decade that followed, resulting in new laws. Today, awareness and action to prevent abuse continues to grow and be applied in new contexts. Holding abusers accountable, no matter how much power and prestige they have, and protecting the safety of those who are vulnerable to abuse is part of the unfinished agenda of the Sixties.

The feminist movement and *Ms. Magazine* also led the struggle to legalize abortion. In 1972 *Ms.* published the names of women who had illegal abortions. I would have added my name if I had known about the list beforehand. In 1973 the Supreme Court issued its decision in Roe v. Wade affirming women's right to choose to end an unwanted pregnancy.[184] The immediate effect was to free women from one last restriction on their expressions of sexuality and

---

184   The Court issued its decision on January 22, 1973, with a 7-to-2 majority vote in favor of Roe, legalizing abortion.

to affirm women's right to control their own bodies. Reproductive freedom, including access to abortion, is essential for women's equality. However, the resistance to this idea has been constant, and now restrictions on women's right to end pregnancy have eroded the 1973 Court's intent. Vigilance is required to protect what remains of these important rights and restore access for all women to reproductive services, including abortion. Without reproductive freedom, the Love's agenda is far from complete.

Love, of course, is larger than sex. Applying the Sixties principle that love is stronger than hate to community and international relations is essential to Love's unfinished agenda. Perhaps remembering the dreams of the past will help us move toward a world where indeed Love is All We Need.

6. EDUCATION = CHANGE

"You who are on the road
Must have a code that you can live by
And so become yourself
Because the past is just a good-bye.
Teach your children well..."

> Graham Nash, recorded by Crosby,
> Stills, Nash, and Young, 1970

My awakening to the possibility of new forms of education came unexpectedly, during my last semester at Pomona College, in a course I would not have taken had I not flunked Economics the semester before.[185] The course was Social Welfare.[186]

When I entered the room, I found myself in a very different environment from most college classes. There were no desks, only a circle of chairs. The professor was a woman and younger than the male professors who taught the rest of my college classes. She seemed friendly and open, and interestingly non-professorial. As we students dutifully took out our notebooks and tried to balance them on our laps, she smiled and suggested that we put them away. It was our choice, but she predicted if we took notes we would not do as well as if we listened with full attention and engaged in discussion. She went on to explain there would be no assigned reading, no texts,

---

185   My advisor told me not to take Economics because it was a difficult course I didn't need, but I wanted to better understand what the graduate students I was hanging out with were talking about so I insisted. I succeeded in learning the big ideas but the tests focused on the details, which I failed to master.

186   More about my experiences in Social Welfare can be found in Culture Shock, Senior Year 1964-65.

and no tests. She pointed to a table full of books at the side of the room. These we could borrow and read, if we wanted to. Or we could find our own resources.

The requirements for the course were to come to class, participate in discussions, and go on field trips. Our grades would be based on class participation and a final project. We were expected to go beyond the usual library resources to investigate a social problem and potential solutions in person.

This class changed forever how I understood the process of education. This was unlike anything else I had experienced, something exciting and new. I felt blessed by some unseen spirit of life for flunking Econ and discovering this new approach to learning. I walked out into a sunny blue-sky afternoon, the kind of winter day that makes southern California seem like a paradise. The air around me was fresh and new. My reality had shifted, and I was grateful be alive in this place at this moment in time. I opened my arms and said aloud my favorite words from the musical, The Fantasticks,[187] "Please God, please, don't let me be normal." I thought to myself, this is a whole new world.

INSPIRATION AND INFLUENCE OF FESTIVAL THEATRE

Although people often told me I would be a good teacher, I resisted the idea. I wanted a career that was more unique and less women-dominated. That's why I chose ministry. But after leaving seminary in early 1966 and trying other possible career paths, I found myself contemplating teaching as perhaps the most practical way for me to support myself, even if it didn't fulfill all of what I hoped to do in life.

My involvement with Festival Theatre helped me see that education involving arts and literature could inspire people to change. Marjorie Casebier, one of its founders, explained the relationship between the arts and religion: "Both theology and

---

187   This musical with music by Harvey Schmidt and lyrics by Tom Jones premiered off-Broadway in May 1960 and ran a total of 42 years and 17,162 performances, making it the longest running musical in history. I saw it in Los Angeles in 1961.

theater are concerned with what life is all about and what it means to be human and alive. Art and religious experience are very close to each other."[188] I was beginning to realize that the theater did a better job than the Church of awakening people to the problems of society, by offering inspiration and role models for social change.

In the summer of 1966, the theater began a new project supported by a federal grant under Title III of the Elementary and Secondary Education Act.[189] In cooperation with the Marin County School Superintendent's Office, the project brought students to the theater, sent actors and directors out to talk to students to prepare them for the experience of live theater and introduce them to the play, and supported post-performance discussions with the students. The theater already produced resource packets about each play. These were expanded and further developed for use in classrooms to help students learn about the plays as literature and explore their implications for society.

This was the first experience of live theater for many young people. The plays engaged them and moved them in ways other media did not, and the opportunity to talk about what they had just seen added depth and perspective to what they learned. Listening to the students' questions and comments inspired me to consider how I might use literature and theater to engage students in discovering meaning in their lives. If I could do this, maybe teaching was the path for me.

The 1966-67 season at Festival Theatre took on the theme of Issues and Concerns of the Sixties. The focus shifted from questions of the individual and the family to those of the larger society, with two productions highlighting the defining issue of the decade: war. For me this concern was personal because of my draft-age brother.

The musical revue *Oh What a Lovely War!* used stories,

---

188   Interview with Marjorie Casebier McCoy by Bea Pixa, "Advantages of talking about death," San Francisco *Sunday Examiner and Chronicle*, Nov. 3, 1974 (Sunday Scene, 6).

189   Project # OE-2703, funded by Title III of the 1965 Elementary and Secondary Education Act, part of President Johnson's War on Poverty. Title III invested in research and educational innovations.

humor, songs, and statistics from the First World War to personalize war and demonstrate its devastating effect on everyone concerned. The show forced the audience to consider the war's effect on future generations and our own. The unique combination of music, fun, and passionate protest opened me to new possibilities for inspiring both students and adults to change their attitudes toward how we solve world problems.

This message continued in the even more radical production of Norman Corwin's *Overkill and Megalove*, a plea in dramatic form for "deeper sensitivity about the unique worth of every individual person and for new awareness of the futility of war," now that we have the capacity for mass destruction with nuclear weapons. The play challenged us to "feel with our minds and think with our hearts, and to explore...every means possible for the achievement of peace—the major concern of the Sixties."[190] Before this, I had not taken the possibility of nuclear annihilation seriously. The production awakened me to the necessity of resistance and moved me to understand the importance of teaching peace.

DECISION TIME: BECOME A HIGH SCHOOL TEACHER?

After searching for a professional position I was qualified for as a college graduate, and trying several short-term jobs that ended nowhere, I decided to become a teacher. In a letter to my family, I explained:

I have arrived at a point where I must realize that the job-hunting business…will lead me to failure…If we can work things out for a more productive direction, then I am ready to move on. I want to go back to school and...get a teaching credential! Despite all my hesitancy in the past, I can finally admit that this is not only the most practical thing for me to do, but also it is what I want to do and what I feel is right for me to do.

I discovered that German, my college major, was not sufficiently in demand to get me a teaching position. English teachers were needed, but I would have to take more courses in the field to

---

190   Marjorie Casebier, Student Study Syllabus for *Overkill and Megalove,* Festival Theatre, Feb. 24-Apr. 2, 1967, 3.

qualify. This would be in addition to the Education courses I needed for a California teaching credential. At this point, with my husband's job at Festival Theatre and my inconsistent work, we barely made enough money to cover basic bills. I needed help if I wanted to return to school. Two weeks later, my mother came through with a $500 loan at no interest, to be paid back when I could.

After investigating well-known schools like Stanford and the University of California in Berkeley, both some distance from where I lived, I learned from my relatives about a nearby college with a teacher training program, a Catholic school run primarily by nuns. I wasn't sure how I would fit in, but Dominican College in San Rafael appeared to be my only viable choice.

I felt more than a little intimidated when I went to my first appointment with the Dean of the Graduate School, a nun who wore a long head-covering and a floor-length white robe with long sleeves. Although the Second Vatican Council in 1962 allowed nuns to change or discard their traditional habits, the Dominican Sisters that ran this college stuck to traditional garb. Sister Martin greeted me with a pleasant if slightly stern smile and invited me to sit down. I gave her my college transcript and explained what I wanted to do.

"I've decided to become a high school teacher, but before I start a teacher training program I want to take enough classes for a major in English, because that's what I want to teach."

She didn't respond right away and I wondered if she thought my idea was crazy. Then I realized she was studying my transcript. It was probably only few minutes but it seemed like forever to me before she asked, "Why do you want to teach English? You only have two courses toward a major in that subject. You will need a total of 24 units for a teaching major."

I explained I was willing to start right away, and that I thought my previous experience in studying literature had prepared me well to be able to handle this new major. "Besides," I said. "This time I won't be reading in another language!"

"Take this catalog home," she responded. "Pick out the courses you want to take, and come see me next week. If what you choose seems adequate for a major, we can consider this, but be advised that the semester starts in less than two months. I would need to know right away that you want to do this and pull some strings to get you in. You must pay for this yourself, since we don't have scholarships for this sort of thing. If you decide to apply for the teacher education program, you should go to summer school to take the prerequisites."

I breathed a sigh of relief, thanked her, and left weighed down with the significance of what I was about to do and the work ahead of me. I knew this choice would set my path at least for the immediate future. Was I ready to do this? I wondered, and felt my heart say yes! I picked out my classes, got them approved, and prepared to begin classes in January 1967.

In the meantime, I had to get a part-time job. Now that I knew I was on a career path to teaching, I could apply for a job I thought would not be too stressful and have flexible hours that could accommodate my class schedule. With that in mind, I got a temporary job for the holiday season at the nearby Macy's. I did well enough that they kept me on, so I had a steady income during my preparation for teaching. Finally, it seemed things were working out. I must be doing what the Universe wants me to do, I thought to myself.

PREPARATION FOR TEACHING AT DOMINICAN COLLEGE, 1967-68

The First Human Be-In, held in San Francisco's Golden Gate Park, occurred on January 14, 1967. I wasn't there for the historic event, but Thomas and I heard about it from people who participated. We later made trips into the city to participate in the spirit of hope and love that lasted throughout the year and into the next. My first classes at Dominican began the day after the Be-In.

The first semester I took primarily undergraduate courses required for the English major. There were many class meetings but the work load was relatively light compared with Pomona College. This was a good thing because I was also leading an active social life, learning about the retail department store business at Macy's, maintaining an apartment and relationship with Thomas, including our mutual open marriage activities, and helping with Festival Theatre productions. In retrospect, I wonder how I found the time and energy to earn the grade of A in every class.

During the Summer of Love in 1967, I entered the world of professional teaching. The orientation course included visits from several principals of area schools, a month of daily observation at one school, and a visit to a unique open space school in Corte Madera with individualized instruction for every child, flexibility in instructional groupings and use of space, cooperative teaching teams, non-graded placement and promotion, and multi-age instructional groups. I was introduced to a very different form of education through a filmstrip,[191] *Classroom Revolution*, which included a description of Summerhill, the school in England that became known as the first radically "free" school.[192] From the beginning I was provided with a vision of what school could be, and this vision shaped what I learned about education after that.

In Sociological Foundations of Education, we started with a question, "what is community?" followed by "what is the purpose of school?" We looked at change as a major factor of our time, asked what affect this had on education, and considered how to help students accept change. We explored elements that together constitute our culture and looked at how culture developed and changed over time. We identified major social problems of power, race, and class, and the continuation of poverty and city slums despite growing affluence. We talked about the importance of democracy and were challenged to assess our biases and analyze our attitudes toward teaching to determine if we could teach in ways that modeled democratic principles. We studied Supreme Court decisions on integration and religion in public schools and considered how we could implement them in our classrooms by promoting positive values of respect, awareness of others' needs, and social responsibility. This one short

---

191   Filmstrips are spooled rolls of 35 mm positive film images in common use from the 1940s through the 1980s, threaded through a simple projector and shown on a screen.

192   A.S. Neill, *Summerhill: A Radical Approach to Child Rearing* (1960) and *Freedom—Not License!* 1966.

course covered just about every topic that would later frame my teaching.

That fall I began a full schedule that included additional English and education courses, student teaching, plus a year-long course in German literature. The Education course in Advanced Composition for Secondary School Teachers of English gave me an opportunity to write as the primary work of a class. Although I disliked having to write commentaries on what I considered inane subjects, what I wrote now provides insight into my thinking process at the time.

In one essay, I responded to the problem identified by some English teachers concerning the amount of time required to "correct students' writing." I suggested a radical departure from the norm. I don't know where I got this idea, as it would be several years before I heard it presented at an English teachers' conference:

Often the simplest answers to problems fail to come to mind because they are so simple…This plan is based on the proposition that not all that a student writes must necessarily be graded or even read for the writing experience to have had value. Many assignments could be given with only those being read which the student would choose to present for consideration by the teacher.

The professor took issue with my idea, noting that the student might "simply repeat errors until they become vices." But that didn't deter me from using this approach in my teaching.

By the time I completed the work for my California secondary school teaching credential, I had learned a great deal about myself, including that I was a better student academically than I managed to be as an undergraduate. I had developed new interests in psychology and sociology and greater awareness of serious issues facing our society, and my responsibility as a teacher and a citizen in a democracy. And, I had encountered radical ideas as to the purposes of education and the need for schools to change. All this was excellent preparation for what I was about to encounter when I began teaching.

GETTING REAL: STUDENT TEACHING

During the fall of 1967 I was a student teacher in a beginning German class at Davidson Junior High School in San Rafael. At the time, the State of California mandated the teaching of foreign language in sixth through eighth grades. Although the class went well and the students were generally good learners, some didn't understand why they were asked to learn a foreign language. "They don't seem able to believe that somewhere in the world people really communicate in such a manner. It all seems rather like a code to them."[193] This led me to write a paper calling for flexible scheduling in English and Foreign Language for a course I was taking on Secondary School Curriculum. I imagined a different way of approaching the subject of language. I suggested first teaching basic principles of language itself, how languages developed in different parts of the world,[194] and how they change over time. Since the purpose of learning foreign languages was to increase students' understanding of different cultures, I proposed making cultural studies central and teaching different languages as part of that experience.

The next semester I student-taught in an honors English class at Drake High School in San Anselmo. Teaching high school English was far more interesting and challenging than teaching beginning language to younger students. This was what I wanted to be doing, engaging in encounters with young people who were formulating their values and deciding how they would live their lives. Here's where I thought I could make a real difference.

I reflected on my experiences in the work I submitted for a correspondence course, Teaching English Literature and Composition in Secondary Schools.[195] Although I started the course

---

193   "Toward a Combined English and Foreign Language Curriculum Using a System of Flexible Scheduling," term paper for English 274, December 7, 1967.
194   I learned about how languages developed and changed over time in English 203, History of the English Language, taught by Ms. Herndon.
195   Problems in Teaching English Literature and Composition in Secondary Schools, University of California Extension, Bertrand Evans and James Lynch, professors. Correspondence courses were the forerunners of today's on-line courses. Course materials included a spiral-bound book with fifteen class sessions and assignments, plus four books I ordered from the Berkeley Book Store,

in April, I did most of the work over the summer, allowing me to reflect on the class I student-taught. Professor Evans kept pushing me to consider the "Big Why" behind what I chose to teach. He wanted me to keep a balance between teaching literature as literature and teaching for the meaning or message the literary selection conveyed. I tended more toward the latter and my grades on the assignments suffered, but I became clearer about why I was teaching.

I described the students I taught as generally middle class, speaking Standard English, with "a high degree of familiarity with books through their families." I was concerned, however, about how influenced they were by their peer group, "particularly in their view of life and of the adult world." It was 1968, and the youth rebellion was well underway. I found it odd to be cast in their view as an adult, when I still felt like a student and was only 24 years old myself. I noted: "Most of them are aware of this influence and have begun to search for independence, but their tendency to go to cliché was great." I hoped my teaching might help them move beyond this stage and become more able to think for themselves. I realize now that I was engaged in a similar process myself.

Day to day interaction with my class changed my idealism about how and what to teach. I was forced to question my assumptions about what was valuable about literature for students. I realized that for them reading was not their only literary form but rather that movies and songs often communicated more to them than books. Eventually I came up with an idea that worked by satisfying both the required curriculum and the students' needs and interests. I chose poems I was supposed to teach and paired them with lyrics of popular songs with related themes. For instance, Leonard Cohen's "Suzanne"[196] and John Keats's "La Belle Dame sans Merci" (The

---

including a text written by the two professors who taught the course. When I finished the reading for a class session and completed the writing assignment, I mailed it to the professors whom I never met or talked with. One of the professors wrote comments on my papers and returned them to me by mail. When I had completed all the assignments, I went to an Extension Center to take my final exam.

196   The first popular version of "Suzanne" was recorded by Judy Collins in 1966.

beautiful lady without mercy) shared similar stories: beautiful women offering food and love but remaining unavailable long term. Reading the popular song lyrics along with the poem helped the poem that was considered "literature" come alive for the students.

Just as we finished discussing the two poems, an announcement came over the loud-speaker in the classroom calling for a moment of silence for Robert Kennedy, who had died that morning after being shot the night before, right after winning the California presidential primary. We sat in stunned silence for a time. Then a student said, "We need mercy right about now! I'll take Suzanne over the other beautiful lady any day." What a sad way to know they got it! Then the bell rang to end class, so there wasn't time for response.

In anticipation of the possible continued discussion, I prepared another pairing of poems: e.e. cummings' "If everything happens that can't be done" and the Beatles' "Fixing a Hole" (Paul McCartney and John Lennon):

I'm taking the time for a number of things
That weren't important yesterday
And I still go
I'm fixing a hole where the rain gets in
And stops my mind from wandering
Where it will go

"I like the lines at the end of the song," a student said. "I feel that way sometimes myself."

"What way is that?" I asked.

"It's like taking time out when something big happens, so you can think about what to do. Like now, when it seems so horrible that the coolest leaders are getting killed.[197] I thought Bobby would make a great president."

They liked the e.e. cummings poem, too, especially the last stanza, because it left them feeling hopeful about the future and their role in it.

we're anything brighter than even the sun
(we're everything greater

---

[197]   Martin Luther King, Jr. had been killed two months earlier, on April 4, 1968.

than books
might mean)
we're everyanything more than believe
(with a spin
leap
alive we're alive)
we're wonderful one times one

"Do you think we really can be more than our parents believe we can be?" another student asked.

"What do you think?" I asked the class.

"We're alive," someone said. "That means there's hope. I like that line 'we're anything brighter than even the sun.'"

"My favorite is 'we're everything greater than books might mean'. That one makes me smile," another said. "Someday maybe I'll write a better book than I've ever read!"

I finally felt they understood the importance of literature. In later reflections on my teaching experience, I wrote: "I can think of no quality other than the ability to humanize the reader that great books might be said to have in common." It shouldn't matter, I thought, if a book or other literary work (according to my broader definition including movies, plays, and songs) had been recognized by literary scholars as great. "If a book has the power to humanize, to speak to people now, to affect people in a positive fashion, then it should be considered great without concern or speculation as to whether succeeding ages will also judge it great." This understanding would guide me in future choices I would make about what to teach.

GETTING A JOB

While I was student teaching and finishing my last semester at Dominican College, I was also searching for a teaching position. I quickly learned there were few openings for new teachers in Marin County, where I had wanted to teach, and none for which I was particularly qualified. Disappointed, I extended my search to the county north of us, Sonoma County, and applied to the closest school district, Petaluma.

In May I was asked to come in for an interview. I began the

interview process at the Petaluma High School District Office in Petaluma, where I was interviewed by the Superintendent, Lesley Meyer. He told me about a job opening at Rohnert Park Junior High School. Although I was hoping for high school, I knew by then this might be my only choice, so I said, "Yes!" He responded without hesitation. "That's good because I already set up an appointment for you." Then he paused to look at his watch, "Oh, you'd better get right on your way, since your appointment is set for a half hour from now!"

When I got to my car, I discovered I had locked my keys inside. I ran back inside the building in a panic. The first person I saw was a custodian.

"Help!" I blurted out. "I mean, can you help me, please? I locked my keys in the car."

"Wait a minute," he said, and left me standing there wondering. He came out a minute later with a wire coat hanger. "Come with me," he motioned. He straightened the hanger wire with a pair of pliers he had in his pocket and in about two minutes had my car open.

"You saved my life! Thank you, thank you, thank you." I said, breathing a huge sigh of relief.

As I drove off, I looked back and saw him standing there, still holding the hanger, chuckling to himself and shaking his head. I wondered how many other teachers he had helped.

With only minutes to spare, I made it to my appointment with Ralph Azevedo. After several questions, which I apparently answered to his satisfaction, he explained, "We need someone to teach a class in first-year German, which you seem qualified to do." I agreed.

"Since we already have enough English teachers," he continued, "you would probably also probably teach Social Studies, since I see you have a minor it that. How does that sound?"

No English! I said to myself. Then I took a deep breath and asked, "Would there be a possibility of teaching English in future years? That's what I have been preparing to teach."

"Maybe," he responded, offering scant hope. "But for now, this is the job we have available. Are you interested?"

I had been looking long enough that I knew this might be my only offer. "Yes," I said quietly, hoping the doubt and disappointment I felt didn't show too much.

"Great," he said, apparently choosing to ignore my less than enthusiastic response. He needed one more teacher to be fully staffed for the year, and I would do. He didn't realize, of course, that I was about to shake up his school with my increasingly radical ideas about education.

"You need to go back to the district office and fill out some paperwork," he said in conclusion. "In the meantime, I will call the superintendent and tell him you are hired."

We shook hands and I smiled to myself as I went back to my car. The day had brightened up. The sky was blue with only a few wispy clouds. I was one step further along my path to becoming a teacher.

My contract arrived in the mail, as promised, a week later. I signed it on June 1, agreeing to a salary of $6669.00,[198] to be paid in 12 installments of $555.75 a month, beginning at the end of September. It doesn't seem like much money now, but it was more than enough to pay back my loans and contribute to our family's needs. For me it was an achievement to be celebrated, even if I wasn't teaching what I had just prepared to teach. Somehow, I had faith, it would all work out.

ENCOUNTERING RADICAL IDEAS ABOUT EDUCATION

Shortly after signing my contract, I attended one more course at Dominican, a symposium for teachers in the community. How could I resist the topic: "Today's Youth: Growing Up Absurd?"[199] The week-long symposium for area teachers was scheduled for the week after the school year ended, when teachers were still somewhat in work mode. The guide for the week was Scott Beach, an actor

198   According to the conversion scale for 2015, $6999.00 in 1968 = $45,903 in 2015.
199   "Today's Youth: Growing Up Absurd?" Dominican College, June 17 to 21, 1968, 9 AM-4 PM.

I knew from Festival Theatre. He pointed out that the root of the word "absurd" was "surd," which means voiceless. It was good that today's youth were making their voices heard. He raised the question, though, as to whether we want to encourage our students to be creative or not, since they might have to suppress their creativity to be successful in society. The panel on creativity that followed helped me resolve any doubts I might have about encouraging student creativity. To allow creativity to emerge, teachers needed to remove barriers and encourage students to express themselves without fear of criticism. If school did not provide this open context, students might not otherwise have this opportunity in their lives.

The most mind-opening part of the symposium was a panel with two men who become my heroes: Peter Marin and James Herndon. Peter Marin directed an alternative free school, Pacific High School, in the Palo Alto hills. His critique of public education left little doubt in my mind as to the resistance I would encounter if I tried to change the way schools worked. "If you don't agree with the system, start your own school," he recommended. "The system is only really changed by groups outside who show them what is possible."[200] Maybe I would come to the same conclusion after I had tried to make it work within the system, but first I had to try.

Fortunately for my sense of self-worth at the time, James Herndon, author of *The Way It Spozed to Be*, offered a more moderate approach. "I'm not yet willing to give up on the system," he said, explaining that he found the system "more bendable and resilient than he once thought it would be." He encouraged me "to stretch it as far as I wanted," and assured me that "all I can do is fail and I might find some new techniques." He had practical suggestions, too, like following the school rules to take roll but then not penalizing students for being absent. I appreciated his faith that "by staying in the system we can change it." More important, he said, "we can provide something to the students we contact that they would

---

200   Peter Marin and James Herndon, panelists, "Just What Is Tried and True in Educating the Young?" June 18, 1968, as recorded on Reaction Cards for Dominican College symposium "Today's Youth: Growing Up Absurd?" Quotes that follow also from the Reaction Cards.

otherwise miss." This is what I wanted to do!

I hoped I could offer alternative, free education within the public-school setting, but I was also attracted to those who managed to break free from the way things were and do things in an utterly new way. The two poles represented by Peter Marin and James Herndon would do battle within me throughout my six-year career in public school teaching. Ultimately what kept me working within the system was practical. I needed a job with a regular salary.

The most far-out presentation in the symposium was Lou Gottlieb's contribution to the panel "Drop Out? Go Along? Fight Back?" I loved his music with the folk duo, The Limeliters. Now he had moved to a place he owned in the country to establish a free land community called Morningstar Ranch, issuing an open invitation to anyone who wanted to come live on the land and support each other in creating community. His was the "drop out" perspective, which he described as "the alternative society." My comments at the time reflect what I would continue to believe as I encountered those in my world who "dropped out" to live a more radical life-style than I was willing or able to live, but which nonetheless attracted me.[201]

In each of us, I believe, is at least a tendency to believe in such a style of life. Most of us, however, are too tied to the things of our own lives to be able to go along with it, or to want to live that way. Yet it is important for us to know just what it is that is being offered and being conceived of as possible. Some of our students will have ideas about joining this "society." We must at least know what it is about, or we will be of little help to those students.

I think it is important that we do not attempt to invalidate what Mr. Gottlieb says…Certainly the criticism he wages against our society has truth in it, and…in attempting to right the wrongs is where our efforts ought to be directed.

If I had any doubt about the radical nature of my preparation for teaching at Dominican College, this symposium settled it. I was beginning to understand the power of education to change the learner. I now understood my potential role, not only as a teacher

---

201   More about my visit to Morningstar in Culture Change, Free Land.

but also as a change agent in the public school

THE REALITY OF PUBLIC SCHOOL TEACHING

I spent a week in late August getting oriented to my new school and setting up my classroom. I was disappointed when I got my class schedule to discover that besides the one German class I was well prepared to teach, I would be teaching two classes in US history and two in geography. I had not taken a class in US history since high school, and had never studied geography. When I pointed this out to Principal Azevedo, he shrugged his shoulders and said, "So, just use the textbook and stay a chapter ahead of the kids. I'm sure you'll do just fine."

Both courses were part of what was called Social Studies. Because I had taken courses at Pomona like sociology of religion, social welfare, and anthropology, and the sociology course at Dominican, I had enough credits for my California teaching credential to list this as a minor, thus officially qualifying me to teach any social studies course. The attitude at the time in many schools was that practically anyone could teach such classes, whether listed on their credential or not.

The first day of school was a shock! Things started out well enough with my German class of only 14 students, but after that I was faced with mostly unruly eighth graders who seemed to care little about learning, and even less about the subject matter at hand. Scenes from the movie, *Up the Down Staircase*,[202] kept flashing though my mind. In this movie, Sandy Dennis played an idealistic first-year teacher in a difficult urban high school. Despite huge obstacles she finally managed to get through to at least a few of her students. I wondered which, if any, of these students I would succeed in reaching.

After school that first day, teachers were invited to a party at the principal's house. When I arrived, a line was waiting outside to greet the principal. When my turn came, I shook his hand and said, "Now I know why teachers go on strike!" The next day I joined

---

202   A 1967 movie based on a 1965 novel by Bel Kaufman about her experiences teaching in urban high schools for 15 years.

the California Federation of Teachers, an affiliate of the American Federation of Teachers just getting started in the district at the time.[203] While I was a member, the union didn't take any actions in our district but lawsuits were filed on behalf of teachers elsewhere in California. It was the only time in my life I was a member of a union, and it felt right to me to be part of a group that stood up for teachers' rights.

In the meantime, I had to figure out how to survive. I remembered advice I had laughed at before: how necessary it was to show the kids who is boss. When I asked experienced teachers at my school how they handled things, they agreed that strict discipline was needed. They told me to establish a well-defined set of rules for student behavior and then enforce those rules with a series of punishments varying in severity. The trouble was, I wasn't that kind of teacher and I didn't want to rule with threats and intimidation.

I looked up the meaning of discipline in the dictionary: "training that develops self-control, character, or orderliness, efficiency." It seemed to me the original meaning had been lost in the current practice of control from the outside. I failed to see how controlling students would help them develop their own potential. I wanted to reach students and inspire them to learn and grow. This would be more difficult to accomplish than I imagined.

I tried using the textbooks, assigning pages for them to read as homework, and engaging them in class discussion the next day. I soon learned that at best only a few students would read the material outside of class, so for a while I tried having them read a section to themselves in class and then asking them questions. That worked to an extent in US History, but not in Geography, since some students could barely read. If I asked them to read aloud, I risked embarrassing and further alienating those students. Besides, the textbooks seemed of little interest to the students and in a couple of weeks I stopped using them except occasionally for reference.

---

203   The California Federation of Teachers, affiliated with the American Federation of Teachers, was at the time more change-oriented than the well-established state professional association, affiliated with the National Education Association.

Instead I tried talking with them about what was going on in the world and in their lives, asking them what they wanted to learn, noticing topics they raised and finding materials that related to their interests. These students were different from those in Marin County, because most did not have the same advantages. They grew up in homes with few, if any, books. Most of their parents had not gone to college and some had dropped out of high school. They did not necessarily expect their kids to do well in school or go to college.

As I got to know the students, I became aware of deeper problems. Compared to the Marin County students I worked with as a student teacher, my new students were more likely to come from working or lower-middle class families. Some had chaotic home lives, with parents who worked long hours, leaving their children to fend for themselves. Kids who were only 13 or 14 were responsible for their younger siblings, or for getting dinner on the table. Some came to school hungry and tired and occasionally with bruises. No wonder they had difficulty concentrating on learning.

Although the state college was only a mile away, there wasn't much emphasis that I could see on college preparation. Instead there seemed to be resentment of the "hippie" college students who were viewed as a potentially corrupting influence on the young people of the community. What was admired and encouraged most by the school and the community was sports, especially football. Students who were not good at sports tended to be put down both by students and even some teachers. Sports supposedly taught good citizenship and teamwork, but I saw it differently:

In general, the students were learning to follow orders, to conform to standards set by others with no questions asked, to ostracize anyone who was different, to try to have as much fun as they could behind the back of any teacher they saw as weak, to cheat on tests whenever possible, to get the best grades they could without really learning anything, to do whatever was easiest. And I wanted to help them become free and open and to think for themselves. Now I know I'm insane![204]

---

204   "Evolution of a Radical Public-School Teacher," hand-written notes, c. 1971.

Dorothy May Emerson

THERE'S GOT TO BE ANOTHER WAY
"Think of a child, healthy and strong, radiating with life's creative energy," I later wrote in my master's thesis. I described the child as "eager to learn about the world and to discover the joy of expanding into the fullness of his/her being." That's how it should be, I thought, but wondered, "Are children ever really like this? The reality is the story of how our schools help society sustain the death blow to this brilliantly emerging happy child within us all."

In school, we learn to follow orders. We learn that somebody else knows what is best for us. We learn to be part of a crowd which is controlled by someone else. We learn to do meaningless work because someone tells us to do it and because it's supposed to be good for us. We learn to avoid making decisions for ourselves and to let others tell us what to do. We accept boredom as an inevitable part of our lives, inflicted upon us by those who are preparing us for lives of mindless drudgery relieved only by our craving for excitement, which we devour in often self-destructive ways. We are sold a façade of self-government, a fantasy of freedom, but our minds are controlled, as is our capacity to learn.[205]

Frustrated at what seemed to be a lack of understanding on the part of teachers and administrators at my school, I took advantage of opportunities to meet teachers from other schools in the district. Recalling my first indication that there were others who saw, as I did, the need for change, I wrote: "Full of questions I arrived one evening at a meeting of social studies teachers. There I learned a great deal of questioning was indeed going on and had already led to the development of a new social studies curriculum. I thought it strange that no one at my school seemed to be aware of these new ideas."

The district Curriculum Coordinator, Eunice Loewke, had organized the meeting. A true change agent operating within the school system, she had the uncanny ability to recognize in teachers she encountered those who might join her in working to create more

205   Dorothy E. Orser, "Alternative Public Education," master's thesis, Humanistic Psychology Institute, 1974, 1-2.

relevant curriculum and better schools. She became my mentor and guide, invited me to participate in district in-service projects, and introduced me to the Marin Social Studies Project.

It is not an overstatement when I say the Marin Social Studies Project and its director Sid Lester saved me from certain disaster as a first-year teacher. The project received funding through the same US government program as Festival Theatre.[206] The purpose was to field test, evaluate, and develop new social studies curricula and provide teachers like me access to the most innovative social studies practices and materials available at the time. The people associated with this project and the materials they shared gave me hope that real education was possible even in public schools.

TEACHING NEW SOCIAL STUDIES

Because I was I playing catch-up in my preparation to teach social studies, I eagerly signed up for a Sonoma State College extension course, Teaching New Social Studies,[207] Sid Lester was offering that spring. Once the course began, I realized how pertinent it was to the dilemma I now faced about how and what to teach that might make a real difference in students' lives. New Social Studies was based on a change in the conceptual foundation of the field. Its goals of developing in students heightened social consciousness matched what I felt called to do in my teaching. How to do this was what I needed to learn. I marveled that I happened to be at the right place at the right time to participate in this innovative movement.

Sid began by introducing us to a definition of education I had not yet heard. "Education equals change," Sid said. "Whatever you learn changes you. If there is no change, then real education has not taken place." This simple but profound equation became my mantra. Sid then introduced two models that described levels of learning and decision-making: Benjamin Bloom's Taxonomy

---

206   Funding was provided by Title III of the 1965 Elementary and Secondary Education Act, part of President Johnson's War on Poverty. Title III invested in research and educational innovations.

207   Education 486, Teaching New Social Studies, Sid Lester, Sonoma State College Extension, Spring 1969.

of Educational Objectives[208] and Lawrence Kohlberg's six levels of moral decision-making.[209] Considering these developmental models helped me understand my students and move them toward higher level processes. Challenging work, but knowing these frameworks gave me a place to start.

Sid shared with us his basic premises about students and our role as teachers. What a contrast to the views I heard expressed by other teachers at my school! Sid suggested that our first responsibility was to study our students, listen to them, understand their problems and their ideas. He claimed that good teachers didn't have discipline problems and that if we did, it was up to us to improve our teaching. He recommended that we focus on learning, not on covering some pre-determined body of material. But his most radical idea may have been that we de-emphasize grades and consider what the kids think they earned.[210]

I spent hours adapting what I was learning into lesson plans and then trying them out. I met with my principal to let him know my plans to use innovative materials. He said, "What you do in your classroom is your business, so long as your students don't cause problems for the rest of the school." He approved my attendance at the spring conference of the California Council for the Social Studies, an organization I would participate in throughout my years as a teacher. The theme of that first conference was "Human Rights: Crisis in Confrontations."[211]

---

208   Benjamin Bloom et al, *Taxonomy of educational objectives: The classification of educational goals. Handbook I: Cognitive domain, 1956.*

209   Some of Lawrence Kohlberg's most important publications have been collected in his *Essays on Moral Development*, Vols. I and II, *The Philosophy of Moral Development* (1981) and *The Psychology of Moral Development* (1984), published by Harper & Row. Later I would discover Carol Gilligan's critique of the model. Her book, *In a Different Voice* (1982), postulates an alternative model for women.

210   Selected and adapted from "Lester's Fourteen Points," handout for Education 486, Teaching New Social Studies, Sonoma State College Extension, Spring 1969.

211   California Council for the Social Studies, 8th Annual Conference, "Human Rights: Crisis in Confrontations," El Cortez Hotel, San Diego, CA, March 21-13, 1969.

THE POLITICS OF SOCIAL STUDIES, 1969

Ironically, my unanticipated role as a social studies teacher led to my first direct engagement in politics. A battle was brewing in California concerning how to teach students to be responsible citizens, a battle that continues today. At the conference, I learned about efforts to establish a new state-wide inquiry-based framework for social studies that would include an emphasis on teaching students to think about public issues and understand the need to protect and promote human rights, especially the rights of minorities. However, State Education Superintendent Max Rafferty was dead-set against the proposal. He blamed progressive education and "secular humanism" for the decline of "morality" among America's youth and advocated teaching a narrow set of moral principles based on so-called traditional values.

The Marin Social Studies Council promised to provide members active support and educational opportunities to learn about "the powerful ideas responsible for the Social Studies Revolution...The forthcoming year promises to be a crucial point in the history of social studies teaching! In this time of social flux, the schools—particularly the portion responsible for teaching about society—come under increasing pressure. Activities of extremist groups are intensifying and expanding. ... Social studies teachers MUST UNITE...if they are to deal effectively with such radical onslaughts."[212]

I had walked right into the middle of a culture clash.

TEAR-GASSED IN BERKELEY

Early in 1969, something happened to Thomas and me that radically changed my understanding of the times we were living in. We were invited to a cocktail party in Berkeley. We dressed up for such events. I wore a black cocktail dress, sparkly jewelry, a bright pink shawl, and high heels. Thomas wore gray wool slacks, a navy-

---

212   Membership invitation, Marin County Council for the Social Studies with attached excerpts from "Guidelines for Moral Instruction in California's Schools," 1969.

blue sport jacket and a maroon ascot, a then popular alternative to a tie. The party was in an elegant home near the university, hosted by actors from Festival Theatre. The hosts served the usual mixed drinks but very little food. After a few drinks, we realized that to avoid getting drunk we needed something to eat. People at the party suggested a gourmet hot dog place nearby called Top Dog, so we excused ourselves and walked a few blocks down Durant Avenue.

Once we got out onto the street, we realized something was going on, probably one of the protests we had heard about. Down the block, we saw police chasing students who were running away from campus. Another group of students ran past us with faces buried in their hands, crying. We could see the hot dog place up ahead, so we continued walking, wary but not afraid. We weren't involved in whatever was going on, which should be obvious, we thought, since we were dressed very differently from the protestors.

But that didn't matter to the police car that slowed as it passed us. The men in the car threw something out of the window that exploded on the ground right beside us. "Oh, my God, Thomas," I screamed. "It's tear gas!" I could barely keep my burning eyes open as we ran for the relative safety of Top Dog. Inside the small brick building tears poured out of nearly everyone's eyes. We still had no idea what the protest was about.

"Listen up," a student protestor called out in the crowded room. "We're under attack and we need to protect ourselves." But how? I wondered. At that point police surrounded the small building. Several pushed their way in carrying clubs.

"Break it up!" the one who seemed to be in charge yelled. "We know you're having a meeting in here and you must leave immediately."

I mustered up my most adult, teacherly voice. "We're only here to get some food. We have a right to eat."

"All right," he barked at me. "Everyone who is not ordering food has to leave. Now!"

I knew that sometimes, in response to protests, cops were called in from communities some distance away and were reported to use overly forceful tactics in an effort to "restore order." I took a deep breath and ventured a challenge. "I would like to see your badge. What police force are you with?"

"We don't have to tell you," he said. "On a night like tonight, you have no rights. We have all the power."

I was stunned, but I finally knew how I would begin teaching about the United States Constitution. We barely tasted our hot dogs as we talked with protestors about what they were doing and why. They told us they were supporting the Third World Liberation Front strike, demanding the university teach ethnic studies. They felt bad we had been caught in the crossfire, but since we were there they hoped we would tell others what was going on. I assured them we would. After an hour or so, our eyes still burned, but we were stone cold sober and made it home safely, shocked by the encounter.

On Monday morning, I got to school early and arranged the desks in a circle for my US History and Geography classes. I watched the door as students saw the circle of desks, stopped talking, and took their seats, understanding that something unusual must be going on. I began by telling them what happened to me in Berkeley. Then, in the US History classes I asked, "What does the Constitution have to do with this situation?" In Geography, I began with, "What would you do if this happened to you?"

I got their attention for once, and the best discussions we had that year followed. The US History students were motivated after that to learn about the Constitution, especially the Bill of Rights, and for the Geography students something shifted in their openness to my approach to teaching. I learned that discussions worked best when we could all see each other. Although it wasn't practical to keep the desks in a circle all the time, I experimented with different room arrangements after that.

VALUES IN CRISIS

Protests on college campuses across the country were growing more violent, although things were relatively quiet at the schools closest to us. When I attended my first conference of the California Social Studies Council, held in San Diego in March, I was looking for resources to use in teaching about the political and cultural conflicts happening in this country. I discovered a teaching tool I would use many times in the next years: a filmstrip series called *Law and Order: Values in Crises.*[213]

The first filmstrip began with stories about societies with opposite values that each considered the only right way to live. For example, two neighboring American Indian tribes had very different practices regarding horses. In one, horses were considered community property, so if you needed a horse and one was nearby, you could take it and then leave it for someone else to use. But in the other, horses were personal property, so if you took a horse it was stealing. Most of the students agreed with the tribe that considered taking things to be stealing. To open them to the possibility of another way of thinking, I described people who lived communally and believed in sharing everything. These people rejected consumerism and the emphasis on accumulating wealth and property. The students were surprised to learn there were people in our society like that.

The filmstrips also showed conflicts between police and protestors. Different eras and protests were pictured, some involving civil rights and others the war in Vietnam. Afterwards, some voiced support for the police and others sided with the demonstrators. Still others weren't sure. We talked about why some people protested and others called the protests un-American. I asked them to consider what, if anything, might lead them to participate in a protest.

Over time, at least some students began to understand social and cultural norms and values as relative and to think in more nuanced terms about clashes between people with different values. This opened the door for them to consider what their own values were and to begin to think for themselves about what was right and wrong.

---

213   The soundtrack was on cassette tapes with beeps to indicate where the pictures were to be changed. The images were still photos, but the accompanying sound was realistic enough to get the students thinking about what it would be like to be there.

THE CONSTITUTION TEST

One of the few requirements the State of California had for eighth-grade graduation was that all students pass a test on the US Constitution. Rather than providing a standardized test, teachers were supposed to make up their own. This left things wide open in terms of what I might choose to teach.

In preparing our study of the Constitution as the basis of the form of government we call representative democracy, I came across the concept of oligarchy and decided to introduce it to my students. The next day I wrote five words on the blackboard: democracy, socialism, communism, monarchy, and oligarchy. They were familiar with the other terms but wanted to know what oligarchy was. I explained it as the rule of the few, who are generally richer and more powerful than the others. Then I asked them to define the other terms and indicate which system we had in this country. They ruled out monarchy and communism, but the more we considered the other definitions and looked at how things worked in this country the less sure they were that democracy was the only system. I doubt this was what the State of California had in mind for the students to learn about the Constitution.

The students were surprised to learn that the Constitution was written by and originally applied to those who at the time were considered citizens, namely white men with property. This motivated them to study the amendments that over time broadened the concept of citizenship and extended the right to vote to more people. It was easy after that to stress the importance of voting, and that, I knew, was one of the things the state wanted students to learn.

For the required test on the Constitution, I made up questions that reflected what the classes had discussed and what I hoped they had learned. The students were pleased that they all passed. I know they learned more about the Constitution than they expected to.

DISCOVERING THE USE OF SIMULATION

I was beginning to feel better about my teaching, but the Geography classes remained an ongoing challenge. Eunice invited me to participate in an in-service project she created in conjunction with Sonoma State College.[214] The goal was to encourage teachers to develop their ideas for new approaches to education by providing relevant resources they might not otherwise have access to. As part of this I attended a seminar on Simulation Games at the Ortega Park Teachers Laboratory of Portola Institute.[215]

At the laboratory-seminar I learned about a simulation[216] called Micro-Society, which I adapted for use in both German and Geography.[217] The simulation involved creating a monetary system of exchange in the classroom. I made "money" using colored card stock left over from my husband's work at a print shop. These paper "chips" were unique enough to discourage students from making copies. I decided to introduce the simulation in my Geography classes by passing out the "chips" (money) without explaining what I was doing or why I was doing it.

When the starting bell rang, I gave one "chip" to each of the students who were in their seats. This created an immediate buzz and kids called out questions, which I ignored. Finally, a couple of students raised their hands and I gave them each another chip. After explaining the idea in response to their questions, I invited them to help decide what sorts of things they could do to earn chips, which they easily recognized as a form of money. They came up with actions that were like behavioral rules I had been trying to get them to follow for months—like being in class on time, sitting in their seats, raising their hands before speaking, waiting to be called on, and completing assignments.

---

214 Funding was provided by the California Teachers Association and the Rosenberg Foundation.

215 Portola Institute was established in 1966 as a nonprofit corporation to encourage, organize, and conduct innovative educational projects. Ortega Park Teachers Laboratory, Simulation Games, Computer Education, and the Whole Earth Catalog were all divisions of Portola Institute.

216 In games, participants try to win within a set of rules. In simulations, participants act as themselves within in an environment that simulates a real-world situation. Games tend to be played for a specific time, while simulations can develop and grow in complexity over time.

217 Dorothy E. Orser, "Teaching German through Simulation Games," INPUT: Independent Projects by Teachers, 1968-69 Projects, 1-5. Dorothy E Orser and Dodi Orser were names I used 1966-75.

Right away they wanted to know what they could use the chips for. Together we decided on things like borrowing a pencil, using special materials like colored pens, running the movie or filmstrip projector, and using the pass to go outside to get a drink of water. I nixed their suggestions that we fine those who were late or talked out of turn, because I only wanted to reward positive behavior. After a while they got creative and started small businesses, such as selling materials or snacks. One group eventually opened a bank, so students didn't have to worry about carrying their money around and possibly losing it. One of the best things about this was that they began working with each other instead of fighting and putting each other down.

We went on with other lessons, including some that related to the official subject of the class, Geography. When I could make a connection with a part of the world that had an impact on their lives, I brought in information and maps and we learned about that country. For instance, they wanted to know more about Vietnam, because of the war there and England, because that's where the Beatles and the Rolling Stones were from. Another geography-related activity involved them in making maps of their lives, drawing the routes they took from home to school, where they went after school and on weekends, where their extended families lived, where they took trips, etc. They enjoyed making their maps but they learned that drawing a map other people could understand wasn't easy.

The money system stayed in place for the rest of the year, because it seemed to help the classes settle down. They were never perfect students, but there was definite improvement. One day I got proof. Each classroom had an intercom that was used for school announcements. One day the principal's voice startled us, "Mrs. Orser, come to the office right away." I looked rather helplessly at the students, who were busy on an assignment and seemed to ignore the announcement and said, "Take care of each other while I'm gone, please." I practically ran to the office, figuring this could only be bad news. When I got to the office, there seemed to be some confusion about why I had been called. After a few minutes, the principal came out and said, "False alarm, I guess."

Confused, I walked hurriedly back. As I approached the room, I heard music. When I got to the door, I saw the room had been rearranged and decorated for a party and someone had brought in a radio. When I saw the cake that said: "Thank you Teacher," I had a hard time not crying. How did they plan this without my finding out? I wondered, amazed that they got the principal and office staff to help them. I knew then how much they had changed from the beginning of the year when they hated most everything about school. I felt so proud of them for the way they must have worked together to do this. I finally felt hopeful that maybe I could survive and make a difference as a teacher!

CREATING NEW COURSES

Toward the end of the school year, I approached Principal Azevedo with an idea for a new course for the following year.

"What I've learned about my students this year is that they want to know more about the world we live in today," I explained. "That's why I'd like to create a new social studies course for next year on the current culture."

"Hmm. Might be possible," he said.

The next week he asked me to come to his office.

"I've been thinking about your idea and have decided we can try it out. We can call the course Contemporary Culture," he said. "I also want you to teach Afro-Asian History. You'll still be teaching German, but this means you won't have Geography or US History. How does that sound?"

"Sure," I said with only slight hesitation. "I'll have to study up on Afro-Asian History this summer, but it should be interesting."

On the way home, I stopped at Dominican College and picked up the list of summer courses. I signed up for a class on African Art and Music.[218]

I realize now how supportive my principal was of my unconventional approach to education. In his evaluation of my teaching that first year, he wrote: "She does not have the easiest

---

218   I also participated in the 1969 symposium for teachers, The Community and Contemporary Arts.

teaching situation in our school. In spite of...the type of classes assigned to her, she is contributing much to her students. Dorothy has one of the strongest assets of anyone in the teaching profession, a real sincere feeling for her students' welfare and progress."[219]

I spread the word about the new course through my current classes, encouraged students to sign up if they were interested, and pass the word around to their friends. Some signed up right away and others over the summer. It would be good to have some students for a second year, since we already knew each other. I was pleased at the response and hoped there would be enough for at least two classes.

At the end of the year I passed my yearbook around during class so students could sign it. I got mostly great reviews. One of my favorite comments was: "I really liked being in your class. You really understand us and try to help us. You are a really cool teacher and please don't ever change because there aren't many like that around anymore." I was amazed at how many students said I was the best teacher they ever had. They also used superlatives like greatest, coolest, grooviest, nicest, sweetest, prettiest, cutest, and my favorite "tuffest."

IN-SERVICE PROJECT ON EDUCATIONAL RELEVANCE

Before the end of my first year of teaching, Eunice invited me to meet with other educators in the district to discuss forming "a standing committee to share and develop innovative educational ideas and practices on an interdisciplinary basis."[220] The reason for doing this was, as stated in our in-service project report: "because we perceived a need to stimulate and initiate planned change in the direction of improved educational quality for Petaluma secondary schools."

We referred to ourselves as "the group," but Eunice insisted we have a formal name for reporting purposes, so we agreed to be called the Project on Educational Relevance. The group included

---

219   Teacher Evaluation Summary, by Ralph Azevedo, January 20, 1969.
220   In-Service Project Report, Educational Relevance, prepared by Dorothy Emerson Orser, January 1970.

teachers, counselors, a school psychologist, a nurse, and the curriculum coordinator. After the first couple of meetings in late May, I became chair. When the district granted us $700 for expenses, our first purchase was thirteen copies of a new book, *Teaching as a Subversive Activity*, by Neil Postman and Charles Weingartner, which we agreed to read over the summer.

Over the next year, we shared more books: *How Children Fail* and *How Children Learn*, by John Holt, *Education and Ecstasy*, by George Leonard, *The Open Classroom*, by Herbert Kohl, *How to Survive in Your Native Land*, by James Herndon, and discussed their implications for our schools. Being part of this group gave me hope that educational change system-wide was possible.

When we met, we shared examples of what worked best in our individual classes. I often took home ideas I could use in my classes. However, our larger goal was system change. We realized that our separate classrooms were a major obstacle to collaboration. "What if we could all work together with one group of students?" I wrote. "What if the learning involved in English, Math, Social Studies, Science, Arts, etc. were combined and put to work on real life problems?"[221] Fortunately, an opportunity presented itself that opened the door to putting our emerging ideas into practice. Planning for a new school was just beginning and a committee to help decide what sort of school to design was being formed. Eunice made sure that five members of "the group" became members of the High School #6 Planning Committee. We took on the responsibility to bring the whole group's input into the planning process. Clearly, I thought, we were in the right place at the right time to make substantive change in the educational system.

SUBVERSIVE TEACHING

Reading *Teaching as a Subversive Activity*[222] validated my criticisms of the educational system and helped me figure out how to teach. Teachers, the book claimed, need to be "subversive," which I

221   Dorothy E. Orser, "Alternative Public Education," 26.
222   Neil Postman and Charles Weingartner, *Teaching as a Subversive Activity*, 1969.

understood to mean that we teachers needed to change schools if we are going to prepare our students for the future. The way education is now, the book explained, sets students up for "future shock [which] occurs when you are confronted by the fact that the world you were educated to believe in doesn't exist."[223] To prepare students to deal with change, education needs to engage students in asking questions and making meaning in their lives, rather than following a set curriculum or teaching content that can be evaluated by tests. Based on my first year of teaching, I couldn't agree more. This book articulated what was in my heart.

Like the New Social Studies, these authors advocated for the use of inquiry as the basic teaching process. The primary goal of education, the authors attest, should be to foster development of "a new kind of person...an actively inquiring, flexible, creative, innovative, tolerant, liberal personality who can face uncertainty and ambiguity without disorientation, who can formulate viable new meanings to meet changes in the environment which threaten individual and mutual survival."[224]

I would later describe this book as my bible, because more than any other it helped shape my desire to create a learning environment that would enhance students' ability to be independent learners and questioners. Two years later, I could describe my approach to lesson planning with greater confidence: "I react to what happens in each class and teach what I think they need to learn next to live together in peace as free people."[225] I could see how that could be considered subversive by those in authority who were invested in the way things had been done in the past.

TEACHING ABOUT OUR CULTURE, 1969-70

Although I was first concerned that kids wouldn't know what Contemporary Culture meant, enough students signed up for three

---

223   *Subversive Activity*, 14. Alvin Toffler's best-selling book, *Future Shock*, was published in 1970.
224   *Subversive Activity*, 218.
225   "Peace, freedom and love," notes taken during World Law Fund workshop, April 15, 1972.

classes. I had gotten what I asked for, but now I needed to figure out what to teach. Here was my chance to create the kind of education I had been dreaming and learning about.

The students would be ninth graders, so I expected them to be somewhat more mature than the eighth graders I had the year before. I looked forward to seeing how former students might change over the summer. Since I had already dealt with virtual nonreaders in my Geography classes, I let the special education teacher know I would accept her students in my classes. I knew issues might arise with the other students, but I figured they would be opportunities for learning.

I decided to start by inviting the kids to make collages about themselves, which would then decorate the classroom. Over the summer, I collected magazines from friends and stacked them up on the counter in the back of the room. My idea was that they would look through the magazines and find pictures and words they connected with, cut them out, and then glue them on the paper as a picture of themselves in relation to their culture.

I arranged the desks on two sides of the room facing each other, rather than in usual rows facing the front. When students first entered the room, they knew this class was going to be different. After the students figured out places to sit, I began: "Welcome to a new class, Contemporary Culture. We are all part of today's culture, but each of us relates to this culture in different ways. We're going to start the year by introducing ourselves to each other using elements of our culture as pictured in magazines. After you finish your collage, you will have a chance to tell us about it and introduce yourself to the class."

They had immediate questions, like what was a collage and why were we doing this. I did my best to answer and then encouraged them to choose a few magazines and get started. Minor chaos reigned while they got supplies.

The next day, students began sharing their collages, while others finished theirs. I asked their permission to post the collages on the bulletin board. Some were shy about this, because they didn't think theirs were any good. I stressed that this was not about artistic ability, and that they were all successful in sharing something about their relationship to the culture we lived in. They weren't used to thinking of themselves as part of culture or as having their own perspectives on what culture is.

I wish I could report that all my teaching was as successful as the collage-making activity, but since I was making up the curriculum as I went along, some things worked better than others. Later I reflected: "I decided to ask each class what they wanted to study and how they wanted to study it. I should have known better. How could they know, since they had never been asked such a question before?" Most of the students had not thought of themselves as wanting to learn. Learning was something they were forced to do by other people. I wanted this class to help them think for themselves and become motivated to learn on their own, but most of the time I found I needed to create specific activities to help them engage with learning about their world.

One of the most accessible cultural resources was popular music, both folk and rock and roll. I managed to get the school to provide a portable record player for my room. At first some students thought it was ridiculous to suggest that songs had any meaning at all. I had to prove it to them by making copies of the lyrics to songs I wanted them to discuss.[226] Once the students could read and share the lyrics with each other, they began to better understand the messages songs conveyed, and paid closer attention to the meanings of the songs they liked.

Word about the new class spread around the school. The student newspaper described it in glowing terms:

Mrs. Orser is the teacher of contemporary culture, a "far out" class everyone agrees. The class analyzes things happening today, now! There are no assigned seats, which the students dig on. The class listens to music during classes. Some music just to enjoy and some to dig on and find out the meaning of the song. Everyone seems to feel the class is going very well and should be continued

---

226   When the Beatles released *Sgt. Pepper's Lonely Hearts Club Band* in 1967, printed lyrics were included for the first time, but for most records it took hours of playing songs over and over to write the lyrics down.

in the future. Everyone learns about history, but we aren't living in history, we're what's happening, and so is this class.[227]

I felt gratified that I was on the right track with my ideas for the course, but figuring out what to do from day to day proved to be a challenge. Fortunately, the workshops I attended provided me with many new ideas I could use right away. When I didn't have new input, I made things up, generally based on whatever had come up in class discussions or in conversations with students outside of class. Often current events provided provocative topics.

The war in Vietnam provided an ongoing rich and controversial topic. Using the *Law and Order: Values in Crisis* filmstrips, I sought to create a framework for discussion that would allow all viewpoints to be expressed and heard. On October 15, 1969, there was a nationwide teach-in and demonstration calling for a moratorium on the war. The next month a huge March on Washington featured many popular performers, like Pete Seeger leading the crowds in John Lennon's new song, "Give Peace a Chance." Although the march was mostly peaceful, tear gas was used when fighting broke out near DuPont Circle. Because I remembered how tear gas felt, I was probably less than neutral in my approach.

When the news broke about mass killings of civilians in a small village in Vietnam months earlier, *Time, Life,* and *Newsweek* all carried stories about what became known as the My Lai Massacre. The pictures they published were chilling. Although this event helped turn public opinion against the war, there were students, especially those who had family members in the military, who voiced continued support for the war. I tried to keep my own feelings in check but it was getting harder for me to do so.

Then in the spring, the US invaded Cambodia. Four students at Kent State University were killed a few days later at one of the many protests happening on college campuses in response to the invasion.[228] I was horrified that the National Guard would shoot

---

227   "Two New Courses Have Been Added," *Rampage*, Rohnert Park Jr. High student newspaper, Oct. 1, 1969.
228   I later learned that two Jackson State students in Mississippi were killed by police in a similar protest. These students were black, whereas the Kent State

unarmed students and that college campuses could no longer be considered safe places for young people. Almost immediately, Crosby, Stills, Nash, and Young released a single of Neil Young's song "Four Dead in Ohio" on one side and Stephen Stills' "Find the Cost of Freedom" on the other. It was painful to listen to these songs and realize how bad things had gotten in this country. Many students joined me in feeling outraged, but for others it was too much to deal with and they played it down.

Although I tried to vary the type of activities, a lot of class time involved discussions. Here was where I faced my biggest challenge. The kids that were more verbal enjoyed talking about whatever the topic was, but others rarely participated and sometimes created disturbances. I tried focusing on those who were engaged, hoping the others would find something of interest and join in. Positive reinforcement with those who actively participated in the class activity worked to an extent, but it wasn't enough to keep those who were not engaged from acting out. I needed to figure how to encourage participation from those who were uninvolved and resistant.

As other teachers heard about my approach to teaching, some felt threatened, perhaps by students asking them to do things differently. In my evaluation that fall, Principal Azevedo suggested I "spend time in discussing with the class that these are [your] methods of instruction and that youngsters should expect to meet varying types of instructional methods." At the same time, he gave me plenty of credit:

Dorothy continues to get results from youngsters which some people would think unattainable.

Her approach to the educational process is different, to say the least, but is effective...It is difficult to say how much subject matter is important to the point where it would exclude contemporary problems and the problems of everyday living.

Mrs. Orser is to be complimented on her professional approach to educational theory and practice in that she spends hundreds of hours beyond the school day in trying to improve her classroom

---

students were white. At the time, the news only covered the Kent State killings.

procedures or for the benefit of the Petaluma High School District.[229]

Although the principal recommended my continuation as a teacher at the school, in his final evaluation for the year he indicated that other teachers had apparently complained about my classes: "As her building principal, I must say that her searching for relevance in the area of curriculum becomes quite 'ticklish' at times."[230]

At the time, I had no friends among the faculty. I got tired of hearing teachers' constant complaints about the horrible students they had. Sometimes I got so depressed listening to their talk that I avoided going to the teachers' room altogether, and ate my lunch outside or in my room. My saving grace, both with the principal and other teachers, was that they knew how hard I worked, and that I participated in district meetings and workshops, something hardly anyone else at my school did.

Student response was mostly positive. One boy wrote in my annual: "To the teacher who had to be brave and patient to put up with us. You took a great big task of teaching Contemporary Culture. Only you could have taught it. Keep up the good work. Thanks for your time." A girl wrote: "It's been great being in your classes and I feel if there were more teachers like you I would learn a lot more. You really have been taking on a big job with these kids but you handled it very well." I was pleased with the comments but I knew I could do better. I wanted to reach all my students.

CREATIVE PROBLEM SOLVING

As a struggling teacher, I was fortunate to have access to workshops and courses that broadened my ability to utilize innovative practices in my teaching. When I learned that Robert Adler, a former associate director of Festival Theatre, was teaching a course in Creative Problem Solving at Dominican, I signed up right away. [231] Bob brought his creative spirit to teaching by starting right

229 Teacher Evaluation, by Ralph Azevedo, principal, Nov. 20, 1969.
230 Teacher Evaluation, Jan. 21, 1970.
231 Education 126: Creative Problem Solving, Robert Adler, Dominican College, Spring 1970.

off engaging us in problem solving. What I learned in this course helped me figure out the next steps in developing my approach to teaching. The processes Bob took us through during each class meeting opened us up to seeing new ways to address the problems we were facing. Plus, the exercises he had us do were lots of fun and I could use some of them in my classes.

Bob encouraged us to work on real life problems using the creative problem-solving methods he was teaching us. I chose to focus on problems I was facing in my Contemporary Culture classes:

- Getting a class to function as an interrelating, supporting, cooperating group, with everyone involved
- Convincing students that their education can be self-directed
- Opening kids up to new ways of learning

Bob defined creativity as the ability to change points of view and see things from new perspectives. How might shifting my point of view help me more creatively deal with these problems? Taking us through different processes during each class meeting opened us up to seeing new ways to address the problems we were facing. Toward the end of the course we were asked to work through the process using our most important real-life challenge. The first step was to describe the situation, or as Bob called it, "the mess." I wrote down what I was beginning to realize would be needed to make open learning possible.

I need to find a structure for my classes. They need to know more about what they are learning. They need to be more aware of what is expected of them. They feel confused...I need a clearer idea of what I'm really trying to accomplish—and I need an outline or structure of the class as a whole.

The next step Bob described as "Fact Finding." In one column, I listed questions related to my situation that might have answers, and in the second column people, organizations, books, and other resources that could provide those answers. The third step was called "Problem Finding." I brainstormed "creative type questions" evolving from the mess I had described. Then I selected the one I thought most central, my last question: How can I run a class so it is a true learning environment?

In the "Idea Finding" step, we were to generate ideas but defer judgment until we had as many ideas as possible. This was the basic rule for brainstorming. I came up with nine ideas, four of which I combined the following summer in developing a unique "book" to use with my classes.[232] The book was at least partially successful in helping me move closer to solving my central challenge in teaching.

CREATING A BOOK, 1970

That summer I assembled ideas I had been developing and materials I had collected during my first two years of teaching into a book called *Open!* In the introduction, I wrote responses to typical questions people raised about the Contemporary Culture class and my teaching philosophy and methods. I explained the difference between assignments and activities and provided formats for activities they could use on their own to explore different aspects of culture. I hoped students would eventually use these formats for their own learning. To some extent this worked, at least for some students.

Knowing what had been weakest in my approach the year before, I wrote An Invitation to Self-Management, my attempt to explain what others called discipline: "The basic work of this class is for you to learn to take care of yourself. In this class, you are being given an opportunity to practice being in charge of yourself. The goal is...for you to learn to set your own goals and work towards them on your own. Self-management means you can control your own actions not only for your own needs but also with an understanding of others." If students were unable to control themselves, I recommended they separate themselves from the group and either write or draw about what was going on for them. I even created a special page to help them think about what was happening.

The last part of my methodology section was about skills I hoped students would develop in the class: critical thinking, locating and gathering information, organizing information, evaluating

---

232   Two additional steps, Solution Finding and Acceptance Finding, are included on the diagram of the process by the Creative Problem-Solving Institute, 1969, distributed by Robert Adler, Spring 1970.

information, group discussion, competency in group participation and human relations, and the ability to understand oneself.[233] As I assembled this section I realized I now had a coherent educational philosophy and methodology. My methods and class structure were still idealistic and varied in how successful they were, but no one could accuse me after this of not knowing what I was doing or why.

The next section of the book contained quotations from a wide range of people on themes I planned to explore in the class, such as society, environment, change, conflict, communication, and values. They could use the quotations as starting ideas for essays, topics for discussions, or themes for collages. They could write a letter to the author or write a report on his or her life. I included ancient philosophers, contemporary writers, poets, politicians, popular song writers, and even controversial figures. A resource section at the end included things I expected to refer to during the year, such as outlines of Propaganda Techniques, Critical Thinking Guidelines, and Decision-Making Processes.

Principal Azevedo supported the project because he was pleased to see me creating a structure for my classes. Two secretaries at school typed the 100 pages of the book on mimeograph masters and ran them off.[234] My family helped, too. When my sister, Mary Lou, visited us that summer, she helped find quotations and then proofread the book. Thomas came up with a brilliant idea to make individualized covers using a technique called marbleizing.[235] Then we put each unique cover on top of a set of assembled pages and

---

233   Adapted from T. Patton and R. Armstead, "A Social Studies Project," Taft Junior High, mimeograph hand-out.

234   These were the days before photocopy machines and personal computers. Each page required a master to be individually typed on a heavy waxed-paper stencil, that was then wrapped around the drum of the mimeograph machine that forced ink out through the cut marks on the stencil. The book was printed on five different colors of paper so it would be easy to find the different sections of the book.

235   The marbleizing process we used involved floating printers' ink on top of a pan of water, blowing on it or using a stick to make swirls, then dipping each book cover in the water, picking up a different design for each one and laying them out on the grass to dry.

bound the books with plastic spiral binding.

USING THE BOOK, 1970-71

On the first day of school, I put the books out on the back counter so their beautiful covers would show. I was very proud of them and invited the students to pick their own book. If they wanted, I said, they could keep them at the end of the year. Sometimes I would see them in the schoolyard showing the books to other students. They made a definite statement that this class was different!

A few weeks later I wrote to my mother:

The book has been well received—both by students and other teachers and some parents. Other parents have made some complaints, but all that happens is that a few have transferred out of my classes. Most have greeted the book with great enthusiasm. I can't describe it all without sounding like I'm boasting. And in class (the really important place) the book and my methods have for the most part been so much better than anything I've done before that I'm almost ashamed about what I've done in the past. What I mean is that I can see real tangible progress! But I also see the immensity and the complexity of the problem I am trying to deal with. After all, what gives me the gall to think that I could solve problems that thousands of others have worked on and not succeeded at solving?

Thanks to the book and the structure it outlined, the Contemporary Culture classes functioned better than my previous classes. Late that fall, the principal stopped by my room after school. "This came for you," he said as he handed me a letter and stood there with a smirk, or was it a smile, on his face while I read it.

I opened the folded letter nervously and saw that it was from a parent, handwritten on notebook paper and addressed to me. As I read the first sentence, I noticed several misspelled words (corrected here). She began by describing how she found my "text-book" among her daughter's possessions and read most of it wondering "how a book of this 'caliber' or a woman of your obvious 'character' is allowed in our public schools at the expense of the taxpayer. I find that your book has insulted many parents' opinions of their teenagers."

"Oh, no," I thought. "What does she mean?" But the next sentence allayed my concerns. "You seem to feel the average 14-year-old child can learn to think beyond the range of a 2-year-old." I breathed a big sigh of relief, smiled at the principal, and read on.

I have most certainly been disgusted, frustrated, disillusioned, and unenthusiastic with our public schools' inability to stimulate creative thinking, mature judgment, controversy, good taste, NOW subjects, dealing with problems...I find your book has included these subjects for discussion, and it has been received with great hope and much appreciation by my daughter and her family, For 30 years I've hated to either go to school or send my children to school. If there were more books like yours, and teachers like you I'm sure I would not feel that the time my family spends in class is wasted.

She went on to say she wished my class were available for younger students, like her fourth-grade son, because she tried to teach her family to think but found they were continually confused in school when it was not expected of them. Then she thanked the principal "for this class and all it can be."

That's quite a letter," I said to the principal.

"Keep up the good work," he said as he turned and left the room.

After he left, I read the letter again and let the tears I had held back flow. In days to come when I felt things were never going to work, I would take out the letter and read it again to give me hope.

Although the book and the structure it outlined helped bring order and purpose to my classes, I still struggled almost daily and often felt frustrated. I wrote to my mother:

Sometimes I don't know whether I'm a really brilliant creative person or a stupid ass! It's so damned hard to know what's right! There's no guide—you can look for help from other people, but basically, you've got to make it on your own. You've got to decide things for yourself.

...There is no one else in education who sees things the way I do—and who is doing the things I'm doing. After all, I wrote that book alone! So, it's hard... and I feel the pressure.

CULTURE CLASH, 1970-71

That year the whole school became openly divided over lifestyle, the hippies versus the straights, or the heads vs. the rah-rahs. I was viewed as being on the hippie side of this divide, which meant that some students found it difficult to respect me, including some in my classes. At the end of the year I recorded my experiences in an unfinished fifteen-page essay, handwritten on pink paper and titled "The Evolution of a Radical Public-School Teacher." Despite their impression of me as a hippie, I wrote:

I managed to make lots of points...I may not have gotten much respect, but I blew some minds that needed blowing. I forced many students to confront their prejudices and to look with new awareness at the society they lived in. The "hippies" (a pitiful minority) saw me as an ally and I tried to help them use their freedom to become strong in their ideas. The "straights" resented many of my ideas but learned that freedom wasn't so bad, that it was all right for them to express their own ideas, and that new ideas could often be quite valuable.

That I was successful in encouraging students to think and express themselves in class and to listen and respect others' opinions I consider among my greatest accomplishments in teaching. Many students affirmed their learning of these two important lessons in their year-end evaluations.

HIGH SCHOOL PLANNING COMMITTEE #6

During the fall of 1970 I served as a member of the district committee formed to plan the new high school. Along with four others from the Educational Relevance group, we advocated for an open-space environment that would allow for maximum flexibility to develop innovative, student-centered, interdisciplinary education. Open space was a relatively new concept for secondary schools at the time. Generally, it involved teams of teachers working together with large numbers of students who were divided into varying groups for different activities. The large open space could be configured in different ways depending on the day's programs. Access to media centers and science labs, plus multi-age groupings were often part of the design.

This was the first and only time I served on an official government committee with an important task whose outcome I might be able to influence. I noted in my master's thesis that membership on this committee gave us "power that most critics of the school system rarely attain."[236] I was impressed with how open district representatives were to the new ideas we presented. They seemed to agree that the new school should represent the future of education rather than simply reflecting the way things had been done in the past, and hired architects who had experience building open-space schools. "They corroborated our vision of open education and managed to sell the notoriously conservative Board of Education on the idea that open-space schools were the ideal of the future, offering the versatility of providing for any type of program the school would wish to develop."

The architects recommended that the committee visit open-space schools to see how they functioned. These trips needed to be made during the school day, requiring special arrangements for substitutes, which meant my principal was aware of my service on this important committee. Perhaps this helped balance out any criticism he received with about my teaching.

Meanwhile our Educational Relevance group continued to meet and read books on education. We put together a possible model for an interdisciplinary program and submitted it to the Board of Education. We stressed the importance of hiring teachers who wanted to teach in an open-space setting and were willing to work together to create or adapt curriculum and teaching processes to function in the new setting. We proposed teachers be hired well before the new school opened, and be given time to plan how they would set up the space and work together. The board appeared to understand our emphasis that the building and the teaching staff needed to fit together for the new school to be successful.

---

236   "Alternative Public Education," 27. This and the following quotation are from my master's thesis.

The input period of the planning process ended in January 1971. I received a letter from the district indicating their appreciation for my input. Later I would doubt that they fully understood our group's recommendations, despite their hopeful words; "Your knowledge, ideas, as well as ideals, have contributed to what we hope will be a fine educational environment...with the campus you have helped design, a good teaching staff will have an excellent opportunity to achieve an outstanding purpose."

THE FREE SCHOOL MOVEMENT

I have often found myself living in more than one culture at the same time. While I was helping design the new public school, I was also learning about alternative, free schools. I saw myself as a bridge person, one foot in the counterculture and the other in the dominant culture. A friend pointed out that fence-sitting is hard on the genitals and I knew it was true, but I still hoped I could bring the new ideas I was encountering into the world of public education. More subversive activity, I suppose.

Sonoma State College Professor Robert Greenway was emerging at the time as a primary advocate of free schools. Also called new schools or alternative schools, these small, grassroots community schools, run by parents, teachers, and the students themselves, sought to change the goals and practices of traditional education in the Sixties. Greenway and his partner, Salli Rasberry, had just self-published a book called *Rasberry Exercises: How to Start a School and Make a Book.* This book inspired me with both vision and practical information about how to create education that would foster creativity and encourage independent learning. They advised adults (parents and teachers) to get out of the kids' way, so children could follow their own natural desires to learn.

I got to know both Salli and Robert, particularly Robert with whom I took several classes and who later rented a room in my house. They were conscious of their roles as pathbreakers, something that resonated deeply with me as I became aware of my own role in creating change. Their explanation of how we move forward toward a vision by creating what does not yet exist has stuck with me all these years: "Every now and then a certain forward reference shows us a place where visions merge. The road we're on...a familiar line, a piece of terrain seen before, emerging...So, we rise above the fear and follow the path we see, doing the best we can."[237]

The goal of most free schools was to create what Salli and Robert called "fear-free un-hassled envelopes of free space deep within the heartlands of the dominant culture." I wanted to be able to do this, even in public school. Most free schools were specifically countercultural in their rejection of dominant practices of competition, materialism, authoritarian control, hierarchy of teachers over students, and the traditional work ethic. They wanted learning to include emotional, intellectual, practical, and spiritual values simultaneously in a free, holistic, democratic environment. In these goals, they were similar to the more structured Waldorf schools I had first encountered in Germany.

Ron Miller's 2002 publication, *Free Schools, Free People*, is the only recent book on the free school movement. He estimates that during the height of the movement, 1967 to 1972, there were 400 to 800 schools, involving thousands of families and teachers. But, he claims, the significance lies not in numbers but in the spread of such schools and their educational ideology. People in the free school movement believed they "could escape the influence of modern culture and begin a new society founded on values of love, joy, passion, freedom, and spontaneity. For them, education should not serve the interests of the state or the economic system, but should instead be entirely devoted to the happiness of the individuals who lived, loved, and played within each intimate community."

I did not think we could completely escape the influence of the culture we were immersed in, but we could create a new society by living the values of equality, freedom, peace, and love. This is what I sought to bring into my public-school classroom. I was challenged, however, by the primary question Salli and Robert posed in the book and highlighted on the back cover: "How long has it been since you taught in a culture in which you fully believed?" I had to say never,

---

237   Robert Greenway and Salli Rasberry, *Rasberry Exercises: How to Start a School and Make a Book*, 1970, iv.

but I dreamed of one day being able to live and work in the ways my friends were exploring and developing in their free schools. In the meantime, maybe I could create at least one free class.

EXPERIMENTAL ENGLISH AND SOCIAL STUDIES, 1970-71

This was my dream class. Visions of love and peace promised by the emerging alternative culture merged with hopes for Beloved Community I had internalized years before in church to inspire me to create what I hoped would be an oasis of freedom within a public school. This was my chance to utilize everything I had been learning about applying the principles of freedom, equality, peace, and love to education.

The class was two periods long and counted for both English and Social Studies credit. Students had to apply to be part of the class and their parents had to give permission. The students needed to be aware that they were participating in an experiment. In retrospect, I am amazed I was allowed to have this class and that more students applied than I could accept. At the end of the previous school year, I interviewed forty students and chose twenty-six. A manageable size, I thought. "I tried to get people who were dissatisfied with what they were getting in school," I noted, "and who seemed to want to learn new ways and ideas."

All summer I had wondered, would those who chose this class be more open to free learning or would I have to "manage" them as I did the others? Later I reflected: "I didn't spend much time planning for the 'experimental' class, because I wanted to let things happen. I hoped the students would be able to evolve their own ways. I wanted to try as many new ideas as I could, and I hope the students would be able to develop their own new ideas, too." I knew I had the book I created as a fallback, so I felt confident things would work out one way or another.

"Once again," I wrote, "I was on new ground, far beyond anything I had conceived of or read about. Quite frankly, much of the time I didn't know what I was doing." I asked them questions no teacher had ever asked before: What do you want to learn? How do you hope the class will be? They hardly knew what to say. I could tell

I had my work cut out for me, if I wanted them to take ownership of the class and of their own choices. Before that could happen, though, a few students began to take advantage of my openness and figured they didn't have to learn anything. I could hear the buzz: "This is going to be an easy class. We can do whatever we want." After a couple of days, I realized we needed to talk about rules.

The next day I wrote the word "Rules" in big letters on the blackboard. Underneath I wrote four statements:
1. Some rules are good. Some are bad.
2. It is important to follow rules.
3. We need some rules but most are unnecessary restrictions.
4. It would be better to have no rules.

I asked them to divide themselves into groups based on which statement best reflected their attitudes about rules. Each group made lists of their beliefs about rules and then presented their ideas to the whole class. Heated discussions followed as students advocated for their points of view. Although we didn't draw conclusions about what to do about rules, everyone could see that we had a wide range of opinions.

Later that same day I invited them to divide into groups based on what they thought of police. These groups differed significantly from the previous ones. The first group thought there were some good police and some bad. The second saw police as protectors and law enforcers, and the third hated police and saw them as causing trouble. They began to understand there were major differences among them that they could express and debate. It was a great way for us all to get to know each other better. I wondered, though, how I could teach such a diverse group, especially since, I was beginning to realize, some of them clearly needed me to be an "enforcer" of rules and others wanted no rules.

A few days later I invited them to group themselves with those they thought were most like them. It was fascinating to watch them figure out which group to join, because many discovered they had more in common with classmates they did not know well in than with their friends. The groups discussed what they thought about important topics in their lives: school, rules, war, crime, drugs, peace, sex, police, hippies, and God. Several decided they weren't like anyone else and wrote their own answers. I also asked them to rank order the following values: love, freedom, security, justice, fun, and progress. As expected, there was little similarity in students' lists, even among those who were in the groups they thought were like them. By the time we finished with these initial discussions, we knew that what we had most in common was difference!

After these initial activities, I faced the challenge of determining how best to create an open context for learning. I hoped to strike a balance between open learning time where students could pursue their own interests and group activities where we would learn something together. "The class began with the premise that there would be no prescribed curriculum, that we would study what the students wanted to study...that we would all participate in deciding what to do with our time."[238] I emphasized that we were all teachers and all learners and that I would learn as much from them as they would from me. This surprised them, since no teacher had ever said this to them before, but since this class was an experiment it made sense that we would be learning together as we went along. To reinforce the idea that we were all equal in the class, I told them they could call me Dodi, the name friends and family called me.

Besides group activities, my primary goal for the students was to engage them in learning what they wanted to learn, but since most had no idea what this might be, I tried different ways to help them find what interested them and encouraged them to develop their interests and concerns into learning activities. This was my interpretation of what others described as individualized instruction. For this to work I had to pay attention to each student and help them find ways to explore what they wanted to learn. During open class time students were free to explore their interests, could read, use the book I had prepared, or develop their own activities. Since most students were not used to following their interests, it took time for them to decide what to do, time an observer might judge to be wasted.

Another challenge was figuring out what to do as a group. I

---

238   "Notes from a Stranger in a Strange Land," handwritten notes, c. 1971.

was reluctant to force students to participate, because it would violate the principles of free learning. So, we had to put up with a certain amount of chaos while a few students did their own thing while most participated in the group activity. I explained the tension between individual freedom and group cooperation: "We existed within a hostile system that could offer us little enlightenment concerning what we should do with our time...Our general conclusion was that alternatives must be offered at every turn. No one must be required to do anything he/she does not want to do, but everyone must be willing sometimes to bend his/her individual desires so that he/she may cooperate with the group."

Despite my best efforts to foster cohesion among the students in the class, the larger social context of the school affected us in significant ways. "The hippie-straight conflict extended into the heart of the class," I later reflected. "To the rest of the school, this was known as 'the hippie class.'" This designation did not apply to over half the students, and they were distressed at being labeled just for being in the class. My challenge was to help them see each other as people, not as members of one group or another, but I couldn't keep the larger culture from seeping in.

Among the most successful group activities were the times we went outside and played "New Games."[239] Developed in response to the violence of the Vietnam War, these interactive cooperative games were designed to bring diverse people together and create understanding. Often what made a game "new" was reversing the goal of a game from competition to cooperation. For instance, one popular game involved two groups of people trying to push a large ball over a line. New Games changed the traditional tug-of-war goal by encouraging those on the winning side to switch to the losing side to keep the ball from moving too far in any direction. At first the group found it difficult to work together to keep the ball in the air, but as they learned to play cooperatively, the game got easier.

---

239   *Whole Earth Catalog* publisher, Stewart Brand, and Esalen Institute head, George Leonard, were early proponents of New Games. I learned about New Games from George Leonard at a social studies conference. *The New Games Book* wasn't published until 1976.

Gradually they learned that joining together and having fun with others was better than winning. They even began to make up their own "new games."

Communication exercises helped to get dialog started and demonstrated the value of honest communication. The idea of learning from each other was new to most of them, but the more we shared about what was going on in our lives and how we viewed what was happening in our society they more they began to appreciate each other's perspectives.

Role playing helped them look at decision making and values in specific situations. I discovered that some students were unable to play roles and could only play themselves. They couldn't imagine playing their father, for instance. Nor could they play the same scene in different ways, so I invited them to watch others do it. After a while, a few of the reluctant ones tried on a role.

Simulation games were another way the class came together as a group. My favorite was Atlantis, which invited them to interpret a past society based on its physical remnants. We began by playing a popular song by Donovan about the mythical and supposedly highly evolved society of Atlantis.[240] The basic ingredients of the simulation included a map of Atlantis denoting several sites of an archeological dig, a brief history of the dig and of Atlantis, and items found at each site (which I enjoyed assembling). The players are divided into teams whose job it is to interpret the findings of the dig. Each team hypothesizes concerning the use of their site in the ancient civilization. Then when the various ideas are brought together, they develop a more complete picture of the civilization. There are no right answers and no winners, but everyone learned a great deal about historical perspective, logical consequences, hypothesis, and proof.

Later in the year, when several students in the class were running for student offices, I suggested a simulation called High School. The players are divided up into radical students, parents, faculty, administration, all of whom are attempting to resolve a

---

240   "Atlantis," by Donovan, released as singe in 1968, became a world-wide hit.

controversy concerning student power. This situation involved them in dealing with problems people encounter in trying to accomplish change. They reflected at the end on how this related to our class and why it was difficult for some to understand and accept what we were doing.

After I participated in a workshop with David Ruhmkorff on a process for group decision-making called Provolution, I brought the idea to the class. I called it a game, "What would it be like in our class if...?" We began by generating a long list of possibilities. Since the premise of brainstorming is to record all ideas without judgment, I had to write on the board everything they came up with. Then they selected the most popular ones and divided into groups to continue the process. For each fantasy selected, they made lists of the best and worst possible consequences, if the fantasy were to come true. Then the class discussed other ways we could achieve the best consequences. Out of this process came the idea that what they wanted most was to feel connected as a group and to talk with everyone in the class and be understood.

I later composed a two-page letter to distribute to other teachers at the school. I hoped my description of the class would allay some of the rumors they had undoubtedly heard.

A major subject of study has been the class itself. The students have participated fully in creating, developing, analyzing, evaluating, and changing the structure of the class. We first sought to discover what we really wanted from the class. The major goals that emerged were 1) to achieve a feeling of togetherness in the class, so that people would be able to trust and care about each other; 2) to learn to express our ideas, so that others would be able to understand us; 3) to learn to study on our own in a context of freedom what was important to us, so that we would be able to continue our learning for ourselves after we left this class.[241]

The class came together best when we worked together to accomplish group goals. The most successful project came from my suggestion that they go as a group to the Dickens Faire. Held in a

241   Dorothy Orser, "Experimental English and Social Studies: 1971-72," a letter to teachers at Rohnert Park Junior High, June 1972.

warehouse in San Francisco, the Dickens Faire recreated Victorian London, with stages for performances, shops selling crafts of the day, food vendors, and wandering musicians. The class loved the idea, but pointed out that many of them did not have enough money to make the trip.

After extensive discussion about how we might raise money, they came up with the idea for a fruit sale. Usually when student groups wanted to raise money they sold candy, but this class wanted to do something different. A girl in the class had a friend at Palace of Fruit, a large roadside fruit stand where we could order apples, oranges, and tangerines. One student wrote: "Usually half the class gets interested, but now the whole class was involved. Everybody took turns selling fruit, during lunch and break. It was a complete success in two ways. One was we made enough money and the second was it brought the whole class together, even though it was just a little while."

They especially liked the idea that they were contributing to the health of the other students, by providing fresh fruit, something that was not generally available in the school cafeteria. "The whole school benefitted from this sale," another student wrote. "They finally got some real live good out of a day at school. They got some vitamins they need. I am very proud that I helped some of my fellow students get something from this place. I hope that more fruit sales are conducted after I am not at this school any longer. At least maybe another generation wouldn't be wasted."

Leading up to the Faire, we read Charles Dickens' *Christmas Carol*, saw films about the life and writings of Dickens, and learned about the historical period. They studied clothing of the time and made costumes, and then they planned the trip. Nearly everyone went and afterwards wrote about their experiences. Later they looked back on this experience as one of the highlights of the year.

Another notable group experience was our plan for a field trip to the beach in February to study the unique rocky terrain and tide pools of Salt Point State Park in Jenner, write about the experience, and finish filming a movie they were in the process of making. The movie idea was brought to us by Joey, a student at Sonoma State

College who joined our class through their Community Involvement Program. Unfortunately, a proposed bond amendment failed to pass and funding for our trip was pulled at the last minute. The kids were angry, as might be expected, but I decided this could be an opportunity for group problem-solving and alternative thinking. Rather than give up the whole idea, the class decided to change the trip to a closer location and go on a Saturday. Although not everyone could come, those who did learned they could still do something even when they ran into a roadblock with their initial plan.

Around this same time, something happened that could have torn the class apart. During open study time, two boys were playing around and one of them threw something at the other. It hit him in the face and left a mark. This kind of behavior would have been grounds for immediate suspension in most classes. I was shocked but did not want to kick either of the boys out, or report the incident to the school. I took the boys outside and asked them what they wanted to do. The one that was injured said it was partly his fault. The other boy apologized for hitting him. I suggested they both go to the library for the rest of class and sit separately and think about what had happened.

Back in class the other students wanted to talk about what happened. They knew that the boy who hurt the other had a difficult time in the class because he came from a military family and when we talked about peace, he felt conflicted. He was a poor reader and had trouble figuring out what to do in class, but I had been helping him find his passion, which turned out to be motorcycle magazines. The students were mostly afraid that the boy who had been hurt would leave the class, so several of them went to the library to talk with him and encourage him to stay. As it turned out both boys stayed in the class and later became friends.

Although this was the most dramatic conflict, there were other times when angry words were exchanged. One girl wrote about how much this hurt not only the person who was the recipient of the anger but for all who witnessed it:

All of a sudden angry shouts are thrown across the room— smash! One hits you in the face with the force of a brick. It slashes

across you and seeps into your body—Down it runs twisting and mourning your insides—perverted and tied until you are no longer feeling yourself as a person you aren't there—you are just an image—you are hurt, shattered and broken, just like a bottle thrown on the concrete.
And I see the hurt.
And I feel the hurt.
Why does it happen in here?
Does it have to?
Why?!?

Toward the end of the year I heard about a peace festival at Sonoma State College and arranged for the students to get out of their afternoon classes so they could go.[242] Most of the class had never been to the college before and had heard negative rumors about what went on there. It was eye-opening for them see the college for themselves. What impressed them most is how happy the college students were to be there. They were excited about learning and glad to talk with them about the school. My students contrasted their attitudes to those at our school who mostly seemed to be there under duress. They observed how free the college students were and how accepting of diversity.

David Harris was a featured speaker at the peace festival. He was famous (or infamous) for two reasons, being married to folk singer Joan Baez and for going to prison for refusing the draft. Many class members wrote about his message. The range of comments reflect their diversity:

- His ideas were anti-American. He talked revolution.
- After I heard him talk I realized the government can't push us around. We are the land of the free.
- He speaks the truth.
- He talked of the people in prison with him and said that they were in there for the same crimes the government was doing every day.

---

242   Field trips were much less regulated in those days. Some students walked the mile or so to the campus, others rode with me in my van or with students who had cars, and a few took advantage of the time off and went home.

- David talked about peace. All I really seemed to catch from what he said is that "If you want to do something worthwhile, then say it so people can hear your ideas."
- Dave talked mostly of people working together to get a certain thing done.

During the last month of the class, I suggested making a class book with something in it from each person in the class. They liked the idea because it meant they would each have something to take with them to remember our experience.[243] The book contained pages about each of our major activities as well as poetry and other reflections on what they had learned. We assembled the books in class and made covers for them from construction paper. Some passed their books around for the others to sign. Mine is a treasured remembrance of an intense and important time of learning, for me and hopefully for the class members as well.

I could see the changes in many students because of the class. Most became more open to the diversity among them and to what we were doing. As they gained a stronger sense of themselves, they grew less afraid of what others outside the class thought. The class became a microcosm of what was happening in the larger society. Despite their discomfort with the reputation of the class, no one left, and each student achieved something visible during the year.

In the explanation I wrote for other teachers, I described what I considered our success. This also summarizes what I was trying to accomplish throughout my six years of public school teaching.

We have all learned, both from our mistakes and our successes. Most important, we have tried something new, something that no one else had done. We used other people's ideas, but we applied them in our own way. In a society where people often feel powerless to control their own lives and solve the society's problems, we

---

243   To create their pages, each student made their own ditto master. Some pages were typed, others hand-written, and some contained drawings. Several students took responsibility for arranging to copy the pages on the ditto machine in the school office. In addition to mimeograph machines, schools regularly used spirit duplicators (made by Ditto, Inc.) to make copies. Ditto masters had a top sheet to type, draw, or write on and a second sheet coated with a layer of colored wax, which created the masters used for printing.

learned we could make our own changes. We learned the limits of our power and learned what we could change within them. We learned what our weaknesses were and how hard we must struggle to overcome them, if we wish to accomplish our goals. We have learned about learning, about communication, about freedom, about sharing, about love. As goals of education, these seem to me to be the most important and valuable.[244]

THE STORY CONTINUES

The following year, 1971-72, there was a second Experimental Class. This time I had several highly motivated, college-bound students who chose this free environment so they could explore what they wanted to learn. Whereas the theme of the first class had been love, the theme for the second class became freedom. Since several of the students were friends with those from the previous year's class, I invited members of both classes to come to my house one evening a week to get to know each other and extend the experience of the class.

This was my last year at Rohnert Park Junior High before transferring to Casa Grande, the new open-space school I helped to design. Reflecting on my four years of experience as a teacher, I could see the truth of Sid Lester's equation, "education = change." I saw real change in many of my students and in myself. In a significant way, we educated each other. It was hard to leave the students, but I was ready to move on to a new challenge.[245]

EDUCATION'S UNFINISHED AGENDA

The possibilities for student-centered, open education so alive in the Sixties were squashed in the decades that followed. Public concern that schools were failing began in the late 1970s when scores on college entrance exams declined. Although the College Board later reported that the scores declined because questions were skewed toward middle-class white students, and now more students

---

244   Letter to teachers at Rohnert Park Junior High, June 1972.
245   More about teaching at Casa Grande in Culture Change, Back to School 1973-74.

of color and those living in poverty were applying for college, the damage had been done. Standardized achievement tests began to be designed to hold students, teachers, and schools accountable for minimum standards of learning at different grade levels.[246]

In the early 1980s, President Reagan commissioned the report, "A Nation at Risk: The Imperative for Educational Reform," which continued to promote the idea that American schools were failing and recommended as a solution further development of standardized tests of achievement at major transition points from one level of schooling to another. By the 1990s most states mandated high-stakes testing, and teachers were forced to teach whatever was expected to be on the tests. Alternative perspectives have focused on changing core curricula, but generally rely on mandated content rather than allowing teachers to develop programs for their student's needs and interests.

One early reader of my manuscript expressed sorrow that she did not encounter the sort of education I describe in this book, saying "I might have gone to college if I had been encouraged to learn." Others who have attended talks I've given have shared memories of their experiences in free schools and in open education programs, saying how grateful they are to have been encouraged to develop their own ways of learning. But nostalgia about the past won't change things now. Advocating for student-centered education requires political action, including getting rid of high-stakes testing.

Fortunately, some public and private schools have continued to encourage students to be self-motivated and creative in their learning. Some teachers implement innovative practices even within testing-dominated systems. Theories and practices that allow teachers to individualize instruction for students with different personality types and learning styles are also sometimes used. More than a few college programs are based on ideas of flexibility and self-directed learning that evolved in the Sixties. Free and holistic education practices have been implemented in the home-schooling movement. Waldorf and Montessori schools have provided structured learning

---

246   Read more at Testing - Standardized Tests And High-stakes Assessment - Students, Standards, Assessments, and Achievement, State University Website.

environments that honor students' individuality and creativity. Because the educational innovations of the Sixties have survived in these forms, they can be resources for current efforts to move away from high-stakes testing and allow for greater diversity in approaches to education.

School funding provides a significant challenge to establishing a level-playing field for all schools and all students. Current funding structures provide significantly more funds to schools in middle and upper-middle class neighborhoods, while urban and rural schools in less affluent areas suffer from lack of resources. Education remains a key mechanism for individual advancement and can be an important means for establishing equality and justice for all. Providing all students access to quality schools remains part of education's unfinished agenda.

Above all, it is essential to support teachers as key players in students' education. Without the resources available through the district-supported curriculum coordinator and the federally-funded Marin Social Studies Project, I would have failed as a teacher. Teachers today need similar resources and support, both in terms of time and funding to pursue continuing education relevant to their own circumstances. Schools need support to institute changes, including experimental programs that have the potential to pave the way to quality education that works for all. All children in this society deserve the opportunity to develop their own abilities and become the best version of themselves. Accomplishing this is education's unfinished agenda. Through education, the Sixties vision of a culture of freedom, equality, justice, love, and peace becomes possible.

7. CULTURE CHANGE:
changing the world

"Like a wave rolling across America, the changes came, sometimes surprising, often shocking. By 1970 the passions of the '60s were being channeled into a social revolution more widespread than anyone could have imagined a decade earlier."
–David Hoffmann[247]

The Sixties gave birth to deep changes in American life and values, changes that are still in process a half a century later. "The times they are a-changing" was our mantra. Growing numbers of people began to confront inequities in our society and address problems we saw crying out for amelioration. We cracked the facades of so-called polite society and perceived possibilities of new ways of being in relationship. We invented new ways of doing things in response to what we saw as wrong in our increasingly mechanized, depersonalized, progress and achievement-oriented, consumption-driven culture. In so doing, we changed the culture around us by our presence and our actions, laying the groundwork for new ways of living the vision of democracy dreamed of by our forebears. For fifty years, many who carry the Sixties spirit have continued to develop strategies and tools that make a better world possible. The emerging new culture has showed up in many forms, including the establishment and operation of business enterprises.

For instance, Anita Roddick, born in England in 1942, founded a highly successful business based on Sixties values. When

---

247   Quoted in David Hoffmann, "Remember the Glory Days" video, part of PBS series "Making Sense of the Sixties," available on YouTube.

she started the Body Shop, she dedicated it "to the pursuit of social and environmental change," a worthy goal, but to make it real she had to change the culture of business as usual. Along the way, she learned what it means to be a revolutionary. She explained:

Every real change, every revolutionary idea, every heartfelt gesture, whether it transforms one life or a thousand, was once seen as eccentric. Leaders are few and followers many for a reason. Change requires bucking the status quo, and bucking the status quo requires a willingness to be perceived as crazy, dangerous, or ridiculous. Revolutionaries, activists, and change-makers of every stripe—just like entrepreneurs—lead because they cannot follow something with which they do not agree or which limits their imaginations. They change the world because their passion and conviction won't allow them not to.[248]

My life has been dedicated to changing the world, because my "passion and commitment" would not allow me to do otherwise. But first I had to dream of a better world. Like Dr. Martin Luther King, Jr.'s dream, it included equality and freedom for all, as well as love and peace.

Change begins with dreams, and Sixties people were dreamers. We knew the old ways needed to change, so we imagined alternatives and some of us set out to create and live them. What we learned shaped us. What began as trickles of change in the Sixties have seeped into many places in subtle and demonstrable ways ever since then. As Thomas Berry writes: "When we look back over our lives, we realize that whatever of significance we have achieved in our own personal lives and in the larger cultural domain has been the fulfillment of thoughts and dreams that we had early in our lives, dreams that sustained us when we encountered difficulties through the years."[249]

---

248   Anita Roddick, "Three cheers for crazy ideas," *Ode*, June 2007. Although she died in 2007, her mission continues as the Anita Roddick Team carries forward her charitable and political work.
249   Thomas Berry, "The Great Community of Earth," *Yes! Magazine*, Winter 2001, from a speech at the UN Summit for Religious and Spiritual Leaders, August 2000.

Over the years, I have been sustained through hard times by my dreams and my faith that a better world is possible. My dreams began in church. I didn't so much have a vision of God directing my life as of the world calling me, like the prophets and Jesus who were called by their times to stop what was wrong and create the Beloved Community. A line from a favorite hymn inspired me: "New occasions teach new duties. Time makes ancient good uncouth."[250] I was lucky to have role models who weren't afraid to speak truth as they understood it and confront power they saw as unjust.

Later, when I saw things that needed to be changed, I wasn't afraid to do things differently. In the Sixties, I invented new courses, curricula, and ways of teaching in public junior and senior high schools, and helped create a self-directed master's program. Others invented new disciplines in consciousness and healing, or took leadership in political change. Increasing numbers of young men refused military service, while others set up draft counseling services, helped those who were applying for conscientious objector status, or provided sanctuary for draft resisters. Still others formed alternative communities in urban and rural settings.

"Beyond the dreams of our personal futures, there are the shared dreams that give shape and form to each of our cultural traditions," wrote Thomas Berry.[251] A line from Jefferson Airplane, "We are the crown of creation,"[252] describes our collective awareness that we were actively co-creating new culture. We could see where our world needed to change and provide alternatives for ourselves and others. We shared a vision of a better world, a world founded on peace, justice, equality, freedom, and love—and we tried to make that vision real in our daily lives and work. Whatever success we achieved came from the depths of our beings, from our willingness to risk being the change we believed was possible. Where we failed was in our naïveté that simply being the change was enough. We

---

250   James Russell Lowell, "The Present Crisis" (1844), set to music as "Once to Every Man and Nation."

251   Berry, "The Great Community of the Earth."

252   Paul Kantner, "Crown of Creation," Jefferson Airplane album of the same name, 1968.

Dorothy May Emerson

underestimated the forces of resistance, the entropy of systems that return to stasis once the change agent stops pushing.

Even those new cultural forms that didn't last, however, have value because they sparked our imaginations and inspired others. Andrew Boyd, author of *Beautiful Trouble: A Toolbox for Revolutions* calls what we did "prefigurative interventions."

> We can't create a better world if we haven't yet imagined it. How much better then, if we are able to touch such a world, experience it directly, even live in it—if only to a partial degree and for a brief moment. This is the idea behind "prefigurative interventions," actions that not only work to stop the next dumb thing the bad guys are up to, but also enact in the here and now the world we actually want to live in.[253]

By the mid-1970s some of us felt burned out (a new term invented in that decade), and moved on from our original places of vision and action. But most of us kept dreaming of the better world we knew in our hearts was possible.

SEARCHING FOR A NEW CULTURE

Knowing that the culture I grew up in had big problems and figuring out how to live in a new way are not the same. Salli Rasberry put it simply: "Breaking free of the bonds of one culture doesn't create the agenda for the next."[254] So where does one look?

Living in the San Francisco area meant I was surrounded by people who were exploring and creating alternatives. Festival Theatre and Open End were model alternative communities. Through the Open End newsletter, I learned of groups across the country that were creating new forms of community. In 1972, I participated in an Open End "encounter day" at Westerbeke Ranch, a retreat center in the Valley of the Moon, a beautiful area near Sonoma, where many alternative gatherings took place. I wrote: "I believe there is spiritual knowledge in the universe that we need only free ourselves to see. Most of us, however, get hung up within ourselves and close off to

---

253   Andrew Boyd, "Don't Wait for the Revolution—Live It," *Yes! Magazine* online, July 3, 2013.
254   Salli Rasberry and Robert Greenway, *The Rasberry Exercises*, 2.

305

what surrounds us. Everything that is alive speaks and illuminates whatever is open to it."[255]

In this spirit, I searched for the new emerging culture, finding models in books, through teachers, at events and conferences, and in communities that were in formation at the time. Theodore Roszak called what was developing a "counter culture," explaining that was "a culture so radically disaffiliated from the mainstream assumptions of our society that it scarcely looks to many as a culture at all."[256]

SUMMER OF LOVE, 1967

The "Summer of Love" was a spontaneous happening in what was being called the new counterculture. The song "San Francisco" was interpreted by young people across the country as an invitation to come where, the song said: "Summertime will be a love-in there."[257] The numbers of visitors to the Haight-Ashbury area that summer varies depending on who was counting, with estimates ranging from 75,000 to 200,000. Tour buses brought tourists to see the young people with "flowers in their hair."

Although I was not an active participant, I wanted to see for myself what was going on. One day, when Thomas was busy at the theater, I decided to go to Golden Gate Park. I drove into the city and parked on a residential street near the Panhandle, a grassy strip of land next to the main park and the center of much of the activity that summer.

It was a warm sunny summer day. I could hear the music from a block away and smiled as I skipped my way to join the celebration. I wore a long dress made from an Indian bedspread, leather sandals, and carried a small cloth bag with my keys and a few coins. I decided to leave my driver's license and the rest of my purse in the car. I wanted to remain anonymous and test myself to see if I could be as free as the others seemed to be. I still looked young enough at twenty-four to fit in with the mostly younger people who had found

---

255   Feb. 19, 1972.
256   Theodore Roszak, *The Making of a Counter Culture*, 1969, 42.
257   "San Francisco," written by John Phillips (with The Mamas and the Papas), sung by Scott MacKenzie. The single sold over seven million copies worldwide.

their way there from all over the country.

I had no plans and figured I would go along with whatever others were doing. I sat in the sun, sang songs, danced to the drums, and shared whatever food, drinks, and smokes were offered to me. I loved the feeling of freedom, love, and sharing. Everyone smiled at each other. The world seemed bright and full of hope.

At one point a couple of people near me got up to go across the street. A teenage girl wearing a flowing madras cloth dress asked, "Do you want to come with us? We're going across the street to panhandle,[258] over there by the stores."

I quickly learned this meant we were going to approach passers-by and ask them to give us money. I had never done anything like this before, but I tried it to see what would happen. I felt uncomfortable, because I was sure they could see right through me and knew I didn't really need the money. I wondered about the others. I had heard on the news that some who came to the city had left homes where they were cared for and could go back to if they chose. Each of us managed to collect a couple of dollars in coins.

One of the guys said, "Let's go buy something with the money we collected."

The girl looked at the coins in her hand and sighed, "I need sunglasses, but they cost more than I've got."

"Why don't you just take them?" someone else said. "That store is ripping people off with their outrageous prices anyway."

This was not what I thought the Summer of Love was about, so I walked away and went back to the park. Later I crossed the street again and bought some potato chips to share with others. From what I heard and read I don't think shoplifting was common practice, but for me this incident was a reminder that there were some things I was not willing to do in the name of freedom.

As dusk approached, people started scrambling for places to sleep. Some young women looked for guys to sleep with. Although I knew I could attract someone in that way, I decided to go home

---

258   Although the origins of the term are unclear, the word seems to have been in use at least since the 1890s to refer to people begging for money. At the time, I thought it referred to the section of the park we were in.

instead. I wasn't really cut out for this life, I realized. It seemed ironic to me later when I was dubbed "the hippie teacher." I had to chuckle to myself because they didn't know what a failure I was at the role, at least the free-spirited version.

However, I was not a failure at embracing the spirit of the Summer of Love. Fifty years later, that spirit is still alive in me and many others. In 2017 over 30,000 people signed up for Facebook groups celebrating the fiftieth anniversary of that historic summer. A proclamation was issued, which begins with these words:

There are moments in time when a word or a thought has such power it changes history; a generation so involved in the moment it becomes unstoppable; a spiritual awakening so profound that its very conception shatters perceptions, halts the world and makes people from all nations take notice.

It began with a single four-letter word—LOVE.[259]

RENAISSANCE FAIRES

In 1968 when I entered the community of the newly created Renaissance Faire, I discovered a very different alternative culture, with a more structured environment where people could also be free to express themselves. David Ossman, who was there at the beginning, observed:

In its first decade, the Renaissance Faire unleashed a multi-colored sub-culture in direct revolt against the monochrome of postwar America. It was a home-grown explosion of fancy dress, Shakespearian improv, hand-made objects both useful and ornamental, and music ancient and obscure, much of it heard for the first time in the dusty lanes of the Faire.[260]

Thomas and I fell in love with the Faire and imagined ourselves becoming part of it. As his involvement with Festival Theatre ended, the Faire became our new community, as well as

---

259   Press Release for the Summer of Love 50th Anniversary, issued by 2B1 Multimedia Inc. and The Council of Light, Jan. 25, 2017.
260   David Ossman, review of *Well Met: Renaissance Faires and the American Counterculture*, by Rachel Lee Rubin, 2012, https://nyupress.org/books/book-details.aspx?bookId=11221

a new way of earning money. As a weaver, he became part of the community of craftspeople that existed within the rich context of living theater. I was delighted to help sell his wares. Setting up our first booth on site in the woods, we could build a simple structure that would give us a private place to sleep and store things. We didn't even need a building permit!

Life at the Faire, especially after closing, gave us a sense of what it might have been like to live in a village long ago. People shared food, drinks, and whatever else they had. We slept on a futon surrounded by curtains hung from a wood frame and open to the sky, and fell asleep listening to drums, singing, and laughter. We felt safe surrounded by a loving community of people who shared our values of peace and freedom. If only we could live like this all the time.

PACIFIC NORTHWEST COUNTERCULTURE, 1970[261]

Travel brought us into contact with counterculture people in other places. In 1970, Thomas and I bought a used Volkswagen van that had already been fixed up for camping. Unlike factory-installed campers, this one had a small upright "ice box," a small three-drawer bureau, a foam mattress on a platform across the back, and shades that pulled down to cover the windows. Its most unique feature was a roof that slid back to create a large opening. Not only could we see the trees and sky, we could also stand up to dress. We bought white sleeping bags we zipped together for the bed. Thomas replaced the torn, plastic shades with a maroon and gold-striped fabric. We would be traveling in style! Although I had gone to summer camps, I had never camped at a public campground, so this was a new experience for me.

That summer we took a three-week trip through the Pacific Northwest, including Vancouver Island. Our first stop was in Portland, where we visited Ruth and Unk, two old and beautiful people who were practically Thomas's only family. One night, Ruth and I got into in an argument. Her ideas of "hippies" and radicals had been formed by the nightly news and a few encounters in their neighborhood.

---

261   I wrote most of this section at the time it was happening.

She saw these people as ungrateful wretches who had been given everything by their parents and society and responded by destroying things and being disrespectful, and she saw me as one of them. I felt compelled to explain, but she was adamant and I ended up in tears.

In Portland and along the road, people noticed us. No matter where we went (outside of the San Francisco Bay area), people saw us as unusual. Small children gave us the peace sign and older children smiled, but adults either shook their heads or openly stared. We obviously represented something to them too. We were the far-out hippies they had heard so much about on TV and in their newspapers and magazines. All but the youngest viewed us with suspicion, mingled with curiosity. People seemed confident that they knew all about us. In Berg's, a department store in Portland, the saleslady was anxious to show me what she thought of as hippie clothes. I obliged by buying a colorful poncho on sale. Later, Thomas was carrying it for me when a lady stopped in the middle of the sidewalk and stared at him with mouth wide open in utter disbelief!

Fortunately, we also encountered people who seemed more like us, like the ones selling copies of a local hip[262] paper who told us, "Go to the Buffalo Party Convention!" From the paper, we learned that the next weekend there was a rock festival in Eatonville, Washington. It was called a political convention to sidestep a state law prohibiting rock festivals. We were very curious about rock festivals, after seeing the movie *Woodstock* and talking with people who had been to two California festivals.

On our trip, we were consciously searching to discover where we fit into this world. Thus far, we had found ourselves stared at or argued with, but we hoped maybe the rock festival was a place we would feel at home. Coincidentally, I had borrowed a copy of *Today's Health* from Unk with a surprisingly objective article about rock festivals, advising parents to let their kids go to them and not to worry too much. We bought our tickets and drove to Seattle for

---

262   At the time, I tended to use the word "hip" to describe what others might refer to as "alternative," "underground," or "counterculture." We did not, however, refer to ourselves as "hippies," preferring instead to call ourselves "freaks."

a day, planning to head out to the festival on the next. Then we heard on the radio that there was a court injunction against the festival. We were disappointed and upset that we had paid $10.00 for an event that might not take place. The promoters of the festival were fighting the injunction, but no final decision had been made. Our plans were up in the air when we pulled in to Saltwater State Park, a half hour south of Seattle. The campers next to us greeted us enthusiastically, and invited us to come over and join them. They were also from California, and we immediately felt at home with each other. That evening we helped build a campfire, shared fairy tales and ghost stories, and felt at home.

In the morning we moved on, still uncertain about the festival. We decided to go to the university area in Seattle, an area that felt familiar to us—a cross between San Rafael and Berkeley. The people looked hip, but hip shops were mingled among more usual stores. We found the Buffalo Party Headquarters closed for the weekend. In the head[263] shop next door we met a woman whose husband had a booth at the convention. She had talked with him on the phone and he said everyone there was acting as if the thing was happening. We checked around with others and no one could say for sure, but everyone had an opinion on what was going to happen. We finally sat down in a tavern over a beer to make our decision. I wanted to go but didn't want to force Thomas. Finally, he said we ought to go, that if we didn't, we would always wonder what it would have been like.

So we bought groceries and headed for Eatonville. The radio continued to blare out uncertainties which we had by then decided to ignore. We saw no one else going our direction until we were practically there. Then the gathering of the clan began. Another car full of people like us called out, "Do you know the way?" And some long-haired boys standing on a corner in town pointed down a road saying, "It's that way!"

AT THE ROCK FESTIVAL

We gave our tickets at the gate and were directed to a spot

---

263   Head shops sold beads, posters and cards, candles, incense, drug paraphernalia, and the like.

to park our van. Everything seemed friendly and perfectly in order. We began to set up camp and went in search of water. The closest water supply seemed to be a waterfall and stream which could only be reached by sliding down a rather treacherous but beautiful path. As we struggled back up the path with our jug of water, we heard the police had set up roadblocks and no one was being permitted in or out of the ranch.

It looked like the festival was defeated. Surely no bands could get in now, and no more people could join us. What would happen? Soon we heard the police were allowing people to leave, but it was already near evening so we decided to stay the night. We moved our camper closer to the lakes, where people were enjoying the freedom to swim nude if they wished. It had been a hot dusty day, and we too went to wash ourselves in the lake. Then exhausted, we fixed supper and collapsed into bed.

In the morning we thought we would probably move on, since we had given up hope that anything resembling a rock festival would take place. But the other people there seemed unconcerned and no one else was leaving. We decided to at least go for a swim before we left. The two lakes were already bustling with activity. People were frolicking in the water or lolling about on the shore. The air was full of the sweet smell of marijuana smoke. Surely this was another world.

During the night, people had continued to work on the construction of the sound stage. Eventually the authorities in charge of keeping folks out relented, and the gates were re-opened. Port-a-potties were delivered, which was a big relief, as up till then we had to make do with a trench dug on the spot when folks realized there were no facilities—an example of the cooperative spirit of the people there.[264]

Finally, the music began.[265] The local people still remember the festival, mostly with fondness, surprised at how polite and well behaved the longhairs were. Everyone agreed it was good

---

264   Crowd estimates ranged from 10,000 to 30,000.

265   According to online remembrances, the James Cotton Band "played late into the night," and there were local groups like The Walters, Don and the Goodtones, and The Sonics.

for business. Before the weekend was over, local stores ran out of beer, wine, ice, cigarettes, and most of the food they had on hand. My favorite moment in the festival happened late one night while the music was playing. In honor of the Fourth of July, someone launched a huge flare into the sky above us. Suddenly the sky was bright. We could see those around us and those at a distance, giving us a sense of the whole gathering. At the time, I had never seen a flare and was unsure what was happening. I'm sure we were stoned, which added to the mystery of the experience, but it seemed like a miracle. While the light lasted, we stood smiling at each other, loving the thousands around us. Were we a new society? Could we maintain this wonderful, peaceful feeling of connection with all who were there? Maybe it was enough just to know that for that one shining moment, we could see ourselves in a new light as a new culture. This was what peace and freedom looked like.

I am grateful that our journey in search of enlightenment led us to this experience. The tribe that gathered there welcomed us as family, and the way people interacted seemed far better than other situations we encountered in our lives. But still, this wasn't quite it, although some of the elements were there. I knew I had still not completely found my culture. The rock festival was a wonderful momentary culture, but I wondered what could sustain it over time.

COMMUNAL LIVING

Communes were a common feature of Sixties culture. Sometimes these group living arrangements formed out of necessity, when people without many resources needed a place to "crash" and found folks who were willing to share whatever space they had. Others formed intentionally, basing their principles of shared living on the emerging values of the times. Most Sixties communes were initially established in cities, where people lived together in large houses, sharing food, chores, and resources. As the urban scene degenerated, some groups moved to rural areas, sharing tracts of land, growing their own food, and sometimes developing products to make and sell to support the group. As children were born into these groups, child care was shared, and some folks experimented with group marriage. Some people may have been aware of the long history of communal living in America among such groups as the Transcendentalists, but others seemed to be inventing new forms as they went along.

The contrast was stark between these new shared living arrangements and the idealized nuclear family of the 1950s, with its single-family house in the suburbs, stay-at-home mother, and father who went off to work each day. The implied subtext of the 1950s ideal was that if the man worked hard, the family would be able to move up in the world, to bigger houses and better neighborhoods.

Thomas and I observed this cultural debate mostly from the outside, except when people came to our place to "crash" for a night or two. Occasionally these visitors criticized us for having what they saw as too many possessions. We loved and collected unique pieces of art and crafts (often used, none expensive), and thanks to the generosity of our wedding guests and families, we had decent housewares. Neither of us had grown up with abundance, so we valued and took good care of what we had. Still, the criticism stung. Especially painful for me was one visitor who called me a "dirty capitalist" when I got up at 6 AM to go teach school after a night of partying and sharing with him the bounty of our lifestyle.

Nevertheless, the ideals of communal living drew us, especially when we moved to Cotati in 1970 and visited rural communes that were forming in the area. Since our new place was on several acres of land and had a barn/garage and another small building, the idea occurred to us that others might someday live there with us.

FREE LAND

I first learned about Free Land in 1968 at the Growing Up Absurd Symposium at Dominican College.[266] Lou Gottlieb talked about Morningstar, the free community he had established in rural Sonoma County. He deeded the land to God and issued an open invitation to anyone who wanted to join him on the land and mutually support each other in creating community. Only minimal

---

266   More about the presentation at Dominican in Education = Change, Encountering Radical Ideas in Education.

housing was available so most people camped out.

When Thomas and I moved to Sonoma County two years later, we heard people talking about Morningstar and decided to visit. Since it was well-known by then as part of the Free Land Movement, we knew we would be welcome. It was a beautiful drive to the ranch, located out toward the coast near Occidental. We found the place, parked our car outside the gate, and walked in. We saw people building small shelters to sleep in, much like the booths at the Renaissance Faire. Another group was working in the large garden. Others were hanging out in the sun, some playing music, some sitting in a circle passing a joint. Here and there a small child played, often naked, running around freely but never far from watchful eyes of adults. Everyone smiled when they saw us, welcoming us. Lou wasn't there but we heard he was planning to build a deck for his grand piano so he could play music outside. Later we learned he played for the tomatoes in the garden, which grew large and delicious.

From the beginning, though, long-time residents of the area objected to this gathering of "hippies." The county came several times and bulldozed the shelters because they were built without permits. The people living there fought back by declaring they were a religious group, Morning Star Faith, and creating Thy Community Church. They defined four truths:

1. The Truth is forever one, naked, nameless, homeless.
2. The Truth is thy own self.
3. (Life = Light = Consciousness) = Love
4. Everything + Everyone + Everywhere = God

Their four "Missions of Planetary Purity" affirmed the rights of all people to open land, open access to all energy sources, recovery of clean air through planting forests and gardens, and open access to all sources of water. Although their ideals were noble, I thought them impractical, given the world we were living in. But then I realized that all religions affirmed impractical ideals, so why should this one be different? Defining themselves as a religious group did not, however, afford them protection from the county bulldozers. Eventually the county restricted the land to Lou's family, and most of the people were forced to leave.

Fortunately, an even larger place opened up nearby, on 340 acres owned by Bill Wheeler. Following Lou Gottlieb's lead, he deeded the land to God and all people. A thriving community developed. Although the bulldozers came there too, the area was larger and more difficult to control. One of my favorite students lived there for many years, and some people still live there today.

While we enjoyed our visits to these and other similar places, we realized that it wasn't for us. We liked having our own space and special things, although we were willing to share. Later we opened our own land to others, albeit on a much more limited basis.

HAPPENINGS AND ROCK CONCERTS

Another place where we encountered new culture was through special events that formed temporary communities for a time. One of the most remarkable and memorable happenings took place in Grace Cathedral in San Francisco in the early 1970s. "Totentanz" took place February 4-5, 1971, produced by Dance Spectrum, with music by Warner Jepson and Carl Orff.

It was dark inside as we followed a long line of people into the massive Gothic building. We were each handed a smooth stone and told to hold onto it. Electronic music was blaring. Incense filled the air. As my eyes adjusted to the darkness I saw occasional streaks of red light, my first experience of lasers. I wandered off on my own. People milled about, going into different areas of the cathedral, mingling with dancers who wove through the crowds. There was no formal program, only encounters, as dancers faced someone and engaged them in movement. The music was at times melodic and other times atonal, surrounding us in an ever-changing soundscape. As the lights changed, I could see the intricate religious art around me, and at other times it disappeared. I felt free to move and join in the dance, finding different partners or groups throughout the long night. I had the sense that I was part of something very new and at the same time participating in a lost ritual from the ancient past. The whole experience was disorienting in a good way. I floated immersed in sensation, mystically connected with the community there and all time and space. Clearly a religious experience in a sacred place.

Later, I thought about the fact that this took place in the cathedral of the Episcopal Diocese of California. What did this mean about how religion was being transformed in the Sixties?

Live rock concerts provided another sort of happening. Whenever and wherever rock musicians played, people gathered. We came to dance, to move our bodies in free response to the beat. We came to greet each other, to see who we were and who we were becoming, to let our freak flags[267] fly. We came together to experience ourselves as part of a larger community, a community of freedom, peace, and love. Back then, rock music wasn't a spectator sport the way it sometimes is today. People came to feel free, to dance, to be whoever they felt like being, knowing they would be accepted and appreciated by other free people. Music created a context for the gathering of the tribes.[268]

The concept of the "gathering of the tribes" was introduced on a poster created for the Human Be-In, January 14, 1967, in Golden Gate Park, and publicized in the reporting of the historic event. The Human Be-In brought together diverse elements that would come to be known as central in the emerging counterculture. Timothy Leary and Richard Alpert (later known as Ram Dass) talked about the enlightening effects of psychedelics. Beat poets Allen Ginsberg, Gary Snyder, and Lawrence Ferlinghetti critiqued the madness of the dominant culture. Dick Gregory and Jerry Rubin talked about the need for political change. Music, always an essential element, affirmed the emerging values of peace, love, and freedom. San Francisco groups provided the soundtrack for the gathering—Jefferson Airplane, Grateful Dead, Big Brother and the Holding Company, and Quicksilver Messenger Service.

Although I missed the Be-In, I had plenty of opportunities

---

267   The term "freak flag" usually referred to long hair, as in the song by David Crosby, "Almost Cut My Hair." The term could also mean any of the identifying clothing or styles we wore. Urban Dictionary defines the term "a characteristic, mannerism, or appearance of a person, either subtle or overt, which implies unique, eccentric, creative, adventurous or unconventional thinking."

268   See, for instance, the PBS history series *American Experience*, produced by WGBH, Boston, 2005.

to hear these groups and more. Every month or so groups of us piled into someone's van and headed off to San Francisco to a rock concert, often held at one of the large ballrooms like the Avalon, the Fillmore, and the Family Dog. Sometimes we took small hits of acid on the way there. Often there was pot to smoke. Perhaps the drugs loosened us up, but mostly it was the music—and the feeling of being part of a community of free people. Few people danced in couples anymore. We moved around the dance floor expressing in movement whatever the music inspired in us. No more dance steps to learn, just free movement. I remembered how to twirl from ballet lessons long ago, and loved spinning around the floor. If I felt tired or dizzy, I just sat down where I was, watching the dancers move around me. Sometimes I sat down because an idea had occurred to me and I wanted to write it down; I kept cards and a pen in my pocket just in case. I don't remember ever fearing that someone would step on me. We may have been in our own worlds, but we were still aware of each other and respectful of their space.

This was a new culture, a new way of living, real hope and promise for the future of what our world could become. I would have liked to live there, but inevitably the music stopped and it was time to go home. The music often stayed in me for days afterwards, along with the buzz in my ears from how loud it was.

HIP COMMUNITIES

My brother Howdy was also searching for his place within the emerging new culture. I got to know him as an adult when he was in Berkeley sharing a house with his childhood friend Adam. Berkeley was an exciting place to be, with its political demonstrations and alternative culture. Howdy worked at West Shop Limited on Telegraph Avenue, the main drag leading to the entrance to the university. The store sold posters and cards, imported baskets, candles and incense, beads, unique clothing, peace symbols, and pipes. People went there to find out what was going on and buy hip things. Howdy and Adam enjoyed their exciting life in the middle of things in Berkeley, and we enjoyed visiting them.

One day, things changed. The frequent political

demonstrations were becoming increasingly contentious. Due to reported shootings in the area, the authorities closed their street even to foot traffic, trapping the two of them in their house. After that, they decided it was time to find a safer, more compatible place to live and work. In the early 1970s, Howdy headed to the far north of California, to Humboldt County. I gave him a hard time, challenging him about how he would support himself. "Are you going to eat pine cone sandwiches?" I remember asking him sarcastically.

It turned out that he was part of a migration of hip people from the Bay Area and elsewhere, who saw the town of Arcata as a place where they could live an alternative life style in relative isolation from the madness of the rest of the country. Thomas and I made the four-hour drive to visit him there for the first time in February 1971.

Arcata impressed us immediately as different from any place we had been before. Their free paper, *Daily Planet*, was mimeographed on ten pages of heavy gray paper. The front page was in brown print with the words written in a spiral so you had to keep turning it around to read. In the center was the key message: "We believe that 'creating a new society within the shell of the old' is more than just a phrase. That the *Daily Planet* is a step toward the Humboldt Free Territory."[269] Definitely different.

The paper highlighted alternative stores in the community: a used record store, a cooperatively-owned vegetarian restaurant, the Neo-American Book Store, Pacific Paraphernalia, and Whole Earth Natural Foods. A sampling of other resources included Equinox Free School, Draft Counseling, Women's Liberation, and Indian Teacher's Education Project. Articles included "In White Amerika" (about racism), "Antidote" (ideas about what the community needs), and a long article examining Gary Snyder's poetry (which the author admired, but also critiqued for Snyder's limited view of women.) Sprinkled throughout were quotes and cartoons. My favorite was the goal statement: "To work toward a society that will be essentially human."

My brother worked in the natural foods store, one of the first of its kind in the country. It was a small place but featured foods we

---

269   *Daily Planet*, Jan. 25, 1971.

had never seen before, like yogurt and hummus. Howdy was already a vegetarian, and here he was learning about new foods and healthy ways to eat. He seemed happier and more relaxed than before. We were glad he had made the move. We looked forward to visiting him again and seeing how things developed in this emerging alternative community.[270] The *Daily Planet's* vision proved true over the years: "Have you noticed how the country has changed in the last few years? If you're reading this, in fact, you're probably one of the changes. We're really starting to get it together, and wouldn't it be great if we could take it all the way! Sort of have a liberated zone up here!"

SONOMA STATE COLLEGE

Some colleges and universities were hotbeds of radical political activity in the Sixties. Others, like Sonoma State College, functioned as a reservoir of resources for the creation of new culture.

Part of the California state college and university system, Sonoma State was founded in 1961, and carried the Sixties spirit throughout much of its early history. Because of the growing reputation of its increasingly radical students, Governor Ronald Reagan took control of student government by appointing a conservative board of overseers who had to approve all decisions and proposed programs. In response, the students voted to disband student government in 1970, even though this meant ending funding for athletics, including football. The school soon became famous for their unique use of the football field—for Frisbee tournaments!

I began taking classes there as soon as I started teaching at Rohnert Park Junior High. The college was on the outskirts of town, surrounded by open fields, with two reservoirs as part of the sprawling 215-acre campus. The buildings would have been more appropriate in an urban setting, with their smooth concrete surfaces. But what the buildings lacked in warmth was more than compensated for by the creative, free-thinking students and faculty the college attracted. The students organized many festivals that were open to the wider

270   With the exception of nine years in West Virginia where he moved for a job, Howdy Emerson has lived in Humboldt County the rest of his life. He is an artist (painter) and musician (Celtic harp).

community, such as the annual World Peace Festival, established in response to the invasion of Cambodia and the killing of students at Kent State in 1970.

Among the college's unique features was the psychology department, one of the first in the country to focus on humanistic psychology. The Freudian psychoanalytic approach or BF Skinner's behaviorism dominated earlier psychology. In the late 1950s new approaches began to emerge with Rollo May and Carl Rogers emphasizing human potential, choice and responsibility, the search for meaning and value, consciousness, and creativity. In the early 1970s, as the human potential movement began to gain a following, hundreds of students applied each year to the master's program in humanistic psychology. The program had been designed to be small and personal, accepting only thirty-five at a time. When they cut that number in half in 1972, someone sent unauthorized letters to those who had been rejected saying to come anyway, because there was a possibility of an external degree program. Students hoping to participate in the new program arrived with few resources beyond a desire to learn, and the college was unprepared to accommodate them. Some camped in the field across from the main entrance, forming what became known as Benson's Grove, an ad hoc community where students lived in campers and other vehicles, despite the lack of facilities.

Fortunately, the Humanistic Psychology Institute (HPI) was founded at Sonoma State the year before, with goals of creating a school that embodied the values of the human growth and potential movement. In response to the unanticipated influx of students, HPI created an external degree program to provide access to Sonoma State's resources on humanistic psychology. It was a heady, creative, and somewhat chaotic time.

I connected with the psychology program in 1970, when I visited a course taught by Robert Greenway, "Psychology of Man and Nature." That class opened my eyes to two concepts from Carl Jung that would become important aspects of my understanding from then on. Greenway began the class by drawing what looked like an iceberg on the chalkboard. The part above the line he labeled our conscious minds. Below the surface is our individual subconscious and unconscious, but deep below is something that connects us with others, the collective unconscious. We can access this deep reservoir of ancient symbols, stories, archetypes, patterns, and memories, by opening ourselves to transcendental experiences like dreams. I felt my own mind expanding and was intrigued with the possibility of connection with others across time and space. Perhaps this was how new cultural forms emerged all over the world at the same time.

The second Jungian theory I learned about from Greenway was psychological types. Without explaining much in advance, the professor distributed copies of the Myers-Briggs Type Indicator[271] and invited us to fill them out. I was amazed to discover how well the description of my type, ENFP (extraverted intuitive with feeling and perception), described me. I was indeed enthusiastic and imaginative, and could do almost anything that interested me. I was quick to suggest solutions, and ready to help anyone with a problem. I especially loved the statement "Can usually find compelling reasons for whatever they want."[272]

The ENFP description also validated aspects of my personality I had thought were negative. For instance, I tended to improvise instead of preparing thoroughly in advance. I also tended to wait until the last minute to complete projects. Understanding what I thought were failings as natural aspects of my type helped me accept and celebrate parts of myself I had previously rejected.[273]

---

271   The Myers-Briggs Type Indicator (MBTI) is a self-report questionnaire designed to indicate psychological preferences in how people perceive the world and make decisions, constructed by Katharine Cook Briggs and her daughter Isabel Briggs Myers during World War II and based on the typological theory proposed by Carl Jung in his book, Psychological Types, published in English in 1923. When I first encountered the MBTI, it was still considered a research instrument, published by the Educational Testing Service. In 1975 Consulting Psychologists Press took over publication and the MBTI became more widely used in psychology, career counseling, and organizational development.

272   Isabel Briggs, Myers, Report Form for Myers-Briggs Type Indicator, Consulting Psychologists Press, 1976.

273   I acquired copies of the questionnaire and scoring keys and gave the MBTI to family members and friends, which helped me understand them better and learn more about the dynamics of type.

Dorothy May Emerson

The following year I arranged with my school for a substitute to cover my classes one afternoon a week, so I could participate in another course with Greenway, "Explorations in Instructional Theory: Inquiry into Educational Alternatives." Greenway and the others in the class were involved with free schools. They referred to the course as a "Free School Teaching Lab." I alone was trying to apply the same principles in a public-school setting. What I learned helped me articulate a rationale to support my radical ideas about education. We did some far-out things in that class, given that this was a college-credit course. Several class sessions took place in the sauna students had built by the lakes. Yes, we were all nude. I sat there in amazement that I was getting time off from school for this experience. Talk about being in more than one culture at once!

Sonoma State became a place I could go to connect with other like-minded people. When I needed affirmation that the world was indeed changing in positive ways, I found it at the campus on the edge of town.

ENCOUNTERS WITH INDIGENOUS PEOPLE: OREGON INDIAN COUNTRY, 1971

On our second trip to the Pacific Northwest the following summer, Thomas and I drove our van on a journey through Oregon. I decided to keep a journal, which I typed up and submitted to the Petaluma School District as a summer study project, giving me credit on the salary scale. I called the journal "The Nature of America."[274] An important theme was encountering indigenous people and culture. Knowing that was part of this journey, I began the journal: "We leave Cotati in Coast Miwok territory. When I get home, I must remember to look into the lives of the native Americans[275] who first loved this

---

274   "The Nature of America: Journal of observations and reflections about nature and modern and native Americans based on a trip through Oregon" (June 27-July 10, 1971) exists now only in faded dittoed copies.
275   In 1971, it was not yet common to refer to indigenous people of America as Native Americans (with both words capitalized). The term Indian was more generally used, as it is today especially by older Indians who have explained to me that neither term is accurate since there is no generic term, only the names of their

land." I realized that except for elementary school lessons, I knew very little about the indigenous people of California or anywhere else, for that matter. What I saw on TV and in movies I suspected was wrong, but who were the real Indians? The trip shifted my consciousness and piqued my interest in learning more both about the history of native peoples and what was happening now.

I began my study at the Portland museum, where I read about the worldview of the original people of the area: "The Northwest Coast Indians believed that in the beginning all living things shared the world in a state of equality and mutual understanding. They spoke the same language and the difference between them was in their superficial external appearance. If, for convenience, this body covering was removed, the form underneath was identical with a human form. This allowed a human to live with birds and animals and return with their secrets to hand on to other people." I commented: "A quaint belief? Amusing animal stories? Or is there not a basic truth here, a truth ignored by the European Americans who plundered nature for their own advancement, thereby leading the world to the brink of ecologic disaster?"

The next evening, we camped at Trillium Lake near Mount Hood and read aloud from a book of Indian legends we bought at the museum. I wrote:

We feel a sense of awe for nature as we watch the sun setting on the mountain, the campfire flickering, the mosquito fish jumping. The Indian tales give us a sense of communion with, and respect for, this lovely place. We could not think of throwing our trash on this spiritual place. And yet a quick look around reveals that someone wasn't so affected by its beauty. What allows a person to dump tin cans, papers, cigarette butts, bottles, Styrofoam cups, pull-top rings, etc. all over the countryside? If he believed, as the Indians apparently did, that the land and the animals had spirits equal to his own, he surely could do no such thing. So who is the primitive? The Indian or the white man?

The next morning, we entered the Warm Springs Indian Reservation. I reflected on the surprising change in the landscape

nations.

soon after entering Indian land: "Instead of the plowed fields and grazing land we have been traveling through, we now find ourselves in the midst of a prairie surrounded by mesas, uncultivated except for the roads and fences lining it...There are many colors of flowers—pinks, reds, purples, yellows, and subtle variations of blue sagebrush. The great expanse of prairie overwhelmed me."

Then we came upon a resort development built by the tribe for tourists. The name seemed ironic given what we found there: Ka-nee-ta, "a beautiful place in the sun." The brochure's description struck me as strange given what we were seeing: "an Indian legend that lives...a hidden valley of eternal sun, natural mineral waters, and crystal streams transformed into a luxury resort by its tribal owners." I wrote:

Transformed into crap, it should have said. There remains nothing of the grandeur of this natural place, only plastic America's homogenized idea of luxury, packaged so that any America will feel comfortable and empty. The only remaining hint that this is Indian is that one can rent a teepee for $7.50 a night, in a row of teepees spanning a concrete parking lot—a teepee motel! How sad, we think, that this is hailed as a great business achievement for the poor native Americans. Look how they've learned to set aside their culture and their beauty to make something plastic and clean enough for the America public. Achievement and success of this sort spells death to all that Indian culture means. I feel cheap and sinful to participate in a culture that could call this good. We can't stay here!

We drove past as quickly as we could. On the Fourth of July, we arrived at Chiloquin, our destination for a "primitive weaving workshop," the reason for this trip. The teacher, Hal Painter, a tapestry weaver Thomas knew from San Francisco, greeted us and showed us to the campground run by his cousin. Since I was not a weaver, or even an artist, I was reluctant to participate, but Hal encouraged me, noting that we were all beginners in this form of weaving.

We gathered the next morning on a point overlooking the Sprague River, where a weaving hut had been constructed in "a circular frame of tree trunks and branches lovingly built by Hal and friends to accommodate 20 or so Navajo style looms." Hal showed us hand-spun yarn we could use, one batch from black sheep and the rest dyed with plants and minerals from the earth. The yarn and the setting inspired me to create "a background of the variations in the colors of earth and sky with a strong dark tree silhouetted against it." However, translating my vision into a weaving proved far more difficult than I imagined.

I wasn't the only one having trouble with the technique. Clearly "primitive" did not mean simple. Sitting next to me was a Klamath Indian woman who lived nearby. I recorded her story:

> She is very concerned about learning to be Indian and is taking this class to learn about her own heritage.[276] More than the others she feels frustrated by her inability to master the techniques...and yet she sticks to it, doggedly determined to discover within herself her Indian abilities. Outside of this class she is one of the leaders of the Indian community here, which is just now coming into awareness of its own needs and learning to develop its own strengths and abilities. Her children are part of a group that is reviving in themselves the lost art of Indian dancing.

That afternoon I joined a group going into town to the local Indian museum, two rooms in an old high school "chock full of the finest examples of beadwork, clothing, pottery, mortars and pestles, along with photographs and documents chronicling the encounter of the Indians with white society," I noted. "There is love in these things which makes them valuable far beyond gold or diamonds or blue-chip stamps. No quantity of factory-produced items could compare with one carefully constructed object from this collection."

That night the dancers came despite the rain. They had to dance inside the meeting hall, not as inspiring as dancing around the campfire would have been, but the twenty kids ranging in age from seven to sixteen brought the spirit of their ancestors alive, dressed in costumes they made themselves. At the end, they invited us to join them in a round dance. "They show us a simple step and we share with them the beauty of moving together in rhythmic harmony," I

---

276   We were learning Navajo-style weaving which was different from crafts done by the Klamath, who were noted for their woven baskets.

wrote. "I'm very glad to be able to share this moment with them and let our moving together affirm our relationship to one another. We are all human beings. We all live on the same earth. We can be brothers [and sisters.]"

Afterwards I talked with some of the dancers, particularly several I thought were probably the ages of my students. After learning more about their traditions and dances, I asked one girl about school. "She told me she was stupid and couldn't learn much. She was afraid of entering high school in the fall. She would have to go through hazing run by the white kids. She knew it would be demeaning and embarrassing but she would do it anyway because otherwise she would be a total social outcast." She went on to talk about the prejudice throughout the school. Teachers and administrators often harshly punished Indian kids for things white kids did. Most expected to drop out. They knew the school didn't care because no one would come after them when they stopped attending. "From my experience as a teacher I could tell that this girl was certainly NOT stupid." She was more able than most others her age "to communicate ideas clearly and intelligently to a stranger. If she thinks she is stupid then there most certainly is something wrong with the school system...Instead of helping her develop her strengths, it has made her think she is weak. The crimes America has committed against the Indians have apparently not stopped."

One afternoon during the workshop, a local white woman came to talk with us about the Klamath Indians. The US government sent her parents to work with the Indian School when the reservation was first established. She told us how the Indians were treated at the school, "how they were robbed of their culture, stripped bare by seemingly well-intentioned whites who wished to bring them into European-American modern society." Her horror stories "made us feel sick to death to be Americans." She went on to explain the situation of the Klamath today. In 1955, they were convinced to sell their reservation. The money each family received was long gone and now they had to struggle to rediscover and maintain their culture without a land base. "How successful the white man was in almost destroying the Indian altogether," I wrote. "We cannot help but feel guilty."

As the end of our workshop week approached, I was still struggling with my design. I wrote: "I continue to work and try to hear what the loom is telling me," I wrote hopefully. "Something in it speaks to something in me and guides my hands." But I could mostly see the imperfections in my weaving. "I see my lack of craft, and yet something comes through...I realize it says something different than I had intended. Is this art or just poor planning? People seem struck by what I have created. It said something to them. They liked the subtle changes of color in the earth and sunset sky. The "tree" became a person standing grand and tall reaching into the setting sun. Someone called it Siddhartha." Coincidentally, I had just read the book *Siddhartha* (by Herman Hesse), about a man who spends his life searching for truth and finds answers in nature.[277]

WARRIORS OF THE RAINBOW

That fall 1971, I had an opportunity to continue learning about indigenous people. Vinson Brown, co-author of *Warriors of the Rainbow: Strange and Prophetic Dreams of the Indians*, was speaking in Sebastopol. When we got there the place was packed, but we managed to find seats in the balcony. I was at first disappointed to see an older white man on stage, as I was hoping the speaker would be Indian, but once he began speaking I was enthralled. He talked about ancient prophecies of native people in many parts of the continent and shared spiritual insights and prophecies, many of which point to a time when the earth would be in peril and would need all kinds of people to come together to bring healing and peace.

When the speaker talked about the Makah people of Neah Bay, Washington, the westernmost point in the continental United States, I felt transported into a new awareness. "The Makah teach the importance of hearing the wave," he explained. "They teach us to pray that the spirit will come back to the people, to let the wave come, and not to be satisfied with small things. The white man puts

---

277   I have carried this weaving with me ever since but never figured out how to hang it properly. Finally, while writing this book I asked some artist friends for advice and together we hung it from a branch. It now hangs in my writing room.

truth in boxes to control it, but we should let it wash over us and bring us back to wholeness."

I had loved ocean waves as long as I could remember. What did I need to do to hear the wave the way the Makah do? When he suggested that we connect with the sacred in nature through dreams, I remembered my childhood dream of staying ahead of the big wave. In contrast, the Makah wisdom said to let the wave come and wash over me. What might that mean for me now?

"Because there are enough of us who see the oneness in all people," Brown said, "we can make the earth beautiful again and help the prophecy come true now." Then he connected the teachings of native people of this continent with spiritual teachings and prophecies all over the world. Every people, he said, must be proud of their past, see the good, and learn from the good. All people should be free to seek truth in their own way.

It was a positive, hopeful message that resonated with me and others there. The book became popular and inspired many followers, including Greenpeace leaders who named one of their ships Rainbow Warrior. More recently, critics have discredited the book as "fakelore," not authentically Indian.[278] But in the Sixties the ideas he and co-author William Willoya, an Aleut from Alaska, inspired us with a vision of people of all colors working together to save the earth—and that was a message we needed to hear. Their book, along with other discredited Sixties classics, such as *Black Elk Speaks* and *Seven Arrows*, encouraged us to more deeply explore and connect with the history, teachings, and practices of indigenous people.

ENCOUNTERING NATURE

I don't remember the first Earth Day on April 22, 1970, but I was already connecting with nature more than I had earlier in my life. Growing up I hadn't been interested in gardening, but in 1969 we moved to a first-floor apartment, with open land right off our patio and I tried planting a few vegetables and flowers. Unfortunately, the deer ate the few plants that managed to grow on the hard-scrabble

---

278   See Wikipedia article.

ground. Then we moved to Cotati where we had plenty of room and better soil for multiple gardens.

Before moving to Cotati, I had never lived in a place where I had land around me. Even though our property backed up to the freeway, a sense of peace came over me there. I loved walking around our three acres, smelling the eucalyptus trees that formed a windbreak between our land and the cow pasture next door, picking wild blackberries that grew along the creek that flowed on the side opposite the freeway, learning to prune the apple and plum trees we inherited, and trimming rose bushes that had been planted before we arrived. It was a new world to me, and I had dreams of turning the place into a productive farm. I did manage to put in a sizable vegetable garden. We even bought a rototiller to prepare the ground. I loved digging in the soil, reveling in the smell of dirt and the physical sensation of being close to the earth.

The second Earth Day is emblazoned in my memory. We awoke to the sounds of chain saws cutting down the trees along our country lane. Fortunately, we convinced the tree-cutters to leave our trees intact. We only later learned that the trees were considered unstable, a potential danger to nearby houses. Today our trees are still there, and are the tallest trees on that road.

The early 1970s saw an awakening of interest and concern about the environment, a relatively new concept in those days, at least in popular culture. The word "ecology" was also new to the cultural consciousness, although it was coined by a German zoologist in the nineteenth century. The word came from the Greek *oikos*, meaning "household," "home," or "place to live." In the Sixties, it took on the meaning of interrelationships, the awareness that we as humans interacted with the environment and were part of the whole ecology of the earth, our home. When we first saw the earth from space, and especially when the photograph of the whole planet was widely disseminated, a new consciousness began to arise, that we were all part of one planet and that we needed to take care of our home.

ENVIRONMENT AND CULTURE

When I first came across an announcement for the course

on American Writers and the Environmental Crisis,[279] I realized
I had no awareness of American authors who wrote about the
environment. I knew German and English authors who wrote about
nature, but was that the same thing? The weekend class was being
held in Mendocino, one of my favorite places, so I signed up right
away.

I received a list of books ahead of time, bought them, and
started to read. I was most fascinated by *Earth House Hold*, by Beat
poet Gary Snyder, especially his poetic reflections about living
in a lookout tower in a national park watching for fires and his
experiences in Zen monasteries in Japan. During the class, though,
what Professor Breslin highlighted were essays at the end of the book
about the concept of "tribe."

Gary Snyder began by describing the "Gathering of the Tribes"
at the 1967 Be-In in San Francisco. He identified the people who
gathered and those like them as part of "the Great Subculture, which
goes back as far perhaps as the late Paleolithic."[280] He explained: "For
several centuries now Western Man has been ponderously preparing
himself for a new look at the inner world and the spiritual realms.
Even in the centers of nineteenth-century materialism there were
dedicated seekers—some within Christianity, some within the arts,
some within occult circles." I thought of German authors who fit that
description, like Goethe and Rilke, and I identified myself as part of
this Subculture. The key concepts he articulated clearly resonated
with me. Humankind's "mother is Nature and Nature should
be tenderly respected...[Human] life and destiny is growth and
enlightenment in self-disciplined freedom...[The] divine has been
made flesh and ...flesh is divine...[We] not only should but do love
one another." Although these views have been "harshly suppressed
in the past as threatening to both Church and State," today these
values, he wrote, "seem almost biologically essential to the survival
of humanity."

---

279   University of California Extension course, taught by James Breslin, Aug.
6-8, 1971, at the Mendocino Art Center.
280   Gary Snyder, "Passage to More than India," in *Earth House Hold,* 1969,
104-105.

SEA CHANGE: *the unfinished agenda of the 1960s*

What a relief to discover that in addition to being part of the Sixties counterculture, I was also part of a larger stream of seekers who defied their culture's focus on greed and materialism, and chose to think and live in alternative ways. Snyder used the concept of Tribe "because it suggests the type of new society now emerging within the industrial nations," which he saw as more like the European Gypsies than the American Indians, because they were "a group without nation or territory which maintains its own values...and religion, no matter what country it may be in."[281] He explained that in the past, "As the number of alienated individuals, creative types and general society misfits grew, they came to recognize each other by various minute signals." This is what Thomas and I experienced on our 1970 trip, when we were invited to the rock festival. I felt my mind opening to the larger significance of the new culture that was emerging around me.

The Great Subculture also promotes "an ecstatically positive vision of spiritual and physical love," Professor Breslin explained. This alternative perspective suggests "that we need not look to a model or rule imposed from outside in searching for the center; and that in following the grain, one is being truly "moral." This reminded me of one of my students' favorite song lines: "Follow your heart, 'cause you know it's your light."[282]

I realized that, although I might be part of the Subculture movement, I had yet to find my own tribe. A year later I wrote in an unfinished and unsent letter to my mother: "It all comes back to living in a culture you don't believe in. There is no place to be except at odds with our surroundings."

SEARCH FOR SELF

As was common for women in the Sixties, a major part of my identity was bound up in my marriage. I had lived on my own for less than six months after college. Thomas and I had been together ever since, so most of who I had become was in partnership with him. As our relationship began to change, I desperately needed to

---

281   Gary Snyder, "Why Tribe," in *Earth House Hold*, 1969, 113-116.
282   Sons of Champlin, "Follow Your Heart." 1971.

discover who I was. I had been writing miscellaneous reflections for years, but had only kept journals when traveling. Thomas gave me my first non-travel journal, but I was intimidated by the empty white pages. Finally, on April Fool's Day 1972, I began to write. We were in Mendocino camping with friends. Because Thomas wasn't feeling well, he stayed in the van while I went off into the woods to find a special place to start my journal. When I saw a hollowed-out tree up ahead, I knew that was the place.

Later I reflected on that day. "The day I started this book, in deeper search for myself, was the beginning of the end of our relationship. Perhaps our great relationship was built only on dependence. Perhaps I couldn't face myself so I was willing to do everything for and with Thomas. But it doesn't work that way anymore."

I didn't record daily thoughts but instead wrote when I needed to sort out my thoughts, and sometimes when I was upset and needed to pour out my feelings. Often, writing reminded me of what was most important and helped me regain a sense of balance. Writing also helped me connect with nature. "Being outside is important to me," I wrote. "I like to write with the sun on my paper. The Indians learned great spirit from being outside and from experiencing all forms of nature. I'm only scratching the surface now."

As I got used to journal writing I discovered a new phenomenon. Sometime words flowed through me, like automatic writing. I didn't know what would come next. I just started to write and then went back to see what I had written as if someone else had written the words. Sometimes poems flowed out of me, sometimes songs. Was this my subconscious speaking? Was any of it from the collective unconscious? Ram Dass described something similar in *Be Here Now*:

There is writing happening
Maybe that's hard for you to understand
I am here. But "I" am not here.
I am writing. But "I" am not writing
Inside of me in the heart cave is a mantra going on that reminds me
Who I really am   over and over   in this inner place   I AM

And even as I write, where this mantra is going on
I'm just watching with
GREAT AWE AND WONDER
The awesome drama of nature unfolds before my very Eye
Before that Eye I
I which sees all and knows all.[283]

Often, but not always, the experience of automatic writing came when I was high on marijuana or LSD. These drugs played an important role in my life. Marijuana opened me up to creative ideas and helped me feel better when I was upset. Pot allowed me to significantly reduce my alcohol consumption, as I far preferred that high. I smoked nearly every day in the early 1970s.

TRANSFORMATION OF CONSCIOUSNESS

LSD gave me an understanding of the oneness of all beings and a direct experience of the natural world. I experienced deep connections with other people and insights into my own mind and heart. The experience of complete merging with another is something I can never forget, even though my last experience with this amazing substance was over forty years ago. Because of my many transformational experiences at that time, I cannot imagine who I might be now without them. Not counting the small amounts we sometimes took when we went to concerts, I probably took around two dozen trips from 1968 through 1973. One of the gurus of acid exploration, Richard Alpert (who later became Ram Dass), wrote:

Now, in our culture we've been trained for individual differences to stand out ... and we get so that we only see others as separate from our selves in the ways in which they're separate, and one of the dramatic characteristics of this experience is being with another person and suddenly seeing the ways in which they are like you, not different from you, and experiencing the fact, that which is essence in you, and essence in me is indeed one, and understanding that there is no other, it is all one.[284]

---

283   Ram Dass (Richard Alpert), *Be Here Now*, 1971, 4.
284   From the conclusion of *Zeitgeist: The Movie*, 2007.

Occasionally the experience was so powerful I remembered it in detail long afterwards. Especially clear in my memory are the two trips I took by myself. Here's the story of the first one, written forty years after the transformational day I spent at Miwok Beach.

In the spring of 1971, I decided to take an acid trip at the beach—alone. I started early in the day and took a small "hit" while driving to Miwok Beach. I was just coming on as I arrived. The sand was sparkling, the churning water deep blue-green. It was one of those perfect days, not too hot, but warm enough to give fire to body and soul. I parked my car on a cliff overlooking the ocean and skipped down the steep path with my blanket to the sand below. I was wearing a leather hat my brother gave me. I later used the hat to shield my eyes from the bright sun as I lay on the sand.

There were a fair number of people on the beach, mostly families. Hearing the children's laughter as they played on the rocks blended into the sounds of the pounding surf. I sat on my blanket looking around at the ever-brightening colors and crystal vibrations from the surf. I had come alone on this trip to seek a vision.

I took my shoes off and ran down to the water. The cold water pierced my toes like sharp needles. I picked up a shell and looked deep into its crevices, seeing the story of its long journey through the sea, as eternity touched my soul. The salt sea air filled my lungs with sunshine. My heart thrilled with excitement and I began to laugh with the joy of being alive.

Back on my blanket, everything else on the beach disappeared from my consciousness, leaving me alone with the sun and the roar of the rolling sea. Even tripping I knew I wasn't supposed to look directly at the sun, but it called me to make connection. I laid back and put my brother's hat over my face to protect my eyes. I could still feel the full force of the sun's energy on my face. My body rose to greet the sun's power, its warmth entered my body like a lover, and I became one with the heart of the sun.

This cosmic union filled my soul with greater power than I had ever known before. At that moment, I knew I could do anything, be anything. Clearly, I had an important destiny for the sun loves me and is now in me. I was on this earth for a reason. But what exactly was the reason?

Gradually the sun drifted down towards the sea. Now the ocean and the sun were becoming one and I was united with both sources of great power. Magical moments drew me into eternity, blessing me with gifts of love and destiny.

Suddenly it was nearly dark. I was alone on the beach and the tide was coming in. The pink light was fading from the tall cliffs behind me. I knew I had to reach higher ground quickly or I might be swallowed by the sea.

I scrambled up the rocky path to the cliffs above. Sighing in relief I looked back down at the sand, at the place where I had made love with the sun. There was my brother's hat, right there on the sand about to be swept out to sea.

I froze in terror at the prospect of going back down into that place of impending doom, but at the same time I knew I needed that hat, my talisman of this day of unity and love. The hat was part of me now. It had protected me and I needed to rescue it.

Could I conquer my fear and go back down the steep path? My logical mind told me the tide was not going to come all the way up to the cliffs, but how could I know for sure? The longer I waited the darker it would become and the harder it would be for me to overcome my fear and make the descent. I reached deep inside to find my place of power, took a deep breath, and ran down the path to get the hat. It was one of the hardest things I have ever done.

I felt a sense of triumph when I was safely back on the cliffs above. I sat on the edge of the cliff and watched the last light fade from the sky.

Then I had to drive home. I realized then that I was still tripping. I had driven plenty of times stoned on pot but had never tried to drive on acid. I waited until it started getting too cold to sit outside anymore and got in my car and tried to remember how to drive.

Fortunately, there was almost no one else on the road. I turned the key, the engine started; I remembered to turn on the lights and slowly pulled out onto the road. I had absolutely no sense of how fast I was moving unless I looked at the speedometer. I decided I needed to go at least 25 miles an hour to be reasonable. I drove the winding road without incident but was shocked to see a bright neon sign of a motel I never noticed was there before. I kept on, and miraculously found my way home, laughing in relief as I found my street and pulled in to my driveway.

Most of my trips were exciting and inspiring, but occasionally I got scared. Toward the end of my second solo trip, in 1973, I got scared. The wind started to howl and seemed to shake the little house I was living in at the time. I called for help and friends came to support me.

The next day I reflected: "I sure didn't know how far I could get into my own fear! I really scared myself and had to ask for help. Ruth, Joann, and Andy came and did portfolios [for the HPI master's program]—a real consciousness-lowering experience. But I was grateful to have people around...I need to be with people, for sure." Then I made a list of what I had learned:

I'm not at all as brave and together as I seem to be

I want to be with people—really with people—all my life—I don't want to be alone

I am a little child inside—I want to be loved and protected by someone

Time is meaningless when you are waiting for it to pass—

People give life meaning—I want to share more fully with people

I would love to have a child

A favorite song line, from Jethro Tull's "Aqualung" kept coming to me: "I await my resurrection feeling fine."

I look into my soul
  a hurricane tears me apart
    a tidal wave smashes me down
      a raging fire burns me up
and I am still alive
the moth does not die in the flame

Resurrection is a hard life
  when you want to be free

> when you care to be love
> when you know to be you
> today is a long way
> from where we could be someday

I didn't make a conscious decision about it at the time, but this was my last LSD trip. By then, LSD researcher Richard Alpert had become Ram Dass and was immersing himself in Eastern religions and meditation. My focus was more external. I knew I needed people and dreamed of finding my tribe.

SYNTHESIS

Ruth Miller[285] created Mercury Conferences to bring people with diverse interests together. Held in a lodge in the Sonoma hills, these semi-spontaneous bimonthly weekend gatherings were exciting opportunities to meet and learn from other explorers and seekers. The program for the weekend was determined by the people who arrived on Friday afternoon. Once it was clear who was coming, the program was set but remained flexible to accommodate people's schedules. We all brought food and somehow there was plenty for everyone. We slept in the lodge or outside in sleeping bags. There was no registration fee or budget, but people chipped in if money was needed. It was amazing to experience how each weekend evolved its own structure and themes, based on synchronicities among the people present and the topics being shared.

After a conference in January 1973, I wrote in my journal that the weekend had brought me love, joy, and great hope for the future. "The kind of group consciousness I had wished for appears to be here," I wrote. "We need each other because we are each other." I was falling in love with a group! A week later, I reflected on what I was continuing to learn from the conference: "Changing so fast, opening huge doors, fasting, loving deeply, working hard, straining all faculties, stretching to grow beyond mind fuck, conscious of everything more intensely, feeling new strength."

---

285   For more on Ruth Miller, see Love is All You Need, Exploring Love with Women.

Ruth also spearheaded the formation of a self-directed master's group connected with the external degree program being developed at Sonoma State by the Humanistic Psychology Institute. At the first meeting in 1972 of what was initially called the Inner Frontiers Club, Ruth proposed that we help each other develop our work by meeting together weekly, sharing ideas, giving reports on our projects, receiving feedback and guidance, and sometimes hearing from guests who would share what they were doing in related fields. Each of us would write up our projects per the requirements HPI was establishing. Later, we would present our projects to HPI to earn our degrees. I had long wanted to go back to school to get a master's and maybe even a doctorate, so this was perfect for me. Not only could I build on what I was already doing as a teacher, but I could more fully explore my interest in psychological type using the Myers-Briggs Type Indicator. After the first meeting, I noted my excitement at the possibility that "I could essentially develop something on my own—within a discipline and structure of purpose to keep me committed." I hoped my work with experimental education could provide a framework for the group's creation of our own process for self-directed learning.

The master's group met frequently, often at our house in Cotati, but some came only sporadically. New people came occasionally but didn't stay. Some were less committed to earning a degree than I was, but came to hear the presentations and discuss the ideas. I noted: "Each of us has to see if it's really worth it to get the degree. We all know what our work is. Will the degree help us get there? It means money, organization, and commitment to a time schedule for writing and getting it completed. I can dig the process, and I know I want to do it." Later I observed, "The group is less of a group and more of a process." We had originally hoped to produce a book, but it never materialized. However, I passed my oral exam in May 1973, and four of us completed the program by July, although our degrees were not official until 1974, when the HPI program was registered with the state. With a signed statement from the four members of my Evaluation Committee, I convinced the school district to give me credit for having a master's, even though the formal degree had not yet been issued.

Putting my degree together on my own was a lot of work, but it helped me clarify my ideas about education and the reality of working within the public-school system. Participating in the group meetings and in Mercury Conferences brought me into contact with innovative teachers and practitioners of a wide range of subjects that came to be known as holistic health and New Age.[286] I was most interested in Ruth's work with biorhythms, which we connected with our mutual interest in Jung's psychological types. I was also intrigued with numerology and telepathy. To improve my health I tried chiropractic, acupuncture, and mega-vitamin therapy. With Ruth's encouragement, I started the Atkins diet (new at the time) and over the next four months lost forty pounds.

Being exposed to such diverse ideas expanded my mind and opened me to new possibilities. Ruth helped me understand how the diverse systems we were exploring were connected. Together we created a slide show exploring the synthesis of knowledge represented by seemingly different ways of understanding life and the human condition.[287] Then we developed a workshop, "Synthesis: Focus on Self-Learning," to further explore themes in the slide show. We presented it at several conferences, and included it as part of our master's projects. A highlight for me was our presentation at the annual conference of the California Council for the Social Studies, in Oakland in March 1973. This enabled me to bring my new work to the larger social studies community.

One of the most innovative contexts for our slide show

---

286   Mercury Conference topics included: astrology, Tarot, numerology, handwriting analysis, palm reading, telepathy, trance work, secrets of the pyramids, astral travel, healing powers of the mind, psychic and faith healing, shamanic healing, Kirlian photography, and chakras. Alternative healing practices included acupuncture, chiropractic, orthomolecular medicine, energy therapy, endocrine and hypoglycemic therapies, iridology, massage, body wisdom, yoga, meditation, biorhythms, and vision training. Humanistic psychology topics included Jungian work with symbols, mandalas, dreams, and psychological type, as well as psychodrama and other humanistic and transformational psychotherapies.

287   We used two carousel slide projectors so we could simultaneously show different but related systems.

and workshop was the Omniversal Symposium at Sonoma State, September 29, 1973. In addition to spiritual teachers and practitioners, academics presented papers on cutting-edge studies in such esoteric subjects as "Embryonic Holography," "Synthetic Telepathy," and "Psychotronic History." Stanley Kripper, noted researcher on dreams, hypnosis, altered states of consciousness, and parapsychology, was one of the hosts. This symposium was the first place much of this emerging knowledge was presented in an academic setting. The fact that Sonoma State hosted this radical conference is another indication of what made that place so remarkable. I was lucky to be there at that time and to be part of such an historic gathering.

Above all, my friendship and work with Ruth empowered me to think in new ways. She encouraged my exploration of psychological types and supported my use of the Myers-Briggs with my students. Our exploration of the relationship between type and biorhythms produced many insights I wish we could have pursued more fully. I would have liked to have continued working with her for many years, but my need to move on with my life eventually took me away from California, and we lost touch. Nevertheless, our relationship had a lasting effect on me. Besides connecting me with systems of knowledge I would have been unlikely to otherwise explore, falling in love with her, even though she wasn't interested, opened me to the possibility of being with a woman as a primary partner.[288]

I had my own ways of integrating what I was learning through my association with Ruth. In the end, it came back to how this knowledge affected the needs of society at the time. I wrote the following in early 1974 during the first major gasoline crisis, when we had to wait in long lines to buy gas and the country went on daylight savings time in the winter to save energy.

Energy and environmental crises have made us realize there is much that has been lacking in our knowledge of ourselves and our ability to solve problems. We have failed to make the systems of democracy and free enterprise work, because they were dependent on a capitalistic need to control and use the environment. Now we must learn to shift our energy into conserving and nurturing

---

288   See Love is All You Need, Falling in Love with Women."

nature, if we are to survive on this planet at all.

To survive we must learn to live in harmony with nature, both inside and outside us. Once we realize that we are part of nature, we can begin to observe our own natural flows and functions. The rhythm of life within us is revealed in cycles of energy which can be utilized to help us realize our full potential in life. Living in harmony with natural cycles releases energy we didn't know we had. The forces of nature can guide us, if we open ourselves to natural rhythms.

COMPARING LOCAL CULTURES, THE NEW PIONEERS

I continued to be intrigued by the culture changes happening around me. Sometimes when I attended an event by myself, I took on the role of cultural observer and recorded what I witnessed. One such occasion was in 1972 at Sonoma County Pioneer Day. Quoted portions are from a story I wrote on site during the day.

Pioneer Day is celebrated in honor of the European Americans who established a community here in 1847. The town still retains much of the loveliness of the original settlement. "Freeways have remained marvelously distant, leaving people to live here who care about their town. Joined by some from miles away, they celebrate the past by infusing it, perhaps subconsciously, with the values they would like to have today, each in their own way."

The day began with a parade, which featured:

...a charming mix of fantasy with fanciful reality: buckskin-fringed Indian families, yippee-yi-yo-ing cowboys, satin-elegant western horse riders, surreys with fringe on top, ladies with parasols, delicate Japanese dancers, crazy gypsies, and children everywhere—all in apparent harmony ... undreamed of in the real beginnings of this town ...

The parade ends gloriously in the lovely plaza in the center of town. Shaded by trees and presided over by the calm grace of mission-style government and commercial buildings, costumes and identities mix in the moment of today. Booths sponsored by different community groups and businesses offer tacos, hot dogs, or a real old-time barbeque dinner. Even Granny's own banana bread and poppy seed dressing are for sale. Kids run the game booths, providing an orderly way to either dunk someone in a tank of water or throw a sponge in someone's face. On the lawn, people gather with friends amidst the divergent crowd.

I was intrigued to notice the way different groups of people gathered and the activities they chose to engage in. For instance, the organizers of the event had set up fenced-off enclosure "for babysitting, three hours maximum, for parents who would like time away from their kids."

In contrast, over near the stage there's a buzzing of child activity on blankets spread on the ground beneath a sign: "Moon Valley School, Stitchery, and Stories." Small children laugh, talk, sit, tumble, and run around the smiling women who seem more or less in charge. On adjoining blankets, still part of the children's activities, lounge a group of people happy, relaxed. I figure these folks are the children's parents and friends.

These were the counterculture people who were often part of community gatherings in those days.

The men have long hair and wear bright shirts. One has a scarf tied gaily around his head. The women wear long skirts and no bras. One woman entranced everyone with a top made of two crocheted doilies tied together tentatively at the sides. Ordinarily the cowboys who dominated much of the crowd would have called these people hippies and might have blamed them for some problems. But today the hippies and the children and the cowboys could play comfortably side by side in remembrance of the glory of pioneering.
Contrasting cultures existed side by side, and each seemed to respect the others.

Then the great American tradition begins of giving awards to participants in the parade. The first category declares the winner of the best costume to be the Gypsy Dancers! A shriek of joy arises amongst the children as the hippies stand en masse to receive their silver cup. They laugh, hug one another, and dance a few gypsy steps back to their beer.

The awards continue and all types of people win. Everyone cheers everyone else. "Everybody did such a good job," the emcee says. "Congratulations to everyone!" When we can see each other's virtues, everyone is a winner. What if our whole society operated like this?

Despite the positive energy of the day, I observed one incident of conflict, and it saddened me. This took place in the Moon Valley School area.

One little boy in diapers stumbles with his toy gun, copying the adults he has seen today. A young man with a beer in hand and frown on his face sits down at the corner of a blanket and writes on a piece of cardboard: "Days of drought. Pray for piss—and rain." He scowls at the diapered gun-slinger. "Come here and I'll beat you up." A woman previously intent upon showing a four-year-old girl how to make a chain stitch quickly lifts her head, listens, and wonders what to do. With a soft word, she leaves the little girl with the stitching and moves over to the scowling young man.

"I don't believe I quite understand you," she says, her gentle eyes searching for some light of recognition or contact. His eyes are red and glazed over, perhaps from too much beer.

"There is no peace in the world, only hate," he claims with quivering assurance.

"You seem to be angry at the world. Why? It can be so beautiful."

"The cops are wearing guns and clubs, even today."

"This is a school. We're trying to learn to live beyond the fears that cause such hate," she explains.

"You're raising your children in a fairy tale world," he counters.

"To me your hate is a fairy tale. This is a school where we can all learn love," she says patiently.

"But I am a part of your school," he points out.

Her loving confidence is visibly shaken by this last remark. His daring assertion is true and she knew it. She believed so strongly in the power of love, and yet hate was always there in the midst of those who were trying to find a new way. If only the children could grow up surrounded by love, perhaps they would have a chance to build permanent peace. She must protect the children.

"Listen, friend," she tries once more, worn-down but firm. "I really do respect your right to hate life, if that's your way, but I would appreciate it very much if you would move your hate elsewhere." He stood, accepting defeat for both of them.

This incident left me feeling sad. It was such a beautiful day, but even the spirit of community unity could not reach everyone, especially those who had long been immersed and influenced by the old culture. That was the problem, as I saw it. Those of us who wanted to change things were still influenced by the old ways. Maybe the children would have the best chance of creating a new culture.

COMPARING INTERNATIONAL CULTURES, EUROPE 1973

When Thomas and I began the separation that would eventually lead to divorce, I was still committed to creative teaching and educational innovation, but I was beginning to realize how slowly the system was changing. I could change things in my classroom, but the rest of the system conspired to maintain the status quo. I felt like Sisyphus pushing a rock up the hill each day, only to have it roll down again at night. Was this how I wanted to spend my entire life?

That summer I decided to go to Europe, my first trip since college days. I needed to see who I would be in a completely new environment.[289] I decided to travel with very little agenda, but carried names and contact information for several people I hoped to visit. I wanted to go back to Marburg to see if I could find the folks I had known ten years before. I also wanted to connect with folks from the International Humanistic Psychology group and the Jung Institute in Zurich.

I was traveling light. I decided not to carry a backpack which was what most Americans used, but instead chose small bag I could carry over my shoulder. My favorite clothes were a pair of purple jeans and a turquoise and purple tie-dyed T shirt. I was ready for adventure, and I found plenty of it along the way.

In a park in Montreux, where I planned to attend the annual Jazz Festival, I met other Americans who were traveling around Europe. Maybe we're all on the same journey, I thought. We're all

---

289   See Love is All You Need for more on this trip.

trying to understand the world and see the connections among places and people. I had a sense of being back in my own culture when they offered to share their hashish with me.[290] Smoking made me feel at home. Being once again part of what I called my brotherhood and sisterhood made me realize how different the culture around me was.

After looking at the Jazz Festival program with the Americans, I decided to buy a ticket for the Saturday night concert with Dr. John and music from New Orleans. However, my host, Philippe, had made other plans. He had arranged for us to go to Lausanne for a folk festival. "What a choice! Blues vs. Swiss tradition," I wrote. "I know which I really want to see, but I don't want to miss the other. I feel the oppressive yet essential conservatism of the Swiss attitude in Philippe. Maybe I should be amazed he's as open as he is. Anyway, I know my culture is open and I'm glad I can be free."

I exchanged my ticket for the Friday night blues concert and was blown away by an unforgettable performance by B.B. King and other mostly older black men who had been playing the blues all their lives, it seemed. The program claimed this was "the classical music of America." It emerged from black culture and was now merging into my culture. What is my culture? I wondered once again.

The next day in Lausanne, Philippe introduced me as "a hippie from California." I didn't like being characterized in that way, but he was so charming in the way he did it that I accepted the description with a smile. The following day he invited me to go hiking in the Alps with a group of his friends. The plan was to hike from Bourg St. Pierre to St. Bernard and back, a five-hour trek each way. Not having hiked before, I was unprepared for the serious business of hiking in mountains. My only shoes were lightweight tennis shoes, completely inadequate for rocky slopes and steep climbs. The others helped me along in the tough places, but by the time we got to our destination, the Hospice of St. Bernard, I was exhausted. The monks, who were famous for training St. Bernard rescue dogs, also made

---

290   Marijuana was generally unavailable at that time in Europe, but hash was plentiful. It was generally broken up, mixed with tobacco, and smoked like a cigarette.

brandy. After a small snifter, I knew there was no way I would make it back. Philippe recognized this and suggest I hitchhike back to St. Pierre, which I gratefully did.

It took less than 20 minutes to get back to our starting point. I found the tavern where we were planning to have dinner, ordered a glass of wine, and began writing in my journal. Before long, the other women in the group appeared. They, too, had hitchhiked back! Then the men came, all except Philippe and one other man. They were too proud to hitch, so the others went back to pick them up so we could get on with the business of the evening—eating the famous Swiss fondue.

My next stop was in Oberrohrdorf, a village near Zurich, where I spent the day with a Swiss family who were part of the International Humanistic Psychology group—Sara, Ken, and their two children. Peter, the person who had given me their address, was away at a meeting. We smoked hash, went to the forest, played hide and seek with the kids, and cooked wurst on a fire. It was an idyllic family gathering, except for the airplane noise and an obnoxious smell from a nearby dump.

Sara had only invited me to stay one night, so I went off the next day to find other Americans. Vicki and her friends invited me to stay with them. Others joined us for a lovely afternoon sitting outside in their yard. Since some of them were part of the Jung Institute, I told them about the Myers-Briggs Type Indicator which I had brought with me. They were immediately interested and wanted to take it.[291] It was great fun. They were surprised when most of them turned out to be similar types. I explained that they fit a common pattern of those interested in counseling. It was the Fourth of July, and our gathering was a perfect way to celebrate.

The next day, I took the train to Zurich with Vicki. We had coffee and pastries before I left on the next leg of my journey. Knowing I was on my way to visit a friend in Liechtenstein, her friends suggested I stop in Trogen, where they knew a group of musicians. They told me that the people in this area were traditionally short so the houses were

---

291   Since some participants spoke primarily German, I agreed to read the questions aloud and translate them, with help from others who were bilingual.

small. With their address in hand, I set off hitchhiking on country roads, sometimes waiting a long time for a ride.

When I arrived in Trogen in mid-afternoon, I discovered that the musicians were away playing a benefit concert for people who were buying land in France to establish a self-sufficient community, an idea I found very enticing. Silvio, their helper, and Maricarmen, his friend, welcomed me anyway. We sat outside in the sun and enjoyed the day. Later we went into town with their other visitors, Helga and Josef from Cologne. Fortunately for me, these two spoke standard German which I could understand much better than the Swiss dialect the others spoke. I loved being out in the country and meeting the people in this unique place. The old buildings were indeed built for short people. I was only 5'6" but I still had to stoop a bit to get through some of the doors.

The next day I went on to Liechtenstein to visit my friend, Charlotte. When I arrived, I was tired and confessed that I wasn't feeling well. She offered to take me to a naturopathic doctor in Appenzell, the only part of Switzerland where the practice is legal. I had previously been introduced to naturopathy along with other alternative healing practices, and this was a great opportunity for me to learn about the tradition in one of the places where it originated. The naturopath diagnosed my condition by reading my eyes and prescribed a homeopathic remedy. Within a week, I was completely healed.

Later, on my visit to Marburg, I discovered that Rudolf's brother and wife, Rene and Erika Spalke, shared many of my interests and ideas about the future. They were interested in parapsychology and dreamed of finding land in a rural area to start a community. I had already encountered such interests at home, and now I was finding them in Europe. I concluded that this was evidence of Snyder's theory of The Great Subculture. My trip to Europe was enlightening and much as I would have liked to continue my journey, I knew it was time to go back home.

BACK TO SCHOOL, 1973-74

Settling back into the routine of school after the summer

in Europe was difficult, but I was excited about the prospect of teaching my third Experimental English and Social Studies class. After four years at Rohnert Park Junior High, I had begun teaching at Casa Grande High School the year before. This was the open-space school I helped design, and I had hoped that the new, more flexible environment would foster collaboration among teachers and innovative approaches to education. What happened became my first major lesson in the challenge of institutional change.

To start with, the proposal to provide training for teachers in the use of open space was ignored. The principal who was hired did not seem interested in developing new forms of teaching to fit the new space. A few teachers understood the new opportunities the space offered, but we were left to develop programming on our own. Other teachers hated having one wall of their classrooms open, because it tended to be noisy and made it hard for them to control their students. After a few months, teachers came in on weekends and built plywood walls! This made me even more determined to find creative ways to make the space work.

Fortunately, I found several teachers who were interested in working together to utilize the unique features of the space. Rick, the head of the English Department, had the space next to mine and we decided to teach some units together. The following year I put a team together with Kathie, who taught both English and History as I did, and a student teacher. They liked the idea of the Experimental English and Social Studies class I created at my previous school, and we were successful in our proposal for a similar interdisciplinary two-period block class open to both ninth and eleventh grade students.[292]

The range of students in the class made it interesting as well as challenging. There were college-bound students who wrote amazing term papers, my favorites being two friends, one of whom researched the Beatles and the other the Rolling Stones. There were

---

292   Tenth graders had a required course that prevented them from participating. Because this was a new school there were no twelfth graders until the following year. The ninth graders were officially registered for Landmarks of American History and Freshman English and the eleventh graders were taking Modern US History and American Short Story.

artists and poets who made books of poetry and drawings. There were virtual non-readers who found books they loved. Especially gratifying were the relationships that developed between the ninth and eleventh graders. I enjoyed having older students, who could delve more deeply into the subjects we were studying and apply what they were learning to their lives.

However, it was hard work to plan and manage the class. The time required for the three of us to work together came on top of all our other class preparations and school responsibilities. Nevertheless, we managed to offer an exciting and innovative program. It was moderately successful and controversial enough that the principal threatened to cancel it half way through the year. By the end of the year, I was exhausted. I knew that continuing to create new programs in a less than hospitable context was more than I could handle. It was time for a change. I applied for a year's leave, but I knew I might never return to this type of teaching. I wrote to my mother: "You know how much I had dreamed of the possibilities for Casa Grande. ... I know I'm not leaving education forever. But to continue the fight here in this situation would be more self-destructive than it would be worth."

Now I can see the important lessons I learned. Institutional change requires a multi-faceted approach and acceptance by all concerned. It's certainly not something I can make happen on my own. Nevertheless, even in a difficult situation, I can make a difference in the lives of those I work with. I keep in my heart comments made by my students.

- I have learned more about myself through you and the people I've talked to in your class. –Betsy
- I was really free to express myself the way I wanted to. –Tim
- The "class" has been fun and worth taking, even though my friends were close-minded about it. Keep on teaching. We need more teachers like you. –Leslie
- This class was the best that I have had all year. Thank you for not being so much a teacher as just being yourself. –Rick
- Some of the things we did made me stop and think. It made me see what being a person in this world really means. –Terri

Dorothy May Emerson

EDUCATION FOR LIFE
My six-year career in public school teaching brought me into contact with people and ideas that shaped the rest of my life, particularly through conference speakers who were on the forefront of new thought. For example, from Alex Haley, at the time engaged in research that would culminate in his novel *Roots*, I realized how important it was acknowledge the previously hidden history of people brought to this country as slaves. From Alvin Toffler, author of *Future Shock*, I gained insight into problems inherent in our rapidly changing culture. From Ralph Nader, I learned about consumer activism. Anais Nin inspired me to value time for introspection. George Leonard, author of *Education and Ecstasy* and a founder of the human potential movement, inspired me with possibilities for transformative education as an avenue for positive social change, inspiring me to write in my journal:

> We're working out our full human potential...Releasing potential is the goal of education. Freeing people to break through the walls that limit them, letting people be themselves. Breaking though to another level is progress, creation, evolution. You become your potential once you KNOW the next challenge.

THE IMPORTANCE OF FEMINISM
To fulfill our full human potential, women need equality. In the Sixties, many women (and some men) realized that equality required changing gender stereotypes. Some counterculture women, especially those living in communes or land-based communities, took on traditional women's roles, but did so with a great deal of independence and respect, defining their own spheres of influence and achievement.[293] For the rest of us, feminism helped us realize the extent to which things needed to change.

As a career woman raised by a career woman, I thought I was already liberated, so awareness of how I was oppressed by living male-dominated world required an awakening. Even though most

---

293   Gretchen Lemke-Santangelo, *Daughters of Aquarius: Women of the Sixties Counterculture*, 2009.

teachers were women, the principals and superintendents I worked with were all men, as were the presidents and most of the leadership of teachers' organizations,[294] and most of the college professors I knew. But what really brought home to me the need for feminism was my disastrous relationship with Wolfgang, when I finally woke up to my emotional dependence on men.

My opportunity to change both myself and the system came when I was asked to coordinate a teachers' conference program on the newly emerging field of Women's Studies. What began as a couple of programs became a mini-conference called "The Female Principle,"[295] when I discovered the number of topics that were relevant, and the many resource people available to offer presentations. Programs spanned three days and included ten workshops, three interactive change labs, two keynote speakers, and a play, *Myth America: How Far Have You Really Come?* On the flyer to promote the program. I explained:

> Although women may be a majority among teachers, sexism is still rampant in our schools and in our society. For too long teachers have failed to recognize this problem, and therefore our effectiveness in correcting it has been limited. Hopefully, this conference program will help to deal with the problem by providing both men and women teachers with the background and the motivation to move toward ending sexism wherever it occurs.

The last line in the program description shows what I was thinking in choosing the title: "Explore with us this passport to change the female principle." I was coming to realize that following the cultural imperative to act according to "the female principle" keeps women, including me, from being our whole selves and keeps

---

294   When Doris Prince became the first woman to serve as president of the California Council for the Social Studies in 1973, she asked me to chair an Affirmative Action Committee. Although the previous presidents knew about affirmative action, it had not occurred to them that organizational action was needed.

295   "The Female Principle" was part of the annual state conference of the California Council for the Social Studies, "Passport to Change," March 14-17, 1974, at the Anaheim Convention Center, Anaheim, CA.

us from being self-sufficient equals to men. In describing the keynote presentation, "Sexism is a Social Disease," I wrote: "the division of human characteristics into categories of masculine and feminine is not only arbitrary and absurd, but also debilitating and dangerous, and moreover creates unbalanced societies." This was the radical understanding I was seeking to internalize for myself, sometimes succeeding, sometimes not.

Recognition of the need to change gender stereotypes was growing in the culture as well. For instance, Ms. Foundation for Women collaborated with actor and author Margo Thomas to produce a unique record album and illustrated book in 1972 and a widely popular television show in 1974, involving many other well-known singers and actors. Free to Be...*You and Me* is a prime example of a creative effort to change cultural attitudes. A children's entertainment project, the stories, poems, songs, and illustrations, encouraged gender equality, by highlighting values such as individuality, tolerance, and comfort with one's identity. A central message was that anyone—whether a boy or a girl—can achieve anything.

The backlash against this life-affirming message showed how deeply sexism is embedded in our culture. This came to the fore in debates about the Equal Rights Amendment and ultimately led to its failure to be ratified. Since then, the idea of gender equality has continued to be questioned and debated. As recently as 2014, an article in the New York Post claimed the *Free to Be...You and Me* project emasculated men.[296]

Since the Sixties, many positive changes have occurred for women, but the change is not yet complete. Feminism is still relevant until equality for women is accepted around the world. This work on behalf of women and girls in our country and world-wide needs to continue as essential to the completion of the Sixties agenda.

LASTING EFFECTS

The Sixties inspired many people to seek lives of meaning

---

[296]   *Kyle Smith,* "How *Free to Be...You and Me* emasculated men," *New York Post*, March 8, 2014.

where we might make a difference in the life of others. To some extent, we have succeeded, but now our work must continue through those who will remain after we are gone. Understanding what the Sixties era accomplished and the challenges that remain has the potential to empower young people in their work for change. Since the Sixties still lives inside us, we might as well take the best of it and use it to build a better future and face the challenges that remain.

Each person who studies and writes about the Sixties highlights different lasting effects they see as most important. The three contributions I would like to highlight are music, cultural divides, and paradigm shifts.

LASTING EFFECT: MUSIC'S IMMORTAL SOUL

The first big contribution is music. Music pervaded our lives in ways that had not been possible before the Sixties. Popular music became global, with new influences from England and Latin America, and then Africa and India and many other places in between. Folk and rock musicians were our poets and sometimes prophets. The music embodied themes of creating something better, part of the same large endeavor of culture change. As I wrote in a letter to my family, "The idealism expressed in these records is part of what we hope for and what leads us on."

One of the most popular and well-known San Francisco bands was Jefferson Airplane, with lead singer Grace Slick. A prime representative of acid rock, their lyrics often laid bare the conflicts we lived with.

In loyalty to their kind
They cannot tolerate our minds
In loyalty to our kind
We cannot tolerate their obstruction

Life is change
How it differs from the rocks
I've seen their ways too often for my liking
New worlds to gain
My life is to survive and be alive

Dorothy May Emerson

For you[297]

My favorite local group was The Sons of Champlin.[298] Bill Champlin's philosophical and spiritual lyrics became music played by a multi-instrument rock band, including a horn section. The songs spoke directly to the struggles we faced in trying to live in new ways.

> When your soul feels heavy
> Overburdened by your daily thing
>> Take time to live
>> Take time to love
>> Take time to give
> Then you will see the lightning in your soul
> The whole world is the lightning in my soul[299]

In addition to rock music, there were many acoustic musicians. Lamb, with singer Barbara Mauritz and instrumentalist Bob Swanson, featured haunting melodies combining jazz and folk styles. I recommended "Traveler's Observation" to my students as a reflection on change.

> Love reaching out to lift my soul
> To the peace of the gods
> Hands warm and strong,
> The hands of the gods ...
> Give the new life made in its birth
> Give peace the reigning power[300]

"The whole world is lightning in my soul," "New worlds to gain," "Give peace the reigning power"—these lines run through my mind still. And many more. This music still pervades my life and

---

297   Paul Kantner, "Crown of Creation," title track recorded by Jefferson Airplane, 1968.
298   Back together after a hiatus, The Sons, with some changes in personnel, still perform today. www.sonsofchamplin.com.
299   Bill Champlain, "Lightnin' " on *Welcome to the Dance*, album by Sons of Champlin, 1973.
300   "Traveler's Observation," on the album *A Sign of Change*, Lamb, 1970.

355

gives me hope.

Thanks to YouTube and other internet sites even the less well-known music of the Sixties is available today. Many Sixties musicians are still making music even in their seventies. The more popular music of the era is still frequently played on the radio and reissued as commemorative albums. The fact that so much of Sixties music survives today and is still popular is a testament to what this era produced. The songs remain relevant fifty years later! Through music, the vision and promise of the Sixties remains alive.

LASTING EFFECT: CULTURAL DIVIDES

The second lasting contribution of the Sixties is less admirable. The Sixties helped create the cultural divides we are challenged with today. I happen to be a person who likes and even craves change, but not everyone does. In the Sixties, many people felt threatened by change and resented advocates for change. Some, but not all of it, was generational.

I first experienced this divide in my family. My father represented the opposite of the changes I embraced. Because we had an otherwise close and loving relationship it was possible for me to disagree with him without risking our connection. At first, we argued about music. Because my father had perfect pitch, he often found fault with folk and rock and roll singers for being flat. Our arguments about value conflicts took a more serious turn, however, during the anti-communism scare,[301] when people were looking for communists everywhere, particularly among artists and movie makers. I could not understand why my father refused to even consider that the government might be wrong in their actions. He thought I was being disloyal to my country. Our arguments lasted late into the night, our voices loud enough that my siblings could

---

301   In 1960 the House Un-American Activities Committee held hearings in San Francisco that led to a riot. Two films were made, both shown amid considerable controversy at my high school. *Operation Abolition* was the more widely known and seen official film, supporting the Committee's actions and the police response. *Operation Correction* used the same footage to tell a different story showing the mistreatment of demonstrators and supporting their right to demonstrate.

hear and thought we were fighting. I honed my ability to hold my own in talking with men in those "discussions."

Later in the Sixties, when demonstrations and mass arrests became common, my father told me he hoped he never saw me across a street with the demonstrators "because he would have to shoot me." I didn't believe him, of course, but I realized our arguments had taken a turn for the worse. There was no going back. We were on opposite sides of what was becoming a cultural divide.

The two conflicting cultures in the 1960s had different slogans, both using the American flag: "America: Love it or leave it!" or "America: Change it or lose it!" The first group emphasized the need to enforce the law to keep things the way they were. Like my father, they supported the police in doing whatever they deemed necessary to keep or restore order. The second group demanded change and was sometimes willing to break laws so their voices would be heard. Stephen Stills described the situation perfectly:
There's battle lines being drawn.
Nobody's right when everybody's wrong.
Young people speaking their minds.
Getting so much resistance from behind.[302]

Nothing was more polarizing than the Vietnam War. While some middle and upper-class white men actively avoided the draft, two-thirds of those who fought were volunteers, many from working-class and poverty backgrounds. These soldiers often blamed the protestors for decreasing support for the war and eventual withdrawal without winning. When they returned home they often received less than the hero's welcome of previous wars. Although some soldiers saw the problems of war and joined Veterans for Peace groups, many others became bitter, even as they struggled with post-traumatic stress and debilitating pain resulting from toxic chemicals used in the war, such as Agent Orange.

The expansion of democracy and civil rights also led to resistance and direct opposition, mostly among white people who refused to accept changes like expanded voting rights, integrated schools, and affirmative action. This opposition has never gone away

302   Stephen Stills, "For What It's Worth," 1967.

and has now become a major force in restricting voting rights and eliminating affirmative action. Many schools have once again become segregated, now generally based on economic status of which race is often a component.

Further splits occurred around women's rights, with vocal opposition and defeat of the Equal Rights Amendment. Reproductive rights and the legalization of abortion that were heralded by some as achievements of Sixties values continue to be questioned by others. Although the struggle for gay and lesbian rights has led to protective legislation and equal marriage, resistance continues. The old battles are still being fought. Laws that were changed to be more progressive and inclusive are being eroded and made more restrictive. The failure to build consensus has led to inevitable backlash.

However, there are hopeful signs that a new culture continues to emerge and grow stronger. Prior to World War II there were two dominant cultural groups, both continuing to exist today. One group is the Modernists, with roots in the Renaissance and values based on progress, industry, capitalism, urbanization, materialism, and meritocracy. The other is the Traditionals, social and religious conservatives who value stability, patriarchal families, and often live in rural areas or small towns. These two groups were already engaged in a culture war when the new group began emerging, the Cultural Creatives. Yale professor Paul H. Ray identified these groups, after surveying over 100,000 people about their values.[303] This new group has joined the battle, especially in relation to human rights and the use of the earth's resources.

Paul Ray explained that Cultural Creatives "take the ideas of ecology very seriously."

They support slowing business growth in order to save the planet. They also take very seriously women's issues and issues of personal growth and relationships. We found that the typical Cultural Creative cares intensely about the issues raised by post–World War II social movements. These movements include those focused on civil rights, the

---

303   Paul H. Ray and Sherry Ruth Anderson, *The Cultural Creatives: How 50 Million People Are Changing the World*, 2001.

environment, women's rights, peace, jobs and social justice, gay and lesbian rights, alternative health care, spirituality, personal growth, and now, of course, stopping corporate globalization. All of those concerns are now converging into a strong concern for the whole planet.[304]

In 2000 the researchers estimated that there were already 50 million Cultural Creatives in the United States, and another 80 million in Western Europe. By 2013, they estimated 80 million in the US, 90 million in Europe, and 25 million in Japan.[305] If this is accurate, there is surely reason for hope that, despite the often bleak news of today, a cultural turning is indeed taking place. This turning could bring the promise of the Sixties to fruition. However, first we need to deal with the cultural divides that pit us against one another.

We are confronted almost daily with the difficulties of systemic change. If our culture remains as divided as it is, it will be almost impossible for the changes we envisioned in the Sixties to be realized. What will it take for our country to come together and move forward as a unified people? Where are the consensus-builders? Where are the peacemakers?

LASTING EFFECT: PARADIGM SHIFTS

The Sixties inspired several important paradigm shifts, an idea initially identified by American physicist and philosopher Thomas Kuhn, in his 1962 book *The Structure of Scientific Revolutions*. Described as a fundamental change in the basic concepts and practices of a scientific discipline, a paradigm shift establishes a new framework, resulting in a scientific revolution. Kuhn states that "awareness is prerequisite to all acceptable changes of theory."[306] Often driven by an external agent of change, a new way of thinking

---

304   Interview with Paul H. Ray by Sarah van Gelder, "A Culture Gets Creative," *Yes! Magazine*, October 2000.
305   Interview with Paul H. Ray by Lisa Reagan, "Same Planet, Different Worlds: How Cultural Creatives are Transcending Alienation and Isolation to Bring Forward the Practical Wisdom of Conscious Living," 2013, www.kindredmedia.org
306   Thomas Kuhn, *The Structure of Scientific Revolutions* (revised and expanded edition, 1970), 67.

emerges, transforming the way we understand the world.

The concept of paradigm shift quickly migrated into popular culture and was applied beyond science to other shifts in thinking. Terms such as consciousness-raising, transformation of consciousness, and mind-expanding, describe similar phenomena. The overall result of the paradigm shifts is what this book refers to as sea change. Shakespeare described this radical transformation symbolically: the father's bones buried in the sea are transformed into coral and pearls.[307]

One of the most dramatic paradigm shifts was sparked by increasing numbers of people seeing images of the earth from space. The most widely distributed image was taken on December 7, 1972, by the Apollo 17 astronauts on their way to the moon. Known as the Blue Marble, this color photograph of the entire earth is one of the most reproduced images in existence. Seeing the whole earth sparked a change in the culture's consciousness, not unlike the change that occurred when people accepted the reality of the earth as round, not flat.

Since then, the idea of wholeness has been applied in many different situations. As one group today explains:

The words "holy," "wholesome," "health" and "healing" are all rooted in the idea of "wholeness." Wholeness involves the entirety of things, which suggests inclusion and seeing the big picture. It involves diversity, but diversity that dances with unity instead of undermining it. It involves cooperation, interaction, dialogue, compassion, and all the other things that "bring us together" without losing our individual "integrity" (another word grounded in wholeness), thus enhancing relationship and interconnectedness. Our essential unity and kinship are powerful factors in wholeness.[308]

---

307   Shakespeare, *The Tempest.*
308   The nonprofit Co-Intelligence Institute, based in Eugene, Oregon, embraces ideas, tools, and methods that promote wholeness and explores and catalyzes their integrated application to democratic renewal, community problems, organizational transformation, national and global crises, and the creation of just, vibrant, sustainable cultures.

Attitudes toward the use of drugs popular in the Sixties is another shift. Back then, the use of psychedelic drugs transformed many people's consciousness. People experienced feelings of unity and kinship, where before they felt separate. Seeing the interconnectedness of all life shifted people's frame of reference. It transformed the way they saw the world, not just during the drug experience but afterwards as well. The majority who took LSD experienced positive results, but for some the loss of a sense of oneself as separate was frightening. Those who were predisposed to mind-opening mystical experiences undoubtedly gained the most insight. Because there were enough such people, the overall effect was a paradigm shift in consciousness.

LSD was originally studied in the 1950s by psychiatrists and other researchers as a potentially powerful treatment for a range of disorders. When it was classified as a Schedule 1 controlled substance in 1970, licenses and research funding were effectively ended. Then in the mid-1990s, the US government began issuing a few licenses for research on LSD and other psychedelics and in the twenty-first century that research continues to expand, with indications of success in treating alcoholism and soothing anxiety in terminally ill patients.[309] We who experienced the value of LSD see this movement toward renewed research on psychedelics as another aspect of paradigm shift.

LSD may have also contributed to another paradigm shift: the invention of personal computers. Steve Jobs, co-founder of Apple Computers, believed that taking LSD was one of the two or three most important things he ever did.[310] Steve and other technology innovators in California participated in early (legal) experiments with LSD research conducted by the International Foundation for Advanced Study. A British software engineer suggested that LSD visions may have helped the California innovators conceive of new uses for computers: "in terms of our view of the universe—perception

---

309   Shauncey Ferro, "Why Doctors Can't Give You LSD (but maybe they should), *Popular Science*, April 16, 2013.
310   John Markoff, *What the Dormouse Said: How the 60s Counterculture Shaped the Personal Computer Industry*, 2005.

can be more powerful than physics can be."[311]
While the use of LSD waned in the late 1970s, marijuana use continued. Today a growing number of states have approved the use of medical marijuana and some have made recreational use legal. This herbal substance, first popular in the Sixties, has proved to be beneficial in many ways.

Another significant shift came as the culture awakened to the ways the earth's resources were being polluted and depleted. Rachel Carson's 1962 book, *Silent Spring,* documenting the detrimental effects on the environment of the indiscriminate use of pesticides, began a process of raising awareness that culminated in the celebration of the first Earth Day in 1970. This shift in consciousness toward understanding the responsibility of human beings to care for the earth, ultimately led over the next few decades to the development of technology to harness renewable energy. Growing acknowledgement of the importance of addressing climate change makes this work of the past fifty years more relevant than ever before.

A related aspect of this shift led to awareness of the problems with ever-increasing consumption and consumerism. *The Whole Earth Catalog,* first published in 1968, provided those who wished to live in greater harmony with the earth with tools and resources for individual and community use. Recycling and reusing materials became common, and led eventually to community-wide recycling programs. Changing personal behavior is one solution to the environmental problem, and has led to growing appreciation for simple living, tiny houses, and reduced energy consumption whenever possible.

Raised awareness of the importance of pesticide-free, minimally processed natural food for healthy living, led people to form local food cooperatives to access and distribute healthy food. This paved the way for the expansion of organic food production, increased availability of organic products, and the natural foods markets of today. Education about the effect of pesticides and growth hormones, on our bodies and on the environment, has awakened

---

311   Mike Lynch, quoted in Wendy M Grossman, "Did the use of psychedelics lead to a computer revolution?" *The Guardian*, Sept. 6, 2011,

consciousness of problems with profit-driven factory farming. However, the challenge remains of making organic foods accessible to people who struggle to put food on their family tables.

Health began to be defined as more than the absence of disease, and the idea of working with the whole person to achieve balance and health grew. New practices emerged, some based on ancient and non-Western sources that were more holistic than allopathic medicine. Now many standard medical facilities offer such alternatives within their facilities, and some health insurance plans provide reimbursement for holistic treatments. Here, too, accessibility for all people is a challenge that remains to be addressed for the vision of equality to be realized.

Another shift occurred in the variety of housing options available. While attempts to establish communes and free land in the Sixties met with mixed results, the ideas of sharing and cooperative living have taken hold. Land trusts, where people build their own houses on land owned by the community, exist now in many parts of the country, making home ownership possible for many who could not otherwise afford it. In some states, cooperatively-owned mobile home parks provide affordable housing and a sense of community. Co-housing, where people have individual living spaces and share community grounds and buildings, provides people with a way to live in community and keep their independence. These innovations have taken Sixties ideals to a new level by creating practical and stable cooperative living alternatives.

There is no doubt that the increasing visibility of the civil rights movement in the Sixties led to significant social transformation. Despite resistance, things changed in ways that can never be reversed. Thanks to television, the world witnessed the power of nonviolent protest, even in the face of violent treatment by those who upheld the status quo. Those lessons are carried forward in many of the protests today. Here, too, the shift is incomplete. Now, as in the Sixties, there are those who are impatient with the failure of things to change, while others believe change will not happen without the use of violence and property destruction.

The Sixties saw a major increase in citizen activism and an

expansion of democracy that continues to inspire disenfranchised groups both here and in other countries. This legacy of the Sixties has changed the face of this country to one of increasing diversity and access. We still have a long way to go to truly fulfill the ideals upon which this country was founded, but thanks to the paradigm shifts of the Sixties, we took a big leap forward.

FULFILLING THE PROMISE

In his first State of the Union Message in January 1961, newly elected President Kennedy promised a turning of the tide, with a return to prosperity, and active engagement in world affairs to promote democracy and maintain peace.[312] Other prophecies foretold of a new age coming, a time of increased consciousness, peace, and love. A spirit of change was in the air and with it hope for a better day, when all people could live together in harmony. A shared vision began to emerge, a vision of a world founded on peace, justice, equality, freedom, and love.

During the years that followed, progress towards that vision was mixed with anger at the country's involvement in war in Southeast Asia. Nevertheless, hope prevailed at least in some places that we were beginning to build a new culture. That new culture grew stronger as different waves gained energy as expressions of a fundamental sea change. One wave was a new acceptance of diversity, and the importance of insuring equal rights of all citizens. Another was faith in individual potential to learn how to contribute to society to the best of one's abilities, abilities that could be enhanced and empowered by education that took individual needs and interests into account. A third wave was citizen activism, with new organizations established to amplify people's voices in matters that affected their lives. A fourth wave was an awakening to the need to care for the earth, to heal the devastation of earlier years and develop new ways to live in harmony with natural resources and forces. A fifth wave was an explosion of creativity, in music, the arts, and new forms of community and religion, that spoke prophetically to our souls about the vision of freedom, equality, love, and peace we could

---

312   John F. Kennedy, State of the Union Message, January 29, 1961.

make real with our lives. These waves are visible manifestations of a deep and lasting sea change that continues in process fifty years later. However, because of the forces of resistance, what we set out to change is incomplete. This is the challenge that remains.

To complete this sea change we need to remember the vision, and add to it the insights of the past half-century. We Sixties people are older now, and aware of the dynamics of change and resistance to change. We have wisdom and skills we can share with those born after us and apply to the ongoing work of the Sixties. The world today is even more seriously in danger than ours was. It is incumbent upon us, even in our later years, to revitalize the vision and co-create, with our younger friends, ways to complete the visionary agenda of the Sixties. Only then will the sea change complete its promise. Only then can we who live now pass on to future generations a culture of freedom, equality, love, and peace.

GRATITUDE

My deepest thanks to my spouse, Donna Clifford, for her love and unwavering support of my work and for her patience with how long it took to finish this book.

Special thanks to my college roommate and longtime friend, Ruth (Tanni) Crowley, who guided me in developing the book and kept insisting that I pay attention to the arc of the narrative.

Many thanks my neighbor, Marilyn Davidson, for volunteering to edit early versions, her many helpful suggestions along the way, returning for final editing, and especially for figuring out how to fix the last section.

This book has been vastly improved by the many people who have read various versions, encouraged me to share this story, corrected places where they were mentioned, and provided important feedback and critique. My deep gratitude to you:

Early readers: Jane Rzepka, Linda Lundin, Andy Stark, Susan Jhirad, Karen Edwards, Robert Ellwood, Susan Altman, Rik Thiesfeld, Gail Seavey, Doug Wilson, Ann Zulliger, Stephen Shick, and my sister and brother, Mary Lou Woodcock and Howdy Emerson.

Pomona College classmates: Jeanne Martin Buckley, Joni Raphael Greathouse, Lew Phelps, and Julie Scott. I changed the names of other classmates mentioned.

Beta version readers: Melody Lee, Jane Dwinell, Margret O'Neill, Mark Morrison-Reed, Gail Tapscott, Ken Brown, Bets Weineke, Cerridwen, Anita Farber-Robertson, and Michelle Walsh.

I am especially thankful to "Twinkle" Marie Manning for her enthusiasm for my book and for agreeing to publish it through Matrika Press. Also to Gretchen Ohmann of Ladyweave for creating the website www.seachange1960s.net and a social media presence for the book.

My deep appreciation to my husband, known as Thomas in the book, who has reservations about his part of my story. I hope he will forgive me someday.

Dorothy May Emerson

I want to acknowledge Don Lattin, whose interview on NPR about his books on the 1960s inspired me to choose this era for my first memoir. Thanks, too, to all the other authors whose books about the Sixties informed my understanding of this era. A special shout-out to the women who have courageously shared their stories. We need more stores of women's lives.

Most of all, I want to thank the people who were in my life in the Sixties and who contributed to this story and to the person I have become. Sometimes I changed your names, and to those I left in, I hope you are pleased with what I wrote about you. Remember your dreams and keep living them.

DATES AND MILESTONES

November 20, 1943—Born at Seaside Hospital, Long Beach, California
1943-50—Lived in Long Beach
1950-56—Moved to Fullerton
    Attended Golden Hill Elementary School, grades 2-6
    Began participation in First Presbyterian Church of Fullerton
1956-58—Attended Wilshire Junior High, grades 7-8
    Presbyterian summer camps at Pacific Palisades—1956, 1957
1958-61—Attended Fullerton Union High School, grades 9-12
    Presbyterian summer camps at Big Bear Lake—1958, 1959
    Commission Conference—1960
    Junior counselor at two summer camps at Pacific Palisades—1960
    Relationship with Carl—1959-61
1961-65—Attended Pomona College, Claremont (BA, German Literature)
    Summer job, Southern California Edison Company—1962-64
    Trip to Seattle for World's Fair—1962
    Semester abroad, Marburg, Germany—1963-1964
    Relationship with Rudolf—1963-64
Summer 1965—Studied Biblical Greek at Claremont Theological School
    Worked at Robbie's Restaurant, West Covina
1965-66—Attended San Francisco Theological Seminary, San Anselmo
March 19, 1966—married Thomas
Lived in Marin City (1966); San Anselmo (1966-69); Terra Linda (1969-70); Cotati (1970-75)
1966—Worked at Marin County Juvenile Detention Center, Novato
1967-68—Attended Dominican College, San Rafael
    Worked at Macy's, San Rafael
1968-72—Teacher, Rohnert Park Junior High
1972-74—Teacher, Casa Grande Junior-Senior High, Petaluma
Summer 1973—Trip to Europe
    Relationship with Wolfgang—1973-74
1972-74—Self-directed degree program, Humanistic Psychology Institute at Sonoma State College (MA, Psychology and Education)

About the Author

Dorothy May Emerson is a semi-retired Unitarian Universalist minister and writer, currently living in Massachusetts with her spouse, Donna Clifford. A native Californian, her experiences in the Sixties helped shape the rest of her work and life. She has served for 30 years as a parish and community minister in New England, and currently offers talks and workshops on the Sixties; Spirit, Money, and Justice; and Class Awareness and Action. More at www.rainbowsolutions.us. Her previous books include *Standing Before Us: Unitarian Universalist Women and Social Reform 1776-1936; Called to Community: New Directions in Unitarian Universalist Ministry;* and the curriculum *Becoming Women of Wisdom: Marking the Passage into the Crone Years.*

For more information, visit:
www.SeaChange1960s.net
www.MatrikaPress.com/Dorothy-May-Emerson

About the Publisher

Matrika Press is an independent publishing house dedicated to publishing works in alignment with Unitarian Universalist Values and principles. Its fiscal sponsor is UU Women and Religion, a 501c3 organization.

Matrika Press publishes anthologies, memoirs, poetry, prayer and ritual manuscripts, and other books to bring meaning and transformation to the world. A primary goal of Matrika Press is to publish stories and works that would otherwise remain untold. We also resurrect out-of-print manuscripts to ensure our historical works remain accessible.

Matrika Press titles are automatically made available to tens of thousands of retailers, libraries, schools, and other distribution and fulfillment partners, including Amazon, Barnes & Noble, Chapters/Indigo (Canada), and other well-known book retailers and wholesalers across North America, and in the United Kingdom, Europe, Australia and New Zealand and other Global partners.

For more information, visit:

www.MatrikaPress.com

Matrika Press

MORE MATRIKA PRESS TITLES

Equinox by Desiray Howes

Where the Sky has No Stars by Wesley Burton

Therese's Dream by Dr. David Austin

Intimate Insights to Revolutionizing Intimacy by Tziporah Kingsbury

Making a Monster by Sue Humphries

a Pocketful of Transcendentalism by Polly Peterson

Be Like the Trees - a Sermon in My Pocket by Rev. "Twinkle" Marie Manning

Women of Spirit, Sacred Paths of Wisdom Keepers Anthology

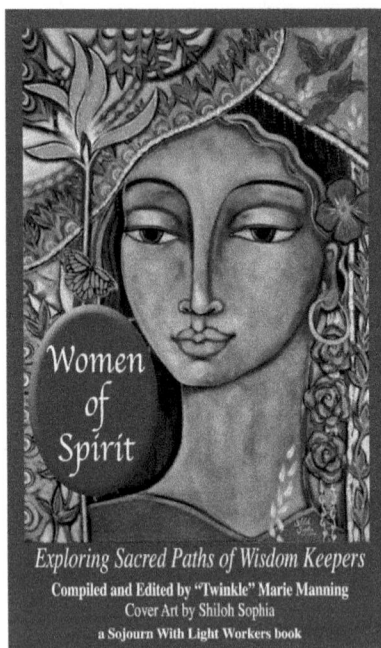

Women
of
Spirit

Exploring Sacred Paths of Wisdom Keepers
Compiled and Edited by "Twinkle" Marie Manning
Cover Art by Shiloh Sophia
a Sojourn With Light Workers book

This book is a compilation of women sojourners, sages, mystics, witches, shaman, medicine women, ministers, philosophers, therapists, life coaches, yogis, and more. Their journeys. Their stories. Their teachings and practices. Essays, Poetry, Art, Rituals and Prayers. This anthology is full of useful tools and powerful messages for everyone who is on a spiritual journey to embrace and enjoy. Beloved Contributors include:
• *Anna Huckabee Tull* • *Bernadette Rombough* • *Deb Elbaum* • *Deborah Diamond* • *Debra Wilson Guttas* • *Grace Ventura* • *Janeen Barnett* • *JoAnne Bassett* • *Judy Ann Foster* • *Julie Matheson* • *Kate Early* • *Kate Kavanagh* • *Katherine Glass*
• *Kris Oster* • *Lea M. Hill* • *Meghan Gilroy* • *Morwen Two Feathers* • *Rustie MacDonald* • *Shamanaca* • *Sharon Hinckley* • *Shawna Allard* • *Shiloh Sophia* • *Susan Feathers* • *Tiffany Cano* • *Tory Londergan* • *"Twinkle" Marie Manning* • *Tziporah Kingsbury* • *Valerie Sorrentino*

www.MatrikaPress.com

Two of our focuses at Matrika Press are to preserve texts and thoughts of our ancestors, and to create publications that share the values and principles of Unitarian Universalism. This allegorical story by David Starr Jordan is a tale about the search for spiritual meaning. Symbolic of Jesus Christ's ministry, it succinctly embodies our Christian heritage and the fourth of the six sources we draw our faith from, namely that which calls us to respond to God's love by loving our neighbors as ourselves.

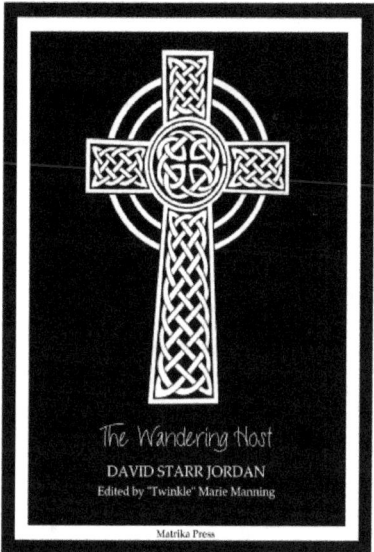

The Wandering Host
DAVID STARR JORDAN
Edited by "Twinkle" Marie Manning

Matrika Press

UU Talks

FIND OUT HOW
YOUR CONGREGATION OR GROUP *CAN HOST*
a local UU Talks in your community. UU Talks is a speakers series, similar to TED Talks, where Speakers will speak about topics aligned with UU Values.
Join Us!
www.UUTalks.org

Above pictured: Inaugural UU Talks event at the UUA Boston, 2017
Peter Bowden, Matt Meyer, Lydia Edwards, Rev. Allison Palm,
Jim Tull, Anna Huckabee Tull, Regie Gibson, Marlon Carey,
Rev. Hank Pierce, "Twinkle" Marie Manning

www.ingramcontent.com/pod-product-compliance
Lightning Source LLC
Chambersburg PA
CBHW051710020426

42333CB00014B/920